INTERNATIONAL HUMANITARIAN LAW

This clear and concise textbook provides an accessible and up-to-date examination of international humanitarian law. With the aid of detailed examples, extracts from relevant cases and useful discussion questions, students are expertly guided through the text. A recommended reading list is included in every chapter to support deeper engagement with the material. Emerging trends in theory and practice are also explored and examined, allowing readers to build on their knowledge and grapple with some of the biggest challenges facing the law of armed conflict in the twenty-first century.

Emily Crawford is a lecturer and Director of the Sydney Centre for International Law (SCIL). She teaches international law and international humanitarian law, and has delivered lectures both locally and overseas on international humanitarian law issues, including the training of military personnel.

Alison Pert lectures at the University of Sydney in international law, specialising in the use of force and international humanitarian law. She is a qualified barrister and has practised as a lawyer in government and the private sector in London, Papua New Guinea and Australia. She has represented Australia at international organisations including Unidroit and UNCITRAL, and in treaty negotiations.

INTERNATIONAL HUMANITARIAN LAW

Emily Crawford and Alison Pert

CAMBRIDGE
UNIVERSITY PRESS

CAMBRIDGE
UNIVERSITY PRESS

University Printing House, Cambridge CB2 8BS, United Kingdom

Cambridge University Press is part of the University of Cambridge.

It furthers the University's mission by disseminating knowledge in the pursuit of
education, learning and research at the highest international levels of excellence.

www.cambridge.org
Information on this title: www.cambridge.org/9781107116177

© Emily Crawford and Alison Pert 2015

First published 2015

Printing in the United Kingdom by TJ International Ltd. Padstow Cornwall

A catalogue record for this publication is available from the British Library

Library of Congress Cataloguing in Publication data
Crawford, Emily (Writer on international law) author.
International humanitarian law / Emily Crawford and Alison Pert.
    pages   cm
ISBN 978-1-107-11617-7 (Hardback : alk. paper) – ISBN 978-1-107-53709-5 (Paperback. : alk. paper)
1. War (International law).   2. Humanitarian law.   3. International criminal law.   I. Pert, Alison, author.
II. Title.
KZ6385.C75 2015
341.6–dc23   2015015426

ISBN 978-1-107-11617-7 Hardback
ISBN 978-1-107-53709-5 Paperback

CONTENTS

PREFACE AND ACKNOWLEDGMENTS

It has become something of a cliché in the general literature on international humanitarian law (IHL – also known as the law of armed conflict, or less frequently, the law of war[1]) to quote Hersch Lauterpacht, who once noted that "if international law is at the vanishing point of law, the law of war is at the vanishing point of international law".[2] To the novice observer, it would seem that there are no rules governing conduct in armed conflicts; that it is absurd to try and regulate the kinds of barbarity we traditionally associate with warfare; and that, even if there are laws of war, no one seems to be abiding by them.[3]

These charges, while compelling, are inaccurate. IHL is one of the oldest branches of international law, and a complex and diverse area of law, covering matters such as the treatment of civilians in times of armed conflict, permissible means and methods of waging such armed conflicts, instruction for occupying forces, rules on the protection of certain kinds of property, such as cultural property and the natural environment, and rules regarding implementation, enforcement and accountability. Research into international humanitarian law indicates that the rules are, for the most part, followed[4] and that States and non-State actors alike are keenly aware of their obligations under IHL.[5]

Sadly, when the rules are broken or ignored, they often result in brutal and inhumane outcomes, as we have seen in recent years in Guantanamo Bay and Abu Ghraib, in the ISIS held territories of Syria and Iraq, in the genocide of Rwanda and the ethnic cleansing of the Former Yugoslavia. The laws governing conduct in

---

[1] The terms IHL, the law of armed conflict and international humanitarian law will be used interchangeably throughout this text.

[2] Hersch Lauterpacht, "The Problem of the Revision of the Law of War" (1952) **29** *BYBIL* 382.

[3] E.g., the US Central Intelligence Agency (CIA) systematically tortured detainees under their control during their operations against al-Qaeda and Taliban forces; former US Vice President Dick Cheney has repeatedly stated that such conduct was acceptable, and that he was unconcerned that innocent persons may have been subject to torture (see Daniel Politi, "Dick Cheney on CIA Torture: 'I'd Do It Again in a Minute'", *Slate*, 14 December 2014, www.slate.com/blogs/the_slatest/2014/12/14/dick_cheney_on_cia_torture_i_d_do_it_a gain_in_a_minute.html).

[4] See research undertaken by James Morrow, "When Do States Follow the Laws of War?" (2007) **101** *American Political Science Review* 559; and (with Hyeran Jo) "Compliance with the Laws of War: Dataset and Coding Rules" (2006) **23** *Conflict Management and Peace Science* 91.

[5] See, e.g., the lengths that US administrations have gone to in order to justify their activities as being in compliance with international law – for instance, President Barack Obama has repeatedly stated that the policy of targeted killings is lawful under IHL. (See remarks by the President at the National Defense University, 23 May 2013, www.whitehouse.gov/the-press-office/2013/05/23/remarks-president-national-defense-university.)

armed conflicts were designed to try and mitigate some of the horrors of warfare. It is unsurprising then that when those rules are violated, horrible outcomes eventuate.

However, part of the process of ensuring that those violations are addressed, and that people are held accountable for such outcomes in some way, is to educate society about the laws of armed conflict, to ensure that people are aware that there are rules that govern conduct in armed conflicts, and that when violations of the rules are brought to light, some public accounting for such acts takes place. This book is a part of that process, and contributes to the process of disseminating the law of armed conflict, and bringing knowledge about its content to society at large. This book looks at this complex and dynamic part of international law, outlining the relevant law, the historical context in which the law developed and emerged, and looks at future challenges to the law.

The authors of this book have many people to thank for helping get this book to publication. First, we must thank our editorial and production team at Cambridge University Press, including Marta Walkowiak, Finola O'Sullivan and Valerie Appleby, who helped shepherd this book in its various incarnations to the work it is today. We also must acknowledge and thank the reviewers of this work, whose thoughtful comments helped shaped and develop the text. Thanks must also go to our colleagues at the Sydney Law School at the University of Sydney, whose collegiality and friendship played no small part in helping us complete the work. Alison Pert is particularly grateful to Lorraine Walsh and Sarah Schwartz for their sterling editorial assistance, and above all to her co-author Emily Crawford for her extraordinary intellectual and personal generosity in all things.

Emily Crawford would like to thank Dr Christian Henderson at the University of Liverpool for his helpful and considerate comments on early drafts of this work, which were immeasurably helpful in improving and developing the manuscript. Acknowledgments must also go to Associate Professor Christopher Michaelsen at UNSW, for his help with an early version of this text. Emily would also like to extend her profound and heartfelt thanks to her co-author, Dr Alison Pert, without whom this text would have never been finished. Emily would like to express her gratitude to her family – Marisa, James, Rebecca, Graham, Daniel, Sofia, Stella, Sadie, Lynn, Phil, Liv, Dem and Lachlan, for their continued support and kindness. Finally, eternal thanks goes to James Ryan, for always making everything better.

TABLE OF CASES

TABLES OF TREATIES, LEGISLATION AND OTHER INSTRUMENTS

LIST OF ABBREVIATIONS

AD	*Annual Digest*
AFL Rev	*Air Force Law Review*
AJIL	*American Journal of International Law*
Am J Public Health	*American Journal of Public Health*
Am U J Int'l L	*American University Journal of International Law*
Am U J Int'l L & Pol'y	*American University Journal of International Law and Policy*
API	Protocol Additional to the Geneva Conventions of 12 August 1949, and Relating to the Protection of Victims of International Armed Conflicts, of 8 June 1977
APII	Protocol Additional to the Geneva Conventions of 12 August 1949, and Relating to the Protection of Victims of Non-International Armed Conflicts, of 8 June 1977
AP Commentary	Yves Sandoz, Christophe Swinarski and Bruno Zimmerman (eds.), *Commentary on the Additional Protocols of 8 June 1977 to the Geneva Conventions of 12 August 1949*, (Geneva: ICRC/Martinus Nijhoff, 1987)
Ariz J Int'l & Comp L	*Arizona Journal of International and Comparative Law*
AULR	*American University Law Review*
AUILR	*American University International Law Review*
BYBIL	*British Yearbook of International Law*
Cal W Int'l LJ	*California Western International Law Journal*
Case W Res JIL	*Case Western Reserve Journal of International Law*
Chicago J Int'l L	*Chicago Journal of International Law*
CDDH	Diplomatic Conference on the Reaffirmation and Development of International Humanitarian Law Applicable in Armed Conflicts (Geneva, 1974–7)
Chinese J Int'l L	*Chinese Journal of International Law*
Colum J Transt'l L	*Columbia Journal of Transnational Law*
Convention I	Geneva Convention (I) for the Amelioration of the Condition of the Wounded and Sick in Armed Forces in the Field, of 12 August 1949
Convention II	Geneva Convention (II) for the Amelioration of the Condition of the Wounded, Sick in Armed Forces at Sea, of 12 August 1949

Convention III	Geneva Convention (III) Relative to the Treatment of Prisoners of War, of 12 August 1949
Convention IV	Geneva Convention (IV) Relative to the Protection of Civilian Persons in Time of War, of 12 August 1949
CTS	*Consolidated Treaty Series*
Denver J Int'l L & Pol'y	*Denver Journal of International Law and Policy*
Dick J Int'l L	*Dickinson Journal of International Law*
DoD	Department of Defense (US)
DPH	Direct Participation in Hostilities
DPHIG	Direct Participation in Hostilities Interpretive Guidance (ICRC)
EJIL	*European Journal of International Law*
ENMOD	United Nations Convention on the Prohibition of Military or Any Other Use of Environmental Modification Techniques 1976
EU	European Union
Fleck (ed.)	Dieter Fleck (ed.), *The Handbook of Humanitarian Law in Armed Conflicts*, 3rd edn (Oxford University Press, 2013)
Final Record	Final Record of the Diplomatic Conference of Geneva of 1949
For Aff	Foreign Affairs
Ga J Int'l & Comp L	*Georgia Journal of International and Comparative Law*
GC	Geneva Convention
GCI Commentary	Pictet (ed), *Commentary to Geneva Convention I for the Amelioration of the Condition of the Wounded and Sick in Armed Forces in the Field*, (Geneva: ICRC, 1952)
GCII Commentary	Pictet (ed), *Commentary to Geneva Convention II for the Amelioration of the Condition of the Wounded, Sick and Shipwrecked Members of the in Armed Forces at Sea*, (Geneva: ICRC, 1960)
GCIII Commentary	Pictet (ed), *Commentary to the Third Geneva Convention Relative to the Treatment of Prisoners of War*, (Geneva: ICRC, 1960)
GCIV Commentary	Pictet (ed), *Commentary to Geneva Convention IV Relative to the Protection of Civilian Persons in Time of War*, (Geneva: ICRC, 1958)
Harv Int'l L J	*Harvard International Law Journal*
HLR	*Harvard Law Review*
Harv Nat Sec J	*Harvard National Security Journal*

HR/Hague Regs	Regulations concerning the Laws and Customs of War on Land, Annex to Convention (IV) Respecting the Laws and Customs of War on Land, of 18 October 1907
IAC	International Armed Conflict
ICC	International Criminal Court
ICJ	International Court of Justice
ICJ Rep.	International Court of Justice, Reports of Judgments
ICLQ	*International and Comparative Law Quarterly*
ICRC	International Committee of the Red Cross
ICRC CIHL Study	Jean-Marie Henckaerts and Louise Doswald-Beck (eds.), *International Committee of the Red Cross: Customary International Humanitarian Law, Volume I: Rules, Volume 2: Practice* (in two parts), (Cambridge University Press, 2005)
ICTR	International Criminal Tribunal for Rwanda
ICTY	International Criminal Tribunal for the Former Yugoslavia
IHL	International Humanitarian Law
IJIL	*Indian Journal of International Law*
ILA	International Law Association
ILC	International Law Commission
IMT	International Military Tribunal (Nuremberg)
IRRC	*International Review of the Red Cross*
ISAF	International Security Assistance Force (in Afghanistan)
IYBHR	*Israeli Yearbook of Human Rights*
J Conf & Sec L	*Journal of Conflict and Security Law*
JICJ	*Journal of International Criminal Justice*
Lieber Code	Instructions for the Government of Armies of the United States in the Field, Prepared By Francis Lieber, Promulgated as General Orders No. 100 by President Lincoln, 24 April 1863
LJIL	*Leiden Journal of International Law*
LNTS	*League of Nations Treaty Series*
LOIAC	Law of International Armed Conflict
Melb U L R	*Melbourne University Law Review*
Mich J Int'l L	*Michigan Journal of International Law*
Mil L R	*Military Law Review*
MJIL	*Melbourne Journal of International Law*
Montreux Document	The Montreux Document on Pertinent International Legal Obligations and Good Practices for States related to Operations of Private Military and Security Companies during Armed Conflict 2008

Neth YB Int'l L	*Netherlands Yearbook of International Law*
New Rules	Michael Bothe, Karl Joseph Partsch and Waldemar Solf (eds.), New Rules for Victims of Armed Conflicts: Commentary on the Two 1977 Protocols Additional to the Geneva Conventions of 1949, Martinus Nijhoff, The Hague/Boston/London, 1982
NIAC	Non-International Armed Conflict
Nordic J Int' L	Nordic Journal of International Law
NYUJ Int' Law & Pol	New York University Journal of International Law and Policy
Official Records	Official Records of the Diplomatic Conference on the Reaffirmation and Development of International Humanitarian Law Applicable in Armed Conflicts Geneva 1974-1977
Pal YB Int'l Law	Palestine Yearbook of International Law
Penn St Int'l L Rev	Pennsylvania State International Law Review
PD	Piskei Din
PMSC	Private Military and Security Contractor
POW	Prisoner of War
Protocol I	Protocol Additional to the Geneva Conventions of 12 August 1949, and Relating to the Protection of Victims of International Armed Conflicts, of 8 June 1977
Protocol II	Protocol Additional to the Geneva Conventions of 12 August 1949, and Relating to the Protection of Victims of Non-International Armed Conflicts, of 8 June 1977
RCADI	Recueil des Cours de l'Academie de Droit International ("Hague Receuil")
RDMDG	Revue de Droit Militaire et de Droit de la Guerre
Res.	Resolution
Rome Statute	Rome Statute of the International Criminal Court
Sassòli, Bouvier and Quintin	Marco Sassòli, Antoine Bouvier and Anne Quintin (eds), *How Does Law Protect in War? Cases, Documents and Teaching Materials*, 3rd edn, (Geneva: ICRC, 2011)
Schindler and Toman	Dietrich Schindler and Jïri Toman (eds.), *The Laws of Armed Conflicts: A Collection of Conventions, Resolutions and Other Documents*, 4th edn, (Leiden: Martinus Nijhoff, 2004)
Stanford LPR	Stanford Law and Policy Review
Tallinn Manual	Michael Schmitt (ed.), *The Tallinn Manual on the International Law Applicable to Cyber Warfare*, Cambridge University Press, New York, 2013

TWC	Trials of War Criminals before the Nuremberg Military Tribunals
UC Davis LR	University of California Davis Law Review
UCLA L Rev	University of California Law Review
UN	United Nations
UNGA	United Nations General Assembly
UN SC	United Nations Security Council
UNTS	United Nations Treaty Series
U Rich L Rev	University of Richmond Law Review
Va J Int'l L	Virginia Journal of International Law
Vand J Transnat'l L	Vandenberg Journal of Transnational Law
YBIHL	Yearbook of International Humanitarian Law

Introduction

When the International Law Commission (ILC) was established in 1947, it was tasked with "the promotion of the progressive development of international law and its codification".[1] At its first meeting in 1949, the Commission set about examining the areas of international law that were in need of such codification or progressive development, and the question of whether the laws of armed conflict should be selected as an area of study was raised.[2] The ILC canvassed a number of opinions, including whether "war having been outlawed, the regulation of its conduct had ceased to be relevant".[3] Ultimately, the ILC decided not to proceed with an examination of the law of armed conflict, on the basis that "if the Commission, at the very beginning of its work, were to undertake this study, public opinion might interpret its action as showing lack of confidence in the efficiency of the means at the disposal of the United Nations for maintaining peace."[4]

The ILC position on the law of armed conflict in 1949 touches on an attitude towards the law that is often expressed by newcomers to the field: how can one "introduce moderation and restraint into an activity uniquely contrary to those qualities"?[5] How can there be laws to regulate and constrain behaviour in situations that are essentially lawless, where injury and death of persons, and damage

---

[1] Article 1(1), Statute of the International Law Commission, Adopted by the General Assembly in resolution 174 (II) of 21 November 1947, as amended by resolutions 485 (V) of 12 December 1950, 984 (X) of 3 December 1955, 985 (X) of 3 December 1955 and 36/39 of 18 November 1981.

[2] Based on memoranda submitted to the ILC by the Secretary-General including: a Survey of International Law in relation to the Work of Codification of the International Law Commission (UN Doc. A/CN.4/1/Rev.l); Preparatory Study concerning a draft Declaration on the Rights and Duties of States (UN Doc. A/CN.4/2); The Charter and Judgment of the Nürnberg Tribunal: History and Analysis (UN Doc. A/CN.4/5); Ways and Means of making the Evidence of Customary International Law more readily available (UN Doc. A/CN.4/6); a Historical Survey of the Question of International Criminal Jurisdiction (UN Doc. A/CN.4/7); and International and National Organizations concerned with Questions of International Law: tentative list (UN Doc. A/CN.4/8).

[3] *Yearbook of the International Law Commission 1949*, p. 281, para. 18.   [4] Ibid.

[5] Gary Solis, *The Law of Armed Conflict: International Humanitarian Law in War* (Cambridge University Press, 2010), p. 8.

and destruction of property are a given, even a hoped-for outcome? Indeed, there is ample evidence throughout history to demonstrate that when wars erupt, barbarous acts have occurred, and the architects and perpetrators of such barbarity often escape without being held accountable for their acts.[6] However, there are also numerous examples throughout history of peoples, groups and States willingly agreeing to conduct their wars in accordance with certain humanitarian dictates and limitations.[7] The reasons for agreeing to constrain wartime conduct vary – they can be for religious, ethical, political or pragmatic reasons. Nevertheless, restraint in warfare has been as much a part of war as lack of restraint. Indeed, as this book demonstrates, States have accepted, and continue to accept and embrace, increasing regulation and sanction on their conduct in armed conflicts.

It is the question of restraint in warfare, and how it is given legal force, that is the focus of this book. Comprising nine chapters, this book looks at the major areas of IHL, putting them in historical context, so as to better understand how the law has evolved. This book also examines the current challenges for and pressures on the existing law, as IHL rules adopted in the time of cavalry and bayonets must adapt to deal with issues like drones, cyber warfare and autonomous weaponry. Chapter 1 looks at the historical development of IHL, from its origins in Europe in the 1850s, and the historical events that have shaped the law through the last century and a half. Chapter 2 then outlines the contemporary legal framework of IHL, examining the treaty and customary laws that govern conduct in armed conflict, and exploring the fundamental principles of the law. Chapter 3 examines the types of armed conflict currently regulated under IHL, and the tests that have developed to determine whether an armed conflict exists.

The book then narrows its focus to examine how individuals are dealt with under the law, and how IHL regulates conduct and provides rights and responsibilities for individuals who participate (or do not participate) in armed conflicts. The first of these chapters, Chapter 4, looks at the concept of combatants and non-combatants, and its connected status, that of prisoner of war (POW). Chapter 4 examines who is entitled under IHL to combatant status, and examines those persons who have been denied combatant and POW status under IHL. Chapter 4 also explores the current legal thinking regarding a contentious area of the law – that of direct participation in hostilities. Chapter 5 looks at the rules regarding the protection of the wounded, sick and shipwrecked members of the armed forces, and those who care for them – medical and religious personnel. This chapter also looks at the law regarding what is perhaps the most recognisable emblem in the world – the Red Cross, and its affiliated emblems, the Red Crescent and Red Crystal.

---

[6] Solis gives the examples of Idi Amin and Josef Mengele as just two instances of persons who were never brought to account for their acts of "butchery" (ibid., p. 8).

[7] See further Chapter 1 for examples of historical limitations on warfare.

How the law defines and protects all those persons who are not designated as combatants or POWs – civilians – forms the focus of Chapter 6, which examines how the law protects civilians who find themselves in the hands of an adverse power in situations of belligerent occupation. Chapter 6 examines the rules that Occupying Powers must observe when, in international armed conflicts, they find themselves in temporary possession of territory that belongs to another sovereign State. Additional rules regarding protecting civilians from the deleterious effects of the conflict provide the focus of Chapter 7, which looks at the law of targeting. Chapter 8 looks at the general rules which apply to means and methods of warfare, and what kinds of weapons have been prohibited under IHL. Chapter 8 also examines a number of means and methods which have been the focus of much attention, but whose legality is highly contested, including the use of nuclear weapons, white phosphorus, depleted uranium munitions, cyber warfare, drone warfare and targeted killing. The final chapter of this book looks at how all these rules are implemented and enforced, and what mechanisms exist to hold violators of the law accountable for their acts.

Certain topics related to the law of armed conflict have not been examined in this book – for example, the law of neutrality, the interaction between IHL and human rights law, and the law on peacekeeping; furthermore, other areas of the law are touched on, but are not examined in specific detail, such as the specific rules on naval and aerial warfare, and international criminal law. This decision was made not because the authors considered the topics insignificant; rather, we wished to provide a detailed but comparatively concise assessment of what we consider to be the core rules of IHL, that would make the law accessible to newcomers to the field, but also to offer something for practitioners also.

1 Historical development of international humanitarian law

1. INTRODUCTION

For thousands of years, different societies have recognised that there are certain acts that are, and others that are not, permissible in war. There is evidence of rules regarding warfare in ancient China, India and what we now call the Middle East, dating back two millennia BC.[1] Hugo Grotius, the great seventeenth century Dutch jurist regarded as the "Father of the Law of Nations",[2] devoted one of the three books comprising his 1625 masterpiece *On the Law of War and Peace* to the rules applicable in war.[3] In it he drew on extensive examples from ancient Roman and Greek practice and literature to conclude that a number of principles were part of the "Law of Nations". Practices that he asserted were forbidden included the use of poison and poisoned weapons,[4] and rape,[5] while destruction and pillage of enemy property were permitted, as was the killing of all those in enemy territory – even women and children, and prisoners.[6] But Grotius drew a distinction between what was legally permissible and what was "right", compiling an extensive list of moral prohibitions that included the killing of women, children, prisoners of war and other categories of non-fighters, and positive requirements of moderation in the conduct of hostilities.[7]

Another great European jurist, Georg Friedrich von Martens, described a similar list of rules of warfare that had become custom by the late eighteenth

---

[1] See e.g. Leslie Green, *The Contemporary Law of Armed Conflict*, 3rd edn, (Manchester University Press, 2008), pp. 26–36.

[2] L. Oppenheim, *International Law: A Treatise*, 1st edn, 2 vols. (London /New York: Longmans, Green and Co., 1905–6), vol. I, p. 58.

[3] Hugo Grotius, *De Jure Belli ac Pacis Libri Tres*, trans. Francis W. Kelsey, in James Brown Scott (ed.) *The Classics of International Law*, (Oxford University Press, 1925), vol. 2.

[4] Ibid., pp. 651–3.   [5] Ibid., pp. 656–7.   [6] Ibid., pp. 646–51, 658.   [7] Ibid., pp. 643, 722–77.

century.[8] Of particular interest in light of subsequent developments are von Martens's views on "the treatment of the vanquished", where he asserted that "[t]he victor, he who remains master of the field of battle, ought to take care of the wounded, and bury the dead. It is against every principle of the laws of war, to refuse or neglect to do either."[9] He described this duty as "dictated by humanity".[10]

While the laws and usages of war continued to evolve, the practice of States was by no means uniform; in many cases these were rules, as Grotius had put it, "if not of all nations, certainly of those of the better sort".[11] By the middle of the nineteenth century, many of these usages may indeed have become customary international law, but they had not been codified in a multilateral treaty. This began to change in 1856 with the Declaration of Paris at the end of the Crimean War, establishing a few short but important rules on maritime law in time of war.[12] But it was in the following decade that the modern law of armed conflict, or international humanitarian law, began to take shape from two quite separate but concurrent developments.

2. HENRI DUNANT AND THE BATTLE OF SOLFERINO

The first was the Battle of Solferino, in June 1859. Fought between the forces of Austria and a French-Piedmontese alliance, involving over 300,000 men, it was one of the great battles in the struggle to unify Italy, and the most bloody: lasting only a day, the battle left 6,000 dead and nearly 40,000 wounded.[13] Henri Dunant was a Swiss businessman who happened to arrive in the nearby town of Castiglione on the day of the battle and witnessed the aftermath. He was so moved by what he saw that he wrote a detailed account of his experiences, published in 1862 under the title "A Memory of Solferino".[14] He described how the army field hospitals were wholly inadequate and soon overwhelmed; in addition to the thousands of dead, many more thousands of wounded and dying men were left on the battlefield without water, food or medical care. It took many days for the wounded to be collected and taken to nearby villages and towns; more than 9,000 were brought into Castiglione where Dunant and the townspeople did what they could to help alleviate the

---

[8] G. F. von Martens, *Summary of the Law of Nations*, trans. William Cobbett (Philadelphia: Thomas Bradford, 1795), pp. 279–97. Georg Friedrich von Martens (1756–1821) was a German jurist and diplomat; to avoid confusion with the Russian Fyodor Fyodorovich Martens (1845–1909), whose name in French and German is translated as "de Martens" and "von Martens" (see e.g. n. 38 below), G. F. von Martens will be referred to in this book as "von Martens", and Fyodor Fyodorovich Martens as simply "Martens".

[9] Ibid., p. 295.   [10] Ibid.   [11] Grotius, *De Jure Belli ac Pacis Libri Tres*, p. 652.

[12] Declaration Respecting Maritime Law, Paris, 16 April 1856, in force 18 April 1858, 115 CTS 1.

[13] François Bugnion, "Birth of an Idea: The Founding of the International Committee of the Red Cross and of the International Red Cross and Red Crescent Movement: From Solferino to the Original Geneva Convention (1859–1864)" (2012) 94 IRRC 1299 at 1301.

[14] Jean-Henri Dunant, *A Memory of Solferino*, 1862, trans. by the American Red Cross (Geneva: ICRC, 1939).

suffering. But there were few medical supplies and fewer doctors, and wounds quickly became infected from the heat, dust and lack of treatment. Dunant organised a group of volunteer helpers, as "[t]he convoys brought a fresh contingent of wounded men into Castiglione every quarter of an hour, and the shortage of assistants, orderlies and helpers was cruelly felt."[15]

After a few days the crisis eased as the wounded were transported to hospitals in larger towns, but as Dunant discovered when he left Castiglione for Brescia, there was a shortage of voluntary orderlies and nurses everywhere.[16] A poignant example of the lack of care cited by Dunant was of a dying soldier who had letters from his family at the post office, that would have brought him great comfort, but the hospital workers refused to fetch them. When well-meaning townspeople brought unsuitable food to the hospitals, access was limited to those with official authorisation, which few were willing to seek, and their "charitable zeal" began to wear off.[17] Dunant saw that "selected and competent volunteers, sent by societies sanctioned and approved by authorities, would easily have overcome all these difficulties".[18] He therefore called, in his 1862 book, for the establishment of societies for the relief of the wounded – organisations of experienced volunteers, recognised and accepted by commanders and armies in the field, who would provide immediate treatment of the wounded on the battlefield – and for States to agree by treaty to grant such access.[19] This would alleviate suffering as early as possible, and prevent the exacerbation of injuries, amputations and deaths that had resulted from neglect and infection at Solferino.[20] This was not an original idea, as Dunant admits, but the instant popularity of his book ensured its wide dissemination.[21]

3. THE 1864 GENEVA CONVENTION

Dunant's suggestions were taken up by the Geneva Society for Public Welfare, and in early 1863 a committee including Dunant was set up to develop these ideas.[22] The committee organised an international conference in Geneva later that year which discussed a draft convention the committee had prepared, and passed a number of resolutions agreeing to the establishment of national committees; these would supply voluntary medical personnel to armies in the field and these volunteers would wear a white armband with a red cross as a uniform, distinctive sign.[23] Another important step was the conference's recommendation that all countries adopt a uniform flag and sign for their medical corps and facilities, and that medical

---

[15] Ibid., p. 60.   [16] Ibid., p. 102.   [17] Ibid.   [18] Ibid., p. 103.   [19] Ibid., pp. 124–6.
[20] Ibid., pp. 116–28.   [21] Ibid., pp. 124, 9.   [22] Ibid., pp. 129–39.
[23] ICRC, "Resolutions of the Geneva International Conference, Geneva, 26–29 October 1863", www.icrc.org/applic/ihl/ihl.nsf/INTRO/115?OpenDocument.

personnel, hospitals and ambulances, as well as the wounded themselves, should be recognised as neutral.[24]

To give effect to these principles, at the behest of the committee the Swiss government invited States to a diplomatic conference which, in August 1864, adopted the landmark Geneva Convention for the Amelioration of the Condition of the Wounded in Armies in the Field. The core provisions of the Convention were neutrality of the wounded and those who care for them, the adoption of the red cross on a white background as the distinctive sign for medical facilities and personnel, and an obligation to collect and care for the wounded and sick on the battlefield, regardless of nationality.[25] These were radical provisions: for the first time, international law applied to an activity – war – which (apart from some maritime questions) had previously been ruled by force; moral ideas of humanity moderated State interests; and international law protected private actors, such as the voluntary relief societies, on the battlefield.[26]

A dozen years after this, the Geneva committee adopted the name by which it is now known: the International Committee of the Red Cross (ICRC).[27] Thus the experiences of one man witnessing the effects of one battle led directly to two milestones in the development of modern international humanitarian law: the 1864 Geneva Convention, and the founding of the Red Cross and Red Crescent Movement. In recognition of his contribution, Dunant was the joint recipient of the first Nobel Peace Prize, in 1901.[28]

4. THE LIEBER CODE 1863

Meanwhile, the other major development arose indirectly out of the Civil War in the United States (1861–5). At the beginning of the war, Francis Lieber was a highly regarded professor at Columbia in New York, writing and lecturing on military law.[29] The war raised difficult legal questions for the Union forces, such as whether the exchange of prisoners, customary in warfare, would amount to recognition of the Confederacy as a belligerent, i.e. a sovereign power, rather than an unlawful rebel force.[30] Lieber published his opinions on these issues, and his advice was regularly sought by the Union government, particularly another international lawyer, Henry Halleck, who was appointed General-in-Chief of the Union armies

---

[24] Ibid.
[25] Convention for the Amelioration of the Condition of the Wounded in Armies in the Field, Geneva, 22 August 1864, in force 22 June 1865, 129 CTS 361.
[26] Jean Pictet (ed.), *Commentary to Geneva Convention I for the Amelioration of the Condition of the Wounded and Sick in Armed Forces in the Field* (Geneva: ICRC, 1952) ("GC I Commentary"), p. 11.
[27] ICRC, Resolutions of the Geneva International Conference.
[28] The Nobel Prize, *The Nobel Peace Prize 1901*, www.nobelprize.org/nobel_prizes/peace/laureates/1901/.
[29] Ernest Nys, "Francis Lieber – His Life and His Work" (1911) 5 AJIL 355 at 355.
[30] Francis Lieber, "The Disposal of Prisoners", letter to *The New York Times*, 19 August 1861.

in 1862.[31] Lieber persuaded Halleck that because the existing army regulations were far from comprehensive, a code of all the laws and usages of war should be drawn up. Halleck agreed, appointing Lieber to a War Department board of five men to prepare such a code. Drafted by Lieber and revised by the board, the "Instructions for the Government of Armies of the United States in the Field" were issued by the Union government as General Orders No. 100 in April 1863.

The "Lieber Code" was the first time a government had set out explicit rules not only on matters of internal discipline, as previous military codes had done, but also on the treatment of enemy forces and civilians.[32] It covered, in its 157 articles, everything from rules on occupation of enemy territory, protection of civilians and civilian objects, and the treatment of prisoners of war, to assassination and the rules applicable in civil war. The Code had a profound influence, being adopted to varying degrees by Great Britain, France, Prussia, Spain, Russia, Serbia, the Netherlands and Argentina.[33] It formed the basis of draft conventions in 1874 and an 1880 manual on the laws of land warfare prepared by the Institute of International Law.[34] More enduringly, it also found expression in the second and fourth Hague Conventions of 1899 and 1907 (discussed below), as well as influencing the later Geneva Conventions.[35]

5. THE 1868 ST PETERSBURG DECLARATION

The 1860s saw another innovation with the 1868 St Petersburg Declaration, the first international agreement to prohibit particular weapons.[36] Bullets had recently been invented that exploded on contact with the target, and were being adopted for military purposes. Because such bullets would cause considerably more damage to the human body than traditional bullets, the Russian government decided that they were an inhumane form of weapon.[37] It invited States to an International Military Commission to discuss the issue and the result was a binding declaration, ratified or acceded to by nineteen states at the time, prohibiting the use in time of war of bullets which were "explosive or charged with fulminating or inflammable substances".[38]

---

[31] Richard Shelly Hartigan, *Lieber's Code and the Law of War* (New York: The Legal Classics Library, 1995), pp. 2–14.

[32] Ibid., pp. 2–5.

[33] Gary Solis, *The Law of Armed Conflict: International Humanitarian Law in War* (Cambridge University Press, 2010), p. 40.

[34] Hartigan, *Lieber's Code*, p. 22.   [35] Ernest Nys, "Francis Lieber – His Life and His Work", 391–2.

[36] Declaration Renouncing the Use, in Time of War, of Explosive Projectiles Under 400 Grammes Weight, Saint Petersburg, in force 29 November/11 December 1868, 138 CTS 297 ("St Petersburg Declaration").

[37] Ibid.

[38] St Petersburg Declaration, first operative paragraph. The Declaration applied to "any [such] projectile of a weight below 400 grammes", thus allowing their use against hard objects such as artillery and gun carriages

With many of that time believing that "the object of making war is to kill",[39] it is of particular significance that the participants noted the need "to conciliate the necessities of war with the laws of humanity", and affirmed that:

the only legitimate object which States should endeavour to accomplish during war is to weaken the military forces of the enemy;

That for this purpose it is sufficient to disable the greatest possible number of men;

That this object would be exceeded by the employment of arms which uselessly aggravate the sufferings of disabled men, or render their death inevitable;

That the employment of such arms would, therefore, be contrary to the laws of humanity.[40]

These concepts of balancing military necessity and humanity, and the avoidance of unnecessary suffering, are at the heart of international humanitarian law. They are discussed further in Chapter 2.

6. THE 1868 ADDITIONAL ARTICLES, 1874 BRUSSELS DECLARATION, 1880 OXFORD MANUAL

Some States attending the St Petersburg conference had been willing to broaden the discussion to consider prohibiting other "barbaric" means of warfare, but this was precluded by other States, notably Great Britain, which insisted on retaining complete freedom in the choice of means.[41] Fundamental divisions between States as to the existence and extent of the laws and customs of war continued for the next thirty years. In 1868 an unsuccessful attempt was made to clarify some of the provisions of the 1864 Geneva Convention and extend them to naval warfare, in the Additional Articles relating to the Condition of the Wounded in War.[42] The Additional Articles did not come into force, but their object was eventually achieved by one of the 1899 Hague Conventions.[43] In the Franco-German War of 1870–1 the belligerents accused each other of violating the laws and customs of war, and public opinion in many European quarters demanded an end to the "uncertainty and anarchy" surrounding these questions.[44]

---

while prohibiting them in small arms: Fyodor de Martens, *La Paix et la Guerre* (Paris: Arthur Rousseau, 1901), p. 88 (note this is the French version of the name of Fyodor Fyodorovich Martens).

[39] "The Emperor of Russia on Projectiles", *The Sydney Morning Herald*, 26 August 1868, p. 6, trove.nla.gov.au/ndp/del/article/13171704.

[40] St Petersburg Declaration, fifth operative paragraph and preamble.

[41] Martens, *La Paix et la Guerre*, pp. 89–91.

[42] Additional Articles relating to the Condition of the Wounded in War, Geneva, 20 October 1868, 138 CTS 189.

[43] Convention for the Adaptation to Maritime Warfare of the Principles of the Geneva Convention of August 22, 1864, The Hague, 29 July 1899, in force 4 September 1900, 187 CTS 443 ("Hague III 1899").

[44] Martens, *La Paix et la Guerre*, p. 98 (Pert translation).

This led to the Russian government again taking the initiative in inviting States to a conference in Brussels in 1874, to discuss a draft code of the laws of war on land.[45] The first draft was prepared by Fyodor Fyodorovich Martens, revised and expanded by a Russian government commission, and submitted to the conference.[46] The conference agreed a draft code in the Brussels Declaration of 1874, drawing in part on the Lieber Code, but States were not ready to commit to binding prescriptions as to how they should conduct war and defend themselves. A major area of disagreement concerned the laws of occupation, a subject of great contention in the recent Franco-German War, and in particular, who would be entitled to combatant status when a population took up arms against an occupier.[47] The Declaration, influenced by States such as Holland and Belgium, recognised as lawful combatants a population that rose *en masse* against an occupier, which Germany could not accept.[48] Great Britain was also obstinately opposed to a binding code, while the smaller powers called it a "code for invasion".[49]

The 1874 Declaration lacked any binding effect but the following year the newly-formed Institute of International Law began work, using the Declaration as a starting point, on ways to restrain the destructive effects of war, while recognising its inevitable necessities.[50] As the rapporteur for the project (Gustave Moynier, a leading member of the original International Committee of the Red Cross) noted, the Institute accepted that an international treaty was perhaps premature; it therefore produced, and adopted at its meeting in Oxford in 1880, a Manual on the Laws of War on Land that it hoped States would use as a basis for national legislation.[51]

7. THE 1899 AND 1907 HAGUE CONVENTIONS

As the nineteenth century continued to see more wars, rapid advances in weaponry and mounting expenditure on arms, the Russian government once more proposed an international conference.[52] In 1898 it invited all States represented in St Petersburg to a conference with the object of seeking means to limit the "progressive increase of military and naval armaments, a question the solution of which becomes evidently more and more urgent in view of the fresh extension given to these

---

[45] Ibid., p. 99.   [46] Ibid., p. 103.

[47] Peter Holquist, *The Russian Empire as a "Civilized State": International Law as Principle and Practice in Imperial Russia, 1874–1878* (Washington: The National Council for Eurasian and East European Research, 2004), p. 13.

[48] Ibid., p. 11; Martens, *La Paix et la Guerre*, pp. 372–3.   [49] Martens, *La Paix et la Guerre*, pp. 100, 121.

[50] Institute of International Law, Resolutions, "Examen de la Déclaration de Bruxelles de 1874", 30 August 1875, www.idi–iil.org/idiF/resolutionsF/1875_haye_02_fr.pdf; Institute of International Law, Manuel des Lois de la Guerre sur Terre, 9 September 1880, www.idi–iil.org/idiF/resolutionsF/1880_oxf_02_fr.pdf, Preface.

[51] Institute of International Law, Manuel 1880, Preface.   [52] Solis, *The Law of Armed Conflict*, p. 51.

armaments", and of "preventing armed conflicts by . . . pacific means".[53] The list of proposed subjects for discussion included the prohibition of new weapons, adapting the Geneva Convention of 1864 to naval war and a revision of the 1874 Brussels Declaration concerning the laws and customs of war. It was thought more conducive to agreement to hold the conference elsewhere than in a Great Power, and the Netherlands obliged by offering The Hague as a venue.[54] Twenty-six States attended what quickly became known as the Peace Conference, in 1899.[55]

The work of the Conference was divided between three commissions: the first on limiting armaments and military expenditure, the second on "the laws governing civilized warfare" (of which Martens was appointed chair) and the third on mediation and arbitration.[56] After two months of meetings, the first commission failed to achieve consensus on disarmament, but the other commissions were more successful, with the conclusion of several important treaties:

- Convention for the Pacific Settlement of International Disputes (Hague I)[57]
- Convention with Respect to the Laws and Customs of War on Land (Hague II)[58]
- Convention for the Adaptation to Maritime Warfare of the Principles of the Geneva Convention of August 22, 1864 (Hague III)[59]
- Declaration on the Launching of Projectiles and Explosives from Balloons[60]
- Declaration on the Use of Projectiles the Object of Which is the Diffusion of Asphyxiating or Deleterious Gases,[61] and
- Declaration on the Use of Bullets Which Expand or Flatten Easily in the Human Body.[62]

In the Convention for the Pacific Settlement of International Disputes, States agreed to "use their best efforts to insure the pacific settlement of international differences" and to establish a Permanent Court of Arbitration to which disputes could be referred. Of even greater significance to the law of armed conflict was the second Hague Convention – the first internationally agreed, legally binding code of (at least

---

[53] Russian Circular Notes Proposing the First Peace Conference, 12 August 1898 and Program of the First Conference, 30 December 1898, in James Brown Scott, *The Hague Conventions and Declarations of 1899 and 1907*, (Washington, DC: Carnegie Endowment for International Peace, 1915), pp. xiv–xvi.

[54] Ibid., p. xvii.   [55] Ibid., pp. vi–vii.   [56] "The Peace Conference", *The New York Times*, 18 May 1899, 1.

[57] Scott, *The Hague Conventions and Declarations of 1899 and 1907*, p. vi; International Convention for the Pacific Settlement of International Disputes, The Hague, 29 July 1899, in force 4 September 1900, 187 CTS 410 ("Hague I 1899").

[58] Convention with Respect to the Laws and Customs of War on Land, The Hague, 29 July 1899, in force 4 September 1900, 187 CTS 429 ("Hague II 1899").

[59] Convention for the Adaptation to Maritime Warfare of the Principles of the Geneva Convention, The Hague, 29 July 1899, in force 4 September 1900, 187 CTS 443 ("Hague III 1899").

[60] Declaration Concerning the Prohibition, for the Term of Five Years, of the Launching of Projectiles and Explosives from Balloons or Other New Methods of a Similar Nature, The Hague, July 29, 1899, in force 4 September 1900, 187 CTS 453 ("Hague IV, 1 1899").

[61] Declaration Concerning the Prohibition of the Use of Projectiles Diffusing Asphyxiating Gases, The Hague, July 29, 1899, in force 4 September 1900, 187 CTS 429 ("Hague IV, 2 1899").

[62] Declaration on the Use of Bullets which Expand or Flatten Easily in the Human Body, The Hague, July 29, 1899, in force 4 September 1900, 187 CTS 459 ("Hague IV, 3 1899") .

some of) the laws and customs of war on land. The detailed rules were based on the 1874 Brussels Declaration which in turn had drawn "its life and spirit" from the Lieber Code.[63] Another success for the conference was the third Convention, finally applying the substance of the 1864 Geneva Convention, and the protections of the Red Cross, to naval warfare.[64] One of the outcomes of the conference that has come to be appreciated more with the passage of time was the Martens clause, discussed in more detail in Chapter 2 below.[65]

A second peace conference was envisaged and with Russia preoccupied with its war with Japan, the United States proposed such a conference in 1904.[66] On the conclusion of the Russia–Japan war in 1905, Russia resumed its previous role and arranged a second conference in 1907, again in The Hague, where forty-four States were represented.[67] One of the aims of the conference was "further developing the humanitarian principles" on which the 1899 conference had been based; it was recognised that many of the provisions agreed in 1899 could be refined and improved, and other aspects of warfare addressed.[68] These aims were achieved: the 1899 Conventions were revised and ten new treaties adopted:

- Hague I – Pacific Settlement of International Disputes
- Hague II – Limitation of Employment of Force for Recovery of Contract Debts
- Hague III – Opening of Hostilities
- Hague IV – Laws and Customs of War on Land
- Hague V – Rights and Duties of Neutral Powers and Persons in Case of War on Land
- Hague VI – Status of Enemy Merchant Ships at the Outbreak of Hostilities
- Hague VII – Conversion of Merchant Ships into War Ships
- Hague VIII – Laying of Automatic Submarine Contact Mines
- Hague IX – Bombardment by Naval Forces in Time of War
- Hague X – Adaptation to Maritime War of the Principles of the Geneva Convention
- Hague XI – Restrictions With Regard to the Exercise of the Right of Capture in Naval War
- Hague XII – Creation of an International Prize Court
- Hague XIII – Rights and Duties of Neutral Powers in Naval War
- Declaration (XIV) prohibiting the Discharge of Projectiles and Explosives from Balloons.[69]

---

[63] James Brown Scott, "The Work of the Second Peace Conference" (1908) 2 AJIL 1 at 11.
[64] Martens, *La Paix et la Guerre*, p. 435.   [65] See p. 47.
[66] Letters from the US Secretary of State to the American diplomatic representatives accredited to the Governments signatory to the acts of the first Hague Conference, 21 October and 16 December 1904, Scott, *The Hague Conventions and Declarations of 1899 and 1907*, pp. xix–xxv.
[67] Scott, *The Hague Conventions and Declarations of 1899 and 1907*, p. viii.
[68] Letter Russian Ambassador to US Secretary of State 12 April 1906, Scott, *The Hague Conventions and Declarations of 1899 and 1907*, pp. xxvi–xxviii.
[69] For the text of each instrument and a useful side-by-side comparison of the 1899 and 1907 conventions and declarations, see Scott, *The Hague Conventions and Declarations of 1899 and 1907*. For analysis and

The fourth convention revised and expanded its 1899 predecessor (Hague II, 1899), and similarly annexed detailed "regulations respecting the laws and customs of war on land"; as explained in Chapter 2, many of these "Hague Regulations" remain core rules on the conduct of armed conflict. Both conventions are still in force, although as between the parties to the 1907 Convention, it replaced the 1899 Convention.[70]

A contemporary commentator summarised the principal achievements of the conference as fourfold:

(i) providing for a third conference within eight years;

(ii) the adoption of a convention for the non-forcible collection of contract debts, "substituting arbitration and an appeal to reason for force and an appeal to arms";

(iii) establishing a prize court to safeguard neutrals; and

(iv) laying the foundations of "a great court of arbitration" – meaning, in addition to the previously established Permanent Court of Arbitration, a new permanent court of justice.[71]

Interestingly, the same commentator regarded the conferences themselves as of even greater importance than the conventions they produced, because they showed that "practically all nations of the world, recognizing and applying international law, could meet together, discuss and debate matters of universal interest, and, just as smaller and more exclusive bodies, reach results of the greatest value to mankind."[72]

8. THE 1949 GENEVA CONVENTIONS

The First World War precluded the holding of the anticipated third Hague Peace Conference, but the international community continued its efforts to "humanize war".[73] One of the recommendations of the 1899 Hague Conference had been the revision of the 1864 Geneva Convention, and this was put into effect by the 1906 Geneva Convention for the Amelioration of the Condition of the Wounded and Sick in Armies in the Field.[74] For the contracting parties, the 1906 Convention

---

commentary on the conference and its outcomes, see the numerous articles in the *American Journal of International Law*, vol. 2 (1908).

[70] Convention Respecting the Laws and Customs of War on Land, The Hague, 18 October 1907, in force 26 January 1910, 187 CTS 227 ('Hague IV 1907'), art. 4. At the time of writing, the latest accession was that of Palestine, in 2014: ICRC, *Treaties and State Parties to Such Treaties*, www.icrc.org/IHL.

[71] Scott, "The Work of the Second Peace Conference", 28. This was not achieved until the Permanent Court of International Justice was created in 1920.

[72] Scott, *The Hague Conventions and Declarations of 1899 and 1907*, pp. viii–ix. Scott's discussion here is interesting in showing that the Hague Conference, which he described as "a recognized international institution" where all States were equal, was in many ways a precursor to the League of Nations.

[73] Scott, "The Work of the Second Peace Conference", 28.

[74] Geneva Convention for the Amelioration of the Condition of the Wounded and Sick in Armies in the Field, Geneva, 6 July 1906, in force 9 August 1907, 202 CTS 144 ("GC 1906").

replaced that of 1864, and was in turn replaced by the 1929 Convention for the Amelioration of the Condition of the Wounded and Sick in Armies in the Field,[75] which among other provisions formally recognised the red crescent and the red lion and sun in addition to the red cross symbol.[76] Also in 1929 the Convention relative to the Treatment of Prisoners of War supplemented the provisions on that subject in the Hague Regulations.[77] Other important treaties were concluded in the inter-war period, such as the 1925 Geneva Gas Protocol,[78] and in the 1930s the ICRC prepared a number of draft treaties revising the 1929 Geneva Convention concerning the wounded and sick, adapting its principles to maritime and air warfare, on hospital and safety zones in time of war, and on the protection of civilians in occupied territory.[79] The intention was to submit the drafts to a diplomatic conference but again war intervened, and in light of the experiences of the Second World War, the drafts were significantly revised. The result was the four draft treaties that became the 1949 Geneva Conventions.

The Geneva Conventions have received universal acceptance, having been ratified or acceded to by more States than there are members of the United Nations.[80] Each convention deals with a distinct topic. The first (GC I) concerns "the Amelioration of the Condition of the Wounded and Sick in Armed Forces in the Field", and replaces the 1864, 1906 and 1929 conventions on the same subject.[81] The title itself is noteworthy in that it refers to "armed forces" rather than "armies" as did its predecessors, reflecting the enlarged scope of protection afforded by the Convention to include, among others, members of "organized resistance movements".[82] As discussed in Chapter 4, this was inspired by the uncertain legal status of partisans or resistance fighters in occupied territory during the Second World War.[83] The Convention is longer and more detailed than the 1929 Convention and its provisions are considered in detail in Chapters 4 and 5 below.

The second Convention (GC II) deals with "the Amelioration of the Condition of Wounded, Sick and Shipwrecked Members of Armed Forces at Sea", and adapts the provisions of the first convention to maritime warfare, replacing the 1907 Hague

---

[75] Convention for the Amelioration of the Condition of the Wounded and Sick in Armies in the Field, Geneva, 27 July 1929, in force 19 June 1931, 118 LNTS 303 ("GC 1929"), art. 34.

[76] Ibid., art. 19; and see below pp. 134–6.

[77] Convention relative to the Treatment of Prisoners of War, Geneva, 27 July 1929, in force 19 June 1931, 118 LNTS 343.

[78] Protocol for the Prohibition of the Use in War of Asphyxiating, Poisonous or Other Gases, and of Bacteriological Methods of Warfare, Geneva, 17 June 1925, in force 8 February 1928, 94 LNTS 65.

[79] ICRC, *Final Act of the Diplomatic Conference of Geneva, 12 August 1949*, www.icrc.org/applic/ihl/ihl.nsf/Treaty.xsp?documentId=A0B2F6B37BB094C7C12563CD002D6ADA&action=openDocument.

[80] The Geneva Conventions have been ratified or acceded to by the Cook Islands, the Holy See and Palestine, none of which is a member of the United Nations (although the Holy See and Palestine are "non-Member Observer States": see www.un.org/en/members/nonmembers.shtml).

[81] Convention for the Amelioration of the Condition of the Wounded and Sick in Armed Forces in the Field, Geneva, 12 August 1949, in force 21 October 1950, 75 UNTS 31 ("GC I"), art. 59.

[82] GC I, art. 13.   [83] GC I Commentary, p. 144.

X Convention.[84] The third (GC III) is a detailed code on the treatment of prisoners of war, the exhaustive detail (143 articles compared with 97 in the 1929 Convention) necessitated by the experience of the Second World War.[85] The 1929 Convention had, for example, applied primarily to members of the armed forces "captured by the enemy", thus excluding prisoner of war status for those surrendering. The 1949 Convention spells out, and to a degree expands, the categories of persons entitled to prisoner of war status, thereby indirectly defining who is entitled to combatant status in armed conflict.

The fourth Convention (GC IV)[86] is on the protection of civilians, primarily in occupied territories, the need for which was made acutely apparent during the Second World War when:

millions of civilians were left without protection at the mercy of the enemy Power and were liable to be deported, taken as hostages, or interned in concentration camps. Hundreds of thousands among their number met with a ghastly death.[87]

The main purpose of GC IV was to protect civilians from arbitrary enemy action, and it contains detailed regulations on the treatment of civilians in occupied territory or who are aliens in the territory of a party to the conflict.[88] The scope and effect of the Convention are examined in detail in Chapter 6 below.

a. Common Article 3

The four 1949 Geneva Conventions have several articles in common. Particularly worth noting here are Common Article 3, discussed in the next paragraph, and Common Article 2, which applies the Conventions to any international armed conflict – that is, a conflict between two or more contracting parties – whether or not the conflict is formally recognised as a "war". The article also applies the Conventions to cases of occupation, even if not resisted by force. Finally, the article provides that the Conventions bind contracting parties not only as between themselves but also, unlike the earlier Geneva Conventions, as between them and any non-party that accepts and applies the relevant Convention's provisions, although this is of less significance today with the universal adoption of the Conventions.

---

[84] Convention for the Amelioration of the Condition of Wounded, Sick and Shipwrecked Members of Armed Forces at Sea, Geneva, 12 August 1949 in force 21 October 1950, 75 UNTS 85 ("GC II").

[85] Convention Relative to the Treatment of Prisoners of War, Geneva, 12 August 1949, in force 21 October 1950, 75 UNTS 135 ("GC III").

[86] Convention (IV) Relative to the Protection of Civilian Persons in Time of War, Geneva, 12 August 1949, in force 21 October 1950, 75 UNTS 287 ("GC IV").

[87] Oscar Uhler and Henri Coursier (eds.), *Commentary on the Geneva Conventions of 12 August 1949, Volume IV* (Geneva: ICRC, 1958) ('GC IV Commentary'), p. 5.

[88] GC IV, art. 4.

Common Article 3 is one of the most important articles of the Conventions. It arose out of pressure from "the Red Cross world" to regulate not just international, but internal, armed conflicts, "the horrors of which sometimes surpass the horrors of international wars by reason of the fratricidal hatred which they engender".[89] In the negotiations for the 1949 Geneva Conventions it was proposed that a provision be inserted, requiring all parties to an internal conflict to implement the principles of the Conventions. Many States opposed this, however, arguing that its effect would be to confer legitimacy and protection on rebels or even common criminals using force against the government.[90] The eventual compromise was Common Article 3, which says in essence that the parties to a non-international armed conflict must respect and apply certain fundamental principles, which are listed.[91] This characteristic led to it being described as a "Convention in miniature", and ensures the application of at least the basic rules of humanity even in internal conflicts.[92]

9. THE 1977 ADDITIONAL PROTOCOLS

The ICRC continued its efforts to expand the content and application of international humanitarian law, and in particular the protection of civilians. In 1956 it published Draft Rules on the protection of civilians in time of war, which would have afforded civilians greater protection from the effects of hostilities and especially from nuclear, chemical and biological weapons.[93] The draft rules attracted little support from States and were not pursued.[94] But over the next few years the wars in Vietnam, Nigeria and the Middle East, and the many violent anti-colonial struggles, reawakened international interest in the need to update and fill some of the gaps in the 1949 Conventions.[95] The Hague Conventions had not been significantly revised since 1907, despite the changes in the nature of war and warfare that had occurred. The ICRC therefore prepared two draft protocols "additional to" the Geneva Conventions, and these were debated at a diplomatic conference in Geneva which sat in four sessions from 1974 to 1977. The two Additional Protocols were adopted in June 1977 and concern the protection of victims of international, and non-international, respectively, armed conflicts.

---

[89] GC IV Commentary, pp. 38–9.   [90] Ibid., pp. 43–4.   [91] See below p. 62.

[92] GC I Commentary, p. 48, quoting an unnamed delegate at the conference.

[93] Draft Rules for the Limitation of the Dangers Incurred by the Civilian Population in Time of War, (Geneva: ICRC, 1956), www.icrc.org/applic/ihl/ihl.nsf/Treaty.xsp?documentId=FEA0B928100D3135C12563CD002 D6C10&action=openDocument.

[94] ICRC, *Final Act of the Diplomatic Conference of Geneva of 1974–1977* (Geneva: ICRC, 1977), pp. 123–4, www.icrc.org/applic/ihl/ihl.nsf/Treaty.xsp?documentId=D7D9F26C38F99332C12563CD002D6CB8&actio n=openDocument.

[95] Ibid.

a. Additional Protocol I, wars of national liberation, and guerrilla fighters

Additional Protocol I (AP I) applies in international armed conflicts, but is radical in including within that term "armed conflicts in which peoples are fighting against colonial domination and alien occupation and against racist régimes in the exercise of their right of self-determination" – commonly known as "wars of national liberation".[96] This had been the dominant form of conflict since the 1950s, as colonial peoples fought their colonists for independence ("colonial domination"), the Palestine Liberation Organisation fought against Israeli occupation ("alien occupation"), and various (mainly guerrilla) groups fought against the apartheid régime in South Africa and Namibia, and the white minority government in Southern Rhodesia ("racist régimes"). These kinds of conflict raised issues not adequately addressed in the 1949 Geneva Conventions or the Hague Regulations, in particular the legal status of guerrilla fighters (or "freedom fighters" more generally) and whether they were entitled to prisoner of war status on capture. The solution adopted in Additional Protocol I was to extend its application to such wars of national liberation, as defined, while expressly stating that this had no effect on the legal status of the parties to the conflict or of any occupied territory.[97]

Over the objections of many Western States, the Protocol relaxes the requirements for combatant – and therefore prisoner of war – status for those engaged in wars of national liberation.[98] The GC III requirements in relation to resistance fighters included that they wear a fixed and distinctive sign, visible at a distance, and that they carry their arms openly.[99] Additional Protocol I recognises that the very nature of guerrilla fighting precludes this, and requires as a minimum only that fighters carry their arms openly during each military engagement.[100] These issues are discussed in detail in Chapter 4, and in part explain why the Protocol has not received the universal acceptance of the Geneva Conventions; by the end of 2014 there were 174 parties, compared to 196 for the Geneva Conventions.

Additional Protocol I was also innovative in including in the one instrument provisions that had hitherto been found in either Geneva Conventions or Hague Conventions, thus to some degree merging "Geneva Law" with "Hague Law"; this is analysed further in Chapter 2.

b. Additional Protocol II

Before 1977, the only rules of international humanitarian law applying to non-international armed conflicts were those contained in Common Article 3 of the

---

[96] Protocol Additional to the Geneva Conventions of 12 August 1949, and relating to the Protection of Victims of International Armed Conflicts, Geneva, 8 June 1977, in force 7 December 1978, 1125 UNTS 3 ("AP I"), art. 1(4).
[97] Ibid., art. 4.   [98] Solis, *The Law of Armed Conflict*, p. 126.   [99] GC III, art. 4(A)(2); below pp. 91–3.
[100] AP I, art. 44(3).

1949 Geneva Conventions. While a breakthrough at the time, that article is far too brief to provide a useful set of rules for what has become the prevalent form of conflict: it is estimated that some 80 per cent of the victims of armed conflicts since 1945 have been victims of non-international conflicts.[101] In the lengthy negotiations on the Protocol, many States were concerned that such a treaty "might affect State sovereignty, prevent governments from effectively maintaining law and order within their borders [or] be invoked to justify outside intervention".[102] But eventually a set of provisions was agreed, albeit far shorter (a mere twenty-eight articles) than its supporters had originally desired.[103] Recognising that the regulation of non-international armed conflicts was a relatively undeveloped area of the law, the Preamble to the Protocol includes a paragraph containing the essence of the Martens clause: "Recalling that, in cases not covered by the law in force, the human person remains under the protection of the principles of humanity and the dictates of the public conscience".

The Protocol is in addition to, not a replacement of, Common Article 3 and the two instruments have slightly different fields of application. Common Article 3 applies to any armed conflict "not of an international character" occurring in the territory of a contracting party, without defining that term. The application of Additional Protocol II is narrower, applying to such a conflict if it occurs between the State's armed forces and either dissident armed forces or other organised armed groups.[104] Further, for the Protocol to apply, those groups must be under responsible command and exercise sufficient control over a part of the State's territory that they are able to carry out "sustained and concerted" military operations and are able to implement the provisions of the Protocol.[105] These qualifications ensure that the Protocol applies only to conflicts of a certain degree of intensity, and application to internal disturbances such as riots or isolated acts of violence is expressly excluded.[106] The requirement of control over territory has meant that in practice the Protocol rarely applies to modern internal armed conflict and is more suited to the type of civil war where the insurgents gradually acquire control over greater portions of State territory.[107] When it does apply, the Protocol includes provisions on the protection of civilians from attack and basic guarantees of humane treatment for those not taking direct part in hostilities.[108] Its specific provisions are considered in relation to particular topics throughout this book.

---

[101] Protocol Additional to the Geneva Conventions of 12 August 1949, and relating to the Protection of Victims of Non-International Armed Conflicts, Geneva, 8 June 1977, in force 7 December 1978, 1125 UNTS 609 ("AP II").

[102] Ibid.

[103] For an interesting summary of the tortuous negotiations see Yves Sandoz, Christophe Swinarski and Bruno Zimmerman (eds.), *Commentary on the Additional Protocols of 8 June 1977 to the Geneva Conventions of 12 August 1949* (Geneva: ICRC/Martinus Nijhoff, 1987) ("AP Commentary"), pp. 1319–36, paras. 4337–418.

[104] AP II, art. 1(1).   [105] Ibid.   [106] AP Commentary, p. 1343; AP II, art. 1(2).

[107] Solis, *The Law of Armed Conflict*, p. 131.   [108] AP II, arts. 7–18.

Like AP I, Additional Protocol II has not received universal acceptance, with 167 parties by the end of 2014. States not party to either Protocol include the United States, India, Pakistan, Sri Lanka, Nepal and Israel. These States are nevertheless bound by the relevant rules of customary international law, as explained in the next chapter, but the extent to which the provisions of the Additional Protocols have attained the status of customary law is contested.

10. OTHER IHL INSTRUMENTS

The above sections trace the history of the principal treaties forming the core of international humanitarian law. In addition there is a growing body of treaty law on particular aspects of armed conflict, including a number of treaties restricting or prohibiting the use of certain weapons or means of warfare, such as chemical weapons, cluster munitions, and anti-personnel mines.[109] These treaties are discussed at relevant places in the text, and especially in Chapter 8.

11. THE DEVELOPMENT OF INTERNATIONAL CRIMINAL LAW – THE ICTY AND ICTR, THE ICC, AND THE HYBRID AND *AD HOC* COURTS AND TRIBUNALS

One final development that should be mentioned here is that of international criminal law and its role in enforcing international humanitarian law. As has been described in this chapter, increasingly detailed rules on the conduct of armed conflict have been developed in customary law and by treaty. But these provisions, particularly before 1949, have very little to say about the consequences of breaching the rules. Broadly speaking, the rules may be breached either directly by the State itself, for example by continuing to produce a prohibited weapon, or by one or more individual participants in the conflict, such as a soldier who kills a prisoner of war. Both kinds of breach engage the State's responsibility in international law: the obligations are legally those of the State concerned, since it is States that are parties to the relevant treaties and subject to customary international law. The detailed prescriptions and prohibitions in the Hague Regulations rest upon the direction to States to "issue instructions to their armed land forces, which shall be in conformity with the [Regulations] annexed to the present Convention".[110] The State's responsibility for a violation of the Regulations by its armed forces is affirmed in the 1907 Hague IV Convention and, in more recent times, in the International Law

---

[109] For a list of these instruments see ICRC, *Treaties by date*, www.icrc.org/applic/ihl/ihl.nsf/vwTreatiesBy Date.xsp.
[110] Hague II 1899, art. 1; Hague IV 1907, art. 1.

Commission's Articles on State Responsibility, most of which are accepted as reflecting customary international law.[111] A State injured by such a violation may either make a claim for compensation or other reparation from the wrongdoing State or, more likely during armed conflict, take reprisals against the wrongdoing State. In earlier times this was the only sanction practically available – as von Martens wrote in 1788:

... in time of war, a prisoner of war may sometimes be put to death in order to punish a nation that has violated the laws of war. .... war being of itself the last state of violence, there often remains no other means of guarding against future violations on the part of the enemy.[112]

As explained in Chapter 8, however, the modern law has progressively shrunk the scope of lawful reprisals almost to extinction.

But what of the individual who violates the law? Again in earlier times, violations of the laws and customs of war were punished in one of two ways. First, the individual could be punished by his own State in accordance with that State's domestic law – usually within its military justice system and in extreme cases even by the death penalty on the battlefield.[113] Second, individuals could lose their entitlement to be treated as belligerents (lawful combatants), and could therefore be severely punished as ordinary criminals if captured by the enemy.[114] By 1905 Oppenheim was referring to "war crimes", which he defined generally as "such hostile or other acts of soldiers or other individuals as may be punished by the enemy on capture of the offenders".[115] The 1949 Geneva Conventions laid the foundation for the modern understanding of "war crimes", as explained in more detail in Chapter 9. They require States to take any measures necessary to suppress contraventions of the Conventions, and in the case of defined "grave breaches", to prosecute or extradite any accused person.[116] Thus the Geneva Conventions confer on States universal jurisdiction to prosecute those accused of grave breaches of the Conventions. But this does not guarantee that alleged war criminals will actually be tried, particularly in their own State.

a. The International Criminal Court

This was one of the reasons why the international community resumed its efforts to establish an international court that would have jurisdiction to prosecute these

---

[111] Hague IV 1907, art. 3; International Law Commission, Draft Articles on Responsibility of States for Internationally Wrongful Acts, November 2001, Supplement No. 10 (A/56/10) ("ILC Articles on State Responsibility"), art. 4; see pp. 308–310 below.

[112] Von Martens, *Summary of the Law of Nations*, p. 269.

[113] Instructions for the Government of Armies of the US in the Field, General Orders, 24 April 1863; promulgated as General Orders No. 100 ("Lieber Code"), art. 44.

[114] William Winthrop, *Military Law and Precedents*, 2nd edn, (Washington, DC: Washington Government Printing Office, 1920), p. 779; Henry Wheaton, *Elements of International Law*, 8th edn, (Boston: Little, Brown and Company, 1866), p. 452.

[115] Oppenheim, *International Law*, 1st edn, vol. II, pp. 263–4.

[116] GC I, arts. 49–50; GC II, arts. 50–1; GC III, arts. 129–30; GC IV, arts. 146–7.

offences.[117] These efforts date back to at least 1920 when the League of Nations considered a proposal for a court to try "crimes against the universal law of nations".[118] The proposal was not taken up, the League taking the view that it was premature because "there is not yet any international penal law recognized by all nations".[119] Similar proposals in the 1920s and 1930s came from international bodies such as the International Law Association, the Inter-Parliamentary Unions and the International Congress of Penal Law, and included the creation of a criminal chamber within the Permanent Court of International Justice: all met the same fate.[120]

The atrocities committed in the Second World War prompted the victorious Allies (US, UK, France and the USSR) to create the Nuremberg and Tokyo military tribunals, at which in 1945–6 German and Japanese "major war criminals" were tried for "crimes against peace, war crimes in the strict sense and crimes against humanity", as defined in the Nuremberg and Tokyo Charters.[121] Establishing ad hoc tribunals was a traditional method by which a victor prosecuted violations of the laws of war committed by the enemy;[122] the significance of the Nuremberg and Tokyo tribunals lay in their detailed definitions of crimes against peace, war crimes and crimes against humanity, and in the principles of law established by the Charters and judgments such as excluding obedience to superior orders or claims of immunity as defences.[123] Proposals for a truly international criminal court continued to be made, for example during the drafting of the Genocide Convention; some States wanted the crime of genocide to be triable in an international court, but agreement could not be reached on the nature of the tribunal envisaged or its precise jurisdiction.

These questions were therefore referred to the International Law Commission (ILC) in 1947, with a direction to "(a) formulate the principles of international law recognized in the Charter of the Nürnberg Tribunal and in the judgment of the

[117] Another reason was the perceived additional "moral effect" of an international, rather than domestic, prosecution: United Nations, *Historical Survey on the Question of International Criminal Jurisdiction*, 1949, UN Doc A/CN.4/7/Rev.1, p. 2.

[118] Calls for a standing international tribunal to investigate violations of the law of armed conflict can be traced even further back, to 1872, when one of the founders of the ICRC, Gustave Moynier, called for such a body – see further Christopher Hall, "The First Proposal for a Permanent International Criminal Court" (1998) 322 IRRC 57; United Nations, *Historical Survey on the Question of International Criminal Jurisdiction*, p. 11.

[119] United Nations, *Historical Survey on the Question of International Criminal Jurisdiction*, p. 11.

[120] Ibid., pp. 12–15.

[121] Agreement for the Prosecution and Punishment of Major War Criminals of the European Axis, and Charter of the International Military Tribunal, London, 8 August 1945, in force 8 August 1945, 82 UNTS 280 ("Charter of the Nürnberg Tribunal"), art. 6; Charter of the International Military Tribunal for the Far East, 19 January 1946, 15 AD 356, art. 5.

[122] See e.g. Hall, "The First Proposal for a Permanent International Criminal Court". Examples range from the trial of Peter de Hagenbach in 1474 for murder, rape and other crimes during his occupation of the town of Breisach, to the attempted trial of the German Emperor at the end of the First World War: Edoardo Greppi, "The Evolution of Individual Criminal Responsibility under International Law" (1999) 835 IRRC 531, www. icrc.org/eng/resources/documents/misc/57jq2x.htm.

[123] See e.g. Charter of the Nürnberg Tribunal, arts. 6–8.

Tribunal, and (b) prepare a draft code of offences against the peace and security of mankind, indicating clearly the place to be accorded to [these] principles." The ILC produced a "Draft Code of Offences against the Peace and Security of Mankind" in 1954, including as offences aggression and various other forms of inter-State force, genocide, inhuman acts against a civilian population and acts in violation of the laws or customs of war.[124] The problem this time was that States could not agree on what constituted "aggression", and it was decided to defer consideration of the Draft Code while the UN General Assembly worked on the question of defining aggression. This took another twenty years[125] and the ILC resumed its work in 1982, producing a revised and updated Draft Code in 1996.[126] The intention behind the code was to codify a body of international criminal law, with States having universal jurisdiction to prosecute the specified international crimes, except for the crime of aggression which could be prosecuted only in an international criminal court.[127] The other specified crimes were genocide, crimes against UN personnel, crimes against humanity and war crimes, the latter two categories being exhaustively defined.[128] No further action was taken on the Draft Code after 1996.

A separate strand of the ILC's work on this topic was the drafting of a statute for an international criminal court. The Commission had briefly considered this in 1950 and a committee of the General Assembly had actually drafted such a statute in 1951; it was then taken up again in 1990 as part of its work on the Draft Code of international crimes, and finalised in 1994.[129] The General Assembly convened a diplomatic conference in Rome in 1998 with a view to adopting a convention establishing an international criminal court, based on the ILC draft as refined by a preparatory committee that met several times in 1997.[130] On 17 July 1998, the Rome Statute of the International Criminal Court ("Rome Statute") was adopted.[131] The crimes covered by the Rome Statute are genocide, war crimes, crimes against humanity and aggression, as discussed in more detail in Chapter 9. The Court's jurisdiction is quite narrow, one constraint being that except where a situation has been referred to the Court by the Security Council, an individual can only be prosecuted if the State where the conduct occurred, or of which the accused is a national, is either a party to the Statute or has accepted the jurisdiction of the

---

[124] ILC, "Draft Code of Offences against the Peace and Security of Mankind with commentaries" (1954) 2 YBILC 134, 151–2.

[125] UN General Assembly, *Definition of Aggression*, UN Doc. A/RES/3314(XXIX), 14 December 1974.

[126] ILC, "Draft Code of Crimes against the Peace and Security of Mankind with commentaries" (1996) 2 YBILC 17.

[127] Ibid., art. 8.   [128] Ibid., arts. 17–20.

[129] See ILC, "Summary – Draft Code of Crimes Against the Peace and Security of Mankind (Part II) – including the draft Statute for an international criminal court", legal.un.org/ilc/summaries/7_4.htm.

[130] Ibid.; UN General Assembly, Resolution 50/46, Establishment of an international criminal court, UN Doc. A/RES/50/46, 11 December 1995.

[131] Rome Statute of the International Criminal Court, 17 July 1998, in force 1 July 2002, 2187 UNTS 90, art. 8 (2)(b)(xiii) ("Rome Statute").

Court.[132] The Court formally came into existence in 2002 and delivered its first conviction in 2012.[133]

In the later stages of drafting the Rome Statute, and in finally reaching agreement after decades of equivocation, States were clearly influenced by the recent establishment of the ad hoc criminal tribunals described below.

b. The *ad hoc* Criminal Tribunals for the former Yugoslavia and Rwanda

In stark contrast to the long gestation period of the International Criminal Court (ICC), the International Criminal Tribunal for the former Yugoslavia (ICTY) [134] was created in a matter of weeks. The Tribunal was the international community's response to the atrocities committed during the many ethnic conflicts that followed the break-up of the Socialist Federal Republic of Yugoslavia, which began in 1991 when two of its six constituent republics, Slovenia and Croatia, declared independence, with Bosnia and Herzegovina and Macedonia following shortly afterwards. By late 1992 reports were emerging of gross violations of international humanitarian law including systematic ethnic cleansing, such as mass deportations, killings and rapes, and the use of concentration camps. The UN Security Council asked the Secretary-General to appoint a Commission of Experts to investigate these allegations, and the Commission's interim report of February 1993 – confirming many atrocities – caused public outrage.[135] The Commission recommended that the Security Council consider establishing an ad hoc war crimes tribunal, to which the Security Council immediately agreed.[136] Barely three months later, in May 1993, the Security Council adopted a resolution establishing the ICTY and approving the statute prepared by the Secretary-General.[137] The judges were

---

[132] Ibid., art. 12. The Security Council has only referred two situations to the Court to date (2014) – Darfur in 2005 and Libya in 2011.

[133] ICC, *Prosecutor* v. *Thomas Lubanga Dyilo*, ICC-01/04–01/06, Judgment, 14 March, 2012. Lubanga was found guilty of "war crimes consisting of: Enlisting and conscripting of children under the age of 15 years into the . . . (FPLC) and using them to participate actively in hostilities in the context of an armed conflict not of an international character": see ICC, Case Information Sheet, *Prosecutor* v. *Thomas Lubanga Dyilo*, www.icccpi.int/en_menus/icc/situations%20and%20cases/situations/situation%20icc%200104/related% 20cases/icc%200104%200106/Pages/democratic%20republic%20of%20the%20congo.aspx.

[134] The full title is Statute of the International Tribunal for the Prosecution of Persons Responsible for Serious Violations of International Humanitarian Law Committed in the Territory of the Former Yugoslavia since 1991, UN Doc. S/25704 at 36, annex (1993) and S/25704/Add.1 (1993), adopted by Security Council on 25 May 1993, UN Doc. S/RES/827 (1993) ("ICTY Statute").

[135] UN Security Council, Interim Report of the Commission of Experts Established Pursuant to Security Council Resolution 780 (1992), UN Doc. S/25274, 10 February 1993.

[136] Ibid., Annex I, paras. 72–4; UN Security Council, Resolution 808, UN Doc. S/RES/808 (1993), 22 February 1993.

[137] UN Security Council, Resolution 827, UN Doc. S/RES/827 (1993), 25 May 1993. The statute was drafted by the Secretary-General's Department taking into account suggestions from States, NGOs, international organisations and private individuals.

appointed in August that year and the first indictment issued in late 1994.[138] By the end of 2014 over 160 individuals had been indicted for "serious violations of international humanitarian law" – grave breaches of the 1949 Geneva Conventions, violations of the laws or customs of war, genocide and crimes against humanity.[139] To meet the aim of completing its work as soon as possible after the initial target of 2010, the Tribunal was directed to concentrate on "the most senior leaders suspected of being most responsible for crimes within the ICTY's jurisdiction", and to transfer other cases to national courts.[140]

As will be apparent from the numerous mentions of ICTY cases in this book, the Tribunal has made a very significant contribution to the development of international humanitarian law and international criminal law more generally. Its major achievements in this context include classifying rape as a form of torture (over seventy individuals have been charged with crimes of sexual violence), and developing the principles governing indirect modes of liability such as command responsibility and joint criminal enterprise.[141] These are examined in Chapter 9.

Like the ICTY, the International Criminal Tribunal for Rwanda (ICTR) was established by Security Council resolution in response to mass atrocities – in Rwanda's case, the genocide of April–July 1994 during which between 800,000 and one million mainly Tutsi victims were killed.[142] The crimes within its jurisdiction are genocide, crimes against humanity and violations of Common Article 3 to the Geneva Conventions and of Additional Protocol II – the genocide being an internal, and not an international, conflict.[143] From commencement in 1995 to its last trial in 2012 the Tribunal indicted ninety-three individuals, and then embarked on a completion strategy similar to that of ICTY. The two tribunals shared a chief prosecutor and appeals chamber, and a common "residual mechanism" to handle the remaining cases.[144] The ICTR has also produced some landmark judgments in international humanitarian law, being the first international tribunal to deliver verdicts in relation to genocide, to define rape in international criminal law, to recognise rape as a means of perpetrating genocide

---

[138] UN Security Council, UN Doc. S/RES/857 (1993), 20 August 1993; ICTY, Case Information Sheet, *Dragan Nikolic*, p. 2, www.icty.org/x/cases/dragan_nikolic/cis/en/cis_nikolic_dragan.pdf.

[139] ICTY Statute, arts. 1–5.

[140] UN Security Council, Resolution 1534 on necessity of trial of persons indicted by the International Tribunal for the Former Yugoslavia and the International Criminal Tribunal for Rwanda, UN Doc. S/RES/1534 (2004), 26 March 2004, operative para. 5.

[141] See e.g. ICTY, *Landmark cases*, www.icty.org/sid/10314.

[142] See www.unictr.org/en/genocide. The Tribunal's formal title is the International Criminal Tribunal for the Prosecution of Persons Responsible for Genocide and Other Serious Violations of International Humanitarian Law Committed in the Territory of Rwanda and Rwandan citizens responsible for genocide and other such violations committed in the territory of neighbouring States, between 1 January 1994 and 31 December 1994: Statute of the International Tribunal for Rwanda, adopted by UN Security Council, Resolution (955), UN Doc. S/RES/955, 8 November 1994, ("ICTR Statute"), Annex, preamble.

[143] ICTR Statute, arts. 2–4.

[144] UN Security Council, Resolution 1966 on the establishment of the International Residual Mechanism for Criminal Tribunals with two branches, UN Doc. S/RES/1966 (2010), 22 December 2010.

and to hold members of the media responsible for broadcasts intended to inflame the public to commit acts of genocide.[145]

c. Hybrid and *ad hoc* courts and tribunals

The trend away from impunity and towards accountability for international crimes continued in the late 1990s with the creation of "hybrid" courts and tribunals – post-conflict bodies with criminal jurisdiction, usually based within a State's judicial system but with a mixture of national and international judges and staff, and applying both international and domestic law. These include the Special Court for Sierra Leone, the special panels of the District Court of Dili, the Special Tribunal for Lebanon and the Extraordinary Chambers in the Courts of Cambodia and the Extraordinary African Chambers.

The Special Court for Sierra Leone was established by agreement between the United Nations and Sierra Leone in 2002, to try "persons who bear the greatest responsibility for serious violations of international humanitarian law and Sierra Leonean law committed in the territory of Sierra Leone since 30 November 1996" – the height of the country's decade-long (1991–2002) civil war. It had a mixture of Sierra Leonean and international judges and tried ten individuals before its closure in 2013, the most notable conviction being of Charles Taylor, the President of Liberia, for crimes against humanity, violations of Common Article 3 and Additional Protocol II, and other serious violations of international humanitarian law, namely conscripting or enlisting child soldiers. A Residual Special Court was established in 2012 to oversee the continuing legal obligations of the Special Court.[146]

In 2000 the United Nations established special panels as part of the Dili District Court to prosecute serious crimes committed in East Timor in the lead-up to the referendum on independence in late 1999.[147] The offences were set out in extensive detail and included genocide, war crimes, crimes against humanity, murder, sexual offences and torture. The panels were composed of two international judges and one East Timorese judge, and the applicable law was that of East Timor and "where appropriate, applicable treaties and recognised principles and norms of international law, including the established principles of the international law of armed conflict".[148] Until their demise in 2005, the panels tried nearly ninety individuals, mainly members of pro-Indonesian militia, for their role in the violence.[149]

---

[145] United Nations International Criminal Tribunal for Rwanda, *The ICTR in Brief,* www.unictr.org/en/tribu nal; see e.g., *The Prosecutor* v. *Jean-Paul Akayesu*, ICTR-96-4-T, Judgment, 2 September 1998.

[146] The Special Court for Sierra Leone and the Residual Special Court for Sierra Leone, www.rscsl.org.

[147] United Nations Transitional Administration in East Timor, *Regulation no. 2000/15 on the Establishment of Panels with Exclusive Jurisdiction Over Serious Criminal Offences,* UN Doc. UNTAET/REG/2000/15, 6 June 2000, www.jornal.gov.tl/lawsTL/UNTAET-Law/Regulations%20English/Reg2000-15.pdf.

[148] Ibid., ss. 1.3, 3.1, 22.

[149] University of California Berkeley, War Crimes Studies Center, *East Timor, Special Panels for Serious Crimes Documents,* wcsc.berkeley.edu/east-timor/east-timor-2/.

The Extraordinary Chambers in the Courts of Cambodia for the Prosecution of Crimes Committed during the Period of Democratic Kampuchea were established by UN–Cambodian agreement in 2003 to try senior leaders of Democratic Kampuchea (the name of the state established by the Khmer Rouge, 1975–9) and those who were most responsible for the crimes and serious violations of Cambodian penal law, international humanitarian law and custom, and international conventions recognised by Cambodia, that were committed from 17 April 1975 to 6 January 1979 – in this period nearly two million Cambodians were executed or died from disease or starvation.[150] Again there are both Cambodian and international judges; as at late 2014 they had convicted three individuals and it is expected there will be no more than ten indictments in total.[151]

In 2007 the Special Tribunal for Lebanon was created by an agreement between the United Nations and Lebanon "to establish a tribunal of an international character" to try all those found responsible for the attack of 14 February 2005 which killed the former Lebanese Prime Minister Rafıq Hariri and twenty-one others.[152] The tribunal's statute provides for a majority of the judges to be international, the remainder Lebanese, but the applicable law is Lebanese.[153]

Finally mention could be made of the Extraordinary African Chambers – a more recent hybrid court established within the courts of Senegal in 2012 by agreement between Senegal and the African Union (AU). The Chambers have a mixture of Senegalese and other AU judges and a mandate to prosecute the person or persons most responsible for international crimes (genocide, crimes against humanity, war crimes and torture) committed in Chad between 7 June 1982 and 1 December 1990 – the dates during which Hissène Habré had been President.[154] The applicable law is the provisions of the Chambers' Statute, supplemented if necessary by Senegalese law.[155] In 2013 Hissène Habré was charged with crimes against humanity, torture and war crimes; he had long been resident in Senegal while resisting efforts by Belgium to prosecute him in that State for the same crimes.[156]

---

[150] Agreement between the United Nations and the Royal Government of Cambodia concerning the Prosecution under Cambodian Law of Crimes committed during the Period of Democratic Kampuchea, 6 June 2003, art. 1 www.eccc.gov.kh/sites/default/files/legal-documents/Agreement_between_UN_and_RGC.pdf.

[151] Ibid., art. 3; Extraordinary Chambers in the Courts of Cambodia, *Case Load,* www.eccc.gov.kh/en/caseload.

[152] UN Security Council, Resolution 1757 (2007) on the Agreement between the United Nations and the Lebanese Republic on the establishment of a Special Tribunal for Lebanon, UN Doc. S/RES/1757 (2007), 30 May 2007.

[153] Ibid., art. 2.

[154] Agreement on the Establishment of the Extraordinary African Chamber within the Senegalese Judicial System between the Government of the Republic of Senegal and the African Union and the Statute of the Chambers, Dakar, 22 August 2012, in force December 2011], 52 ILM 1024 ("Statute of the Extraordinary African Chamber"), arts. 2-4, 11 within the courts of Senegal created to prosecute international crimes committed in Chad between 7 June 1982 and 1 December 1990, arts. 2-4, 11, www.hrw.org/news/2013/09/02/statute-extraordinary-african-chambers.

[155] Ibid., art. 16.

[156] *Questions relating to the Obligation to Prosecute or Extradite (Belgium* v. *Senegal),* Judgment, ICJ Rep. 2012, p. 422.

These international and hybrid courts and tribunals vary considerably in their material scope, but there are strong similarities in the "internationalisation" of the judiciary and of the applicable law. Some have been, or are likely to be, much more successful than others. All are extraordinarily expensive. But their mere existence is an indication of the international community's increasing preparedness to impose and enforce international criminal responsibility. However, each of the courts and tribunals described above, with the exception of the Extraordinary African Chambers, would not have been created without Security Council approval – meaning, of course, that if a new Cold War were to descend, prosecution of individuals will be limited to the International Criminal Court, if it has jurisdiction, or to domestic courts.

12. CONCLUSION

This chapter has outlined how and why international humanitarian law has developed. It has been seen that significant changes or developments in the law have been the international community's response to a war or other calamity; the law is therefore sometimes criticised for being "one war behind reality".[157] But this is unjustified, for at least two reasons. In the first place "the law" is only what States are prepared to make it, whether by treaty or by custom – it does not have a mind or life of its own. Second, through the strenuous efforts of certain individuals and organisations such as the International Committee of the Red Cross, there are in fact provisions designed to ensure that the law does apply to new and unforeseen situations – the Martens clause being the prominent example.

Nevertheless, there are areas of the law, such as that governing non-international armed conflict, which remain far less developed than others. The history summarised in this chapter has shown that over the years the body of law governing armed conflict has grown, along with mechanisms for its enforcement and a growing acceptance of individual accountability for violations. The next chapter provides an overview of the law, and explains the fundamental purposes, principles and sources of that law.

FURTHER READING

Dunant, Jean-Henry, *A Memory of Solferino, 1862,* trans. by the American Red Cross (Geneva: ICRC 1939)

[157] Marco Sassòli, Antoine Bouvier and Anne Quintin, *How Does Law Protect in War? Cases, Documents and Teaching Materials on Contemporary Practice in International Humanitarian Law,* 3rd edn, (Geneva: ICRC, 2011), pp. 52, 60.

Hartigan, Richard Shelly, *Lieber's Code and the Law of War* (New York: The Legal Classics Library 1995)

Gillespie, Alexander, *A History of the Laws of War* (Oxford: Hart Publishing 2011)

Posner, Eric A. "A Theory of the Laws of War", (2003) 70 *University of Chicago Law Review* 297, www.law.uchicago.edu/Lawecon/index.html

Schindler, D. and J. Toman, *The Laws of Armed Conflicts*, 3rd edn, (Dordrecht/Geneva: Martinus Nijhoff Publishers/Henry Dunant Institute 1988)

DISCUSSION QUESTIONS

1. If Henri Dunant had not chanced upon the Battle of Solferino, would the course of development of IHL have been any different? Would it have developed at all?
2. Is the accusation that IHL is "one war behind reality" justified?
3. Are States reluctant to regulate warfare? If so, why?
4. Is the steady increase in treaty law relating to IHL a positive development?

2 The contemporary legal basis of international humanitarian law and its fundamental principles

1. INTRODUCTION

As noted in Chapter 1, international humanitarian law (IHL) or the *jus in bello* (law in war) is one of the oldest bodies of international law and aims to regulate the conduct of States and individual participants in an armed conflict, and to protect people and property. The law seeks to balance twin objectives: the needs of the armed forces of a State (or non-State group) to prosecute the armed conflict, and the humanitarian need to protect those who do not, or no longer, take direct part in the hostilities (known as *hors de combat* or "out of combat").

Initially, the law only regulated the conduct of States in international armed conflicts; now, the law governs the conduct of States and non-State actors, in international and non-international armed conflicts, and contains a plethora of rules, drawn from treaties, customary international law and other sources, covering weapons, methods of warfare, targeting and the treatment of persons *hors de combat*. All of these rules find their origins in more general overarching principles of IHL; it is these general principles and specific sources that are explored in this chapter.

2. THE LAW OF ARMED CONFLICT: PURPOSE, CONCEPTS, SCOPE, APPLICATION

As stated above, IHL seeks to regulate conduct in armed conflicts. At first glance, such an aim would seem nonsensical – how can one regulate warfare? How can you prohibit certain kinds of killing, wounding and property destruction, while permitting other kinds of violence? Indeed, this very sentiment was expressed by Admiral Lord Fisher, First Sea Lord of the Royal Navy: "the humanizing of War! You might as well talk of the humanizing of Hell ... As if war could be civilized! If I'm in command when war breaks out I shall issue my order – 'The essence of war is violence. Moderation in war is imbecility. Hit first, hit hard, and hit everywhere.'"[1]

However, contrary to Fisher's bleak outlook, history has shown that over the centuries many societies, from many different parts of the globe, have attempted to place limitations on conduct in armed conflict.[2] Indeed, IHL, in its modern incarnation, is fundamentally pragmatic in its approach – though the use of force by States is circumscribed by the UN Charter, armed conflicts will inevitably occur. IHL aims to limit the brutality of the conflict, imposing restrictions and rules on those who participate in the armed conflicts.[3] As Solis has argued, "the idea of war as indiscriminate violence suggests violence as an end in itself, and that is antithetical to the fact that war is a goal-oriented activity directed to attaining political objectives."[4]

In order to achieve its objectives, IHL is governed by some fundamental principles, analysed in more detail in the second half of this chapter. However, there are some additional concepts that need to be explored regarding IHL – namely, the principle of the separation of the law on resort to force and the law of armed conflict, and the concept of "Hague Law" and "Geneva Law".

a. The separation of *jus ad bellum* and *jus in bello*

The law of armed conflict developed during a period where resort to force was a legitimate tool of State policy.[5] However, when the UN Charter was adopted in 1945, States sought to prohibit unilateral acts of force by States in their international relations. Thus, resort to force between States – war – was prohibited in Article 2(4), which states that "All members shall refrain in their international relations from the threat or use of force against the territorial integrity or political independence of any state, or in any other manner inconsistent with the Purposes of the United Nations".

Despite the prohibition on the use of force, the community of nations, under the auspices of the Swiss Government and the International Committee of the Red Cross

---

[1] Quoted in Sir Reginald Bacon, *The Life of Lord Fisher of Kilverstone, Admiral of the Fleet*, 2 vols. (New York: Doubleday, Doran & Co., 1929) vol. 1, pp. 120–1. See similar comments made by Carl von Clausewitz in *Vom Kriege [On War]*, trans. J. J. Graham 1873 (London: Penguin Classics, 1982) Book I, Chapter 1, ss. 2, 3, 75.

[2] See generally Alexander Gillespie, *A History of the Laws of War*, 3 vols., (Oxford: Hart Publishing, 2011); see also M. Sassòli, Antoine Bouvier and Anne Quintin, *How Does Law Protect in War? Cases, Documents and Teaching Materials on Contemporary Practice in International Humanitarian Law*, 3rd edn (Geneva: ICRC, 2011), pp. 3–7.

[3] As Sassòli, *et al.* bluntly put it, "although armed conflicts are prohibited, they happen": *How Does Law Protect in War?*, p. 114.

[4] G. Solis, *The Law of Armed Conflict: International Humanitarian Law in War*, (Cambridge University Press, 2010), p. 7.

[5] Sassòli, *et al.*, *How Does Law Protect in War?*, p. 114.

(ICRC)[6] and in response to the devastation of the Second World War, recognised that armed conflicts may yet occur. It was felt that the failure to observe the rules with regard to the use of force (*jus ad bellum*) should not lead to a failure to observe *any* rules in the conduct of war, nor should those States who unlawfully use force deprive their soldiers and civilians of any legal protection, due to the acts of their leaders and sovereigns. As Sassòli *et al.* argue "from the humanitarian point of view, the victims of the conflict on both sides need and deserve the same protection, and they are not necessarily responsible for the violation of *jus ad bellum* committed by 'their' party".[7]

As such, the law of armed conflict applies to all sides to the armed conflict, regardless of whether a party to the conflict violated the *jus ad bellum* to start the war – this is the idea of "equality of belligerents". This is explicitly acknowledged in the preamble to Protocol I Additional to the Geneva Conventions, which notes that "the provisions of the Geneva Conventions of 12 August 1949 and of this Protocol must be fully applied in all circumstances to all persons who are protected by those instruments, without any adverse distinction based on the nature or origin of the armed conflict or on the causes espoused by or attributed to the Parties to the conflict."[8] This position has been affirmed in State practice: during the 2003 Iraq War, the US Department of Defense stated:

the four 1949 Geneva Conventions specifically state in there that it doesn't make any difference who started the war, who is the party who was first off or what have you; that in any case, the conventions will apply. That's to sort of keep people from saying, "well, he started it, and therefore, I don't have to follow the law of war." Regardless of who started the conflict, each side has an obligation to follow the law of war.[9]

The need to reaffirm this strict division has been highlighted in recent years as some public discourse and State practice, especially in the context of counter-terrorism operations, seem to suggest that those who violate the law on the use of force (or, indeed, the laws of armed conflict themselves) are not entitled to *any* protections under international law.[10] This was highlighted in the case law of the Special Court

---

[6] See Communications from the Swiss Federal Political Department to States Which Were Parties to the Geneva Conventions of 1929 or to the Xth Hague Convention of 1907, in *Final Record of the Diplomatic Conference of Geneva of 1949*, 3 vols. (Berne: Federal Political Department, 1949) ("Final Record 1949"), vol. I, pp. 147 ff. See also François Bugnion, *The ICRC and the Protection of War Victims* (Geneva: ICRC, 2003), pp. 313–315.

[7] Sassòli, *et al, How Does Law Protect in War?*, p. 115.

[8] AP I, Preamble; see also Articles 1 and 2 common to the Geneva Conventions, which affirm the applicability of the rules to all belligerents.

[9] US Department of Defense, "Briefing on Geneva Convention, EPWs [Enemy Prisoners of War] and War Crimes", 7 April 2003, www.defense.gov/Transcripts/Transcript.aspx?TranscriptID=2281. See further Vaios Koutroulis, "And Yet It Exists: In Defence of the 'Equality of Belligerents' Principle" (2013) 26 LJIL 449 at 547–60 for examples of State practice on the independence of *jus ad bellum* and *jus in bello*.

[10] See further Adam Roberts, "The Equal Application of the Laws of War" (2008) 90 IRRC 931 at 946ff for an overview of State practice regarding advocacy for unequal application of the laws of war.

for Sierra Leone and in the ICTY, where the Court noted that "many perpetrators believe that violations of binding international norms can be lawfully committed, because they are fighting for a 'just cause'. Those people have to understand that international law is applicable to everybody, in particular during times of war"[11] and that "the political motivations of a combatant do not alter the demands on that combatant to ensure their conduct complies with the law ... consideration of political motive by a court applying international humanitarian law not only contravenes, but would undermine a bedrock principle of that law".[12]

b. Hague Law and Geneva Law

It is common in IHL literature to see reference to "Hague Law" and "Geneva Law".[13] This division of the law into two theoretical streams places the law into two categories – Hague Law, which regulates the conduct of hostilities, and Geneva Law, which generally relates to the treatment of those *hors de combat*. The names given to these theoretical strands are drawn from the locations where the major treaties of these strands were debated and adopted; thus, Hague Law relates to the Hague Conventions of 1899 and 1907, while Geneva Law relates to the various Geneva Conventions. An effective "merging" of Hague and Geneva laws occurred with the adoption in 1977 of the Additional Protocols, specifically Additional Protocol I (AP I),[14] with AP I covering rules regarding means and methods as well as rules on the protection of civilians, the *hors de combat*, and the wounded, sick and shipwrecked.[15] Useful as descriptive, but essentially non-legal terms, "Hague and Geneva Law" efficiently summarises the dual aims of IHL – the balancing of military needs with humanitarian objectives.

c. Terminology: wars vs. armed conflicts, law of armed conflict vs. international humanitarian law

A note should also be made at this point regarding terminology. The literature on the law of armed conflict often employs a number of terms, sometimes in the same

---

[11] *Prosecutor* v. *Kordić and Čerkez*, IT-95–14/2-A, Appeal Judgment, 17 December 2004, para. 1082.

[12] *Prosecutor* v. *Fofana and Kondewa*, SCSL-04–14-A, Appeal Judgment, 28 May 2008, paras. 530–1.

[13] See, e.g., Solis, *The Law of Armed Conflict*, p. 24; François Bugnion, "Droit de Genève et droit de La Haye" (2001) 83 IRRC 901; Richard John Erickson, "Protocol I: A Merging of the Hague and Geneva Law of Armed Conflict" (1979) 19 Va J Int'l L 557; Yoram Dinstein, *The Conduct of Hostilities under the Law of International Armed Conflict,* 2nd edn, (Cambridge University Press, 2010), pp. 14–15.

[14] See Christian Tomuschat, *Human Rights: Between Idealism and Realism* (Oxford University Press, 2003), p. 247; Erickson, "Protocol I: A Merging of The Hague and Geneva Law of Armed Conflict", 559.

[15] This was noted in *Legality of the Threat or Use of Nuclear Weapons*, Advisory Opinion, ICJ Rep. 1996, p. 226 at 256 ("*Nuclear Weapons*") para. 75, where the Court states that the law of The Hague and the law of Geneva have "become so closely interrelated that they are considered to have gradually formed one single complex system, known today as international humanitarian law".

text, to describe its subject matter (such as war, warfare and armed conflict) and the legal system established to regulate it (varying between the law of armed conflict, the law of war and international humanitarian law).[16] Are these phrases coterminous or mutually exclusive? Do they describe the same things or are there differences?

In some respects, the changing terminology has been by specific design. The Geneva Conventions of 1949 intentionally moved from using the word "war", replacing it with "armed conflict". The Commentaries to the Conventions make it clear that in changing the terminology from "war" to "armed conflict", States parties to the Conventions were attempting to ensure that no one could argue that the Conventions were inapplicable due to the absence of an acknowledged and declared "war".[17] The idea was that the Conventions must apply in all situations "from the moment hostilities have actually broken out, even if no declaration of war has been made",[18] including situations of belligerent occupation even "in the absence of any state of war".[19]

Likewise, with the move from the term "law of war" to "international humanitarian law", this has partially been done to reflect the growing influence of human rights and humanitarian aims of IHL.[20] The phrase "international humanitarian law" is not used in the Geneva Conventions, but is connected to the Additional Protocols, the drafting conferences of which were entitled the "Diplomatic Conference on the Reaffirmation and Development of International Humanitarian Law Applicable in Armed Conflicts".[21]

Some publicists use the terms "law of armed conflict" and "international humanitarian law" interchangeably;[22] however, some see "international humanitarian law" as a potentially narrower area of international law, one that relates only to the laws in armed conflict that are "designed to regulate the treatment of persons – civilian or military, wounded or active – in armed conflicts".[23] Indeed, the "tireless defender

---

[16] See, e.g., Solis, *The Law of Armed Conflict*; Sassòli *et al.*, *How Does Law Protect in War?*; Laurie Blank and Gregory Noone, *International Law and Armed Conflict: Fundamental Principles and Contemporary Challenges in the Law of War* (New York: Wolters Kluwer, 2013).

[17] See generally the commentary to Article 2 in GC I Commentary, pp. 27–33.

[18] ICRC, *Report on the Work of the Preliminary Conference of National Red Cross Societies for the Study of the Conventions and of Various Problems Relative to the Red Cross, 26 July–3 August 1946* (Geneva: ICRC, 1947), p. 15.

[19] ICRC, *Report on the Work of the Conference of Government Experts for the Study of the Conventions for the Protection of War Victims, 14–26 April 1947* (Geneva: ICRC, 1947), p. 8.

[20] See Mary Ellen O'Connell, "Historical Development and Legal Basis", in Dieter Fleck (ed.) *The Handbook of International Humanitarian Law*, 3rd edn (Oxford University Press, 2013), pp. 11–13, and Solis, *The Law of Armed Conflict*, pp. 22–6, on this phenomenon.

[21] See *Official Records of the Diplomatic Conference on the Reaffirmation and Development of International Humanitarian Law Applicable in Armed Conflicts*, 16 vols. (Bern: Swiss Federal Political Department, 1978) ("Official Records").

[22] Solis (*The Law of Armed Conflict*, p. 23) cites as one example Helen Durham's "International Humanitarian Law: The Story of Athena Versus Ares" (2007) 8 Melb J Int'l L 248.

[23] O'Connell, "Historical Development and Legal Basis", p. 11; though O'Connell goes on to include rules on means, methods and occupation as forming part of humanitarian law. See also Solis, *The Law of Armed Conflict*, p. 23, where he describes IHL and LOAC as "fraternal twins".

and advocate of international humanitarian law",[24] Jean Pictet was himself reticent regarding the employment of the term "international humanitarian law", arguing that the term:

> could be thought to exclude some parts of the laws of war ... whose primary purpose is not humanitarian. Indeed, the term "international humanitarian law" could be seen as implying that the laws of war have an exclusively humanitarian purpose, when their evolution has in fact reflected various practical concerns of states and their armed forces on grounds other than those which may be considered humanitarian.[25]

d. Scope and application of the law of armed conflict

Chapter 3 of this text examines the different types of armed conflict in more detail, but it is useful to make a few preliminary comments on this topic. The aim of the modern law of armed conflict is to ensure that "the rules on the conduct of hostilities apply equally to all hostilities in international armed conflicts and all victims benefit equally from them. The law of non-international armed conflicts by definition protects persons against their fellow citizens, i.e., it applies equally to all persons equally affected by such a conflict."[26] More specifically, the law of armed conflict binds States, non-State actors and individuals. The idea is thus that in times of armed conflict, all persons who may be affected by the conflict, on any side, in any way, are covered by the ambit of the law – this includes combatants and prisoners of war,[27] the wounded, sick and shipwrecked,[28] and civilians.[29]

With regards to temporal scope applicability of the law of armed conflict, IHL is objectively triggered whenever there is "armed conflict". The precise scope of the term "armed conflict" differs according to whether the conflict is international or non-international in scope – this is discussed in more detail in Chapter 3. The temporal scope of the law of armed conflict also depends on the treaties to which the participants to the conflict are party – for instance, a State may be party to a treaty that has not come into force yet, or because the State has signed, but not ratified the treaty in question. While the Geneva Conventions have been ratified by every State in the world, many other IHL treaties do not enjoy similarly high levels of ratification. As such, these treaties may not (or not yet) apply to parties to hostilities.[30] The law of armed conflict is generally deemed to no longer be applicable when there is a general close of military operations,[31] an end of captivity or

---

[24] As described by Sassòli, et al., in their dedication to How Does Law Protect in War?
[25] Jean Pictet, Humanitarian Law and the Protection of War Victims (Leyden: AW Sijthoff, 1975), p. 11.
[26] Sassòli, et al, How Does Law Protect in War?, p. 133.   [27] See further Chapter 4.
[28] See further Chapter 5.   [29] See further Chapters 6 and 7.
[30] See, generally, Robert Kolb and Richard Hyde, An Introduction to the International Law of Armed Conflicts (Oxford: Hart, 2008), pp. 99–101 on temporal scope of application of armed conflicts.
[31] GC IV, art. 6(2); AP I, art. 3(b).

detention under Geneva Convention III relating to prisoners of war (POWs),[32] and/or an end of military occupation, which may be one year after the general close of military operations,[33] except in cases where the occupying power continues to exercise the functions of government.[34]

The situation regarding the cessation of applicability of the law in non-international armed conflicts is less clear. Additional Protocol II only makes reference to the "end of the armed conflict";[35] however, the ICTY in *Tadić* has held that once the necessary threshold for a non-international armed conflict has been reached, the law of armed conflict applies until "a peaceful settlement is achieved".[36] The difficulty in determining the exact end of hostilities has been noted by Sassòli *et al.*, who argue:

in an international society where the use of force is outlawed, armed conflicts seldom end with the *debellatio* (total defeat) of one side or a genuine peace. Most frequently, contemporary armed conflicts result in unstable cease-fires, continue at a lower intensity, or are frozen by an armed intervention by outside forces or by the international community. Hostilities, or at least acts of violence with serious humanitarian consequences, often break out again later. It is difficult for humanitarian actors to plead with parties that have made declarations ending the conflict that the fighting in reality continues.[37]

Finally, a brief comment should be made regarding the spatial scope of application of the law of armed conflict. As noted by Kolb and Hyde, when it comes to spatial scope of application of IHL, "the principle of effectiveness dominates. It means that the LOAC will apply in all areas covered by the state of war, by actual armed conflict, or by belligerent occupation."[38] Thus, IHL applies to the territory of the belligerent States – i.e., the States engaged in the armed conflict. It applies in areas of belligerent occupation, even if such occupation meets with no armed resistance and there are no active hostilities in the occupied territory.[39] It applies in all areas where there are actual hostilities or any form of belligerency between parties outside the territory or territorial control of the belligerents – for instance, on the high seas.[40] The law of armed conflict will also apply to "special areas" such as neutralised zones – which are areas which may be established in neutral territory for the care and protection of persons *hors de combat*.[41]

---

[32] GC III, art. 5(1).   [33] GC IV, art. 6(1).

[34] Ibid., art. 6(3). Cf Hague IV 1907, art. 42, which holds that the regulations apply for as long as there is *de facto* occupation of territory.

[35] AP II, art. 2(2).

[36] *Prosecutor* v. *Dusko Tadić*, IT-94-1, Decision on the Defence Motion for Interlocutory Appeal on Jurisdiction, 2 October 1995 ("*Tadić Jurisdiction*"), para. 70.

[37] Sassòli, *et al.*, *How Does Law Protect in War?*, p. 134.

[38] Kolb and Hyde, *The International Law of Armed Conflicts*, p. 94.   [39] GC IV, art. 2.

[40] See Jann Kleffner, "Scope of Application of International Humanitarian Law", in D. Fleck (ed.), *The Handbook of International Humanitarian Law* 3rd edn (Oxford University Press, 2013), pp. 56–7.

[41] GC IV, art. 15.

With regards to the spatial scope in both international and non-international armed conflicts, the "principle of the unity of territory"[42] applies – that even if the fighting is localised in one area, the law of armed conflict applies in the entirety of the territory, even in areas where no active hostilities take place. This was affirmed in the context of non-international armed conflicts in the ICTR decision of *Akayesu*,[43] and in the context of international armed conflicts by the ICTY in *Tadić*.[44]

However, the spatial scope of the law of armed conflict and its applicability is more complex in non-international armed conflicts where the hostilities and the belligerents are not localised within the internal borders of a State; i.e., where a non-State group fighting against a State or other non-State group crosses international borders to commit acts of hostility. This raises questions regarding the potential internationalisation of the conflict (discussed in more detail in Chapter 3) and the possibility of the armed conflict existing on a far more global scale (discussed in more detail in the context of targeted killing in Chapter 8).

3. SOURCES OF THE LAW OF ARMED CONFLICT

As a subsection of international law, IHL is primarily found in treaties and custom. Treaties, written agreements between States governed by international law, include conventions, agreements and instruments;[45] treaties that relate to previously adopted treaties are often called protocols. The common factor in all these documents, regardless of nomenclature, is that they expressly set out binding obligations for States who are parties to the document.[46] Treaties also usually require a certain number of States to ratify the instrument before it can have legal effect.[47]

Customary international law is a form of law that derives from two elements; the first is State practice, which is the conduct of States in their dealings, both domestically and on the international plane; the second element is what is known as *opinio juris* – the belief that the State practice in question is required by law.[48] Identifying custom relies on looking to certain factors including the degree of consistency and uniformity of the State practice and the generality and duration of the practice.[49]

---

[42] Kolb and Hyde, *The International Law of Armed Conflicts*, p. 95.

[43] *Prosecutor* v. *Akayesu*, ICTR-96-4-T, Trial Judgment, 2 September 1998, para. 635.

[44] *Tadić Jurisdiction*, para. 68.

[45] See the International Law Commission (ILC), "Commentary to the Vienna Convention on the Law of Treaties" (1966) 2 *Yearbook of the International Law Commission*, 188.

[46] See generally ILC, "Fourth Report on the Law of Treaties" (1965) 2 *Yearbook of the International Law Commission*, 12 on the binding nature of treaties.

[47] Vienna Convention on the Law of Treaties, Vienna, 23 May 1969, in force 27 January 1980, 1155 UNTS 331, art. 24.

[48] For a detailed analysis of the concept of customary international law, see *North Sea Continental Shelf Cases (Germany v. Denmark; Germany v. The Netherlands)* Judgment, ICJ Rep. 1969, p. 43, pp. 71–7.

[49] See James Crawford, *Brownlie's Principles of Public International Law*, 8th edn (Oxford University Press, 2012), pp. 23–30.

While there are a multitude of treaties relating to armed conflict, the importance of customary international humanitarian law should not be overlooked. Customary international law can evolve and develop at a faster pace than treaty law, and binds States where treaty law does not; customary international law thus allows for universal application of certain rules. Customary international law can also serve to fill in the gaps where the treaty law is scant, generalised in its wording, or otherwise non-existent – as is often the case with the laws relating to non-international armed conflict. Most of the substantive treaty rules of international humanitarian law are considered as having customary status.

Also important in IHL is so-called "soft law"; non-binding instruments such as UN resolutions or declarations, codes of conduct issued by international organisations, and other instruments such as manuals or interpretive guidance documents. These instruments, while not legally binding, provide useful instructions and guidance for States and non-State actors, and often reiterate or elucidate existing international law norms.

a. Treaties

The treaties of IHL form a comprehensive set of rules governing numerous facets of armed conflict including protection of the wounded, sick and shipwrecked, rules regarding occupied territory, permissible means and methods of armed conflict, and rules regarding criminal sanctions for violations of IHL. Indeed, IHL is one of the most codified areas of international law, and among the most widely accepted by States – the Geneva Conventions of 1949 were the first treaties in history to enjoy universal acceptance, with Palestine acceding in 2014.[50]

i. The treaty law distinction between international and non-international armed conflict

Though this issue will be explored in more detail in the next chapter, it is worthwhile to note, at this introductory stage, that the treaty laws that relate to non-international armed conflicts are considerably less comprehensive than those relating to international armed conflicts. International armed conflicts – wars fought between two or more States – are subject to more treaty provisions than those wars fought between a State and a non-State armed opposition group, or between two or more non-State armed groups – wars known as "non-international armed conflicts". The origins of this dichotomy in the law can be traced back to the earliest writings[51]

---

[50] See further Chapter 1 on the historical development of IHL treaties.

[51] See Laura Perna, *The Formation of the Treaty Law of Non-International Armed Conflicts* (Leiden: Martinus Nijhoff, 2006), pp. 15–23 on the early writings of international lawyers regarding non-international armed conflicts.

on the place of law in the conduct of armed conflicts, which were almost uniform in stating that only *international* armed conflicts were to be subject to international law. Non-international armed conflicts – civil wars – were illegal rebellions against legitimate and sovereign authorities.[52] As noted by the ICTY, States:

preferred to regard internal strife as rebellion, mutiny and treason coming within the purview of national criminal law and, by the same token, to exclude any possible intrusion by other States into their own domestic jurisdiction. This dichotomy was clearly sovereignty-oriented and reflected the traditional configuration of the international community, based on the coexistence of sovereign States more inclined to look after their own interests than community concerns or humanitarian demands.[53]

However, when the 1949 Geneva Conventions were being debated, the brutality of the recent Spanish Civil War was impetus for calls for the application of international law to non-international armed conflicts. In response, the international community adopted Common Article 3, which for the first time, codified an international law applicable in non-international armed conflicts, defining such conflicts as "armed conflict not of an international character occurring in the territory of one of the High Contracting Parties". When the laws of war were revisited in the 1970s, it was determined that there should be more laws regulating non-international armed conflicts. Thus, Additional Protocol II was adopted, which supplements and develops Common Article 3, giving more detail to the provisions outlined in Common Article 3.[54] However, while there are now more detailed provisions for non-international armed conflicts, the treaty law of non-international armed conflict still lags behind the law of international armed conflict considerably.

b. Custom

Although many of the rules of the law of armed conflict are extensively codified, and the relevant treaties enjoy widespread acceptance, there are still areas of conduct in armed conflict that have few, if any, rules. In this respect, customary international law is an important and dynamic source of IHL; its universal applicability binds States who are not party to treaties, often the case in the treaty law of non-international armed conflict.[55] Many of the treaty provisions of the Geneva

---

[52] Anthony Cullen, *The Concept of Non-International Armed Conflict in International Humanitarian Law* (Cambridge University Press, 2010), p. 9.

[53] *Tadić Jurisdiction*, para. 96.

[54] For more detailed analysis of the relevant provisions on non-international armed conflicts, see Chapter 3.

[55] E.g., while the Geneva Conventions are universally ratified, only 168 States are party to AP II: ICRC, *Treaties and State Parties to Such Treaties*, www.icrc.org/IHL. However, Daniel Bethlehem argues that we "must be hesitant about engaging in the crystallisation of custom simply with the object of remedying the defect of non-participation by States in a treaty regime. If States have objections to particular treaty-based

Conventions and Additional Protocols have been acknowledged as declaratory of customary international law – for instance the ten-year long study into customary international law undertaken by the ICRC[56] suggests that most of the provisions of the Conventions and Protocols are customary international law.

However, a note of caution must be sounded when considering customary international law in the context of armed conflict. While customary international law offers the promise of universal applicability and the potential to evolve and develop at a faster pace than treaty law, there are, nonetheless, problems in accurately identifying customary international law, especially in the context of international armed conflicts. First, as highlighted by Blank and Noone, only a handful of States are (or have been) regular participants in armed conflicts.[57] This is problematic when one considers that customary law is meant to reflect the practice of many States, rather than just a select few. Furthermore, the ability to accurately assess what a State does in the context of an armed conflict can be remarkably difficult. There is what a State says it does, and then what it actually does; for example, the US claims it does not engage in torture, and yet, it engaged in a number of techniques, such as waterboarding, that have amounted to torture. As Sassòli *et al.* note:

[the] actual practice of belligerents is difficult to identify, particularly as it often consists of omissions ... war propaganda manipulates truth and secrecy makes it impossible to know which objectives were targeted and whether their destruction was deliberate. Finally, States are responsible for the behaviour of individual soldiers even if the latter did not act in conformity with their instructions, but this does not imply that such behaviour is also State practice constitutive of customary law. It is therefore particularly difficult to determine which acts of soldiers count as State practice.[58]

Indeed, this was one of the common critiques of the ICRC CIHL Study – that it focused too much on statements and sources that could have been driven more by policy, rather than being a statement of binding legal obligation. For example, the Study focused on "official practice" – that is, official State declarations, in the form of public statements and military manuals.[59] Criticisms of the Study have argued that such an approach fails to make the distinction between acts (or instructions) that are done for reasons of policy or expediency, as opposed to acts done because the State in question feels that it *must* act in a particular way.

---

rules, those objections will subsist as regards the formulation of the rules in a customary format": "The Methodological Framework of the Study" in Elizabeth Wilmshurst and Susan Breau (eds.), *Perspectives on the ICRC Study on Customary International Humanitarian Law* (Cambridge University Press, 2007), p. 7.

[56] Jean-Marie Henckaerts and Louise Doswald-Beck (eds.), *International Committee of the Red Cross: Customary International Humanitarian Law*, 2 vols. (Cambridge University Press, 2005) ("ICRC CIHL Study").

[57] Blank and Noone, *International Law and Armed Conflict*, p. 14.

[58] Sassòli, *et al.*, *How Does Law Protect in War?*, pp. 152–3.

[59] ICRC CIHL Study, Introduction vol. I, p. xxxiii.

The conflation of practice and *opinio juris* in the Study has thus been subject to considerable criticism.[60]

As such, caution must be exercised in identifying State practice for the purposes of determining customary international humanitarian law. The approach taken in this text book is one of cautious acceptance of the ICRC CIHL Study. Where there is little controversy about the customary status of a particular principle (the principle of distinction for example), the ICRC position will be taken. However, in the case of more controversial positions – the customary status of parts of Additional Protocol I relating to guerrilla fighters for instance – the ICRC position is noted with caution, and additional supporting practice is sought.

c. Other sources – soft law

An additional source of influence on conduct in armed conflict can be categorised as "soft law". These sources – in the form of case law, guiding principles, military manuals and so on – are not law in *sensu stricto*. Under international law, only treaties, custom, and general principles of law can be sources of law.[61] However, it is often the case that States and judicial organs will look to these soft laws to assist in shaping their own conduct or guiding their decision-making processes. As such, soft law can be enormously important; as Boyle and Chinkin note:

> some of the forms of "soft law" ... are potentially law-making. The proposition is not that non-binding instruments or resolutions of the General Assembly or any other soft law instrument are invariably law per se, but that they may be evidence of existing law, or formative of the *opinio juris* or state practice that generates new law ... [soft law] can and does contribute to the corpus of international law.[62]

Over the past quarter of a century, there has been a wealth of new forms of soft law that have helped in the understanding and development of the law of armed conflict. The jurisprudence of the International Criminal Court, the ICTY and ICTR, as well as of other tribunals such as the Special Court for Sierra Leone, and the hybrid and specialised courts in Cambodia, Timor-Leste, Lebanon, and Bosnia and

---

[60] For critiques of the ICRC CIHL Study, see George Aldrich, "Customary International Humanitarian Law – an Interpretation on Behalf of the International Committee of the Red Cross", (2005) 76 BYBIL 503; W. Hays Parks, "The ICRC Customary Law Study: A Preliminary Assessment" (2005) 99 *ASIL Proceedings* 208; Yoram Dinstein, "The ICRC Customary International Humanitarian Law Study" (2006) 36 IYBHR 1.

[61] Under art. 38(1) of the Statute of the International Court of Justice, San Francisco, 26 June 1945, in force 24 October 1945, 33 UNTS 993 ("ICJ Statute"), the Court will look to treaties, custom and general principles of law as recognised by "civilized nations" as sources for its determinations; it may also look to judicial decisions and the "teachings of the most highly qualified publicists of the various nations" to assist in its decision-making. While other courts and tribunals may examine other documents and instruments for guidance, in practice, generally only treaties and custom are considered to be binding sources of international law.

[62] Alan Boyle and Christine Chinkin, *The Making of International Law* (Oxford University Press, 2007), p. 212.

Herzegovina, have provided important interpretations of the law of armed conflict in both treaty and customary forms. While there is no doctrine of *stare decisis* in international law, the jurisprudence of these bodies has nonetheless been an invaluable interpretative tool in the law of armed conflict.[63]

In addition to the output of these courts and tribunals, there has been a proliferation of international manuals, guidelines and codes of conduct that have contributed to the general understanding and application of the laws of armed conflict to the conduct of armed conflicts. These manuals and codes are frequently the product of a collaborative expert process, whereby experts in the field, drawn from government, industry, academia and the military, meet to discuss and agree upon a set of rules regarding a particular area of armed conflict. They are often drafted in response to perceived lacunae in the law, and aim to apply the existing rules of the law of armed conflict to new situations.[64] Thus, over the last twenty-five years we have seen the production of, among other instruments, the San Remo Manual on International Law Applicable to Armed Conflicts at Sea (1994), the ICRC Study on Customary International Humanitarian Law (2006), the Montreux Document on Private Military and Security Companies (2008), the ICRC Interpretive Guidance on the Notion of Direct Participation in Hostilities (2009), the Harvard University Manual on International Law Applicable to Air and Missile Warfare (2010) and the Tallinn Manual on the International Law of Cyber Warfare (2013). While there are often debates over the merits of such documents, they remain valuable tools with which to better understand IHL.[65]

4. THE FUNDAMENTAL PRINCIPLES OF THE LAW OF ARMED CONFLICT

The next section of this chapter examines the fundamental principles of the law of armed conflict, from which all the substantive rules of the IHL are derived.

a. The principle of distinction

The principle of distinction is enunciated in Article 48 of Additional Protocol I: "In order to ensure respect for and protection of the civilian population and civilian

---

[63] ICJ Statute, art. 38(1)(d) states that judicial decisions are a "subsidiary means for the determination of rules of law", subject to Article 59 that states that "the decision of the Court has no binding force except between the parties and in respect of that particular case".

[64] See, generally, William Boothby, *Conflict Law: The Influence of New Weapons Technology, Human Rights and Emerging Actors* (The Hague: Springer, 2014), specifically Chapter 3, which examines the status of international manuals under international law.

[65] See Chapter 4 on the disputes surrounding the ICRC Interpretive Guidance on the Notion of Direct Participation in Hostilities.

objects, the Parties to the conflict shall at all times distinguish between the civilian population and combatants and between civilian objects and military objectives and accordingly shall direct their operations only against military objectives."[66] The principle of distinction is considered customary international law,[67] and has been acknowledged as one of the "cardinal principles"[68] of IHL. Indeed, the idea that civilians are not legitimate objects of attack – unless they take part in the hostilities – developed from some of the earliest writings of international law publicists. As Grotius argued, "by the law of war armed men and those who offer resistance are killed … [it] is right that in war those who have taken up arms should pay the penalty, but that the guiltless should not be injured".[69]

Observing the principle of distinction is a two-fold obligation. First, parties to the armed conflict must at all times distinguish between civilians and combatants. Combatants are liable to targeting due to their status as combatants;[70] civilians must not be made the object of attack.[71] Likewise, attacks must only be directed against military objects and objectives; civilian objects must not be targeted.[72] A simple example would be that a military installation, such as an army base, would be lawfully targetable, while a *prima facie* civilian building, like a religious installation (a church, mosque or synagogue) or school, would not be lawfully targetable.[73] The corollary to this injunction is the obligation on parties not to "blur" the lines between military and civilian. Thus, combatants must distinguish themselves from the civilian population through use of uniforms and other visible insignia that mark them as military in nature.[74]

Military installations must not be located in civilian-dense areas as a means to immunise them from attack. This provision is contained in Article 58(b) of Protocol I, which provides that parties to the conflict "shall, to the maximum extent feasible … avoid locating military objectives within or near densely populated areas". As noted in the Commentary to the Additional Protocols:

This article is a corollary to the numerous articles contained in the Protocol for the benefit of the population of enemy countries. It is not concerned with laying down rules for the conduct to be observed in attacks on territory under the control of the adversary, but with

---

[66] AP I, art. 48.

[67] See Geoffrey Best, "The Restraint of War in Historical and Philosophic Perspective" in Astrid Delissen and Gerard Tanja (eds.), *Humanitarian Law of Armed Conflict – Challenges Ahead* (Dordrecht: Martinus Nijhoff, 1991), p. 17, who states that the principle of distinction was "no doubt customary law before it received positive formulation in the 1860s".

[68] *Nuclear Weapons,* para. 78.

[69] Hugo Grotius, *De Jure Belli ac Pacis Libri Tres,* trans. Francis W. Kelsey, in James Brown Scott (ed.), *The Classics of International Law* (Oxford University Press, 1925), Book III, Chapter XI, Section X.

[70] See further Chapter 4.   [71] See further Chapter 6.

[72] See Chapter 7 on targeting, and the definition of military and civilian objects and objectives.

[73] However, there are situations where targeting a civilian building is permissible – see further Chapter 7.

[74] See GC III, art. 4(A)(2)(b) relating to the requirement for combatants to wear a "fixed distinctive sign recognisable at a distance".

measures which every Power must take in its own territory in favour of its nationals, or in territory under its control. Belligerents may expect their adversaries to conduct themselves fully in accordance with their treaty obligations and to respect the civilian population, but they themselves must also cooperate by taking all possible precautions for the benefit of their own population as is in any case in their own interest.[75]

This builds on Article 51(7) of the Protocol, which provides that:

The presence or movements of the civilian population or individual civilians shall not be used to render certain points or areas immune from military operations, in particular in attempts to shield military objectives from attacks or to shield, favour or impede military operations. The Parties to the conflict shall not direct the movement of the civilian population or individual civilians in order to attempt to shield military objectives from attacks or to shield military operations.[76]

Putting the principle of distinction into practice is most often seen in the rules regarding targeting.[77] The principle of distinction can be found at the core of many of the laws of armed conflict, and indeed forms part of (or can be seen as part of) other fundamental principles, such as the principle of discrimination, military necessity, and even proportionality.

i. The principle of discrimination (prohibition on indiscriminate attacks)

Connected to the principle of distinction is the principle of discrimination. It is often the case that rules on distinction are worded in terms of a prohibition on indiscriminate tactics. Thus, Article 51(4) of Protocol I states that indiscriminate attacks are prohibited, defining indiscriminate attacks as attacks which are not directed at a specific military objective, which employ a means or method which cannot be directed at a specific military objective, or which employ a means or method the effects of which cannot be limited, and which are "of a nature to strike military objectives and civilians or civilian objects without distinction".[78] Examples of an indiscriminate attack include launching an attack without aiming at a specific military target, or treating a number of distinct military targets as a single target and carpet-bombing the sites as if they were one target. Discrimination is thus a corollary of distinction, in that an attack that fails to observe the principle of distinction will be considered an indiscriminate attack.[79]

b. Military necessity

The principle of military necessity requires that the parties to the conflict only adopt the measures necessary to weaken the enemy and achieve their surrender; it is not

---

[75] AP Commentary, p. 692, paras. 2239–40.   [76] AP I, art. 51(7).   [77] See further Chapter 7.

[78] AP I, art. 51(4).   [79] The prohibition on indiscriminate attacks is examined in more detail in Chapter 7.

necessary to bring about total destruction of the enemy, its armed forces or its property.[80] The concept of military necessity was first codified by Francis Lieber:[81] the Lieber Code, in Article 14, set out the definition of military necessity, which "consists in the necessity of those measures which are indispensable for securing the ends of the war, and which are lawful according to the modern law and usages of war."[82]

A more exhaustive explanation of the concept of military necessity can be found in the Second World War war crimes case *US* v. *List*:

Military necessity permits a belligerent, subject to the laws of war, to apply any amount and kind of force to compel the complete submission of the enemy with the least possible expenditure of time, life and money. In general . . . it permits the destruction of life of armed enemies and other persons whose destruction is incidentally unavoidable by the armed conflicts of the war . . . but it does not permit the killing of innocent inhabitants for the purposes of revenge or the satisfaction of a lust to kill. The destruction of property to be lawful must be imperatively demanded by the necessities of war. Destruction as an end in itself is a violation of international law. There must be some reasonable connection between the destruction of property and the overcoming of the enemy forces.[83]

The principle of military necessity is not outlined in either the Geneva Conventions or AP I, but the essence of the principle of military necessity finds expression in the rule on proportionality. The concept of military necessity is found in the 1907 Hague Regulations[84] and the Rome Statute for the International Criminal Court.[85]

c. The principle of proportionality

The principle of proportionality requires that any military measures taken by parties to the conflict must be proportionate – the military advantage obtained by a particular operation must outweigh the damage caused to civilians and civilian objects. This principle is more often understood in the negative; an attack will be considered disproportionate if it is expected to (or does) cause incidental loss of civilian life, injury to civilians or damage to civilian objects, or a combination thereof, which would be excessive in relation to the concrete and direct military advantage anticipated.

---

[80] See generally Burrus Carnahan, "Lincoln, Lieber and the Laws of War: The Origins and Limits of the Principle of Military Necessity" (1998) 92 AJIL 213.

[81] See further Chapter 1 on the historical development of IHL.   [82] Lieber Code, art. 14.

[83] *United States* v. *Wilhelm List et al.* ("the Hostage Case"), US Military Tribunal Nuremberg, IX TWC 757 (19 February 1948), pp. 1253–4.

[84] Hague IV 1907, art. 23(g).

[85] Rome Statute of the International Criminal Court, 17 July 1998, in force 1 July 2002, 2187 UNTS 90, art. 8 (2)(b)(xiii) ("Rome Statute") provides that destruction or seizure of enemy property when not "imperatively demanded by the necessities of war" constitutes a war crime. See further Chapter 7 on the concept of military necessity in targeting.

The principle of proportionality is outlined in AP I, which states in Article 51(b) that a violation of the principle of proportionality is "an attack which may be expected to cause incidental loss of civilian life, injury to civilians, damage to civilian objects, or a combination thereof, which would be excessive in relation to the concrete and direct military advantage anticipated".[86] A key term in the provision is "incidental". Thus, some collateral civilian casualties will not render an attack *prima facie* disproportionate: as Gardam has noted, the law of armed conflict accepts "the incidence of some civilian casualties"[87] as a result of military action. Rather the principle of proportionality will only be violated if the "collateral civilian casualties would be disproportionate to the specific military gain from the attack".[88] Proportionality is closely linked to the principles of distinction and necessity, in that it seeks to limit, as far as possible, damage, injury and death to civilians and civilian objects, while still allowing for the needs of the military campaign to be met.

d. The prohibition on causing unnecessary suffering and superfluous injury

The law of armed conflict prohibits the use of means or methods of warfare that result in superfluous injury or unnecessary suffering. The principle, which underpins the majority of the weapons treaties, prohibits any injury against combatants greater than that strictly necessary to achieve the military objectives, which uselessly aggravate the suffering of wounded personnel, or otherwise render their death inevitable. The principle sits as a counter to the principle of military necessity; the preamble to the St Petersburg Declaration provides an illustration:

Considering: That the progress of civilization should have the effect of alleviating as much as possible the calamities of war; That the only legitimate object which States should endeavour to accomplish during war is to weaken the military forces of the enemy; That for this purpose it is sufficient to disable the greatest possible number of men; *That this object would be exceeded by the employment of arms which uselessly aggravate the sufferings of disabled men, or render their death inevitable;* That the employment of such arms would, therefore, be contrary to the laws of humanity.[89]

The prohibition on causing superfluous injury or unnecessary suffering is contained in a number of IHL documents, including the 1907 Hague Regulations[90] and AP I[91] and is the underlying philosophy of the 1980 Convention on Prohibition or

---

[86] AP I, art. 51(5)(b).
[87] Judith Gardam, "Necessity and Proportionality in Jus ad Bellum and Jus in Bello", in Laurence Boisson de Chazournes and Philippe Sands (eds), *International Law, the International Court of Justice and Nuclear Weapons* (Cambridge University Press, 1999), p. 283.
[88] See also *Nuclear Weapons*, para. 936 (dissenting opinion of Judge Higgins).
[89] St Petersburg Declaration, Preamble, emphasis added.   [90] Hague IV 1907, art. 23.   [91] AP I, art. 36.

Restrictions on the Use of Certain Conventional Weapons Which May be Deemed to be Excessively Injurious or to Have Indiscriminate Effects.[92] The principle of unnecessary suffering and superfluous injury is designed to apply to combatants, rather than civilians. How exactly "superfluous injury and unnecessary suffering" is formulated is explored in more detail, with practical examples, in Chapter 7 on means and methods. As a general rule however, the idea is that the injury or suffering caused by a particular weapon must be "substantially disproportional to the military advantage gained".[93]

e. The principle of neutrality

The principle of neutrality provides that, upon commencement of an armed conflict, all States not already party to the conflict must decide whether to join the hostilities, or not become involved – that is, be neutral. States that choose not to become a party to the conflict enjoy certain fundamental rights that attach to their neutrality, including that their territory is inviolable – neutral States may not be attacked.[94] Belligerent parties must respect the neutrality of such nations.

However, in order to enjoy the rights of neutrality, certain fundamental principles must be observed by the neutral State. These include:

- *Duty of abstention* – it is incumbent upon States wishing to stay neutral in an armed conflict that they abstain from participating in the conflict, either directly or indirectly. Thus, neutral States must not engage in any acts of hostilities against parties involved in the conflict and must not allow their territory to be used by a party to the conflict for any purpose whatsoever – such as transit through the neutral territory, or using the neutral territory as a base from which to launch attacks.
- *Duty of impartiality* – neutral States must not show any preference to any of the belligerent States. Commercial arrangements and treaties that existed before the commencement of hostilities may, generally speaking, continue to be observed, but neutral States must refrain from initiating new commercial transactions that would benefit one party over another.
- *Duty of prevention* – neutral States are required to assert their neutrality, by defending themselves against any belligerent power that may seek to violate such neutrality. A neutral power must defend, through force, if necessary, its neutral

---

[92] Also known as the Conventional Weapons Convention, 10 October 1980, in force 2 December 1983, 1342 UNTS 137.

[93] Solis, *The Law of Armed Conflict*, p. 272.

[94] Hague Convention (V) Respecting the Rights and Duties of Neutral Powers and Persons in Case of War on Land, The Hague, 18 October 1907, in force 26 January 1910, 105 CTS 305, art. 1 ("Hague V 1907"). See also Hague Convention (XIII) concerning the Rights and Duties of Neutral Powers in Naval War, The Hague, 18 October 1907, in force 26 January 1910, 205 CTS 395 ("Hague XIII 1907").

status – failure to do so gives rise to the right of a belligerent power to enter the territory of the neutral power and ensure performance of the act the neutral State should have performed.

The principle of neutrality is contained in a number of IHL treaties, such as Articles 54 and 57–60 of the Regulations annexed to the 1899 Hague Convention II on land warfare. The rules on neutrality were codified more extensively in the 1907 Hague Convention V Respecting the Rights and Duties of Neutral Powers and Persons in Case of War on Land. Continued references to the principle of neutrality are included in the Geneva Conventions and Additional Protocols.[95]

The principle of neutrality establishes the rules for the parameters of the conflict – that is, where the conflict geographically begins and ends: "neutrality law leads to a geographic-based framework in which belligerents can fight on belligerent territory or the commons [the High Seas] but must refrain from any operations on neutral territory".[96]

f. The principle of humanity

Finally, note should be made regarding the principle of humanity, which is also at the core of many of the laws of armed conflict; it is an "essential counterbalance to the principle of military necessity and serves as a central principle of constraint".[97] It is possible to see the principle of humanity as part of the prohibition on causing unnecessary suffering and superfluous injury, as well as in the rules that prohibit the targeting of the *hors de combat*.[98] However, charting the exact contours of "human-ity" as a concept, let alone a "principle", is not straightforward. Indeed, as Larsen *et al.* have noted, "the concept of a 'principle of humanity' is vague in several respects . . . is it a 'principle' in the same sense as other general principles in IHL? . . . [or] is this 'principle' more a form of consideration, as opposed to a legal principle, the violation of which would result in some form of reaction?"[99]

While the principle of humanity may arguably not have the same kind of binding force as the principles of proportionality and distinction, considerations of human-ity have been an important influence on IHL, and are perhaps best understood with reference to perhaps the most famous acknowledgement of humanity in times of armed conflict – the Martens clause. Included in the preambles to both the 1899 and the 1907 Regulations, the Martens clause emerged from debate at the 1899 Confer-ence, over the status of resistance fighters who take up arms against an occupying authority. Debate was divided over whether those who forcibly resisted an invading

---

[95] See, e.g., GC III, arts. 4(B)(2) and 122; AP I, art. 19.

[96] Blank and Noone, *International Law and Armed Conflict*, p. 129.   [97] Ibid., p. 41.   [98] Ibid.

[99] Kjetil Larsen, Camilla Cooper and Gro Nystuen, "Is There a 'Principle of Humanity' in International Humanitarian Law?" in Kjetil Larsen, Camilla Cooper and Gro Nystuen (eds.), *Searching for a "Principle of Humanity" in International Humanitarian Law* (Cambridge University Press, 2012), p. 1.

army could be considered legitimate combatants or should be treated as criminals. A compromise was suggested by the Russian delegate, Fyodor Fyodorovich Martens, who proposed the inclusion of a clause in the Regulations which stated that:

Until a more complete code of the laws of war is issued, the High Contracting Parties think it right to declare that in cases not included in the Regulations adopted by them, populations and belligerents remain under the protection and empire of the principles of international law, as they result from the usages established between civilised nations, from the laws of humanity, and the requirements of the public conscience.[100]

The Martens clause has been a profound influence on IHL, far beyond the Hague Regulations, and is found in the Geneva Conventions and Additional Protocols[101] and has been cited in numerous tribunals and Courts, including the International Court of Justice, as an important foundational principle of the law of armed conflict.[102]

The idea of "humanity" as an influence on the laws of armed conflict is thus best understood as a limiting factor – the idea that there are, and should be, limits on what one does in times of armed conflict. It is an explicit rejection of the nineteenth century doctrine of *Kriegsraison* – the idea that in times of war, the need to achieve military success should override all other laws and customs that restrain one's conduct;[103] that "belligerents, even individual combatants, [have] the right to do whatever is required to prevail in armed conflict; to do whatever they believe is required to win. *Kriegsraison*, then, is the unlimited application of military necessity."[104] The principle of humanity seeks to place a limit on such an approach.[105]

5. CONCLUSION

This chapter has set the stage for the remainder of this textbook, examining the sources of the law of armed conflict, and the fundamental principles that have

---

[100] See further Antonio Cassese, "The Martens Clause: Half a Loaf or Simply Pie in the Sky?" (2000) 11 EJIL 187 at 193–8; and Jean Pictet (ed.), *Commentary to the Third Geneva Convention Relative to the Treatment of Prisoners of War* (Geneva: ICRC, 1960) pp. 46–7 ("GC III Commentary").

[101] The Martens clause is included in arts. 63(4)/62(4)/142(4)/158(4) of the Four Geneva Conventions of 1949, art. 1(2) AP I and in the Preamble to AP II. It is also found in paragraph 5 of the Conventional Weapons Convention.

[102] See *Nuclear Weapons*, para. 226; see also the written statement of the United Kingdom, *Nuclear Weapons*, ICJ Pleadings 1996 reprinted in BYBIL 712 (1995); and *Compilation of Written Statements*, UN AW/95/31, pp. 47–8, para. 3.58. See also the ICTY cases *Prosecutor v. Kupreškić et al.*, IT-95-16-T, Judgment, 14 January 2000, para. 527; *Prosecutor v. Martić*, IT-95-11-R61, Review of the Indictment Pursuant to Rule 61, 13 March 1996, para. 13; and *Prosecutor v. Furundžija*, IT-95-17/1-T, Judgment, 10 December 1998, para. 137.

[103] For an analysis of the *Kriegsraison* theorists, see Jesse Reeves, "The Neutralisation of Belgium and the Doctrine of Kriegsraison" (1914–15) 13 *Michigan Law Review* 179.

[104] Solis, *The Law of Armed Conflict*, p. 266.

[105] See Michael Walzer, *Just and Unjust Wars*, 3rd edn, (New York: Basic Books, 2000), p. 8.

shaped and influenced the law as it exists today. In the next chapters, we will explore how these principles are given practical effect, and IHL is observed and implemented.

SUGGESTED READING

Crowe, Jonathan and Kylie Weston-Scheuber, *Principles of International Humanitarian Law* (Cheltenham: Elgar 2013).

Meron, Theodor, *Human Rights and Humanitarian Norms as Customary Law* (Oxford: Clarendon 1989).

Pictet, Jean, *The Development and Principles of International Humanitarian Law* (The Hague: Martinus Nijhoff 1985).

Thürer, Daniel, "International Humanitarian Law: Theory, Practice, Context", *Recueil des Cours* Vol. 338 (2008).

Wilmshurst, Elizabeth and Susan Breau (eds.), *Perspectives on the ICRC Study on Customary International Humanitarian Law* (Cambridge University Press, 2007).

DISCUSSION QUESTIONS

1. Is the "principle of humanity" truly a legal principle, in the same way as, for example, the principle of distinction?
2. What are the benefits and drawbacks of the increasing influence of "soft law" on the development of the law of armed conflict?
3. Is there any utility in continuing to refer to "Hague Law" and "Geneva Law"?
4. What are the arguments for and against the idea of *Kriegsraison*?
5. Given that the Martens clause was never intended to have any sort of norm-generating impact, how do you account for its enduring legacy? Should the Martens clause hold such a significant position in the law of armed conflict, given its origins?

3   Types of armed conflicts

1. INTRODUCTION

The law of armed conflict does not apply to every situation in which armed force or other violence is employed; it applies only to certain kinds of conflict. And as mentioned in the previous chapters, the laws regulating international armed conflict are not the same as those regulating non-international armed conflict. Broadly speaking the full panoply of IHL treaty law, other than Additional Protocol II, will apply in an international armed conflict, while a non-international armed conflict (NIAC) will be subject only to Common Article 3 of the 1949 Geneva Conventions, Additional Protocol II, and some of the more recent treaties on the means and methods of warfare, as elaborated below.[1] The body of customary law applying to NIACs is undoubtedly wider than the treaty law, but its exact content and limits are unclear. The ICRC, in its landmark study on customary international humanitarian law (CIHL), concluded that of the 161 rules of CIHL it identified, 140 were applicable to NIACs and a further eight were "arguably" applicable to NIACs.[2] Not all States or writers agree that CIHL relating to NIAC is quite so extensive, but even on the ICRC view, there are still significant differences between the law applicable to inter-national and non-international conflicts in some areas. In order to determine what law applies, it is therefore necessary to determine the nature of the relevant conflict.

---

[1] For a concise summary, see e.g. Dieter Fleck, "The Law of Non-International Armed Conflict", in Dieter Fleck (ed.), *The Handbook of International Humanitarian Law* 3rd edn, (Oxford University Press, 2013), pp. 603–5.

[2] Jean-Marie Henckaerts and Louise Doswald-Beck (eds.), *International Committee of the Red Cross: Custom-ary International Humanitarian Law*, 2 vols. (Cambridge University Press, 2005) ("ICRC CIHL Study"). From this the Geneva Academy has produced a list of the customary rules applying to non-international armed conflicts: Geneva Academy of International Humanitarian Law and Human Rights, "Customary Rules of International Humanitarian Law Applicable in Armed Conflicts of a Non-International Character" (undated) www.geneva-academy.ch/RULAC/pdf_state/Summary-of-the-rules-applicable-in-armed-conflicts-of-a-non-international-character.pdf.

This chapter describes the different types of conflict and focuses in particular on the distinction between international and non-international armed conflicts. Although the term "international armed conflict" is now used universally, it is not defined in any IHL treaty; indeed it does not appear in The Hague or Geneva Conventions, first appearing in Additional Protocol I in 1977.[3] As explained in the next section, international armed conflicts now encompass not only those between States, but also situations where territory is occupied, and conflicts between government forces and national liberation movements.

2. INTERNATIONAL ARMED CONFLICTS

a. Common Article 2 armed conflicts

Article 2 common to the four 1949 Geneva Conventions provides that the Conventions apply in three potentially distinct situations: declared war (with or without actual hostilities), inter-State armed conflict, and where territory is occupied:

ART. 2. – In addition to the provisions which shall be implemented in peacetime, the present Convention shall apply to all cases of declared war or of any other armed conflict which may arise between two or more of the High Contracting Parties, even if the state of war is not recognized by one of them.

   The Convention shall also apply to all cases of partial or total occupation of the territory of a High Contracting Party, even if the said occupation meets with no armed resistance. . . .

i. "War" vs. "armed conflict"

The early treaties on the LOAC applied only between States, and only in situations of "war". The 1899 Hague Regulations, for example, stipulated that "[t]he provisions contained in the Regulations mentioned in Article I are only binding on the Contracting Powers, in case of war between two or more of them."[4] This latter requirement presented no difficulties when States formally declared war on each other, but there were many instances of military actions that were indistinguishable from war, yet had not been preceded by any declaration – such as Japan's operations in China in the 1930s, and Italy's invasion of Ethiopia in 1935.[5] In the absence of any definition of "war", States could easily, if they wished, portray their conflicts as involving forcible measures short of war, and thereby avoid the legal consequences of being at war such as the application of the LOAC.

---

[3] AP I, Title and art. 72.   [4] Hague II 1899, art. 2.
[5] See e.g. C. G. Fenwick, "War without a Declaration" (1937) 31(4) AJIL 694 at 694.

With the creation of the United Nations in 1945 the international community agreed to outlaw the use of armed force in inter-State relations, except if authorised by the UN Security Council or in self-defence.[6] Thereafter no State could declare war (except possibly in the limited circumstances of permissible self-defence)[7] without violating the UN Charter – another reason for States to avoid formal declarations of war.

The States meeting in 1949 to finalise the texts of the Geneva Conventions took account of these developments and agreed that the Conventions would apply not only to "all cases of declared war" but also to "any other armed conflict which may arise between two or more of the High Contracting Parties, even if the state of war is not recognized by one of them".[8] This wording ensures that the Conventions apply following any declaration of war, even if there is no actual fighting, as well as to any armed conflict between States, regardless of whether war is declared or recognised. The other situations in which the Conventions apply are discussed below.

ii. What is an "armed conflict"?

There is no definition of "armed conflict" in LOAC treaty law. A body of jurisprudence and State practice has built up in relation to non-international armed conflicts, as explained in Section 3 below, but opinions differ as to what constitutes an armed conflict in the international context.

The ICRC position is that an armed conflict exists as soon as there is "resort to armed force between two or more States".[9] This formulation follows the International Criminal Tribunal for the former Yugoslavia (ICTY) *Tadić* judgment[10] and is interpreted by the ICRC as meaning "recourse to armed force [by one State] against another State, regardless of the reasons or the intensity of this confrontation".[11] This is similar to the Commentary to the Geneva Conventions, which explains that an armed conflict is "any difference arising between two States and leading to the intervention of armed forces [regardless of] how long the conflict lasts, or how much slaughter takes place."[12] According to the ICRC, an armed conflict exists as soon as one State uses armed force against another, and the

---

[6] Charter of the United Nations, San Francisco, 26 June 1945, in force 24 October 1945, 1 UNTS XVI ("UN Charter"), arts. 2(4), 42, 51.

[7] Self-defence is lawful only in response to "an armed attack" and as a temporary measure until the Security Council can act: UN Charter, art. 51; *Military and Paramilitary Activities in and Against Nicaragua (Nicaragua v. United States)* Judgment, ICJ Rep. 1986, p. 14 ("*Nicaragua*"), paras. 115, 216, 255 and 256.

[8] Article 2 common to the four 1949 Geneva Conventions.

[9] ICRC, "How is the Term 'Armed Conflict' Defined in International Humanitarian Law?", ICRC Opinion Paper, March 2008, p. 5 www.icrc.org/eng/assets/files/other/opinion-paper-armed-conflict.pdf.

[10] *Tadić Jurisdiction*, para. 70.   [11] ICRC, "How is the Term 'Armed Conflict' Defined", p. 1.

[12] GC I Commentary, p. 32.

duration and intensity of the conflict are irrelevant.[13] Some writers refer to this as the "first-shot" theory, according to which an armed conflict exists, and therefore IHL applies, from the first moment that force is used.[14] One of the reasons for this view is that if the violence must reach a certain degree of intensity or duration before it qualifies as an armed conflict, there might be a period in which force is being used but is not regulated by IHL. The ICRC in particular is obviously concerned to ensure that IHL applies to the greatest possible extent, from the earliest possible moment.

The International Law Commission (ILC) also followed the *Tadić* formulation in its 2011 Draft Articles on the effects of armed conflicts on treaties, defining (international) armed conflict as "a situation in which there is resort to armed force between States".[15] No threshold requirement is recommended by the ILC, but in any event the commentary to the Draft Articles makes it clear that the use of this definition is for the purposes of treaty law, which is the subject of the Draft Articles, and is not intended to affect the rules of international humanitarian law.[16]

Others consider that isolated incidents or minor skirmishes, even involving armed forces, do not constitute armed conflict, and that minimum requirements of duration, intensity and the intention of the parties, must be met. The UK Ministry of Defence, for example, notes that an accidental bombing or unintentional border incursion would not constitute an armed conflict.[17] Solis and Dinstein take the view that a border incident would not be an armed conflict provided it is over quickly and that neither party intends to engage in armed conflict.[18] The International Law Association (ILA) concluded in 2010 that "State practice and *opinio juris,* judicial opinion, and the majority of commentators support the position that hostilities must reach a certain level of intensity to qualify as an armed conflict."[19] The ILA sought to address the concern that this approach would leave a legal gap where inter-State violence was not governed by IHL, suggesting that in practice, IHL can be and is on occasion applied by States even in the absence of an armed conflict.[20] This is not a complete answer, however, since it appears to leave the application of the law to the discretion of the States concerned.

[13] ICRC, "International Humanitarian Law and the Challenges of Contemporary Armed Conflicts", Geneva, October 2011, pp. 7–8, www.icrc.org/eng/assets/files/red-cross-crescent-movement/31st-international-conference/31-int-conference-ihl-challenges-report-11-5-1-2-en.pdf.

[14] See e.g. Jann Kleffner, "Scope of Application of Humanitarian Law", in D. Fleck (ed.) *The Handbook of International Humanitarian Law,* 3rd edn, (Oxford University Press, 2013), pp. 44–5.

[15] ILC, *Draft Articles on the effects of armed conflicts on treaties with commentaries,* 2011, art. 2(b), legal.un.org/ilc/texts/instruments/english/commentaries/1_10_2011.pdf.

[16] Ibid., commentary to art. 2, para (4).

[17] UK Ministry of Defence, *The Manual of the Law of Armed Conflict,* (Oxford University Press, 2004), p. 29.

[18] Yoram Dinstein, *War, Aggression and Self-Defence,* 5th edn (Cambridge University Press, 2011), p. 11; Gary Solis, *The Law of Armed Conflict: International Humanitarian Law in War* (Cambridge University Press, 2010), pp. 151–2.

[19] International Law Association, Use of Force Committee, *Final Report on the Meaning of Armed Conflict in International Law,* p. 29, www.ila-hq.org/en/committees/index.cfm/cid/1022.

[20] Ibid., p. 30.

Still other writers attempt to reconcile these positions. They prefer the view that an armed conflict exists as soon as there is resort to armed force between States, so that there can be no legal vacuum in the period between that moment and the hostilities reaching the threshold requirements discussed above.[21] They see no reason why IHL should not be applicable in all circumstances. But they point out that in practice only the rules of IHL that are relevant to the particular circumstances will apply. So in a short, minor border incident very few rules of IHL will be relevant; but if during the incident a member of the opposing armed forces were taken prisoner, the rules on prisoners of war will govern that person's treatment; and so on.[22]

iii. Occupation

In addition to declared war and actual armed conflict, Common Article 2 extends the Geneva Conventions to all situations of belligerent occupation – where territory is occupied by a foreign army, whether or not the occupation is resisted. If territory is occupied during armed hostilities, the situation is covered by the first paragraph of Common Article 2 – declared war or other armed conflict.[23] Occasionally, however, territory is occupied without any accompanying hostilities. The States negotiating the Geneva Conventions were conscious that during the Second World War territories such as Denmark had decided not to resist German occupation, believing resistance to be futile. In drafting the Geneva Conventions, therefore, the second paragraph was added to Common Article 2 to exclude the possibility of an Occupying Power refusing to adhere to the laws and customs of war on the ground that the occupation was not part of a war or other armed conflict.[24]

b. Wars of national liberation

Additional Protocol 1 to the Geneva Conventions builds upon Common Article 2 and applies the Conventions and the Protocol not only to conflicts as described in that article, but also to:

1(4) . . .. armed conflicts in which peoples are fighting against colonial domination and alien occupation and against racist régimes in the exercise of their right of self-determination, as enshrined in the Charter of the United Nations and the Declaration on Principles of International Law concerning Friendly Relations and Co-operation among States in accordance with the Charter of the United Nations.[25]

---

[21] See e.g. Kleffner, "Scope of Application of International Humanitarian Law", pp. 44–5.   [22] Ibid.
[23] GC IV Commentary, p 21.   [24] Ibid.   [25] AP I, art. 1(4).

When the Protocol (AP I) was adopted in 1977, these kinds of conflict – wars of national liberation – had been prevalent since the late 1940s as colonies fought for independence from their reluctant metropolitan Powers.[26] Such conflicts had traditionally been considered to be internal matters for the metropolitan Powers concerned, not international conflicts, and therefore largely beyond the reach of international humanitarian law. In the protracted negotiations culminating in the 1977 Additional Protocols, however, developing States succeeded in having these conflicts classified as international in AP I, with the result that the rules of IHL, and in particular those relating to prisoners of war and occupation, would apply to their struggles for independence.[27]

Many States objected to this development.[28] The principal objections were that the wording of Article 1(4) was vague and that it introduced subjective and political concepts into international humanitarian law, basing the law's application on the motives of the armed group.[29] The deep divisions between negotiating States were exacerbated when a vote was called on this provision, rather than following the usual route of consensus adoption, and this obvious lack of agreement substantially weakened the authority of the provision and, some argue, the Protocol as a whole.[30] While over time most States have adhered to the Protocol, some significant States are not parties; these include India, Indonesia, Iran, Israel, Malaysia, Myanmar, Nepal, Pakistan, Sri Lanka, Thailand, Turkey and the United States, many of which were or are experiencing separatist conflicts.[31] In addition, a number of States have made reservations to various provisions in the Protocol.[32]

The Protocol does not apply automatically in a war of national liberation: its application requires satisfaction not only of the criteria in Article 1(4) set out above but also those in Article 96(3) of the Protocol.[33] This provides that the authority representing the relevant "people" (i.e. those fighting the war of national liberation) may submit a declaration to the Swiss government as depositary of the Protocol, undertaking to apply the Geneva Conventions and AP I in their conflict. If such a declaration is made, the authority making it immediately becomes a party to the conflict and subject to all the rights and obligations of those treaties.[34] While not

---

[26] AP Commentary, para 68.   [27] Ibid.

[28] For the drafting history of AP I see *Official Records of the Diplomatic Conference on the Reaffirmation and Development of International Humanitarian law Applicable in Armed Conflicts, Geneva (1974–1977)* 16 vols., (Bern: Federal Political Department, 1978) ("Official Records"); for a summary of the debates on art. 1(4), see e.g. Anthony Cullen, *The Concept of Non-International Armed Conflict in International Humanitarian Law* (Cambridge University Press, 2010), pp. 66–86.

[29] See e.g. Solis, *The Law of Armed Conflict*, p. 132, citing the US Department of State in 1988, and Cullen, *The Concept of Non-International Armed Conflict*, pp. 73–9.

[30] Cullen, *The Concept of Non-International Armed Conflict*, p. 80. The vote was 70 in favour, 21 against, and 13 abstentions: Official Records, Vol. VIII, p. 102.

[31] See table of parties at ICRC, *Table of Treaties and State Parties to Such Treaties*, www.icrc.org/IHL.

[32] These are summarised in Julie Gaudreau, "The Reservations to the Protocols Additional to the Geneva Conventions for the Protection of War Victims' (2003) 849 IRRC 143; see also Solis, *The Law of Armed Conflict*, pp. 123–9.

[33] For a contrary view see Fleck, *The Law of Non-International Armed Conflict*, p. 583.   [34] AP I, art. 96(3).

expressly stated in AP I, majority opinion is that an Article 96(3) declaration is a prerequisite for the application of the Protocol to an Article 1(4) conflict.[35] Through Article 96(3), national liberation movements have "the right to choose whether or not to submit to international humanitarian law, insofar as it goes beyond customary law."[36] Thus if no declaration is made, the Geneva Conventions and AP I do not apply to the conflict.[37]

But a further requirement of Article 96(3) is that the State against which the armed conflict is being waged must be a party to the Protocol.[38] If the State is not a party to the Protocol, the declaration may (possibly) have the effect of a unilateral commitment by the national liberation movement to the obligations in the Conventions and the Protocol, but will have no effect on the State.[39] Since all the States to which Article 1(4) was originally likely to apply either did not become parties until after the armed struggle was over, or are still not parties, its potential field of application was and remains narrow.[40] Not surprisingly, therefore, few Article 96(3) declarations have been made and none has been accepted as effective by the depositary.[41] A rare example of a publicly documented declaration is that made by the National Democratic Front of the Philippines (NDFP) in 1996;[42] at the time the

---

[35] AP Commentary, para 68; Sandesh Sivakumaran, *The Law of Non-International Armed Conflict*, (Oxford University Press, 2012), pp. 220–1; Solis, *The Law of Armed Conflict*, p. 128.

[36] AP Commentary, para. 3765.

[37] With the exception of the potential application of Common Article 3 and subject to note 39 below.

[38] AP I, art. 96(3).

[39] AP Commentary, paras. 3770–5. The Commentary notes the view held by some States that national liberation movements could be regarded as "Powers" within the meaning of Common Article 2, para. 3 of the 1949 Conventions, which provides that parties to the Conventions will be bound by them in their relations with a non-party Power (i.e. a national liberation movement) if the latter "accepts and applies" their provisions. Thus on this view, if an NLM makes a declaration under art. 96(3) but the territorial State is not a party to AP I, the declaration could be interpreted as an acceptance under CA 2, and the Geneva Conventions – but not AP I – will apply as between them: Ibid. paras. 3771–4. However, the view that "Powers" in Common Article 2, para. 3 means anything other than States may be strongly doubted.

[40] E.g., of the colonial States the United Kingdom became a party in 1998, Portugal 1992 and France 2001; South Africa became a party in 1995; and Israel is not a party: see table of parties at ICRC, Table of Treaties, www.icrc.org/IHL.

[41] Swiss Federal Department of Foreign Affairs, e-mail 15 January 2015, on file with the authors. A 1989 communication to the depositary from the Palestine Liberation Organization is sometimes referred to as an example of an attempted Article 96(3) declaration: see e.g. Leslie Green, *The Contemporary Law of Armed Conflict*, 3rd edn, (Manchester University Press, 2008), p. 70, n. 27. But this communication describes itself as an "instrument of accession of the State of Palestine" to each of the 1949 Geneva Conventions and both Additional Protocols, and makes no reference to Article 96(3). The closest it comes to such a declaration is in stating that government of Palestine "hereby undertakes to respect" the Conventions and Protocols, and to ensure their respect in all circumstances – implicitly, with immediate effect. In any event the depositary treated the communication as a purported accession, not a declaration, but was unable to decide if the accession was valid, due to "the uncertainty within the international community as to the existence or non-existence of a State of Palestine": Communication to the Swiss Federal Council from the Permanent Representative of Palestine to the United Nations dated 14 June 1989. The communication and the depositary's response are set out in the *1989 Palestine Yearbook of International Law*: (1989) 5 Pal. Y.B. Int'l L. 318.

[42] National Democratic Front of the Philippines, *NDFP Declaration of Undertaking to Apply the Geneva Conventions of 1949 and Protocol I of 1977*, 5 July 1996, www.ndfpmc.com/gob/sites/default/files/publications/Booklet%206.pdf.

Philippines was not a party to the Protocol and the declaration was not accepted by the depositary.[43] An added problem for the NDFP was that it is generally agreed that Article 1(4) does not apply to every kind of separatist or other rebel movement; the list of types of conflict in Article 1(4) is exhaustive and confined to those clearly in the minds of the negotiating States in 1977: those against colonial domination, alien occupation and racist régimes.[44] For all these reasons some writers dismiss Article 1(4) as obsolete,[45] but others note that its future application is by no means impossible: colonies (or "non-self-governing territories") still exist, and an alien occupation or a racist régime might be established somewhere.[46] Even in the present day there are conflicts that arguably fall within the scope of Article 1(4).[47]

Table 3.1 below is a simplified summary of the effect of Articles 1(4) and 96(3), according to whether or not the armed group is a national liberation movement

Table 3.1 Effect of AP I Articles 1(4) and 96(3)

Armed group is an NLM	Yes	Yes	Yes	Yes	No
State is a party to AP I	Yes	Yes	No	No	Yes or no
Art. 96(3) declaration made	Yes	No	Yes	No	N/A (only an NLM can make an Art. 96(3) declaration)
Effect	GCs and AP I apply to both parties	GCs* and AP I do not apply to the conflict	GCs and AP I apply only to the NLM[48]	GCs* and AP I do not apply to the conflict	GCs* and AP I do not apply to the conflict

*Other than Common Article 3, which will apply in any non-international armed conflict.[49]

---

[43] Swiss Federal Department of Foreign Affairs, e-mail of 15 January 2015, on file with the authors. The Philippines ratified AP I in 2012: ICRC, Table of Treaties, www.icrc.org/IHL.

[44] AP Commentary, paras. 111–113; Sivakumaran, *The Law of Non-International Armed Conflict*, pp. 217–220.

[45] E.g. Kolb and Hyde, *An Introduction to the International Law of Armed Conflicts*, p. 77. For a list of non-self-governing territories see UN, *The United Nations and Decolonization*, www.un.org/en/decolonization/nonselfgovterritories.shtml.

[46] E.g. Sivakumaran, *The Law of Non-International Armed Conflict*, p. 219.

[47] The obvious current example is the Israeli occupation of the Palestinian territories; others are West Papua and Western Sahara (see e.g. UN Security Council, Letter dated 29 January 2002 from the Legal Counsel to the President of the Security Council, 12 February 2002, UN Doc. S/2002/161, and the latest annual General Assembly resolution, 16 December 2014, UN Doc. A/RES/69/101.

[48] Subject to the argument that the declaration might qualify as an undertaking under Common Article 2: see note 39 above.

[49] AP Commentary, para. 3765.

(NLM) as defined in Article 1(4), the State is a party to AP I and the movement has made a declaration under Article 96(3).

In the situations where the Conventions and Protocol do not apply to the conflict, the effect is that the conflict will not be subject to the customary and treaty laws governing international armed conflict. This is because it is only through Articles 1 (4) and 96(3) that wars of national liberation can be classed as international armed conflicts. However, it does not mean that the conflict is not governed by IHL. On the contrary, the conflict is likely to be classified as a non-international armed conflict and will be subject to the growing body of both treaty and customary law applicable to such conflicts. This is described in the next section.

3. NON-INTERNATIONAL ARMED CONFLICTS

Before looking at how non-international armed conflicts are identified today, it is worth briefly recalling the legal position in the pre-1945 era, and in particular the effect of a civil war on a foreign State and the recognition of belligerency. Although no longer practised, it will be seen that the criteria for recognition of belligerency have significantly influenced our contemporary understanding of non-international armed conflict.

As outlined in Chapter 1, purely internal conflicts were not regulated by international humanitarian law at all prior to 1949. An intrinsic quality of State sovereignty was (and is) that "foreign nations hav[e] not the least right to interfere in arrangements which are purely domestic",[50] such as how and by whom the State should be governed, and how it deals with internal unrest. This had been the law of nations for centuries. There were exceptions to this general principle, but opinions on what those exceptions were varied markedly between jurists and over time.[51] They included intervention pursuant to, or in order to uphold, a treaty obligation or an acquired right, or as a measure of self-preservation where the violence threatened the territory or nationals of the intervening State.[52] The writers Hall in 1890 and Oppenheim in 1905 admitted the right of other States to intervene in a State that had violated universally recognised principles of the law of nations, or in order to restore the balance of power, or in the interests of humanity – for example to stop religious persecution or prevent excessive cruelties in war.[53] Hall lamented:

---

[50] G. E. von Martens, *Summary of the Law of Nations*, trans. William Cobbett (Philadelphia: Thomas Bradford, 1795), p. 69.

[51] See e.g. Ibid., pp. 77–81; William Edward Hall, *A Treatise on International Law* (Oxford: Clarendon Press, 1880) pp. 245–9; John Westlake, *International Law*, vol. 1 (London: Sweet and Maxwell, 1904), p. 305; L. Oppenheim, *International Law: A Treatise*, 1st edn, vol. I (London / New York: Longmans, Green and Co, 1905-6), pp. 182–6.

[52] See e.g. von Martens, *Summary of the Law of Nations*, p. 71; Oppenheim, *International Law* 1st edn, vol. I, pp. 183–4.

[53] Oppenheim, *International Law* 1st edn, vol. I, pp. 185–6.

It is unfortunate that publicists have not laid down broadly and unanimously that no intervention is legal, except for the purpose of self-preservation, unless a breach of the law as between states has taken place, or unless the whole body of civilised states have concurred in authorising it.[54]

Subject to these exceptions, an insurrection or other conflict within a State was regarded as an internal matter for that State and outside the purview of international law. However, an internal conflict of protracted duration and some intensity might affect other States: their nationals might find themselves in territory controlled by an insurgent group, a contiguous State might wish to prevent its territory from being used in the fighting, and if the conflict was conducted at sea as well on land, the ships and ports of other maritime States would be affected. In these situations the foreign State might need to determine its legal relationship with the warring parties, by deciding whether or not to recognise the insurgent forces[55] as belligerents. The difficulties that can be posed for third States were put succinctly by the British government in 1825:

the character of belligerency was not so much a principle as a fact; that a certain degree of force and consistency, acquired by any mass of population engaged in war entitled that population to be treated as a belligerent, and, even if their title were questionable, rendered it the interest well understood of all civilized nations so to treat them; for what was the alternative? A Power or a community (call it which you will) which was at war with another, and which covered the sea with its cruisers, must either be acknowledged as a belligerent, or dealt with as a pirate.[56]

Recognition of belligerency turned a civil conflict into a real war and had several important legal effects.[57] First, as between the insurgents and the recognising State it conferred on the insurgents the same rights and duties, relating to the conduct of the conflict, as a State.[58] Second the State fighting the insurgency (the territorial State) was required to treat the recognising State as a neutral in the conflict, with all the extensive rights and duties attaching to neutrality.[59] Third, it relieved the

---

[54] Hall, *A Treatise on International Law*, p. 288.

[55] This applied equally to recognition of groups fighting each other for control of the State.

[56] Lord Russell, British Foreign Secretary, quoting the government's response to a Turkish protest at Britain allowing Greece belligerent rights during the Greek war of independence (1821–32): Parl. Deb., vol. 162, p. 1566, 6 May 1861.

[57] Oppenheim, *International Law*, 1st edn, vol. II, pp. 321–2.

[58] E.g. Hall, *A Treatise on International Law*, pp. 25–6.

[59] Ibid., p. 26. Oppenheim asserted that the territorial State was not obliged to treat the recognising State as a neutral unless it (the territorial State) had recognised the insurgents as belligerents, but that this usually occurred in practice where foreign States had recognised belligerency: Oppenheim, *International Law*, 1st edn, vol. II, p. 322. For accounts of the law of neutrality, see e.g. von Martens, *Summary of the Law of Nations*, pp. 310–28; Wheaton, *Elements of International Law* (London: Sampson Low, 1866), pp. 508–710; Hall, *A Treatise on International Law*, pp. 574–745; Oppenheim, *International Law*, 1st edn, vol. II, pp. 285–480; L. Oppenheim, *A Treatise on International Law*, 3rd edn, 2 vols. (London, New York: Longmans, Green and Co., 1920–1921), vol. II, pp. 383–644.

territorial State from any responsibility for injury suffered by the recognising State or its nationals as a consequence of the acts of the insurgents or the territorial State's inability to perform its international obligations in areas not under its actual control.[60] If belligerency were recognised by the territorial State, the laws of neutrality then applied as between the territorial State and the foreign State, and the laws of war applied as between the territorial State and the insurgents.[61]

Because of the legal significance of the recognition of belligerency, it was essential to determine when such recognition by a foreign State would be justified. There was broad agreement that in the first place, the foreign State's interests must be so affected by the hostilities that recognition of belligerency would be a reasonable measure of self-protection, as mentioned above.[62] In addition, the recognition was of an existing fact, and therefore the hostilities must in fact amount to a war – the parties must be actually exercising the powers and rights of war in the conflict. The tests for determining this included the following criteria:

(i) the existence of a *de facto* political organisation of the insurgents, with character, population and resources sufficient to constitute it a State if left to itself, reasonably capable of discharging the duties of a State;

(ii) actual employment of military forces on each side, acting in accordance with the rules and customs of war such as the use of flags of truce, exchanging prisoners and the territorial State treating captured insurgents as prisoners of war; and

(iii) at sea – insurgents using commissioned cruisers, the government exercising rights of blockade of insurgent ports against neutral commerce, and stopping and searching neutral vessels at sea.[63]

Oppenheim summarised the position:

It is a customary rule of the Law of Nations that any State may recognise insurgents as a belligerent Power, provided (1) they are in possession of a certain part of the territory of the legitimate Government; (2) they have set up a Government of their own; and (3) they conduct their armed contention with the legitimate Government according to the law and usages of war.[64]

There have been few instances of recognition of belligerency: a handful in the nineteenth century, and none since then.[65] Apart from these rare cases, rebellions,

---

[60] Hall, *A Treatise on International Law*, p. 26. Although many writers denied the responsibility in international law of a State for the acts of insurgents and rioters, recognition of belligerency in this connection removed any doubt: Oppenheim, *International Law*, 1st edn, vol. I, pp. 212–13; Westlake, *International Law*, p. 53.

[61] Oppenheim, *International Law*, 1st edn, vol. II, pp. 65–6; Hall, *A Treatise on International Law*, p. 32.

[62] Hall, *A Treatise on International Law*, 1890, p. 35; Wheaton, *Elements of International Law*, p. 34.

[63] Wheaton, *Elements of International Law*, p. 35.

[64] Oppenheim, *International Law*, 3rd edn, vol. II, p. 101.

[65] See e.g. Joseph Beale, "The Recognition of Cuban Belligerency" (1896) 9(6) *Harvard Law Review* 406; Sivakumaran, *The Law of Non-International Armed Conflict*, pp. 17–20.

insurgencies and even civil wars remained internal affairs for the State concerned, beyond the reach of regulation by international law. This was still the position when States met to negotiate the 1949 Geneva Conventions.

a. Common Article 3 armed conflicts

When the negotiating parties convened in Geneva in 1949, fresh in their minds were not only the recently concluded Second World War but also the 1936–9 Spanish Civil War. Although in Spain both the republican government (implicitly) and the nationalist rebels (explicitly) had to some degree undertaken to comply with at least the principles contained in the 1929 Geneva Conventions, there were atrocities on both sides, including the aerial bombing of undefended towns – civilians – such as Guernica.[66] But the fact that the undertakings were given, and the work the Red Cross was able to do in Spain as a result, encouraged the ICRC to continue its efforts towards the full application of IHL in civil war.[67] In 1946, therefore, a preliminary conference of national Red Cross Societies, preparing early drafts of new Geneva Conventions, proposed that the Conventions should apply to the parties in a civil war unless one of them expressly refused.[68] However, this and similar proposals were rejected by most governments. The Commentary to Common Article 3 summarises the main arguments against the application of the Conventions to civil war:

It was said that it would cover all forms of insurrections, rebellion, and the break-up of States, and even plain brigandage. Attempts to protect individuals might well prove to be at the expense of the equally legitimate protection of the State. To compel the Government of a State in the throes of internal conflict to apply to such a conflict the whole of the provisions of a Convention expressly concluded to cover the case of war would mean giving its enemies, who might be no more than a handful of rebels or common brigands, the status of belligerents, and possibly even a certain degree of legal recognition. There was also a risk of ordinary criminals being encouraged to give themselves a semblance of organization as a pretext for claiming the benefit of the Convention, representing their crimes as "acts of war" in order to escape punishment for them. A rebel party, however small, would be entitled under the Convention to ask for the assistance and intervention of a Protecting Power. Moreover, it was asked, would not the *de jure* Government be compelled to release captured rebels as soon as order was re-established, since the application of the Convention would place them on the same footing as prisoners of war? Any such proposals giving insurgents a legal status, and consequently support, would hamper the Government in its measures of legitimate repression.[69]

One of the many contentious issues was how to define the kind of conflict to which the Conventions would apply, and who would have the authority to decide if the

---

[66] Frédéric Siordet, "The Geneva Conventions and Civil War" (1950) 3 IRRC Supplement at 112–14.
[67] Ibid., 114.   [68] GC I Commentary, p. 42.   [69] Ibid., pp. 43–4.

conditions in any definition were satisfied. Another was that few States were willing to accept the application of the anticipated Conventions in their entirety to internal conflicts. The solution eventually adopted was to apply the principles of the Conventions, rather than the Conventions themselves, to the relevant conflict, and to omit any detailed definition of that conflict.[70] Common Article 3 thus simply applies to an "armed conflict not of an international character", the full text being:

In the case of armed conflict not of an international character occurring in the territory of one of the High Contracting Parties, each Party to the conflict shall be bound to apply, as a minimum, the following provisions:

(1) Persons taking no active part in the hostilities, including members of armed forces who have laid down their arms and those placed "*hors de combat*" by sickness, wounds, detention, or any other cause, shall in all circumstances be treated humanely, without any adverse distinction founded on race, colour, religion or faith, sex, birth or wealth, or any other similar criteria.
　　To this end, the following acts are and shall remain prohibited at any time and in any place whatsoever with respect to the above-mentioned persons:
(a) violence to life and person, in particular murder of all kinds, mutilation, cruel treatment and torture;
(b) taking of hostages;
(c) outrages upon personal dignity, in particular humiliating and degrading treatment;
(d) the passing of sentences and the carrying out of executions without previous judgment pronounced by a regularly constituted court, affording all the judicial guarantees which are recognized as indispensable by civilized peoples.
(2) The wounded and sick shall be collected and cared for.

An impartial humanitarian body, such as the International Committee of the Red Cross, may offer its services to the Parties to the conflict.

The Parties to the conflict should further endeavour to bring into force, by means of special agreements, all or part of the other provisions of the present Convention.

The application of the preceding provisions shall not affect the legal status of the Parties to the conflict.

What, then, is an "armed conflict not of an international character"? A preliminary issue to note is that while those negotiating the 1949 Conventions were clearly thinking primarily of a civil war – i.e. a conflict between the State and an insurgent force of some kind – the wording of Common Article 3 is broader than this, and encompasses conflicts between armed groups even without State involvement.

　　There is no definition of "armed conflict not of an international character" in the Conventions; as noted above, no definition could be agreed. Many States wanted to differentiate between internal armed conflicts and other forms of internal unrest

---

[70] Ibid., pp. 46–7.

ranging from rebellion to "plain banditry".[71] Various criteria to make this distinction were put forward in the negotiations; while ultimately rejected, they were summarised in the Commentary to the Conventions as factors that, if present, might indicate the existence of an armed conflict rather than mere unrest.[72] They are as follows:

(1) That the Party in revolt against the *de jure* Government possesses an organized military force, an authority responsible for its acts, acting within a determinate territory and having the means of respecting and ensuring respect for the Convention.

(2) That the legal Government is obliged to have recourse to the regular military forces against insurgents organized as military and in possession of a part of the national territory.

(3) (a) That the *de jure* Government has recognized the insurgents as belligerents; or
   (b) that it has claimed for itself the rights of a belligerent; or
   (c) that it has accorded the insurgents recognition as belligerents for the purposes only of the present Convention; or
   (d) that the dispute has been admitted to the agenda of the Security Council or the General Assembly of the United Nations as being a threat to international peace, a breach of the peace, or an act of aggression.

(4) (a) That the insurgents have an organization purporting to have the characteristics of a State.
   (b) That the insurgent civil authority exercises *de facto* authority over persons within a determinate territory.
   (c) That the armed forces act under the direction of the organized civil authority and are prepared to observe the ordinary laws of war.
   (d) That the insurgent civil authority agrees to be bound by the provisions of the Convention.

The essence of these criteria is that the insurgents are organised, with control over some territory, and are able to obey the laws of war – clear echoes of the criteria for the recognition of belligerency as described above. The Commentary implicitly acknowledged that Common Article 3 would not apply if none of these criteria was satisfied, but somewhat confusingly proceeded to argue that in practice it should apply in all cases of internal strife because of the fundamentally humane nature of the Article's provisions.[73] However, this view has not been followed, and it is now well settled that Common Article 3 applies to an "armed conflict" and not to lesser forms of internal disturbances such as riots or sporadic violence.[74]

i. Intensity and organisation

More specific criteria for identifying a Common Article 3 conflict have been developed by international courts and tribunals, especially ICTY. In the early case

---

[71] Ibid., p. 49.   [72] Ibid.   [73] Ibid., p. 50.
[74] See e.g. Sylvain Vité, "Typology of Armed Conflicts in International Humanitarian Law: Legal Concepts and Actual Situations" (2009) 91 IRRC 69 at 76.

of *Tadić*, the defendant challenged the jurisdiction of the Tribunal on a number of grounds, including the absence of an "armed conflict" in the region of Bosnia at the time of his alleged offences.[75] The Tribunal rejected the appeal, holding:

> ... we find that an armed conflict exists whenever there is a resort to armed force between States or protracted armed violence between governmental authorities and organized armed groups or between such groups within a State. [76]

This test has been followed in a number of cases. Thus for a non-international armed conflict to exist, there must first be protracted armed violence. This means that the conflict must be of a certain intensity, measured by factors such as those in the Commentary to the Geneva Conventions, listed above.[77] The ICTY listed other factors that tribunals have considered in assessing intensity:[78]

The criterion of protracted armed violence has therefore been interpreted in practice, including by the *Tadić* Trial Chamber itself, as referring more to the intensity of the armed violence than to its duration. Trial Chambers have relied on indicative factors relevant for assessing the "intensity" criterion, none of which are, in themselves, essential to establish that the criterion is satisfied. These indicative factors include the number, duration and intensity of individual confrontations; the type of weapons and other military equipment used; the number and calibre of munitions fired; the number of persons and type of forces partaking in the fighting; the number of casualties; the extent of material destruction; and the number of civilians fleeing combat zones. The involvement of the UN Security Council may also be a reflection of the intensity of a conflict.[79]

Second, for a situation to qualify as a non-international armed conflict, the armed group must be organised: "non-governmental groups involved in the conflict must be considered as 'parties to the conflict', meaning that they possess organised armed forces".[80] Where the conflict is between armed groups, each of these groups must satisfy the test of organisation: it must have a degree of internal structure and organisation that enables it to plan and carry out sustained military operations[81] and be able to meet at least the basic requirements of IHL.[82] Organisation may also establish the collective nature of the violence, as opposed to random individual attacks.[83]

---

[75] *Tadić Jurisdiction*, para. 66.   [76] Ibid., para. 70.

[77] *Prosecutor v. Dusko Tadić*, IT-94–1-T, Judgment, 7 May 1997 ("*Tadić Trial Judgment*"), para. 562.

[78] See also e.g. Sivakumaran, *The Law of Non-International Armed Conflict*, p. 168.

[79] *Prosecutor v. Haradinaj, Balaj and Brahimaj*, IT-04–84-T, Judgment, 3 April 2008, para. 49.

[80] ICRC, "How is the Term 'Armed Conflict' Defined", p. 3.

[81] *Prosecutor v. Thomas Lubanga Dyilo*, ICC-01/04–01/06, Decision on the Confirmation of Charges, 29 January 2007 ("*Dyilo Decision*"), para. 234. This particular criterion is made explicit in AP II, discussed below.

[82] Dietrich Schindler, *The Different Types of Armed Conflicts According to the Geneva Conventions and Protocols, Collected Courses*, vol. 163, 1979-II, p. 147, cited in ICRC, "How is the Term 'Armed Conflict' Defined", p. 5.

[83] Ibid.

As with the assessment of intensity, there are no set criteria for measuring the requisite level of organisation. Factors that the tribunals have found relevant include the existence of headquarters, designated zones of operation and the ability of the group to procure, transport and distribute arms.[84] Other indicators would be a command structure, internal disciplinary system, wearing uniforms, military training and ability to control territory.[85] The degree of organisation required for a Common Article 3 conflict has been described as "minimal", and is certainly lower than that required for an Additional Protocol II conflict (discussed below).[86]

Whether a situation does or does not amount to a non-international armed conflict is a question of fact, to be determined according to actual position of the parties and the nature of the hostilities. However, there is no designated authority to make that determination. Courts and tribunals, particularly but by no means exclusively the international criminal tribunals, are often required to classify the situation in order to establish jurisdiction or to identify the applicable law. As this usually occurs months or years after the situation has arisen and the conflict might have long since concluded, it is of no assistance to those involved in the conflict at the time. The ICRC does classify the conflict, but only privately; a rare exception was its publicly naming the Libyan uprising in 2011 a "civil war" and an "armed conflict".[87]

States are often reluctant to acknowledge that Common Article 3 applies to an internal problem, in case this confers some kind of legitimacy on the armed group or constrains the State's ability to act against those the State regards as criminals or terrorists.[88] It was for this reason that the last paragraph was included in the Article ("[t]he application of the preceding provisions shall not affect the legal status of the Parties to the conflict"), but whatever the legal situation, States may still wish to avoid the political implications of recognising a NIAC. There are many examples of conflicts which appear to have satisfied the intensity and organisation criteria for Common Article 3 but which have not been acknowledged as NIACs by the State concerned, such as the campaign from 1969 to 1997 by the Irish Republican Army (IRA) against the United Kingdom, demanding independence, or reunification with

---

[84] *Prosecutor* v. *Limaj, Bala and Musliu*, IT-03–66-T, Judgment, 30 November 2005, para. 90.

[85] See e.g. *Prosecutor* v. *Boskoski and Tarculovski*, IT-04–82-T, Judgment, 10 July 2008 ("*Boskoski Judgment*"), paras. 199–289; Sivakumaran, *The Law of Non-International Armed Conflict*, pp. 170–1.

[86] *Boskoski Judgment*, para. 197; and see e.g. Sivakumaran, *The Law of Non-International Armed Conflict*, pp. 184–5; Vité, "Typology of Armed Conflicts", 78.

[87] "ICRC Seeks Access to All of Libya as Conflict Intensifies", *Voice of America*, 9 March 2011, www.voanews. com/content/international-red-cross-president-libya-in-civil-war-117725988/136289.html. "The ICRC most often makes this communication by way of a letter or memorandum submitted directly to the parties to a conflict, in a bilateral and confidential manner. Where contact with one or more of the parties is not possible, it could be done through a public press release.": ICRC, "Increasing Respect for International Humanitarian Law in Non-International Armed Conflicts", February 2008, p. 15, www.icrc.org/eng/assets/files/other/icrc_002_0923.pdf.

[88] UK Ministry of Defence, *The Manual of Armed Conflict 2004*, p. 386; Solis, *The Law of Armed Conflict*, p. 102.

Eire, for Northern Ireland.[89] Despite the duration (nearly thirty years) and the number of casualties (over 600 service personnel killed and more than 6,000 injured), the UK regarded the operation as one of law enforcement against terrorism.[90]

ii. Geographical field of application

Common Article 3 applies to an "armed conflict . . . occurring in the territory of one of the High Contracting Parties". The use of the word "one" has given rise to debate as to whether the Article applies only where the conflict is confined to a single State, or whether it applies equally where the conflict occurs in more than one State.[91] On the one hand the Commentary to Common Article 3 seems to interpret the wording literally:

> Speaking generally, it must be recognized that the conflicts referred to in Article 3 are armed conflicts, with armed forces on either side engaged in hostilities – conflicts, in short, which are in many respects similar to an international war, but take place *within the confines of a single country.*[92]

On the other hand, many argue that the word "one" was simply a reflection of the fact that each Convention would only bind the States party to it, and that Common Article 3 would naturally not apply to conflicts within the territory of a State not a party to the Convention.[93] This view seems to be prevailing, and has been followed in practice for example by the US Supreme Court in *Hamdan* v. *Rumsfeld*.[94] There the Court rejected the Bush administration's argument that the "war on terror" against Al Qaeda fell outside Common Article 3 because, *inter alia*, the conflict was occurring in several States.[95] Additional Protocol II (discussed below) avoids this issue by referring to "a High Contracting Party" instead of "one of the High Contracting Parties" in describing its field of application.[96]

The potential legal effects of armed groups operating across borders, or in more than one State, are discussed further in section 4 below on internationalisation of the conflict.

---

[89] Up to 30,000 troops were deployed in Northern Ireland: UK Ministry of Defence, "UK Defence Statistics 2008", p. 155: webarchive.nationalarchives.gov.uk/20140116142443/http://www.dasa.mod.uk/publications/UK-defence-statistics-compendium/2008/2008.pdf.

[90] Ibid., p. 150. Other examples include uprisings against the UK colonial government in Kenya, Malaya and Cyprus in the 1950s and against Portugal in Mozambique and Angola in the 1960s and 1970s, in the continuing conflict between Turkey and the PKK, between Russia and Chechnyan separatists, and between Colombia and various internal groups, both military/political and quasi-military drug cartels: Sivakumaran, *The Law of Non-International Armed Conflict*, p. 201. Sivakumaran (pp. 202–4) also cites examples of where States have implicitly or explicitly recognised a NIAC.

[91] Vité, "Typology of Armed Conflicts", 78; Rogier Bartels, "Timelines, Borderlines and Conflicts: The Historical Evolution of the Legal Divide between International and non-International Armed Conflicts" (2009) 91(873) IRRC 35 at 61–4.

[92] GC III Commentary, pp. 36–7 (emphasis added).

[93] Vité, "Typology of Armed Conflicts", 78; Bartels, "Timelines, Borderlines and Conflicts", 60.

[94] *Hamdan* v. *Rumsfeld* 548 US 557 (2006).   [95] Ibid., pp. 630–2, 718–19.   [96] AP II, art. 1(1).

iii. The shortcomings of Common Article 3

In summary, the criteria for identifying a Common Article 3 conflict are now tolerably clear, but many uncertainties remain in its application. And at heart the Article, while of great importance, was drafted in 1949 in the most general terms. Within twenty years the lack of detailed regulation of non-international armed conflict had become painfully apparent. The judicial guarantees referred to in Common Article 3 are not spelt out; there are no provisions on protection of medical personnel or the emblem; there are no rules on sparing civilians during the hostilities; and the absence of provisions guaranteeing access for relief actions has led to difficulties in setting up relief operations in practice.[97] In 1965 the ICRC began a concerted push towards addressing the lack of development of IHL in non-international armed conflict and in particular, the inadequacy of the protection of civilians.[98] From 1969 to 1973 the ICRC consulted and convened committees of experts to draw up some rules that would supplement and clarify Common Article 3, eventually producing a draft Protocol that was put to the 1974–1977 Diplomatic Conference.[99] This is the subject of the next section.

b. Additional Protocol II armed conflicts

The formal title of Additional Protocol II is "Protocol Additional to the Geneva Conventions of 12 August 1949, and relating to the Protection of Victims of Non-International Armed Conflicts (Protocol II), 8 June 1977". The final version was less detailed and comprehensive than the ICRC and many delegations had hoped for, but it was only in this form that a treaty could be concluded at all.[100] Many of the same concerns that had accompanied the drafting of Common Article 3 were repeated from 1974 to 1977. The two main concerns were that the earlier drafts did not adequately guarantee respect for national sovereignty and non-interference in internal affairs, and that some of the rules were too detailed to be either realistic or actually applied in an internal armed conflict.[101]

The first of these concerns was addressed in Article 3 of the Protocol, which expressly states that nothing in the Protocol affects the sovereignty of the State or its ability to legitimately maintain law and order or defend its "national unity and territorial integrity".[102] It further provides that the Protocol cannot be invoked as a justification for intervening, even indirectly, in the armed conflict or in the internal or external affairs of the State concerned.[103] The second concern was addressed by reducing the number of provisions in the Protocol. As finally agreed, AP II contains only fifteen articles on specific protections, covering humane

---

[97] AP Commentary, paras. 4363–6.   [98] Ibid., paras. 4370–2.   [99] Ibid., paras. 4372–403.
[100] Ibid., paras. 4412–18.   [101] Ibid., para. 4412.   [102] AP II, art. 3(1).   [103] Ibid., art. 3(2).

treatment in general, protection of the wounded, sick and shipwrecked, and protection of the civilian population.[104]

i. Material field of application

As noted earlier, the absence of any definition of "armed conflict" in Common Article 3 has given rise to much debate and uncertainty as to whether it applies in any given situation. Those drafting AP II therefore hoped to provide a definition for the purposes of the Protocol, or at least identify some objective criteria for its applicability, but this proved extremely difficult given the wide range of views.[105] Article 1, "a delicate compromise", contains the following cumulative elements setting out the Protocol's application:

   (i) It "develops and supplements" Common Article 3, which means that AP II may apply in addition to, but does not affect, Common Article 3. Several delegations were concerned that defining the scope of the Protocol's application might affect how Common Article 3 was interpreted and undermine even the modest achievement it represented; the wording of Article 1 makes it clear that Common Article 3 is unaffected.[106] This also means that in some situations both Common Article 3 and AP II will apply, and in others, only Common Article 3.[107] This is explained further below.[108]

   (ii) It applies to "armed conflicts ....". As with Common Article 3, this term is not defined. The ICRC Commentary to AP II interprets it as meaning "open hostilities between armed forces which are organized to a greater or lesser degree", without citing any authority for this view.[109] But the other provisions of Article 1 help to give the term a more precise meaning than in Common Article 3, and show that the Protocol is intended to apply only to conflicts of a certain degree of intensity.[110] In the drafting negotiations there were many different views on whether or not the full spectrum of internal violence should be covered, from local rioting to a general war-like uprising against the government.[111] Article 1 therefore sets upper and lower thresholds for its application, as explained in paragraphs (iii) and (vii) below.

   (iii) The Protocol applies to "armed conflicts which are not covered by [AP I]". This sets the upper limit of its application, by providing that the Protocol will apply to all armed conflicts that are not international armed conflicts as defined in AP I.[112] Put differently, it ensures that at the upper limit of severity there is no gap between AP I and AP II through which an armed conflict can fall – it will be either an international armed conflict under AP I, or a non-international armed conflict under AP II.

---

[104] Ibid., arts. 4–6, 7–12, 13–18.   [105] AP Commentary, paras. 4446–50.   [106] Ibid., para. 4454.
[107] Ibid., para. 4457.   [108] See p. 71 below.   [109] AP Commentary, para. 4341.
[110] Ibid., paras. 4438, 4447.   [111] Ibid., paras. 4340, 4450.   [112] Ibid., para. 4458.

(iv) The armed conflict must take place "in the territory of a High Contracting Party", limiting AP II to conflicts within the 168 (to date) States party to the Protocol. This wording avoids the problems of interpretation caused by the Common Article 3 reference to "one of the High Contracting Parties" discussed above (the potential legal effects of armed groups operating across borders, or in more than one State, are discussed in section 4 below on international-isation of the conflict).

(v) The conflict must be "between [that State's] armed forces and dissident armed forces or other organized armed groups ...".[113] This immediately excludes conflicts between two or more armed groups, where the State's armed forces are not involved,[114] and is a major difference to Common Article 3 which does not have this qualification; Common Article 3 applies both between the State's armed forces and other armed groups, and between armed groups.

(vi) These forces or groups must satisfy two criteria which enable them to imple-ment the Protocol:[115]

A. First, they must be under "responsible command". There is no definition of this term; at its simplest, it is just a shorthand form of the phrase "commanded by a person responsible for his subordinates" – one of the elements of the definition of a lawful combatant under the Hague Regula-tions and Geneva Conventions.[116] It does not necessarily require a hier-archical structure: the ICRC Commentary to the Protocol says that this requirement in AP II "implies some degree of organization", which it summarises as meaning "an organization capable, on the one hand, of planning and carrying out sustained and concerted military operations, and on the other, of imposing discipline in the name of a *de facto* author-ity."[117] It might be noted here that "responsible command" is closely related to, but is not the same as, "command responsibility": "the concept of responsible command looks to the duties comprised in the idea of command, whereas that of command responsibility looks at liability flowing from breach of those duties. But ... the elements of command responsibility are derived from the elements of responsible command."[118] Command responsibility is discussed in Chapter 9.

B. Second, there must be some territorial control: the force or group must "exercise such control over a part of its territory as to enable them to carry out sustained and concerted military operations and to implement this

---

[113] AP II, art. 1(1).   [114] AP Commentary, para. 4461.   [115] Ibid., para. 4470.

[116] Hague II 1899, Annex, art. 1(1); Hague IV 1907, Annex, art. 1(1); GC II, art. 13(2)(a); GC III, art. 4(2)(a). AP I, art. 43(1), uses similar wording in its definition of combatant: "under a command responsible to [the Party to which the forces belong] for the conduct of its subordinates".

[117] AP Commentary, para. 4463; Sivakumaran, *The Law of Non-International Armed Conflict*, p. 175.

[118] *Prosecutor* v. *Hadzihasanovic, Alagic and Kubura*, IT-01-47-AR72, Decision on Interlocutory Appeal Challenging Jurisdiction in Relation to Command Responsibility, 16 July 2003, para. 22.

Protocol."[119] No minimum area of territory is specified, but it must be enough to allow the group to satisfy the two conditions:

1. *To carry out sustained and concerted military operations:* the ICRC Commentary interprets the words "sustained and concerted" according to their ordinary diction- ary meaning, i.e. the operations must be continuous and "done in agreement according to a plan".[120] The Commentary makes the logical point that these requirements will rarely be satisfied at the beginning of a conflict, in which case only Common Article 3 will apply at that time.[121]

2. *To implement this Protocol:* although not settled, this probably means that the group must be able to implement the Protocol, rather than that it must actually do so.[122] In terms of how much territory is required for a group to implement the Protocol, this too is open to interpretation and will inevitably depend on the particular facts. For example, the keeping of prisoners or tending to the wounded or sick requires physical space somewhere; but as some writers posit, if the group makes arrangements to immediately transfer prisoners and wounded to a sympa- thetic neighbouring State, then arguably little or no territory need be controlled.[123]

Despite this, the reference to control over territory tends to be interpreted more literally, as requiring at least some territorial control, and has meant that in practice the Protocol has rarely been applied to modern internal armed conflict.[124] Thus lack of territorial control has precluded many long-running military campaigns such as those in Northern Ireland (IRA) and Spain (ETA) from being treated as AP II conflicts, although it may also be argued that an additional problem is that such groups' guerrilla (or "terrorist") tactics are not persuasive evidence of an ability to carry out sustained and concerted military operations as required by the Protocol.

A notable exception, however, is the Libyan internal conflict that began in February 2011 between government and anti-Gaddafi armed forces. Within a month the ICRC declared the existence of a non-international armed conflict, and it is strongly arguable that it very quickly satisfied all the conditions of AP II.[125]

(vii) The lower limit of the Protocol's application is set by Article 1(2), which excludes its application to "situations of internal disturbances and tensions, such as riots, isolated and sporadic acts of violence and other acts of a similar nature, as not being armed conflicts". While not subject to international humanitarian law, such situations are covered by the law of human rights.[126]

---

[119] AP II, art. 1(1).   [120] AP Commentary, para. 4469.   [121] Ibid.

[122] See Sivakumaran, *The Law of Non-International Armed Conflict*, p. 189, pointing out that the alternative interpretation would be circular: the Protocol would only apply if the group were implementing the Protocol. See also AP Commentary, para. 4470, and *Boskoski Judgment*, para. 205.

[123] Sivakumaran, *The Law of Non-International Armed Conflict*, p. 186.

[124] Solis, *The Law of Armed Conflict*, p. 131.

[125] Richard Dalton, "Libya", in Chatham House, "The Legal Classification of the Armed Conflicts in Syria, Yemen and Libya", (2014) 1 *International Law PP*, 38. Libya became a party to the Protocol in 1978.

[126] AP Commentary, para. 4479.

Together the conditions set out in Article 1 mean that the Protocol's scope of application is narrower than that of Common Article 3, in two major respects. First, the Protocol only applies to a conflict between a State's armed forces and either dissident armed forces or other organised armed groups.[127] Common Article 3 applies to any armed conflict "not of an international character" occurring in the territory of a contracting party, without defining that term, and so applies to conflicts between armed groups whether or not the State's forces are involved. Second, the requirement of territorial control – as generally interpreted – does not apply to a Common Article 3 conflict. The ICRC view is that taken together, the AP II criteria of responsible command, territorial control and ability to carry out sustained and concerted military operations and implement the Protocol, "restrict the applicability of the Protocol to conflicts of a certain [higher] degree of intensity. This means that not all cases of non-international armed conflict are covered, as is the case in common Article 3."[128] In other words, while Common Article 3 applies to the whole range of internal armed conflict from short-lived rebellion to a full civil war, AP II applies only to the "upper segment" of this range.[129]

A third factor affecting the Protocol's application is that unlike the Geneva Conventions, it has not attracted universal adherence, with 168 parties by early 2015. Of the States not party to the Protocol, several have experienced conflicts that might have come within the scope of the Protocol, including India, Pakistan, Sri Lanka, Nepal and Turkey.

To a considerable extent, this gap between AP II and Common Article 3 is narrowed because most, and perhaps all, of the substantive provisions of AP II are now regarded as having the status of customary international law.[130] Indeed, many now argue that there is a substantial body of customary law that applies to all armed conflicts, whether international or internal, and whether strictly covered by Common Article 3 or the narrower AP II.[131] Those in this school include the ICRC in its 2005 study on customary international humanitarian law, and much of the jurisprudence of ICTY.[132] In essence their approach has been to apply most of the rules applicable in international armed conflict to non-international armed conflicts, on the basis that "what is inhumane and consequently proscribed, in international wars, cannot but be inhumane in civil strife".[133] This almost blanket application of customary law is by no means agreed or settled, but it is clear that the weight of opinion is generally favouring a growing body of customary international humanitarian law.[134]

---

[127] AP II, art. 1(1).   [128] AP Commentary, para. 4453.

[129] Frits Karlshoven and Liesbeth Zegveld, *Constraints on the Waging of War: an Introduction to International Humanitarian Law*, 4th edn (Cambridge University Press, 2011), p. 143.

[130] *Tadić Jurisdiction*, para. 117.   [131] Ibid., paras. 117–26.

[132] See e.g. Sivakumaran, *The Law of Non-International Armed Conflict*, pp. 55–61.

[133] Ibid., p. 57; *Tadić Jurisdiction*, paras. 70, 119.

[134] See, e.g., Sivakumaran, *The Law of Non-International Armed Conflict*, pp. 66–7.

4. INTERNATIONALISED AND "TRANSNATIONAL" ARMED CONFLICTS

The rules for classifying conflicts as international or non-international, discussed in the previous sections, are obviously easiest to apply when the conflict is clearly between two (or more) States, or within one State. Assuming the other threshold criteria are satisfied (also discussed above), a conflict between the forces of two or more States will be international, while a conflict within one State between a State and an armed group will be non-international.[135] But many conflicts cannot be so neatly categorised: to name but a few possibilities, the fighting may spill across national borders; an armed group might be fighting in one State but based in another; or a government might be overtly or covertly supporting one of the parties to a civil war in another State. A vivid example is the Democratic Republic of Congo (DRC), which since 1994 has been suffering extreme levels of violence, especially in its remote eastern provinces. At one time referred to as "Africa's world war", the conflict has involved government troops from Angola, the DRC, Namibia, Rwanda, Sudan, Uganda and Zimbabwe, as well as a host of armed groups of varying aims, nationalities, State backing and areas of operation.[136]

In situations where there is some transnational element, the conflict might be international, or non-international, or indeed both – there might be concurrently an international armed conflict between certain parties and a non-international conflict between others. Or a conflict may change from international to non-international (or vice versa) over time, as occurred in Afghanistan from 2001.[137] The focus of this section is on conflicts involving both State and non-State parties, and in particular the legal effect of foreign involvement in a non-international armed conflict. The situations are usually discussed under two broad headings, although the terminology is not always consistent and there is some overlap

---

[135] Unless the armed group is a national liberation movement – see above, pp. 54–8.

[136] One 2014 estimate was of 54 armed groups operating in the east of DRC: IRIN (an independent non-profit news and information service) report, "Briefing: DDR in Eastern DRC – Try, Try Again", 4 March 2014, www.irinnews.org/report/99741/briefing-ddr-in-eastern-drc-try-try-again. For other accounts of the extremely complicated situation in DRC, see e.g. *Armed Activities on the Territory of the Congo (Democratic Republic of the Congo v. Uganda)*, Judgment, ICJ Rep. 2005, p. 168; International Coalition for the Responsibility to Protect, "Crisis in the Democratic Republic of Congo" (undated), www.responsibilityto protect.org/index.php/crises/crisis-in-drc; IRIN, 'Briefing: Armed groups in eastern DRC', 31 October 2013, www.irinnews.org/report/99037/briefing-armed-groups-in-eastern-drc.

[137] Initially (following the 2001 invasion) an international armed conflict between the US-led coalition and the Taliban, as the government of Afghanistan, on the election of an Afghan government in June 2002 it became a non-international armed conflict between the Afghan government, supported by US and other foreign forces, and the Taliban and other insurgents: Annyssa Bellal, Gilles Giacca and Stuart Casey-Maslen, "International Law and armed non-state actors in Afghanistan" (2011) 93(881) IRRC 51 at 51–2 (but see also the contrary views referred to at Ibid., notes 21–2); Geneva Academy of International Humanitarian Law and Human Rights, "Afghanistan: Applicable International Law", 14 June 2012, www.geneva-academy.ch/RULAC/applicable_international_law.php?id_state=1.

between the two. The first is "internationalised" conflicts, where a non-international armed conflict may change into an international armed conflict through the involvement of another State; the second is "transnational", "extra-State" or "extra-territorial" armed conflicts, which considers the legal effect of a non-international armed conflict taking place in more than one State.

a. Internationalised armed conflicts

A non-international armed conflict can be "internationalised" in one of two ways: "if (i) another State intervenes in that conflict through its troops, or alternatively if (ii) some of the participants in the internal armed conflict act on behalf of that other State."[138] Each of these is discussed below.

i. Military intervention by a foreign State in a NIAC

If there is a non-international armed conflict between a State and an armed group operating within that State, satisfying all relevant criteria such as intensity and organisation, what is the legal effect of military intervention – such as the sending of troops – by a foreign State?[139] There is a range of views, described below.

A. The conflict becomes an IAC, regardless of which side the foreign State supports

A few writers take the view, as has the ICRC in the past,[140] that whether the foreign State intervenes to support the established territorial State or an armed group, the whole conflict becomes an international armed conflict because an international element has been introduced – the conflict is no longer only between a single State and an armed group, or between armed groups.[141] Certain ICTY jurisprudence is usually cited in support of this view, such as *Rajic*, *Blaskic* and *Kordic*,[142] but whether these cases do support such a contention is questionable.[143] They each concern the complicated wars that broke out in Bosnia and Herzegovina following

---

[138] ICTY, *Prosecutor* v. *Dusko Tadić*, IT-94-1 Appeals Judgment, 15 July 1999 ("*Tadić Appeal Judgment*"), para. 84.

[139] The effect of less direct forms of intervention, particularly the exercise of control by a foreign State over the armed group, is considered below, pp. 76–9.

[140] ICRC, "Protection of Victims of Non-International Armed Conflicts", Document presented at the Conference of Government Experts on the Reaffirmation and Development of International Humanitarian Law Applicable in Armed Conflicts, vol. V, Geneva, 24 May–12 June 1971, p. 17.

[141] See e.g. Dietrich Schindler, "International Humanitarian Law and Internationalized Internal Armed Conflicts" (1982) 22(230) IRRC 255 at 256.

[142] ICTY, *Prosecutor* v. *Rajić*, IT-95-12-R61, Review of Indictment, 13 September 1996, ("*Rajić Review of Indictment*") paras. 10–21; ICTY, *Prosecutor* v. *Blaškić*, IT-95-14-T, Judgment, 3 March 2000, paras. 76, 83–94; ICTY, *Prosecutor* v. *Kordić and Čerkez*, IT-95-14/2-T, Judgment, 26 February 2001 ("*Kordić Judgment*"), paras. 66–7, 79, 108–9.

[143] See e.g. Sivakumaran, *The Law of Non-International Armed Conflict*, pp. 223–4.

its declaration of independence in 1992, and Croatia's military support of Bosnian Croatian troops in their conflict with the (mainly Muslim) Bosnian government forces. Several comments by the Tribunal are to the effect that any involvement of foreign troops renders a conflict international, for example in *Blaškić*: "[a]n armed conflict which erupts in the territory of a single State and which is thus at first sight internal may be deemed international where the troops of another State intervene in the conflict …".[144] However, although the situation in Bosnia and Herzegovina was extremely complex, with different breakaway entities proclaiming statehood and forming their own armed forces at various times, the foreign intervention in question in each case was in support of the party opposing the government at the time – not in support of the government party, or of both parties.[145] As noted below, it is widely accepted that foreign military intervention in aid of a non-government party renders the conflict international.[146]

B. If the foreign State supports the territorial State, the conflict remains non-international

If the foreign State intervenes to assist the territorial State, the general view is that the conflict remains non-international, on the basis that there is no conflict between two or more States – only between one State supported by another, and an armed group.[147] There would be a question as to what treaty law would apply, because while Common Article 3 applies to all NIACs, AP II might not apply as between the foreign State and the armed group. On one view, AP II would not apply (even if other conditions for its applicability were satisfied) because on its literal wording it is confined to conflicts between the armed group and the armed forces of the territorial State (the State on which the conflict is occurring). Another view is that the words "its armed forces" in Article 1 of AP II should be read more broadly, as covering any State assisting the territorial State.[148] At the very least, the rules of customary international law applicable to NIACs would apply.

---

[144] See also Human Rights Watch, "Genocide, War Crimes and Crimes Against Humanity: Topical Digests of the Case Law of the International Criminal Tribunal for Rwanda and the International Criminal Tribunal for the Former Yugoslavia", February 2004, Listing of Cases included, www.hrw.org/reports/2004/ij/icty/2.htm.

[145] See e.g. *Rajić Review of Indictment*, para. 11.   [146] See below, pp. 75–9.

[147] Geneva Academy of International Humanitarian Law and Human Rights, Rule of Law in Armed Conflict (RULAC), "Qualification of Armed Conflicts", 13 June 2012, section 1(A), www.geneva-academy.ch/RULAC/qualification_of_armed_conflict.php; Sivakumaran, *The Law of Non-International Armed Conflict*, p. 222; Schindler, "International Humanitarian Law and Internationalized Internal Armed Conflicts", 261; Christopher Phillips, "Syria", in Chatham House, "The Legal Classification of the Armed Conflicts in Syria, Yemen and Libya", (2014) 1 *International Law PP*, 19.

[148] Vité, "Typology of Armed Conflicts", 80.

C. If the foreign State supports the armed group, the conflict between the foreign State and the territorial State is international; that between the armed group and the territorial State remains non-international

When a foreign State intervenes militarily in an internal conflict on the side of the rebel armed group, the currently prevailing view is that there are two parallel conflicts.[149] One is the non-international armed conflict between the territorial State and the armed group, and the other is the international armed conflict between the territorial State and the foreign State.[150] This is how the ICJ appeared to analyse the position in the *Nicaragua* case: the conflict between the rebel *contras* and Nicaragua was non-international, while the military action between the US, which was supporting the *contras*, and Nicaragua was international in character.[151]

D. If the foreign State supports the armed group, the whole conflict becomes international

This is similar to (A) above, but is confined to foreign military support in aid of the armed group only, and is a more commonly advanced view.[152]

As noted, the views at (B) and (C) are the most widely accepted at present: that foreign military intervention to aid the government does not alter the status of a non-international armed conflict, while aid to the insurgents will (probably) create parallel international and non-international armed conflicts. However, in some situations the view at (D) might in fact be more appropriate, for example where the relationship between the foreign State and the armed group is so close that there is effectively only one conflict, with the foreign State and the armed group on one side, and the territorial State on the other.[153]

For completeness, a fifth category of intervention might be mentioned: where the foreign State intervenes in an internal conflict between two (or more) armed groups, in support of one armed group against another. The legal effect of this will depend on the reaction of the territorial State; if it consents or acquiesces in the foreign State's actions, there is no conflict between two opposing States and – if the view at (C) above is accepted – the conflict remains non-international. If the territorial State objects, then as a matter of international law, force is being used on the territory of another State without its consent, even if that force is not directed at the State itself.[154] If the territorial State does not respond with force, however, there may be no armed conflict of any kind between the two States because the requisite threshold has not been reached. If there is a forcible response, then any armed conflict between them will obviously be international in character.

---

[149] Geneva Academy, Qualification of Armed Conflicts, section 1(A); Phillips, "Syria", 19.

[150] See e.g. Solis, *The Law of Armed Conflict*, p. 155; Sivakumaran, *The Law of Non-International Armed Conflict*, p. 223.

[151] *Nicaragua*, para. 219.   [152] Geneva Academy, Qualification of Armed Conflicts, section 1(A).

[153] Sivakumaran, *The Law of Non-International Armed Conflict*, pp. 224–5.

[154] Fleck, "The Law of Non-International Armed Conflict", p. 585.

ii. One of the parties is acting on behalf of a foreign State

This is the second main way in which a non-international armed conflict can become internationalised through foreign State intervention (the first being direct intervention through the provision of troops by a foreign State, as described above).[155] On innumerable occasions foreign States have meddled in other States' internal conflicts, whether openly or covertly. What degree of indirect intervention will amount legally to an armed conflict between the foreign State and the territorial State? The question has arisen in a number of international cases where the tribunal had to characterise the relationship between an armed group and a foreign State. This has led to a divergence of opinion between the International Court of Justice and the ICTY, as explained below.

A. The *Nicaragua* test – effective control

The 1986 *Nicaragua* case[156] arose out of the United States' involvement with the *contras*, an insurgent group fighting to overthrow the left-wing Sandinista government in Nicaragua in the early 1980s. Nicaragua brought a claim against the US in the International Court of Justice, complaining that the United States had breached international law in a number of ways, including by using force against Nicaragua directly, and indirectly through the *contras*. Nicaragua also alleged that the US was responsible in international law for the breaches of international humanitarian law allegedly committed by the *contras*.[157] It argued that the relationship between the US and the *contras* was such that the acts of the *contras* were essentially the acts of the United States.[158] In examining Nicaragua's claims, the Court found that the US had fostered and aided the *contras* over the years in a number of ways:

> ... it is in the Court's view established that the support of the United States authorities for the activities of the *contras* took various forms over the years, such as logistic support, the supply of information on the location and movements of the Sandinista troops, the use of sophisticated methods of communication, the deployment of field broadcasting networks, radar coverage, etc. The Court finds it clear that a number of military and paramilitary operations by this force were decided and planned, if not actually by United States advisers, then at least in close collaboration with them, and on the basis of the intelligence and logistic support which the United States was able to offer, particularly the supply aircraft provided to the *contras* by the United States.[159]

While the Court found that there was no US "direct and critical combat support" provided to the *contras*, it did find that they were "largely financed, trained, equipped, armed and organized" by the US.[160] In considering whether generally

---

[155] *Tadić Appeal Judgment*, para. 84.   [156] *Nicaragua*, para. 106.   [157] Ibid., paras. 113–15.
[158] Ibid., para. 114.   [159] Ibid., para. 106.   [160] Ibid., para. 108.

the *contras* could be regarded as an organ of the US government, for the purposes of the law of state responsibility,[161] the Court concluded otherwise:

despite the heavy subsidies and other support provided to them by the United States, there is no clear evidence of the United States having actually exercised such a degree of control in all fields as to justify treating the *contras* as acting on its behalf.[162]

The Court accepted that the US clearly exerted some control over the *contras*, but the question was the degree of that control, and this was central to claim that the US was responsible for the *contras*' alleged violations of international humanitarian law.[163] The Court set a very high threshold for this:

All the forms of United States participation mentioned above, and even the general control by the [US] over a force with a high degree of dependency on it, would not in themselves mean, without further evidence, that the United States directed or enforced the perpetration of the acts contrary to human rights and humanitarian law alleged by [Nicaragua]. Such acts could well be committed by members of the *contras* without the control of the United States. *For this conduct to give rise to legal responsibility of the United States, it would in principle have to be proved that that State had effective control of the military or paramilitary operations in the course of which the alleged violations were committed.*[164]

On the evidence before it, the Court was not satisfied that such effective control had been exercised by the US.[165] The "effective control" test was, however, disregarded by the ICTY in 1995 in the *Tadić* case, discussed in the next section.

B. The *Tadić* test – overall control

The degree of control became an issue in the *Tadić* case because the charges against Tadić included grave breaches of the Geneva Conventions where, relevantly, the victims of the crimes had to be persons "in the hands of a Party to the conflict ... of which they are not nationals".[166] The victims were Bosnians in the hands of Bosnian Serb forces (the VRS), and therefore apparently excluded from the above provision. But if the VRS could be equated in some legal way to the forces of another State – Serbia and Montenegro (FRY) – the conflict would be rendered international and the charges could stand. The ICTY Appeals Chamber in 1999 considered what degree of control would have to be exercised by a State over a military group for this to occur, and concluded:

In order to attribute the acts of a military or paramilitary group to a State, it must be proved that the State wields *overall control* over the group, not only by equipping and financing the group, but also by coordinating or helping in the general planning of its military activity.[167]

---

[161] See e.g. ILC Articles on State Responsibility, art. 4.   [162] *Nicaragua*, para. 109.
[163] Ibid., paras. 110–13.   [164] Ibid., para. 115 (emphasis added).   [165] Ibid., para. 115, *dipositif* para. 9.
[166] *Tadić Trial Judgment*, para. 578, citing GC IV, art. 4.
[167] *Tadić Appeal Judgment*, para. 131 (emphasis added).

The Chamber made it clear that this test, which it summarised as "generally directing or helping plan [the military group's] actions",[168] was less stringent than the ICJ's "effective control" test:

... control by a State over subordinate *armed forces or militias or paramilitary units* may be of an overall character (and must comprise more than the mere provision of financial assistance or military equipment or training). This requirement, however, does not go so far as to include the issuing of specific orders by the State, or its direction of each individual operation. Under international law it is by no means necessary that the controlling authorities should plan all the operations of the units dependent on them, choose their targets, or give specific instructions concerning the conduct of military operations and any alleged violations of international humanitarian law. The control required by international law may be deemed to exist when a State (or, in the context of an armed conflict, the Party to the conflict) *has a role in organising, coordinating or planning the military actions* of the military group, in addition to financing, training and equipping or providing operational support to that group. Acts performed by the group or members thereof may be regarded as acts of *de facto* State organs regardless of any specific instruction by the controlling State concerning the commission of each of those acts.[169]

The Appeals Chamber was satisfied on the evidence that "the [VRS] were to be regarded as acting under the overall control of and on behalf of the FRY. Hence ... the armed conflict in Bosnia and Herzegovina between the Bosnian Serbs and the central authorities of Bosnia and Herzegovina must be classified as an *international* armed conflict."[170] Thus while the ICJ effective control test required the foreign State to be in fairly direct control of individual operations, the ICTY overall control test required only a more general role in planning and organising the group's operations.

The ICJ had the opportunity to respond to the *Tadić* judgment in 2007 in the *Bosnian Genocide* case.[171] There the issue was identical – the relationship between the VRS and the FRY – but for the purpose of determining whether the genocide carried out by the VRS at Srebenica in 1995 could be attributed to the FRY, the respondent in the case.[172] This again turned on the degree of control exerted, and the Court took as its starting point the customary rule of state responsibility as reflected in Article 8 of the International Law Commission's articles on state responsibility, dealing with conduct directed or controlled by a State.[173] The Court reiterated its "effective control" test from *Nicaragua*, and rejected the *Tadić* reasoning, stating that while the "overall control" test might be appropriate in the context of determining whether or not an armed conflict was international, it was

---

[168] Ibid., para. 138.   [169] Ibid., para. 137; see also para. 145.   [170] Ibid., para. 162.

[171] *Application of the Convention on the Prevention and Punishment of the Crime of Genocide (Bosnia and Herzegovina v. Serbia and Montenegro)*, Judgment, ICJ Rep. 2007, p. 43 ("*Bosnian Genocide Case*").

[172] Ibid., paras. 297, 376.   [173] ILC Articles on State Responsibility, art. 8.

certainly not appropriate for determining issues of State responsibility.[174] The Court therefore applied its "settled jurisprudence" on state responsibility and concluded that the FRY did not exercise effective control over the operations in the course of which the genocide was perpetrated; "the decision to kill the adult male population of the Muslim community in Srebrenica was taken by some members of the VRS Main Staff, but without instructions from or effective control by the FRY."[175]

Nevertheless, the ICTY has maintained the correctness of its "overall control" test and has applied it in several cases since *Tadić*;[176] it has also been applied by the International Criminal Court for the same purpose – determining whether or not an armed conflict is international.[177] It is thus increasingly accepted that the overall control test is indeed appropriate for this purpose. And as the ICJ itself noted, there is no logical reason why the test should be the same for both issues, which are quite different: one is assessing the international character of a conflict, the other is determining whether a State is responsible for a specific act committed in that conflict.[178] The ICJ emphasised however that the overall control test was not appropriate for the latter purpose, because it would unacceptably broaden the scope of State responsibility, the core principle of which is that a State should only be responsible for its own conduct.[179]

b. "Transnational" armed conflicts

In addition to armed conflicts becoming internationalised through foreign State intervention, as described in the previous section, problems with classification can arise when a non-international armed conflict involves the territory of more than one State. The different ways in which this can occur are explored below. It is useful to keep in mind the relevant wording of Common Article 3 and AP II defining their application:

Common Article 3 applies to non-international armed conflicts "occurring in the territory of one of the High Contracting Parties", with no further qualification presently relevant.

AP II applies to non-international armed conflicts with a number of relevant qualifications:
"which take place in the territory of a High Contracting Party";
"between [that State's] armed forces and [organised armed groups etc]";
"[the groups must] exercise ... control over a part of [that State's] territory ...".[180]

---

[174] *Bosnian Genocide Case*, para. 404.   [175] Ibid., paras. 407, 413.
[176] See e.g. *Kordić Judgment*, para. 111; ICTY, *Prosecutor v. Delalić et al.*, IT-96-21 (Appeals Chamber), 20 February 2001, para. 26; ICTY, *Prosecutor v. Aleksovski*, IT-95-14/1 (Appeals Chamber), 24 March 2000, paras. 134, 145.
[177] *Dyilo Decision*, paras. 210–11.   [178] *Bosnian Genocide Case*, paras. 404–5.   [179] Ibid., para. 406.
[180] AP II, art. 1(1).

The wording of Common Article 3 does not appear to require that the conflict take place on, or only on, the territory of the State party to the conflict. That of AP II, however, interpreted literally, requires that:

the conflict take place on (and possibly only on) the territory of the State party to the conflict;
    that State must be a party to the Protocol; and
    the armed group must have control of territory in that State.

Thus even AP II may apply comfortably where the armed conflict takes place wholly within a State party to the Protocol and without any foreign intervention, but many conflicts are more complex. The following are some of the complications that arise in practice; it will be seen that in many cases the law is not settled and that there are a range of opinions as to what the law is and ought to be. In each case, State A is fighting armed group X, and it is assumed that the relevant threshold requirements of intensity and organisation are met (see above pp. 64–6). It is also assumed that armed group X is not subject to the control of another State (as discussed in the previous section, control by a foreign State may render the conflict international), and that there is no actual fighting between States, as this will itself be an international armed conflict. The examples raise the question of whether there can be a non-international armed conflict that occurs in, or involves, more than one State.

i. Conflict between State A and armed group X based in State A, fighting in State A

This is the simplest form of non-international armed conflict, included here for completeness and as a reference point. It involves a classic armed conflict which is wholly internal to State A. The law applicable to the conflict would be at least Common Article 3 and customary international law. In addition, if State A were a party to AP II and group X satisfied the Protocol's requirements of territorial control, AP II would apply to the conflict.

ii. Conflict between State A and armed group X based in State B, fighting in State A

This is a common variation of the simplest form of NIAC in (i) above. The conflict is between State A and armed group X and the fighting takes place in State A, but X has its base in (usually) neighbouring State B, for example in the border area. From this base in State B, group X crosses into State A and engages State A's armed forces there. The prevailing view is that this is still a non-international armed conflict and that it makes no difference that group

X operates from across the border in State B:[181] the fighting is still confined to State A.

As to the applicable law, Common Article 3 and customary international law would apply as in the previous example. Additional Protocol II could in theory also apply, but if group X is based in neighbouring State B, it is unlikely to be able to satisfy the requirement of controlling territory in the State where the conflict is taking place, i.e. State A.[182]

iii. Conflict between State A and armed group X, fighting in A spills across border into State B

The fighting between State A and armed group X might spill into neighbouring State B or, for example, X might have a base in State B and be pursued there by State A. Because the fighting has straddled an international border, this kind of conflict has been referred to as a "transnational" or "extraterritorial" non-international armed conflict.[183] There are many views as to the legal consequences.

The first is that these consequences depend on the nature of State A's military action in State B: if it is limited to attacking armed group X and its military infrastructure, then the conflict remains non-international, on the basis that there is no conflict between States A and B. If on the other hand State A's attacks are against, or also against, State B's infrastructure, the whole conflict becomes international because there is now a conflict between the two States.[184]

The second view is similar, but turns on whether State B has consented to, or at least acquiesced in, State A's use of force in State B's territory. If it has, then the conflict remains non-international, for the same reason as in the previous paragraph – there is no conflict between the two States. If State B has not consented or acquiesced, then the situation is that there are two parallel armed conflicts: a non-international armed conflict between State A and X, and an international armed conflict between State A and State B.[185] This for example was the ICRC's view of the conflict between Israel and Hezbollah in 2006: that there was a NIAC between Israel and Hezbollah, who were operating from Lebanon, and an international armed conflict between Israel and Lebanon.[186]

---

[181] See e.g. Marco Sassòli, "Transnational Armed Groups and International Humanitarian Law", Program on Humanitarian Policy and Conflict Research, Harvard University, *Occasional Paper Series*, Winter 2006, No. 6, pp. 8–9; Geneva Academy, Qualification of Armed Conflicts, section II(C).

[182] If group X were only partly based in State B, this might be overcome: as Sivakumaran points out, FARC was able to control territory in Colombia even though it was partly based in Venezuela: Sivakumaran, *The Law of Non-International Armed Conflict*, p. 231.

[183] Vité, "Typology of Armed Conflicts", 89.

[184] Geneva Academy, Qualification of Armed Conflicts, section II(C).   [185] Ibid.

[186] ICRC, "International Humanitarian Law and the Challenges of Contemporary Armed Conflicts", Geneva, October 2011, p. 10 www.icrc.org/eng/assets/files/red-cross-crescent-movement/31st-international-conference/31-int-conference-ihl-challenges-report-11-5-1-2-en.pdf.

In each of these cases, where the conflict is considered to be non-international, the fact that it is not geographically confined to a single State is deemed immaterial, notwithstanding the wording of CA 3 and AP II set out above. Proponents acknowledge that this wording appears to limit a non-international armed conflict to the territory of a single State, but say that this would be an incorrect interpretation; what is critical, they argue, is not the territorial aspect but the nature of the belligerents.[187] Examples abound of internal conflicts spilling over borders, with the operations of FARC against Colombia being frequently cited, where the non-international character of the conflict is generally accepted.[188] Consequently, Common Article 3 and customary international law relevant to non-international armed conflict would apply.[189] As to AP II, they say that provided some part of the hostilities take place in State A (and assuming A to be a party to the Protocol), there is no reason to regard the applicability of AP II as stopping at the border with State B; it should apply equally to that part of the conflict taking place in B. In short, once the Protocol is applicable to one part of the conflict, it applies to all.[190]

A third view is that the situation between State A and group X does not fit neatly into either type of armed conflict – international or non-international. The conflict is not international, because it is not between States, but neither is it non-international because another State and its territory are involved. Proponents of this view argue that there should be a new, third category of armed conflict and that rules should be developed specifically for these kinds of situations.[191]

iv. Conflict between State A and armed group X based in neighbouring State B, fighting in B only

The critical distinction between this and the last example is that there is no fighting taking place in State A at all; there has been no spillover or spread of an existing conflict. As between State A and group X, some say that since the conflict would be non-international if it moved into the territory of State A (on the same reasoning as in the previous example), there is no logical reason for not classifying it as non-international while in State B.

---

[187] Vité, "Typology of Armed Conflicts", 92; Sivakumaran, *The Law of Non-International Armed Conflict*, p. 232.

[188] Sivakumaran, *The Law of Non-International Armed Conflict*, p. 230. Another current, extreme, example is that of ISIL (the Islamic State in Iraq and the Levant, also known as ISIS and Al-Qaeda in the Arabian Peninsula), which since 2013 has gained control of large areas of territory in Syria and Iraq.

[189] This is also the ICRC view of "spillover" NIACs: ICRC, "International Humanitarian Law and the Challenges of Contemporary Armed Conflicts", 9–10.

[190] Sivakumaran, *The Law of Non-International Armed Conflict*, p. 231: "a non-international armed conflict can have overspill, and the overspill remains part of the core conflict".

[191] Vité, "Typology of Armed Conflicts", 89, citing R. S. Schöndorf, "Extra-State Armed Conflicts: Is there a Need for a New Legal Regime?" (2004) **37** *New York University Journal of International Law and Politics* 41 and G. S. Corn, "Hamdan, Lebanon, and the Regulation of Armed Conflict: The Need to Recognize a Hybrid Category of Armed Conflict" (2007) **40** *Vanderbilt Journal of Transnational Law* 295.

Other views on how this should be classified are the same as in the previous example, but the issue of territory becomes more difficult, particularly for the potential application of AP II. It is hard to see how AP II could apply to any part of the conflict, even if both States A and B were parties to the Protocol. The fighting is taking place within State B, but not between "its" armed forces and armed group X. Conversely, the fighting is taking place between X and State A's armed forces, but not on the territory of State A.

v. Conflict between State A and armed group X based in State C (and elsewhere), fighting in various States

This is a more extreme version of the previous example: here a State is involved in a conflict with an armed group that has one or many foreign bases, where the hostilities are taking place in different States. These States may be anywhere in the world; there is no question of the spillover of a local conflict. It is particularly relevant in the context of international terrorism and the US-declared "war on terror" against, primarily, Al-Qaeda.

Al-Qaeda is a loose network of militant extremists that has been declared a terrorist organisation by the United Nations and other international organisations. It operates, or has affiliates, in a number of States, and since the 1990s has been responsible for a number of high-profile terrorist attacks around the world, most notoriously those in the United States on 11 September 2001. In 2002 the United States began referring to a "war on terror" against Al-Qaeda and since then has at different times characterised this as an armed conflict that was neither international nor non-international, a non-international armed conflict, or simply a global armed conflict without specifying its nature.[192] The US Supreme Court in its 2006 decision in *Hamdan* v. *Rumsfeld* deemed it to be a non-international armed conflict, essentially because it was an armed conflict which was not international since it was not between nations.[193]

There have been many analyses of the legal nature of the continuing conflict between Al-Qaeda and its affiliates on the one hand, and the United States and its allies, on the other. There is little consensus. Two critical questions are whether Al-Qaeda is an armed group and whether its activities qualify as an armed conflict. One of the difficulties in reaching a firm conclusion is the shadowy and changing nature of the organisation, and the lack of verifiable information on the true relationship between the various offshoots that from time to time emerge and claim

---

[192] Sivakumaran, *The Law of Non-International Armed Conflict*, p. 232. See below, pp. 102–5.
[193] *Hamdan* v. *Rumsfeld* 548 US 557 (2006), 630. The judgment has been criticised for its lack of rigour on this point: see e.g. Sivakumaran, *The Law of Non-International Armed Conflict*, p. 232.

to be Al-Qaeda affiliates.[194] As always, much depends on the actual facts. If the US is correct and there is one global armed conflict between the US (primarily) and Al-Qaeda, the various attacks and hostile responses in different locations could be aggregated to determine if the intensity requirement for an armed conflict is satisfied.[195]

The weight of opinion, however, is that there is legally no such thing as a global war on terror, or global armed conflict, but rather a number of separate situations, each of which has to be analysed separately. As the ICRC puts it, "[the 'war on terror'] is a term used to describe a range of measures and operations aimed at preventing and combatting further terrorist attacks. These measures could include armed conflict."[196] Thus the 2001 US-led attack on Al-Qaeda and the Taliban, the *de facto* government of Afghanistan at the time, was an international armed conflict;[197] following the overthrow of the Taliban, the continuing conflict with Al-Qaeda became non-international.[198] The US attacks on Al-Qaeda bases in border areas of Pakistan could be seen as an overspill of that non-international armed conflict.[199] Other situations might not amount to armed conflicts at all but acts of terrorism only: the United Kingdom (and many others) denies that terrorist acts per se can be an armed conflict, as recorded in its reservation when ratifying AP I in 1998.[200] The ICRC has doubted "whether these groups and networks can be characterised as party to any type of armed conflict, including 'transnational'".[201]

While some situations are accepted as a NIAC or terrorist acts, at either end of the spectrum, in the middle is an increasing number of instances of hostilities between the US (and its partners) and Al-Qaeda and its affiliates – in Yemen, Somalia and Syria to name but a few. There is no geographical connection between these States and the US, raising the question of whether such conflicts can really be "non-international". Many commentators, however, say that there is no difference in principle between this situation and the example in (iv) above – whether the location of the hostilities is a neighbouring State or on the other side of the world

---

[194] For a description of the network in 2011, see e.g. US National Strategy for Counterterrorism, June 2011, www.whitehouse.gov/sites/default/files/counterterrorism_strategy.pdf.

[195] Sivakumaran, *The Law of Non-International Armed Conflict*, p. 233. See also Solis, *The Law of Armed Conflict*, pp. 216–19.

[196] ICRC, "What is ICRC's Position on Terrorism?", 15 November 2002, www.icrc.org/eng/resources/documents/faq/5fmf6k.htm.

[197] ICRC, "International Humanitarian Law and the Challenges of Contemporary Armed Conflicts", p. 10.

[198] See above, n. 133.   [199] E.g. Sivakumaran, *The Law of Non-International Armed Conflict*, p. 233.

[200] "It is the understanding of the United Kingdom that the term 'armed conflict' of itself and in its context denotes a situation of a kind which is not constituted by the commission of ordinary crimes including acts of terrorism whether concerted or in isolation": see AP I, Reservations, United Kingdom of Great Britain and Northern Ireland, www.icrc.org/applic/ihl/ihl.nsf/Notification.xsp?action=openDocument&documentId=0A9E03F0F2EE757CC1256402003FB6D2.

[201] ICRC, "International Humanitarian Law and Terrorism: Questions and Answers", 1 January 2011, www.icrc.org/eng/resources/documents/faq/terrorism-faq-050504.htm.

from the State party to the conflict, what matters is the nature of the parties and not the geography.[202]

5. CONCLUSION

While the body of customary international humanitarian law is growing, there are still differences in the law applicable to international, and non-international, armed conflicts. This difference is even more marked in relation to the treaty provisions applicable. It can therefore be essential to identify the nature of an armed conflict, as this will in turn determine the specific rules that apply to the participants and, for example, the treatment of any prisoners. This chapter has outlined the tests by which the two types of conflict can be identified.

The characterisation of non-international armed conflicts in particular can be very difficult. There are uncertainties and strong differences of legal opinion on almost every aspect from the meaning of "armed conflict" (which also affects international armed conflicts) to the apparent paradox of regarding a conflict between one State and an armed group located thousands of kilometres away as "non-international". Those drafting the Geneva Conventions in 1949 seemed to have the traditional civil war in mind when drafting Common Article 3; those drafting AP II in 1977 confined its scope even further by imposing reasonably specific territorial limitations. There is clearly a trend towards reading these definitions of non-international armed conflict as liberally as possible, and not as limited to the territory of a single State. The principal basis for this reading is that the application of CA 3 (and even AP II, to the extent possible) should depend not on the location of the fighting but on the nature of the parties – State v. non-State. Whether this will be universally accepted when stretched to the extreme, as may be said to be occurring with the US actions against Al-Qaeda and its affiliates worldwide, remains to be seen.

The next chapter examines the status of individual participants in armed conflict.

SUGGESTED READING

Crawford, Emily, *The Treatment of Combatants and Insurgents under the Law of Armed Conflict,* (Oxford University Press, 2010).

Lubell, Noam, *Extra-Territorial Use of Force against Non-State Actors,* (Oxford University Press, 2010).

Sivakumaran, Sandesh, *The Law of Non-International Armed Conflict,* (Oxford University Press, 2012).

Wilmshurst, Elizabeth (ed.), *International Law and the Classification of Conflicts* (Oxford University Press, 2012).

---

[202] See, e.g., Michael Schmitt, "Charting the Legal Geography of Non-International Armed Conflict", (2014) **90** *Int. L Studies* 1 at 6.

DISCUSSION QUESTIONS

1. What are the main differences between an IAC and a NIAC?
2. Are those differences justified?
3. What are the tests for internationalisation of an armed conflict?
4. Of the tests for internationalisation/state responsibility laid down by ICTY and the ICJ, which is to be preferred?
5. How should we characterise conflicts involving armed groups crossing borders, or taking place in more than one State? Does the law need amending?

4 Individual status in armed conflict – combatants, non-combatants, direct participation in hostilities and prisoners of war

1. INTRODUCTION

As noted in Chapter 2, one of the fundamental principles of the law of armed conflict is the principle of distinction – parties to a conflict must "at all times distinguish between the civilian population and combatants and between civilian objects and military objectives and accordingly shall direct their operations only against military objectives."[1] In order to carry out such assessments, one must therefore be able to identify a combatant, as distinct from a member of the civilian population.

Important consequences flow from designation as either a combatant or a civilian. Combatants are lawfully permitted to take direct part in the hostilities.[2] If captured by an adverse party, combatants are also entitled to prisoner of war (POW) status, which brings special rights and privileges. Combatants also enjoy what is known as "combatant immunity"; a lawful combatant, so designated under IHL, will not face prosecution for his or her war-like acts at the cessation of hostilities, provided that they conducted such acts in accordance with the laws of armed conflict.[3]

The "trade-off" for this right of participation, POW status and combatant immunity, is that combatants may be targeted with lethal force at any time, by virtue of their status as combatants.[4] Failure to comply with the laws regarding

---

[1] AP I, art. 48; see also ICRC CIHL Study, r. 1.

[2] Knut Ipsen, "Combatants and Non-Combatants" in Dieter Fleck (ed.), *The Handbook of International Humanitarian Law in Armed Conflicts* 3rd edn (Oxford University Press, 2013), p. 82.

[3] Waldemar Solf, "The Status of Combatants in Non-International Armed Conflicts under Domestic Law and Transnational Practice" (1983–4) 33 AULR 53 at 57–8.

[4] As Solis notes, "a combatant remains a combatant when he/she is not actually fighting. When a soldier is bivouacked and sleeping she remains a combatant and so remains a legitimate target": *The Law of Armed Conflict*, p. 188.

combatant status may result in severe penalties, including denial of POW status or combatant immunity. In contrast, civilians may not be targeted in an armed conflict, so long as they do not directly participate in hostilities. However, if a civilian takes direct part in the hostilities, they lose their immunity from targeting.

This chapter will examine the law relating to combatants and POWs, and the rights, privileges and responsibilities that follow from one's categorisation under international law. This chapter will also examine the complicated question of how and why a civilian loses their immunity from attack and the attempts in recent years to expressly define the parameters of direct participation in hostilities.

2. COMBATANT STATUS – CRITERIA, PRIVILEGES AND RESPONSIBILITIES

The defining elements of combatant status are the dual rights of combatant immunity and POW treatment. Though the phrase "combatant immunity" is not explicitly used in the Geneva Conventions, it is found in Article 43(2) of Protocol I, which states that "combatants ... have the right to participate directly in hostilities".[5] As outlined in the Commentary to Additional Protocol I:

> ... the combatants' privilege ... provides immunity from the application of municipal law prohibitions against homicides, wounding and maiming, or capturing persons and destruction of property, so long as these acts are done as acts of war and do not transgress the restraints of the rules of international law applicable in armed conflict. Those who enjoy the combatant's privilege are also legitimate targets for the adversary's attacks until they become *hors de combat* or prisoners of war. The essence of prisoner of war status under the Third Convention is the obligation imposed on a Detaining Power to respect the privilege of combatants who have fallen into its power.[6]

Because of the privileges and responsibilities that attach to combatant status, defining who may and may not participate in armed conflicts under international law is thus of critical importance.

---

[5] The idea of combatant immunity has been recognised in a number of fora, such as the Nuremburg Trials (*United States* v. *Wilhelm List et al.* ("the Hostage case"), US Military Tribunal Nuremburg, IX TWC 757, (19 February 1948), 788). Though not specifically mentioned in the Conventions, the notion of combatant immunity can be inferred from provisions in the Conventions themselves, namely arts. 82 and 87–9 of GC III. See Derek Jinks, "Protective Parity and the Laws of War" (2004) 79 *Notre Dame Law Review* 1493 at 1502.

[6] Michael Bothe, Karl Partsch and Waldemar Solf (eds.), *New Rules for Victims of Armed Conflicts: Commentary on the Two 1977 Protocols Additional to the Geneva Conventions of 1949* 2nd edn, (Leiden: Koninkliike Brill NV, 2013), pp. 277–8.

a. Early rules on combatant status – the US Civil War to the Geneva Conventions of 1949

Determining who could take part in hostilities was the concern of some of the earliest documents relating to armed conflicts. For example, the Lieber Code, in Article 57, provided that: "so soon as a man is armed by a sovereign government and takes the soldier's oath of fidelity, he is a belligerent; his killing, wounding, or other warlike acts are not individual crimes or offenses."[7] Attempts continued throughout the late nineteenth and early twentieth centuries to adopt criteria for combatant status, including endeavours at the Brussels Conference of 1874 and the 1880 *Oxford Manual on the Laws of War* – neither of which was adopted as a binding international agreement.[8] However, the influence of both these documents is evident in the eventual definition of combatants that was accepted in The Hague Regulations of 1899 and 1907.[9] Under Article 1 of the Regulations Respecting the Laws and Customs of War on Land, "belligerents" must fulfil the following criteria:

1. to be commanded by a person responsible for his subordinates;
2. to have a fixed distinctive emblem recognisable at a distance;
3. to carry arms openly; and
4. to conduct their operations in accordance with the laws and customs of war.[10]

The re-evaluation of the laws of war that took place following the Second World War prompted a re-evaluation of the criteria for combatant status, especially in light of the widespread partisan and resistance warfare that occurred throughout occupied Europe.[11] Re-evaluation of the law in the 1970s also brought changes to the law on combatants. The substance of these provisions is explored in the next section of this chapter.

3. THE CURRENT LAW REGARDING COMBATANT STATUS

The relevant treaty provisions regarding combatant status are contained in Article 13(1)–(2) of Geneva Convention I,[12] Article 13(1)–(2) of Geneva Convention II,[13] Articles 4A(1)–(3) and (6) of Geneva Convention II[14] and Articles 43–44 of

---

[7] Lieber Code, art. 57.

[8] See Christopher Greenwood, "Scope of Application of International Humanitarian Law", in Dieter Fleck (ed.), *The Handbook of International Humanitarian Law*, 2nd edn, (Oxford University Press, 2008), p. 24.

[9] Hague IV 1907, arts. 1–2.   [10] Ibid., art. 1

[11] GC I Commentary, pp. 52–64; see also ICRC, *Report of the International Committee of the Red Cross on its activities during the Second World War*, vol I. (Geneva: ICRC, 1948), pp. 517–35, and ICRC, *Report on the Work of the Conference of Government Experts* (Geneva: ICRC, 1947), pp. 103–10.

[12] GC I.   [13] GC II.   [14] GC III, art. 6.

Additional Protocol I. Article 4A of GC III is considered to outline the fundamental provisions for combatant status. Combatants include:

1. Members of the armed forces of a Party to the conflict as well as members of militias or volunteer corps forming part of such armed forces.
2. Members of other militias and members of other volunteer corps, including those of organised resistance movements, belonging to a Party to the conflict and operating in or outside their own territory, even if this territory is occupied, provided that such militias or volunteer corps, including such organised resistance movements, fulfil the following conditions
    i. that of being commanded by a person responsible for his subordinates
    ii. that of having a fixed distinctive sign recognisable at a distance
    iii. that of carrying arms openly
    iv. that of conducting their operations in accordance with the laws and customs of war
3. Members of regular armed forces who profess allegiance to a government or an authority not recognised by the Detaining Power.

    . . .

6. Inhabitants of a non-occupied territory, who on the approach of the enemy spontaneously take up arms to resist the invading forces, without having had the time to form themselves into regular armed units, provided they carry arms openly and respect the laws and customs of war.[15]

a. Members of the armed forces

Members of the armed forces comprise the main category of combatant in IHL – they are all persons belonging to the armed forces of a party to the conflict who are entitled to take direct part in the hostilities.[16] This definition includes members of militia and volunteer forces, where such forces operate either as part of the armed forces proper, or in addition to the armed forces. Military reserve and National Guard organisations are examples of militias or volunteer forces.[17]

Members of the armed forces who are *not* permitted to take direct part in the hostilities (such as medical or religious personnel or other persons who have no "combat mission"[18]) are considered non-combatants. Such persons are nonetheless entitled to treatment as POWs if captured – the law on non-combatants is discussed in more detail below.

[15] GC II, art. 4A.   [16] Ipsen, "Combatants and Non-Combatants", p. 81.
[17] E.g., in the US, volunteer forces include the National Guard and the US Coast Guard.
[18] Ipsen, "Combatants and Non-Combatants", p. 97.

b. Partisan and resistance fighters

As noted above, when the 1949 Geneva Conventions were being debated, the experience of partisan and resistance fighters during the Second World War prompted a re-evaluation of the status of such fighters under international law.[19] During the War, captured partisans and resistance fighters in occupied territory were routinely denied any sort of legal protection, and either summarily executed or sent to concentration camps.[20] During the Geneva Diplomatic Conference that adopted the Conventions, the question of whether resistance fighters operating in already occupied territory should be granted international legal recognition was raised. Debate was divided between those States who wanted to expand the categories of combatant and POW to include partisans and resistance fighters[21] and those States who were considerably more reluctant to embrace such an expansion.[22] The former approach prevailed, and members of organised resistance movements were thus included in the category of combatant, under Article 4 (A)(2) of GC III.

However, in order to be recognised as combatants, and to enjoy POW rights on capture, resistance fighters must comply with certain requirements, such as operating under responsible command,[23] wearing a fixed distinctive sign recognisable at a distance,[24] carrying their arms openly[25] and conducting their operations in accordance with the laws and customs of war.[26]

i. Being commanded by a person responsible for his subordinates

In an international armed conflict, any resistance force must be commanded by a person who is ultimately responsible for their conduct. This provision serves multiple functions. First, it enables parties to the conflict to conduct their operations according to an internal disciplinary system in compliance with the laws of armed conflict.[27] Second, an internal disciplinary system provides for a chain of command and accountability which has important implications regarding command responsibility.[28] Finally, an organised command structure excludes private individuals who

---

[19] See further GC III Commentary, pp. 49–50, 52–64 especially, regarding the protracted debates which took place during the preparatory work and the Diplomatic Conference itself, regarding recognition of partisan and resistance fighters. The advocacy of the ICRC during the Second World War did much to further the cause of the resistance and partisan fighter – at least at the Diplomatic Conferences. See further ICRC, Report on its Activities During the Second World War.

[20] See Bugnion, *The ICRC and the Protection of War Victims*, pp. 192–4. See also *United States* v. *Otto Ohlendorf et al.* ("the *Einsatzgruppen* case") US Military Tribunal Nuremburg, IV TWC 1 (9 April 1948).

[21] See GC III Commentary, pp. 52–55.   [22] See ICRC, Final Record 1949, Vol. IIA, p. 469.

[23] GC III, art. 4(A)(2)(a).   [24] Ibid., art. 4(A)(2)(b).   [25] Ibid., art. 4(A)(2)(c).   [26] Ibid., art. 4(A)(2)(d).

[27] Geoffrey Corn, Victor Hansen, Richard Jackson, Chris Jenks, Eric Talbot Jensen and James Schoettler, Jr., *The Law of Armed Conflict: An Operational Approach* (New York: Wolters Kluwer, 2012), p. 137.

[28] Ibid.

take up arms in "private wars"[29] from being protected and recognised under IHL. The "organised command" requirement thus acts as a disincentive for individuals to unilaterally take direct part in the hostilities without doing so according to established and sanctioned pathways, such as the armed forces or volunteer corps.

ii. Having a fixed distinctive sign

The distinctive sign can take any number of forms. It can include a complete uniform, or can be as small as an arm band or some other distinctive emblem. However, the distinctive sign must be the same for all members of the group, be used only by them and be visible at a distance. The critical element is visibility *as a combatant* – rather than just visibility *per se* – as Dinstein notes, the central issue regarding a distinctive sign is not so much whether combatants can be seen, "but the lack of desire on their part to create the false impression that they are civilians."[30] Combatants must therefore be identifiable *as combatants*, and not as civilians who might be carrying arms.

iii. Carrying arms openly

The requirement of carrying arms openly is underpinned by a philosophy essentially similar to that of the fixed distinctive sign – both stem from the need for all persons in a conflict zone to be able to identify members of the armed forces or armed groups. However, defining the precise parameters of "carrying arms openly" is more difficult. "Carrying arms openly" does not literally mean the constant visible carriage of firearms or weapons; the Commentary to Convention III makes it clear that Article 4A(2) "is not an attempt to prescribe that a hand-grenade or a revolver must be carried at belt or shoulder rather than in a pocket or under a coat."[31]

However, this had led some commentators to pose the question: "how can a weapon be carried openly, yet not visibly?"[32] The Commentaries to the Conventions attempt to clarify their position, stating that:

although the difference may seem slight, there must be no confusion between carrying arms "openly" and carrying them "visibly" or "ostensibly"... The enemy must be able to recognise partisans as combatants in the same way as members of regular armed forces, whatever their weapons. Thus, a civilian could not enter a military post on a false pretext and then open fire, having taken unfair advantage of his adversaries.[33]

---

[29] Gary Solis, *The Law of Armed Conflict: International Humanitarian Law in War,* (Cambridge University Press, 2010), p. 196.

[30] Yoram Dinstein, *The Conduct of Hostilities under the Law of International Armed Conflict* (Cambridge University Press, 2010), p. 38.

[31] Solis, *The Law of Armed Conflict,* p. 196.   [32] Ibid.   [33] GC III Commentary, p. 61.

As with the distinctive sign, the relevant element of the provision seems to rest on the ability of an observer to identify someone as a direct participant in the hostilities; thus, a participant must "abstain from creating the false impression that he is an innocent civilian ... he must carry his arms openly in a reasonable way, depending on the nature of the weapon and the prevailing circumstances."[34]

iv. Obeying the laws of war

The remaining criterion for combatant status for partisan and resistance fighters is the requirement that all participants conduct their operations in accordance with the laws and customs of war. This restates the requirement placed on all members of the armed forces – both regular and irregular; all are "bound to conform in the conduct of their operations to the recognized standards of the international humanitarian law".[35]

c. National liberation and guerrilla fighters under Protocol I

Protocol I provides combatant status for irregulars engaged in national liberation wars. Combatants in Additional Protocol I are defined in Article 43(1) as:

The armed forces of a Party to a conflict consist of all organized armed forces, groups and units which are under a command responsible to that Party for the conduct of its subordinates, even if that Party is represented by a government or an authority not recognized by an adverse Party. Such armed forces shall be subject to an internal disciplinary system which, *inter alia*, shall enforce compliance with the rules of international law applicable in armed conflict.

Chapter 1 of this book noted the historical context surrounding the adoption of Protocol I – that of national liberation movements and decolonisation. In the context of combatant status in Protocol I, it is necessary to detail a few more elements that help account for how the law was amended.

In the debates that took place in the UN and in civil society more generally in the lead-up to the adoption of the Protocols, a common argument was that the existing law was inadequate to appropriately regulate these new types of armed conflicts.[36]

---

[34] Dinstein, *The Conduct of Hostilities*, p. 39.

[35] W. Thomas Mallison and Sally Mallison, "The Juridical Status of Irregular Combatants under the International Humanitarian Law of Armed Conflict" (1977) 9 Case W Res JIL 39 at 59.

[36] See debates regarding the shortcomings of the provisions for dealing with resistance fighters, both generally and in the context of national liberation wars, in ICRC, *Report of the Conference of Government Experts on the Reaffirmation and Development of International Humanitarian Law Applicable in Armed Conflicts*, (Geneva: ICRC, 1971) ("CE 1971, Report"), p. 68, and ICRC, *Report on the Conference of Government Experts on the Reaffirmation and Development of International Humanitarian Law Applicable in Armed Conflicts*, 2 vols. (Geneva: ICRC, 1972), vol. 1 ("CE 1972, Report"), pp. 133–5.

As noted above, the 1949 Geneva criteria for irregular fighters provide that in order to be granted combatant status such irregulars must carry their arms openly and wear a fixed, distinctive insignia, recognisable at a distance. However, during the Diplomatic Conferences in the 1970s, it was pointed out that such provisions were incompatible with guerrilla warfare – a strategy of warfare which was reliant on stealth and subterfuge for success. If the new Protocol was intended to better regulate guerrilla warfare, then the requirement of wearing a fixed visible insignia would be untenable and counter-productive.[37] As noted in the Commentary to the Protocols:

> As a practical matter, it was recognised early ... that the prerequisites that members of such movements bear fixed distinctive signs visible at a distance, and that they carry arms openly, virtually precludes the use of the provision ... In order to accomplish their mission, they must work secretly, wear no uniform or distinguishing sign, and withhold their identity prior to their attack. Realisation of the inadequacy of this provision to provide privileged combatant status for those who fight regular military forces in colonial wars and struggles for self-determination gave rise to strong initiatives to relax or abolish the 1949 Geneva Conventions standards for "freedom fighters".[38]

Given this background, AP I moderates combatant requirements notably – Article 44(3) recognises that "there are situations in armed conflicts where, owing to the nature of the hostilities an armed combatant cannot so distinguish himself" and provides that such a combatant will not lose his combatant status so long as he "carries his arms openly (a) during each military engagement, and (b) during such time as he is visible to the adversary while he is engaged in a military deployment preceding the launching of an attack in which he is to participate."[39] This article does not extend the right to engage in guerrilla tactics to regular armies; as noted in Article 44(7), the article is "not intended to change the generally accepted practice of States with respect to the wearing of the uniform by combatants assigned to the regular, uniformed armed units of a Party to the conflict."[40]

The ICRC Commentary to the Protocols makes it clear that the intent behind Articles 43–44 and Additional Protocol I as a whole was to acknowledge and regulate wars of national liberation and those who fought in them, in the hope that such acknowledgement would encourage greater respect for the law by guerrilla groups and by those who fought against them.[41] However, the adoption of these

---

[37] For the debate at the Diplomatic Conference regarding the exact meaning of insignia that is "visible at a distance", see Official Records XV, CDDH/III/SR.55–56, pp. 155–87; also, the comments from the French delegation in Committee III at the 2nd Session of the Diplomatic Conference, regarding the unrealistic nature of distinction requirements for resistance fighters as outlined in the GC III, art. 4A(2), Official Records XIV, CDDH/III/SR.33-SR.36, Annex, pp. 537–8. See further Bothe *et al*, *New Rules*, p. 245.

[38] Bothe *et al*, *New Rules*, p. 245.   [39] AP I, art. 44(3)(a)–(b).

[40] See further AP Commentary, p. 542.   [41] Ibid., para. 1684.

new rules on combatant status came in for intense criticism from States such as the US, Israel, India and Pakistan,[42] with some commentators calling the Protocol "law in the service of terror".[43] Protocol I remains a contentious treaty, and a number of States still have not ratified the instrument.[44]

Despite these concerns, Rules 4 and 106 of the ICRC CIHL Study state that Articles 43 and 44 are customary – though this assessment should be treated with some caution.[45] As of this writing, 174 States are parties to Additional Protocol I, with thirteen States having lodged reservations relating to Article 44[46] and twenty-three States not ratifying the Protocol.[47]

d. Levée en masse

The final category of persons entitled to combatant and POW status are those persons participating in a *levée en masse*. *Levée en masse* was a concept that originated in the years following the French Revolution;[48] in IHL, it refers to a situation where, upon the approach of an invading army, the civilians of the threatened territory spontaneously take up arms in order to resist the invasion. *Levée en masse* is recognised under Article 13(6) of Convention I, Article 13(6) of Convention II and Article 4(A)(6) of Convention III.[49] In order to qualify for combatant/POW status, participants in a *levée* must carry their arms openly and

---

[42] See comments in Official Records VI, CDDH/SR.40 and 41, pp. 121–55, 178–81, 183–6, 189–92 and Official Records XV, CDDH/III/SR.55 and 56, pp. 155–87.

[43] Douglas Feith, "Law in the Service of Terror – The Strange Case of the Additional Protocol" (1985) 1 *National Interest* 36 at 36. See also Abraham Sofaer, "Terrorism and the Law" (1985–6) 64 *Foreign Affairs* 901 at 912–15. Indeed, it was this very concern that stopped US President Ronald Reagan from submitting Protocol I to the Senate for ratification, stating concerns regarding an instrument which would "... grant combatant status to irregular forces even if they do not satisfy the traditional requirements to distinguish themselves from the civilian population and otherwise comply with the laws of war. This would endanger civilians among whom terrorists and other irregulars attempt to conceal themselves. These problems are so fundamental in character that they cannot be remedied through reservations... we must not, and need not, give recognition and protection to terrorist groups as a price for progress in humanitarian law": Message from the President of the United States transmitting the Protocol II Additional to the Geneva Conventions of August 12, 1949, and Relating to the Protection of Victims of Noninternational Armed Conflicts, Concluded at Geneva on June 10, 1977 (29 January 1987).

[44] See Letter from John Bellinger III, Legal Adviser to the US Department of States and William Haynes II, General Counsel, U.S. Department of Defense, Initial response of US to ICRC study on Customary International Humanitarian Law with Illustrative Comments, 3 November 2006, www.state.gov/s/l/2006/98860.htm.

[45] ICRC CIHL Study, rr. 4, 106.

[46] Argentina, Australia, Canada, France, Germany, Ireland, Italy, Japan, South Korea, The Netherlands, New Zealand, Spain and the UK.

[47] Andorra, Azerbaijan, Bhutan, Eritrea, India, Indonesia, Iran, Israel, Kiribati, Malaysia, Marshall Islands, Myanmar, Nepal, Niue, Pakistan, Papua New Guinea, Singapore, Somalia, Sri Lanka, Thailand, Turkey, Tuvalu and the US.

[48] See Alan Forrest, "La Patrie en Danger: The French Revolution and the First *Levée en Masse*" in Daniel Moran and Arthur Waldron (eds.), *The People in Arms: Military Myth and National Mobilisation since the French Revolution* (Cambridge University Press, 2003), p. 9.

[49] See also GC III Commentary, pp. 67–8.

obey the laws of armed conflict.[50] Unlike irregulars in Article 4A(2), there is no requirement for participants in a *levée* to have some kind of fixed distinctive sign or organisational structure; indeed, the fundamental character of the *levée* is its spontaneous, unorganised nature.

Levée en masse remains something of an outlier in the law of armed conflict. As noted by Ipsen, "in modern-day armed conflicts the *levée en masse* has become less significant because, as a rule, the regular armed forces of an attacking party are armed to a degree that simply cannot be countered with the weapons available to a spontaneous resistance (such as hunting weapons)."[51] Since its adoption into international law with the Hague Regulations,[52] there have been only a few instances of recognised *levées en masse*, the most famous being the *levée* that took place on the island of Crete during the Second World War, where local inhabitants held off the German paratroop invasion force for nearly ten days.[53]

Despite the practice of *levée en masse* falling into desuetude, it continues to have a place in modern international law. *Levée en masse* partially underpins Article 9 of the Draft Articles on State Responsibility, that of "conduct carried out in the absence or default of the official authorities".[54] A considerable number of States continue to include *levée en masse* in their domestic military manuals,[55] and the ICRC has affirmed the customary status of the principle of *levée en masse*, acknowledging that, "despite its limited current application"[56] it remains the only exception to Rule 5, which states that "civilians are persons who are not members of the armed forces".[57]

e. Participants in non-international armed conflicts

There is no combatant status for non-State participants in non-international armed conflicts. Participation by non-State actors in a non-international armed conflict is not an internationally wrongful act,[58] but neither Common Article 3 nor

---

[50] For an example of national case law regarding *levée en masse*, see the Israeli case *Military Prosecutor* v. *Omar Mahmud Kassem and Others*, April 13 1969, 42 ILR 470.

[51] Ipsen, "Combatants and Non-Combatants", p. 93.

[52] *Levée en masse* was actually included in the Lieber Code in Articles 51 and 52; the first international instrument to contemplate legitimising *levée en masse* was the Brussels Declaration of 1874 in art. 10.

[53] Nearly as many Cretan civilians were killed as British and German military during the invasion – almost 3,500. However, the bulk of the civilian casualties happened after the Germans occupied the island, in the form of arbitrary mass executions conducted by the Germans in reprisal for the resistance. See generally Antony Beevor, *Crete: The Battle and the Resistance* (London: John Murray Ltd, 1991).

[54] See James Crawford, *The International Law Commission's Articles on State Responsibility: Introduction, Text and Commentaries* (Cambridge University Press, 2002), p. 114.

[55] For a complete listing, see ICRC CIHL Study, vol. I, p. 387.　　[56] Ibid., p. 18.　　[57] Ibid.

[58] R. R. Baxter, "So-Called 'Unprivileged Belligerency': Spies, Guerrillas, and Saboteurs" (1951) 28 BYBIL 323 at 344. Berman concurs, stating that "engagement in combat by those not covered by the combatants' privilege, assuming no war crimes have been committed, is not illegal *per se* under *international* law. Rather, since such acts are not immunised by international law, the contending parties are free to punish

Protocol II legitimises or immunises such participation. Furthermore, participants in non-international armed conflicts do not enjoy the same extensive protections that are provided for combatants in an international armed conflict, such as POW rights.[59]

4. NON-COMBATANTS ENTITLED TO POW STATUS AND TREATMENT

Non-combatants are persons who have no combat function but are nonetheless entitled to POW status and treatment if captured. Such non-combatants can include members of the armed forces' judicial or administrative corps, war correspondents embedded with a military unit or the civilian crew of a military aircraft.

The provisions which relate to non-combatants are contained in Article 4A(4)–(5) of Geneva Convention III, which itself builds on Article 3 of the Hague Regulations of 1899 and 1907. The Hague Regulations provide that "the armed forces of the belligerent parties may consist of combatants and non-combatants. In the case of capture by the enemy, both have the right to be treated as prisoners of war."[60] This was developed in the 1949 Conventions to delineate particular types of non-combatant. These are:

(4) Persons who accompany the armed forces without actually being members thereof, such as civilian members of military aircraft crews, war correspondents, supply contractors, members of labour units or of services responsible for the welfare of the armed forces, provided that they have received authorization from the armed forces which they accompany, who shall provide them for that purpose with an identity card similar to the annexed model.

(5) Members of crews, including masters, pilots and apprentices, of the merchant marine and the crews of civil aircraft of the Parties to the conflict, who do not benefit by more favourable treatment under any other provisions of international law.[61]

The term "non-combatant" was not included in AP I, however, during the Diplomatic Conference, it was affirmed that the term "members of the armed forces", as used in Article 43(1) of Protocol I, "is all inclusive and includes both combatants and non-combatants".[62]

---

individuals engaged in such activities under their own law" in "Privileging Combat? Contemporary Conflict and the Legal Construction of War" (2004) 43 Colum J Transntl L 1 at 14.

[59] See Emily Crawford, *The Treatment of Combatants and Insurgents Under the Law of Armed Conflict* (Oxford University Press, 2010), specifically Chapter 3.

[60] Hague II 1899/Hague IV 1907, art. 3.

[61] Note that those included in GC III art 4A (4)-(5) are in the unusual position of being civilians who, while not entitled to combatant privilege, are entitled to POW status if captured.

[62] Official Records XV, CDDH/236/Rev.1, p. 390.

5. IRREGULARS IN HOSTILITIES NOT ENTITLED TO COMBATANT STATUS

The law of armed conflict precludes certain categories of persons from claiming combatant status and POW rights, even if they comply with all the conditions outlined in Article 4A of Convention III and Articles 43–44 of AP I. Those persons pre-emptively denied combatant and POW rights include spies, mercenaries, civilians who take direct part in hostilities, and, *prima facie*, employees of private military and security firms.[63]

a. Spies

Under IHL, spies who are captured whilst engaged in clandestine activities and not wearing the uniform of their armed forces, are considered unlawful combatants and not entitled to combatant immunity or POW rights. This applies to both civilians who act as spies, as well as members of the armed forces who don civilian attire and are captured whilst engaged in acts of espionage in enemy territory. While civilian spies are, in any event, denied combatant status and POW rights by dint of their civilian status, the loss of such a status for combatants has more serious consequences.[64]

The rules relating to espionage in armed conflict are found in Article 29 of the Hague Regulations and Article 46 of Protocol I. Article 29 provides:

A person can only be considered a spy when, acting clandestinely or on false pretences, he obtains or endeavours to obtain information in the zone of operations of a belligerent, with the intention of communicating it to the hostile party.

Thus, soldiers not wearing a disguise who have penetrated into the zone of operations of the hostile army, for the purpose of obtaining information, are not considered spies. Similarly, the following are not considered spies: Soldiers and civilians, carrying out their mission openly, entrusted with the delivery of despatches intended either for their own army or for the enemy's army. To this class belong likewise persons sent in balloons for the purpose of carrying despatches and, generally, of maintaining communications between the different parts of an army or a territory.

Article 46 of Protocol I provides:

1. Notwithstanding any other provision of the Conventions or of this Protocol, any member of the armed forces of a Party to the conflict who falls into the power of

---

[63] This does not include the civilians covered by GC III art 4A (4)-(5), who retain their POW rights – see n61 above.

[64] See generally A. John Radsan, "The Unresolved Equation of Espionage and International Law" (2007) 28 Mich J Int'l L 595; Geoffrey Demarest, "Espionage in International Law" (1995–6) 24 Denver J Int'l L & Pol'y 321.

an adverse Party while engaging in espionage shall not have the right to the status of prisoner of war and may be treated as a spy.

2. A member of the armed forces of a Party to the conflict who, on behalf of that Party and in territory controlled by an adverse Party, gathers or attempts to gather information shall not be considered as engaging in espionage if, while so acting, he is in the uniform of his armed forces.

3. A member of the armed forces of a Party to the conflict who is a resident of territory occupied by an adverse Party and who, on behalf of the Party on which he depends, gathers or attempts to gather information of military value within that territory shall not be considered as engaging in espionage unless he does so through an act of false pretences or deliberately in a clandestine manner. Moreover, such a resident shall not lose his right to the status of prisoner of war and may not be treated as a spy unless he is captured while engaging in espionage.

4. A member of the armed forces of a Party to the conflict who is not a resident of territory occupied by an adverse Party and who has engaged in espionage in that territory shall not lose his right to the status of prisoner of war and may not be treated as a spy unless he is captured before he has rejoined the armed forces to which he belongs.

What is central to both these instruments is the element of being captured out of uniform whilst engaging in espionage. Both Article 29 and Article 46 provide that soldiers engaged in espionage while *in uniform* continue to enjoy combatant status and POW rights if captured. Likewise, soldiers who remove their uniform to spy and manage to return to their own lines following such a clandestine deployment, regain their combatant privileges. It is only the act of being captured after having removed one's uniform that renders the soldier an unlawful combatant, and strips him or her of protected status under international law.[65]

This is not to say, however, that the act of espionage is a violation of IHL or international law. As noted by the Dutch Special Court of Cassation in *Flesche*, "espionage ... is a recognised means of warfare and therefore is neither an international delinquency on the part of the State employing the spy nor a war crime proper on the part of the individual concerned."[66] Denial of combatant and POW status does not, furthermore, result in a loss of all protections and rights under the law of armed conflict. Spies, whether civilians or members of the armed forces out of uniform, are still protected by the relevant laws relating to civilians who have been detained in armed conflict, such as Article 75 of Protocol I.[67]

---

[65] See Chapter 2 on the principle of distinction.
[66] *Re Flesche*, Dutch Special Court of Cassation [1949] 16 AD 266, 272.   [67] See further Chapter 6.

b. Mercenaries

Like spies, mercenaries are one of the few categories of persons unilaterally determined to be unlawful combatants, with no rights to combatant or prisoner of war status. This absolute injunction is a comparatively recent development in international law, emerging at the same time as changes to IHL during the 1970s, largely in response to the use of mercenaries by colonial powers against national liberation movements during the decolonisation wars of that period.[68]

The Organisation of African Unity (OAU) first prohibited the use of mercenaries, in the 1967 Resolution AHG/Res. 49 (IV) which appealed "to all States of the world to enact laws declaring the recruitment and training of mercenaries in their territories a punishable crime and deterring their citizens from enlisting as mercenaries."[69] This was followed by a draft convention in 1971,[70] eventually adopted by the OAU in 1977.[71] The OAU Convention does not include any mention of financial gain as a prerequisite for mercenary status, but instead centres on the concept of a person who is "not a national of the state against which his actions are directed"; the monetary gain for such acts is deemed irrelevant for classification as a mercenary – which would seem contrary to "conventional" understanding of mercenaries as "soldiers of fortune … men who have fought for money and plunder rather than for cause or patriotism."[72]

At this same time, the larger international community was also looking into the issue of mercenaries under international law, in the context of the reaffirmation and development of international humanitarian law taking place during the Geneva Diplomatic Conferences. During the Diplomatic Conferences, the Working Group of Committee III examined a proposal by the Nigerian delegation to define mercenaries and prohibit their use in armed conflicts under Protocol I.[73] While that proposal was not adopted, a 1977 debate on the issue resulted in the adoption of Article 47, which defined a mercenary as any person who:

---

[68] See Marie-France Major, "Mercenaries and International Law" (1992) 22 Ga J Int'l & Comp L 103 at 103, for a listing of UN Resolutions regarding the use of mercenaries in suppressing national liberation movements. See also the UN Office of the High Commissioner for Human Rights, *Working Group on the Use of Mercenaries as a Means of Violating Human Rights and Impeding the Exercise of the Right of Peoples to Self-Determination*, www.ohchr.org/EN/Issues/Mercenaries/WGMercenaries/Pages/WGMercenariesIndex. aspx.

[69] Organisation of African Unity (OAU), Resolution AHG/Res. 49 (IV), Congo, 11–14 September 1967, www. africa-union.org/Official_documents/Heads%20of%20State%20Summits/hog/eHoGAssembly1967.pdf.

[70] OAU Council of Ministers' Committee of Legal Experts, Doc CM/1/33/Ref. 1 (1972).

[71] OAU, Convention for the Elimination of Mercenarism in Africa, OAU Doc CM/433/Rev. L, Annex I (1972).

[72] Michael Lee Lanning, *Mercenaries: Soldiers of Fortune, from Ancient Greece to Today's Private Military Companies* (New York: Presidio Press, 2005), p. 1.

[73] Official Records III, CDDH/III/GT/82 (1976), p. 92.

(a) is specially recruited locally or abroad in order to fight in an armed conflict;

(b) does, in fact, take a direct part in the hostilities;

(c) is motivated to take part in the hostilities essentially by the desire for private gain and, in fact, is promised, by or on behalf of a Party to the conflict, material compensation substantially in excess of that promised or paid to combatants of similar ranks and functions in the armed forces of that Party;

(d) is neither a national of a Party to the conflict nor a resident of territory controlled by a Party to the conflict;

(e) is not a member of the armed forces of a Party to the conflict; and

(f) has not been sent by a State which is not a Party to the conflict on official duty as a member of its armed forces.

The test outlined in Article 47 is cumulative; if a person does not meet one of the requirements, they cannot be classified as a mercenary. The denial of combatant and POW status to mercenaries under Article 47 of Protocol I is considered to be customary international law.[74]

Finally, an additional piece of law exists in the UN Mercenaries Convention,[75] adopted in 1989. Under Article 1 of the Convention, a mercenary is defined as any person who:

(a) Is specially recruited locally or abroad in order to fight in an armed conflict;

(b) Is motivated to take part in the hostilities essentially by the desire for private gain and, in fact, is promised, by or on behalf of a party to the conflict, material compensation substantially in excess of that promised or paid to combatants of similar rank and function in the armed forces of that party;

(c) Is neither a national of a party to the conflict nor a resident of territory controlled by a party to the conflict;

(d) Is not a member of the armed forces of a party to the conflict; and

(e) Has not been sent by a State which is not a party to the conflict on official duty as a member of its armed forces.

So far, the Convention simply replicates the main elements of Article 47 of Protocol I. However, in paragraph 2 of Article 1, additional elements are required – elements which hark back to the OAU Convention:

2. A mercenary is also any person who, in any other situation:

    (a) Is specially recruited locally or abroad for the purpose of participating in a concerted act of violence aimed at:

        (i) Overthrowing a Government or otherwise undermining the constitutional order of a State; or

        (ii) Undermining the territorial integrity of a State;

---

[74] ICRC CIHL Study, r. 108.

[75] International Convention Against the Recruitment, Use, Financing and Training of Mercenaries, New York, 4 December 1989, in force 20 October 2001, 2163 UNTS 75.

(b) Is motivated to take part therein essentially by the desire for significant private gain and is prompted by the promise or payment of material compensation;

(c) Is neither a national nor a resident of the State against which such an act is directed . . .

The addition of Article 1(2) means that the use of mercenaries even in situations not amounting to armed conflict is also prohibited under international law, for those States party to the Convention.[76]

c. "Unlawful" combatants

A person who takes direct part in hostilities without falling under any of the categories enumerated in Article 4A of Convention III or Articles 43–4 of Protocol I will not be considered a lawful combatant – someone entitled to the combatant's privilege and POW status. As noted above, under the Conventions and Protocol I only two categories of person are pre-emptively designated as "unlawful combatants" - spies[77] and mercenaries.[78] However, neither the Conventions nor the Protocols explicitly use the term "unlawful combatant" – it is not a legal term in IHL.

The term "unlawful combatant" is instead a creation of domestic State practice. One of the earliest usages of the term is found in the US Supreme Court case *ex parte Quirin*.[79] In 1942, eight German servicemen had covertly entered the US, abandoned their uniforms and carried out acts of sabotage. They were captured, tried by a military tribunal for violating the laws of war and the death penalty pronounced for some of their number. The choice of military tribunal, rather than domestic court, was challenged by defence attorneys as unconstitutional.[80] In their ruling, the US Supreme Court stated, *inter alia*, that there was a legal category of unlawful combatant:

By universal agreement and practice, the law of war draws a distinction between the armed forces and the peaceful populations of belligerent nations and also between those who are lawful and unlawful combatants. Lawful combatants are subject to capture and detention as prisoners of war by opposing military forces. Unlawful combatants are likewise subject to capture and detention, but in addition they are subject to trial and punishment by military tribunals for acts which render their belligerency unlawful.[81]

---

[76] Currently only thirty-three States.   [77] See also Hague IV 1907, arts. 29–31 re: spies.

[78] AP I, arts. 46(1) and 47(1); see Leslie Green, "The Status of Mercenaries in International Law" (1978) 8 IYBHR 9.

[79] *Ex parte Quirin et al.*, 317 US 1 (1942).

[80] For a detailed accounting of the facts leading up to and surrounding the Quirin case, see further Louis Fisher, *Nazi Saboteurs on Trial: Military Tribunal and American Law*, 2nd edn, (Lawrence: University Press of Kansas, 2005).

[81] *Ex parte Quirin*, pp. 30–1.

Over sixty years later, the US reaffirmed the concept of unlawful combatancy, in the US Military Commissions Act of 2009, amending the Military Commissions Act of 2006. The act refers to "unprivileged enemy belligerent" in § 948a, defining such a person as:

an individual (other than a privileged belligerent) who–
    (A) has engaged in hostilities against the United States or its coalition partners;
    (B) has purposefully and materially supported hostilities against the United States or its coalition partners;
    or
    (C) was a part of al Qaeda at the time of the alleged offense under this chapter.[82]

Israeli domestic law also recognises the category of "unlawful combatant", in their Detention of Unlawful Combatants Law of 2002,[83] defining an unlawful combatant as "anyone taking part – directly or indirectly – in hostilities against the State of Israel, who is not entitled to a prisoner of war status under Geneva Convention (III)".[84] The law allows for administrative detention of unlawful combatants on the grounds of State security, subject to periodic judicial review. An unlawful combatant can be held in detention as long as hostilities involving his or her force continue.[85]

The US and Israel seem to be outliers in suggesting that there is a "third status" in IHL – additional to civilian and combatant. Over the past decade, the US has employed the term, both in a legal sense and as a descriptive phrase, in relation to al-Qaeda and associated forces.[86] By designating captured al-Qaeda fighters as "unlawful", the US seemed to be attempting to deny any recourse to the law – domestic and international – that such persons might have otherwise enjoyed. Neither combatant nor civilian, such persons deserved none of the

---

[82] Military Commissions Act of 2009, 10 USC §§ 948a et seq.

[83] Detention of Unlawful Combatants Law, 2002, 1834 Sefer Hahukim [Laws of the State of Israel, Hebrew] 192.

[84] Dinstein, *The Conduct of Hostilities*, p. 31.

[85] Ibid., p. 32. The intent of the Israeli law, in denying combatant status and providing for indefinite detention, is to ensure that suspects are unable to claim that their acts are committed in the context of an armed struggle against the State of Israel. The definition of unlawful combatant under the Israeli law is thus quite wide, encompassing both terrorist organisations and those who cause harm to the State of Israel. Indeed, an Israeli case, *Barghouti*, made reference to unlawful combatants as a category which includes terrorist organisation members and enemy forces who take direct part in terrorist and hostile acts against Israelis, but who, if captured, are not entitled to POW status. See *State of Israel* v. *Marwan Barghouti*, District Court of Tel Aviv and Jaffa, Criminal Case No. 092134/02, 12 December 2002, para. 11.2.

[86] See the White House Fact Sheet, *Status of Detainees at Guantánamo*; www.whitehouse.gov/news/releases/2002/02/20020207-13.html (7 February 2002). The US Government agreed to apply GC III to captured Taliban, but not al-Qaeda, detainees. This is despite US Department of Justice advice to Alberto Gonzalez, Counsel to the President, that neither Taliban nor al-Qaeda detainees warranted Geneva protections. See the Memo to Alberto Gonzalez from the Office of the Assistant Attorney General, excerpted in Karen Greenberg and Joshua Dratel, *The Torture Papers: The Road to Abu Ghraib* (Cambridge University Press, 2005), pp. 136–43.

protections available to either combatants or civilians under IHL. As noted by Fletcher and Ohlin:

when combatants are unlawful, the argument goes, they are subject to the burdens of combatancy (they can be killed), but they have no reciprocal rights ... the phrase unlawful combatant as used today combines the aspect of unlawful from the law of crime and the concept of combatant from the law of war. For those thus labelled, it is the worst of all possible worlds.[87]

Unsurprisingly, there was almost uniform resistance to US attempts to assert a legal status of "unlawful enemy combatant".[88] The overwhelming response was that the US had over-reached in trying to restrict the applicability of international law in their conflict with al-Qaeda[89] by creating a category of persons without rights under the law.[90] Indeed, attempts by the US Government to limit the protections and remedies offered for persons deprived of their liberty, both under international and US domestic law, were challenged several times in the US Supreme Court. These challenges came in the cases *Hamdi* v. *Rumsfeld*,[91] *Rasul* v. *Bush*[92] and *Rumsfeld* v. *Padilla*,[93] and culminated in two cases, *Hamdan* v. *Rumsfeld*[94] and *Boumediene* v. *Bush*,[95] where the Supreme Court rejected the US Government's attempt to deny access to petitions for a writ of *habeas corpus*, affirmed the universality of Common Article 3, in international as well as non-international armed conflicts, and held that the provisions of Common Article 3 are applicable as a basic set of fundamental rules to be observed in all armed conflicts.[96] Partly in response to these court decisions, the US Obama Administration changed the

---

[87] George Fletcher and Jens David Ohlin, *Defending Humanity* (New York: Oxford University Press, 2008), p. 183.

[88] See statements by Amnesty International, *USA: Close Guantánamo – Symbol Of Injustice*, www.amnesty. org/en/library/asset/AMR51/001/2007/en/ebd331a0-d3c4–11dd-8743-d305bea2b2c7/amr510012007en. html; Human Rights Watch, "US: Give Guantanamo Detainees Fair Process", 4 December 2007, www.hrw. org/news/2007/12/03/us-give-guantanamo-detainees-fair-process; UN Commission on Human Rights, *Situation of Detainees at Guantánamo Bay*, 27 February 2006, E/CN.4/2006/120; UN Human Rights Council, *Report of the Special Rapporteur on the Promotion and Protection of Human Rights and Fundamental Freedoms while Countering Terrorism, Martin Scheinin: addendum: mission to the United States of America*, 22 November 2007, UN Doc. A/HRC/6/17/Add.3; and the European Union, "Euro MPs urge Guantanamo closure", *BBC News*, 13 June 2006, news.bbc.co.uk/1/hi/world/americas/5074216.stm.

[89] See generally Sylvia Borelli, "Casting Light on the Legal Black Hole: International Law and Detentions Abroad in the 'War on Terror'" (2005) 87 IRRC 39; and Marco Sassòli, "The Status of Persons Held in Guantánamo under International Humanitarian Law" (2004) 2 JICJ 96.

[90] See the UK Court of Appeal in *R (Abbasi and another)* v. *Secretary of State for Foreign and Commonwealth Affairs* [2002] EWCA Civ 158, in which the Court states that Guantánamo detainees have been "arbitrarily detained in a legal black-hole" (para. 64).

[91] *Hamdi* v. *Rumsfeld*, 542 US 507 (2004).   [92] *Rasul* v. *Bush*, 542 US 446 (2004).

[93] *Rumsfeld* v. *Padilla*, 542 US 426 (2004). For an assessment of the 2004 cases, see Terry Gill and Elies Van Sliedregt, "Guantánamo Bay: A Reflection on the Legal Status and Rights of 'Unlawful Enemy Combatants'"(2005) 1 *Utrecht Law Review* 28.

[94] *Hamdan* v. *Rumsfeld*, 548 US 557 (2006).   [95] *Boumediene* v. *Bush*, 553 US 723 (2008).

[96] See Stevens J in *Hamdan* v. *Rumsfeld*, 66–9.

legislative terminology from "unlawful combatant" to "unprivileged enemy belligerent".[97]

It is uncontroversial to say that persons who participate in armed conflict without fulfilling the criteria for combatancy do not enjoy the combatant's privilege or POW rights.[98] However, to reach the conclusion that such persons have no legal rights whatsoever is unsustainable. It should be noted that a single case in a domestic judicial system, *ex parte Quirin* (a case decided several years before the adoption of the Geneva Conventions), is insufficient grounds for the creation of an entirely new status in IHL. Indeed, even the Israeli Supreme Court declined to recognise the existence of an international status of "unlawful combatants", stating that neither the treaty nor the customary law of armed conflict provides any basis for proclaiming such a category.[99] Indeed, the Commentary to the Conventions makes this point:[100]

Every person in enemy hands must have some status under international law: he is either a prisoner of war and, as such, covered by the Third Convention, a civilian covered by the Fourth Convention, [or] a member of the medical personnel of the armed forces who is covered by the First Convention. *There is no intermediate status*; nobody in enemy hands can fall outside the law.[101]

As such, so-called "unlawful combatants" in an international armed conflict will find international legal protection under another instrument, most likely the Fourth Convention. As Dörmann argues, "a textual interpretation of the Conventions can only lead to the conclusion that all persons who are not protected by GC I-III, thus also persons who do not respect the conditions which would entitle them to POW status/treatment, are covered by GCIV".[102]

d. Private military and security contractors

Private military and security contractors (PMSCs) have been the focus of international attention in recent years, largely due to their prominent role in the conflicts in Iraq and Afghanistan.[103] However, States have long contracted out certain military and security services to private corporations, especially in times of high

---

[97] See the change in terminology from the Military Commissions Act of 2006 to the Military Commissions Act of 2009.

[98] Except for those civilians covered by GC III art 4A (4)-(5), who retain their POW rights – see n61 above.

[99] *The Public Committee Against Torture in Israel et al.* v. *the Government of Israel*, HCJ 769/02, 14 December 2006, para. 28. See also William Fenrick, 'The *Targeted Killings* Judgment and the Scope of Direct Participation in Hostilities' (2007) 5 JICJ 332 at 334.

[100] Antonio Cassese, *International Law*, 2nd edn, (Oxford University Press, 2005), p. 410.

[101] GC IV Commentary, p. 51 – emphasis in original.

[102] Dörmann, "The Legal Situation of 'Unlawful/Unprivileged Combatants'", 48–9.

[103] David Johnston and John. M. Border, "F.B.I. Says Guards Killed 14 Iraqis Without Cause", *The New York Times*, 13 November 2007, www.nytimes.com/2007/11/14/world/middleeast/14blackwater.html.

demand, such as during armed conflicts.[104] The privatisation and outsourcing of military functions became widespread in the years following the end of the Cold War,[105] as numerous States undertook to downsize their armed forces.[106]

However, such outsourcing and downsizing left notable vacancies in defence forces, vacancies which PMSCs have been called on to fill. PMSCs thus carry out a range of duties and functions, such as operating mess halls, executing cleaning and janitorial duties, and carrying out administrative functions for armed forces across the world.[107] Some PMSCs also carry out duties which require them to be armed, such as the guarding of convoys, installations and personnel. It is in this latter role that the modern PMSC has become best known – during the 2003 US invasion of Iraq, PMSCs, including nearly 30,000 armed contractors, at one point outnumbered conventional military personnel 180,000 to 165,000.[108] As McDonald has noted, "there is almost no area of the US Armed Forces where civilian subcontractors do not play a vital role".[109]

PMSCs are, *prima facie*, civilians. Unless incorporated in the armed forces under Article 4A of the Geneva Conventions, PMSCs are entitled to all the protections that follow from such status. However, if they take direct part in hostilities, they lose their immunity from targeting for as long as they take direct part. Furthermore, despite some commentators' charges,[110] PMSCs are not mercenaries. The multi-stage, cumulative test for mercenary status contained in Protocol I and the Mercenaries Convention would exclude the large bulk of PMSCs from the definition of

---

[104] See generally Mark Harrison, "Resource Mobilisation for World War II: the USA, UK, USSR and Germany, 1938–1945" (1988) 41 *Economic History Review* 171.

[105] See generally Michael Likosky, "The Privatization of Violence", in Simon Chesterman and Angelina Fisher (eds) *Private Security, Public Order: The Outsourcing of Public Service and Its Limits* (Oxford University Press, 2009).

[106] P. W. Singer, "Outsourcing War" (2005) 84 For Aff 119 at 120.

[107] P. W. Singer, "Outsourcing the Fight", *Forbes*, 5 June 2008, www.brookings.edu/research/opinions/2008/06/05-military-contractors-singer. See also P. W. Singer, *Corporate Warriors: The Rise of the Privatized Military Industry* (Ithaca, NY: Cornell University Press, 2003), p. 88.

[108] Accurate figures regarding the numbers of contractors deployed in Iraq are hard to come by; the US Government Accountability Office's 2005 Report to Congress on PMSCs cited Department of Defense figures to put the number of PMSCs at over sixty companies, with nearly 25,000 employees (US Government Accountability Office (USGAO), *2005 United States Government Accountability Office Report*, July 2005, GAO-05-7370). The 2006 report cites the Director of the Private Security Company Association of Iraq's estimate of 181 PMSCs and around 48,000 employees (*Rebuilding Iraq: Actions Still Needed to Improve Use of Private Security Providers*, USGAO, Testimony before the Subcommittee on National Security, Emerging Threats, and International Relations, Committee on Government Reform, 13 June 2006, GAO-06-865T). However, a census undertaken of all PMSC employees, including US, Iraqi and third State nationals came to a figure of 100,000: Renae Marie, "Census Counts 100,000 Contractors in Iraq", *The Washington Post*, 5 December 2006.

[109] Avril McDonald, "The Challenges to International Humanitarian Law and the Principles of Distinction and Protection from the Increased Participation of Civilians in Hostilities" Paper Presented at the University of Teheran at a Round Table on the Interplay Between International International Human Rights Law, April 2004, para. 2.3.2.1.

[110] See, e.g., Zoe Salzman, "Private Military Contractors and the Taint of a Mercenary Reputation" (2008) 40 NYU J Int'l L & Pol 853, and Abdel-Fatau Musah and Kayode Fayemi, *Mercenaries: An African Security Dilemma* (London: Pluto, 2000) quoted in Singer, *Corporate Warriors*, p.44.

mercenary – at the minimum because most PMSCs "are not *de jure* or *de facto* incorporated into the armed forces of a party and are therefore not combatants but civilians".[111]

However, the situation becomes complicated under IHL when PMSCs are hired to provide quasi-military functions, such as providing protection to legitimate military targets such as military personnel and transports. If those objects, transports or personnel constitute legitimate targets, then any person involved in guarding said objects will be taking direct part in hostilities: "a civilian government employee or private contractor defending military personnel or military objectives from enemy attack directly participates in hostilities. His or her actions are indistinguishable from the quintessential duties of combat personnel."[112]

Using armed PMSCs in war zones can thus make it difficult for parties to an armed conflict to observe IHL rules, such as the principle of distinction – it is often hard to distinguish between regular armed forces and PMSCs. As noted by Ridlon, PMSCs "operate and are equipped much like military units ... [they use] sophisticated military equipment. Some even employ armoured vehicles and helicopters in support of their operations."[113]

An awareness of the possible legal problems arising from the use of PMSCs in conflict zones has led to adoption of the non-binding Montreux Document on Pertinent International Legal Obligations and Good Practices for States related to Operations of Private Military and Security Companies during Armed Conflict.[114] The Montreux Document was developed on the basis of four intergovernmental meetings between 2006 and 2008, involving experts from government, industry and civil society. Finalised in 2008 by seventeen States by consensus,[115] the Montreux Document was the first international document to outline the relevant international law regarding the use and practice of PMSCs in situations of armed conflict.

The document includes a compilation of good practices "designed to assist states in implementing their obligations under international law through a series of national measures".[116] It affirms that international law, and IHL, is the law that governs the acts of PMSCs and the States that hire them. The document contains two parts. Part I differentiates between Contracting States, Territorial States and

---

[111] Marco Sassòli, Antoine Bouvier and Anne Quintin, *How Does Law Protect In War? Cases, Documents and Teaching Materials on Contemporary Practice in International Humanitarian Law*, 3rd edn, (Geneva: ICRC, 2011), p. 172.

[112] Michael Schmitt, "Humanitarian Law and Direct Participation in Hostilities by Private Contractors or Civilian Employees" (2004–5) 5 Chicago J Int'l L 511, 538.

[113] Daniel Ridlon, "Contractors or Illegal Combatants? The Status of Armed Contractors in Iraq" (2008) 62 AFL Rev 199 at 217–18.

[114] The Montreux Document on Pertinent International Legal Obligations and Good Practices for States related to Operations of Private Military and Security Companies during Armed Conflict, UN Doc A/63/467, S/2008/636, 17 September 2008.

[115] Afghanistan, Angola, Australia, Austria, Canada, China, France, Germany, Iraq, Poland, Sierra Leone, South Africa, Sweden, Switzerland, the United Kingdom, Ukraine, and the USA.

[116] Swiss Federal Department of Foreign Affairs, "The Montreux Document", www.eda.admin.ch/psc.

Home States – for each category of States, Part I reaffirms the relevant law of armed conflict as well as international human rights law. The question of attribution of private conduct to the State under customary international law is also addressed. Part I also outlines the relevant international legal obligations of "all other States", the duties of PMSCs and their personnel, and also covers issues relating to superior responsibility.

Part II of the Montreux Document deals with "best practices" in dealing with PMSCs, also differentiating between Contracting States, Territorial States and Home States. These best practices include "transparent licensing régimes and ensuring better supervision and accountability – so that only PMSCs which are likely to respect international humanitarian law and human rights law, through appropriate training, internal procedures and supervision, can provide services during armed conflict."[117] The document is designed to reaffirm the relevant international law obligations of States, especially those that arise under the law of State responsibility. As such, neither NGOs nor companies can "join" the Montreux Document. Such non-State actors are nonetheless "encouraged to use it as a reference in their own relations with PMSCs."[118]

For the purposes of determining the status of PMSCs under international law, the relevant articles are Articles 22–26 of Part I, specifically Article 24 which states that:

the status of personnel of PMSCs is determined by international humanitarian law, on a case-by-case basis, in particular according to the nature and circumstances of the functions in which they are involved.

Article 25 of the Montreux Document affirms that if PMSCs are civilians under the law of armed conflict, such personnel may not be the object of attack, unless and for such time as they directly participate in hostilities. Article 26 provides that the personnel of PMSCs:

(a) are obliged, regardless of their status, to comply with applicable international humanitarian law;
(b) are protected as civilians under international humanitarian law, unless they are incorporated into the regular armed forces of a State or are members of organised armed forces, groups or units under a command responsible to the State; or otherwise lose their protection as determined by international humanitarian law;
(c) are entitled to prisoner of war status in international armed conflict if they are persons accompanying the armed forces meeting the requirements of Article 4A(4) of the Third Geneva Convention;

---

[117] Swiss Government, "Informal Summary of the Montreux Document", para. 4, www.eda.admin.ch/content/dam/eda/en/documents/topics/Montreux-document-4_en.pdf.
[118] Swiss Federal Department of Foreign Affairs, Brochure on the Montreux Document, www.eda.admin.ch/content/dam/eda/en/documents/topics/Montreux-Broschuere_en.pdf, p. 4.

(d) to the extent they exercise governmental authority, have to comply with the State's obligations under international human rights law;

(e) are subject to prosecution if they commit conduct recognised as crimes under applicable national or international law.[119]

The Montreux Document does not create new law; it simply draws attention to pre-existing legal obligations. However, it is a valuable tool, as it draws together the relevant international legal obligations for PMSCs into one document.

Some issues regarding PMSCs remain unresolved – the Montreux Document does not prohibit the use of PMSCs in active hostilities; also unresolved is the question of whether PMSCs can use weaponry defensively, which can cause problems when PMSCs are involved defending legitimate military objectives, when they "may not claim defense of others when they provide cover or assistance to military forces under attack, even in cases of ambush".[120] Furthermore, for regular armed forces, the presence of PMSCs in active hostilities can be highly disruptive. PMSCs, wearing fatigues and camouflage similar to regular armed forces, guarding convoys and installations, can complicate the already complicated process of targeting. As Schmitt has argued:

> The more armed civilians in an area, the more difficult it is for lawful combatants to distinguish between unlawful combatants and those who are merely armed for defensive purposes. This in turn endangers the civilian population by eroding the practical implementation of the principle of distinction. Soldiers may be more inclined to employ force against civilians who they feel pose a threat. Alternatively, soldiers may refrain from the use of force when it is appropriate, thereby assuming greater risk than necessary.[121]

As such, the use of PMSCs will remain a complicated issue under IHL.

e. Civilians taking direct part in hostilities

A final category of persons who do not qualify as Article 4A combatants are civilians who take direct part in hostilities. Article 51(3) of Protocol I provides that "civilians shall enjoy the protection afforded by this Section [i.e., immunity from direct targeting], unless and for such time as they take a direct part in hostilities". Civilians who take direct part in hostilities (DPH) may be targeted for such DPH. Furthermore, they are not entitled to any POW rights if captured. DPH is codified in Article 13(3) of Protocol II, and is worded similarly to Article 51(3) of Protocol I.[122]

---

[119] Montreux Document, art. 26.

[120] Schmitt, "Humanitarian Law and Direct Participation in Hostilities by Private Contractors or Civilian Employees", 538.

[121] Ibid., 539.

[122] Except for those civilians covered by GC III art 4A (4)-(5), who retain their POW rights – see n61 above.

Article 51 of Protocol I does not provide a definition of the scope of the phrase "direct part in hostilities". The Commentary to the Additional Protocols states that:

The immunity afforded individual civilians is subject to an overriding condition, namely, on their abstaining from all hostile acts. Hostile acts should be understood to be acts which by their nature and purpose are intended to cause actual harm to the personnel and equipment of the armed forces.

The indistinct parameters of Article 51 led the authors of the ICRC CIHL Study to state that "a precise definition of the term 'direct participation in hostilities' does not exist".[123] However, over the last decade, a number of institutions have attempted to define the parameters of DPH. One of the first was the Israeli Supreme Court in the 2006 case *The Public Committee Against Torture in Israel* v. *The Government of Israel*.[124]

The so-called *Targeted Killings* case was brought as a challenge to the legality of the Israeli policy of targeted killings against suspected terrorist leaders.[125] In order to determine whether targeted killings were legal, the Court had to examine when civilians were deemed to be taking direct part in hostilities. Thus, the scope of Article 51(3) of Protocol I regarding DPH comprised a major portion of the decision.

The Court identified certain categories of persons who could be considered as taking direct part in hostilities, including persons collecting intelligence; persons transporting participants or ammunition to or from the place where hostilities are occurring; persons who operate weapons, supervise their operation or service them; and persons acting as voluntary human shields.[126] The Court explained that the "direct character of the part taken should not be narrowed merely to the person committing the physical act of attack. Those who have sent him, as well, take 'a direct part'. The same goes for the person who decided upon the act, and the person who planned it."[127]

The Court stated that a person who has ceased taking a direct part in hostilities regains his or her protection, but they were unable to come to a definitive position regarding when precisely such protection was lost and regained.[128] However, they stated that a distinction should be made between a person who takes part in hostilities sporadically (or only once), and those persons who have actively joined a "terrorist organisation" and who commit a series of hostile acts, even if there are short "rest" periods between acts. Such rest periods did not constitute a cessation of

---

[123] ICRC CIHL Study, vol. I, p. 22.

[124] *The Public Committee Against Torture in Israel et al* v. *the Government of Israel*, HCJ 769/02, 14 December 2006 ("*Targeted Killings*").

[125] The challenge was brought by the Public Committee Against Torture in Israel and the Palestinian Society for the Protection of Human Rights and the Environment. For a background and summary of the decision, see Michelle Lesh, "The Public Committee Against Torture in Israel v The Government Of Israel: The Israeli High Court of Justice Targeted Killing Decision" (2007) 8 MJIL 373.

[126] *Targeted Killings*, §§ 35–6.   [127] Ibid., § 37.   [128] Ibid., § 39.

active participation, but rather a brief interlude prior to the commission of or participation in the next hostile act.[129] As such, the direct participation in hostilities was considered to be on-going.[130] The Israeli Supreme Court did not undertake a detailed examination of what constituted membership of a terrorist group or assumption of combat function.

The ICRC has also looked at the question of DPH. Their DPH "Interpretive Guidance"[131] was framed around three questions: who is a civilian for the purposes of the principle of distinction; what conduct amounts to direct participation in hostilities; and what modalities govern the loss of protection against direct attack?

The Guidance defines civilians in international armed conflicts as "all persons who are neither members of the armed forces of a party to the conflict nor participants in a *levée en masse*". Such persons are "entitled to protection against direct attack unless and for such time as they take a direct part in hostilities".[132] The ICRC Guidance then defines civilians in non-international armed conflicts:

All persons who are not members of State armed forces or organised armed groups of a party to the conflict are civilians and, therefore, entitled to protection against direct attack unless and for such time as they take a direct part in hostilities. In non-international armed conflict, armed groups constitute the armed forces of a non-State party to the conflict and consist only of individuals whose continuous function is to take a direct part in hostilities ("continuous combat function").[133]

Exactly what acts amount to DPH is defined by the Guidance as any specific act that meets three cumulative criteria:

(1) the act must be likely to adversely affect the military operations or military capacity of a party to an armed conflict or, alternatively, to inflict death, injury, or destruction on persons or objects protected against direct attack (threshold of harm);

(2) there must be a direct causal link between the act and the harm likely to result either from that act, or from a coordinated military operation of which that act constitutes an integral part (direct causation);

(3) the act must be specifically designed to directly cause the required threshold of harm in support of a party to the conflict and to the detriment of another (belligerent nexus).[134]

Civilians lose their protected status for the duration of each act of DPH but regain protection upon cessation of DPH; high-level members of organised groups do not regain protected status as long as they assume a continuous combat function.[135] Travel to and from an act of DPH is included in the window for loss of protection.[136]

---

[129] Ibid., §§ 34, 39.   [130] Ibid., §§ 39–40.

[131] ICRC, "Interpretive Guidance on the Notion of Direct Participation in Hostilities Under International Humanitarian Law", (2008) 90 IRRC 991.

[132] Ibid., 997.   [133] Ibid., 1002.   [134] Ibid., 1016.   [135] Ibid., 1034–5.   [136] Ibid., 1031.

The ICRC Interpretive Guidance was the result of a five year long process, involving questionnaires, reports, background papers and expert meetings. However, the process was marred by controversy in the latter stages. Towards the end of the Expert Process, nearly a third of the approximately forty experts involved in the discussions requested that their names be removed from the final document "lest inclusion be misinterpreted as support for the Interpretive Guidance's propositions".[137] Dispute arose over a number of sections in the Guidance, including the addition of Section IX in the final document,[138] the temporal dimension to direct participation[139] and the definition of membership of armed groups.[140] The ICRC eventually "took back" the Guidance, and issued it as an ICRC document.[141] The Interpretive Guidance is thus not an expert guidance but rather the ICRC's own position on what constitutes DPH.[142]

The Interpretive Guidance has been criticised for taking too liberal an approach to determining DPH, presenting a "normative paradigm that states that actually go to war cannot countenance."[143] The lack of "official" State responses to the Guidance have made it difficult to assess the degree to which the Guidance has been accepted or rejected by States in practice.[144] The wealth of commentary from academics and practitioners suggests a cautious approach to the Interpretive Guidance, acknowledging the scholarship of the Guidance,[145] but emphasising that it remains the opinion of the ICRC alone, and is not necessarily reflective of customary law.[146]

In addition to the Israeli Supreme Court and the ICRC, an additional perspective on DPH can be found in the jurisprudence of the ICTY which examined DPH in the *Strugar* case.[147] The Chamber defined DPH as "acts of war which by their nature or purpose are intended to cause actual harm to the personnel or equipment of the

---

[137] Michael Schmitt, "The Interpretive Guidance on the Notion of Direct Participation in Hostilities: A Critical Analysis" (2010) 1 Harv Nat Sec J 5 at 6.

[138] Section IX related to "General Restraints on the Use of Force in Attack" – a section added towards the end of the process and apparently to the surprise of the participants, who had not expected nor debated such an inclusion. In a scathing article, one of the experts involved, W. Hays Parks, dubbed Section IX as having "no mandate, no expertise and legally incorrect": see W. Hays Parks, "Part IX of the ICRC 'Direct Participation in Hostilities' Study: No Mandate, No Expertise, and Legally Incorrect" (2010) 42 NYU J Int'l L & Pol 769.

[139] Bill Boothby, "'And for Such Time As': The Time Dimension to Direct Participation in Hostilities" (2010) 42 NYU J Int'l L & Pol 741.

[140] Kenneth Watkin, "Opportunity Lost: Organised Armed Groups and the ICRC 'Direct Participation in Hostilities Interpretive Guidance'" (2010) 42 NYU J Int'l L & Pol 641.

[141] ICRC, "Interpretive Guidance", 992.   [142] Ibid.

[143] Schmitt, "The Interpretive Guidance on the Notion of Direct Participation in Hostilities", 44.

[144] See e.g. J. Jeremy Marsh and Scott Glabe, "Time for the United States to Directly Participate" (2011) 1 Va J Int'l L Online 13, in which the authors note that the absence of state responses to the Interpretive Guidance is creating the possibility for the Guidance to become the authoritative statement on direct participation (14).

[145] Schmitt, "The Interpretive Guidance on the Notion of Direct Participation in Hostilities", 6.

[146] Boothby, "'And for Such Time As'"; Parks, "Part IX of the ICRC 'Direct Participation in Hostilities' Study"; Schmitt, "The Interpretive Guidance on the Notion of Direct Participation in Hostilities".

[147] *Prosecutor* v. *Strugar*, IT-01-42-A, Appeals Chamber Judgment, (17 July 2008) ("*Strugar*").

enemy's armed forces".[148] The Chamber drew on numerous sources in support of its statement, including military manuals from numerous countries, international tribunal judgments, US Military Commission decisions, State practice and reports and decisions of human rights bodies, such as the Inter-American Commission on Human Rights.[149] The *Strugar* approach seems to be the most measured approach, and the one most likely consonant with current State practice.

6. PRISONER OF WAR STATUS

As noted above, combatants and certain categories of civilians are entitled to prisoner of war status if they are captured during an armed conflict. Prisoner of war captivity is not punishment for participation in the hostilities, but a preventative measure only:[150] as noted by the US 9th Circuit Court in *In Re Territo*: "the object of capture is to prevent the captured individual from serving the enemy. He is disarmed and from then on he must be removed as completely as practicable from the front, treated humanely and in time exchanged, repatriated or otherwise released."[151]

The rules pertaining to POWs are found Geneva Convention III, which grants fundamental protections for captured combatants both during and following an armed conflict.[152]

a. Determining prisoner of war status

Prima facie, all persons who claim POW status are to be afforded such status as soon as they are captured. Article 5 of Geneva Convention III provides:

The present Convention shall apply to the persons referred to in Article 4 from the time they fall into the power of the enemy and until their final release and repatriation.

If there is doubt that the person claiming POW status is entitled to do so, detainees will enjoy the rights and privileges of the Conventions until a competent tribunal

---

[148] Ibid., §§ 176–9.

[149] See Inter-Am. CHR, Third Report on the Human Rights Situation in Colombia, OEA/Ser.L/V/II.102, doc. 9 rev. 1 ch. 4, para. 53 (26 February 1999) ("It is generally understood in humanitarian law that the phrase 'direct participation in hostilities' means acts which, by their nature or purpose, are intended to cause actual harm to enemy personnel and material").

[150] See Allan Rosas, *The Legal Status of Prisoners of War: A Study in International Humanitarian Law Applicable in Armed Conflicts* (Helsinki: Suomalainen tiedeakatemia, 1976) p. 82.

[151] *In re Territo*, 156 F.2d 142, 145 (9th Cir 1946).

[152] These rules apply unless the captured combatant is a national of the Detaining Power or owes an allegiance to the Detaining Power; see further *Public Prosecutor* v. *Oie Hee Koi* [1968] AC 829, pp. 856–8.

can assess their status. A "competent tribunal" need not be a military tribunal,[153] though in practice, such tribunals have generally been military in nature.[154]

Article 5 tribunals have attracted attention in recent years as a result of the wars in Afghanistan and Iraq. Following the US invasion of Afghanistan, the US government stated that captured Taliban and al-Qaeda fighters would be unilaterally denied POW status; as such, Article 5 hearings would be unwarranted in a conflict where the Geneva Conventions did not apply. In a number of memoranda to the Department of Defense on the applicability of the Conventions regarding Taliban and al-Qaeda fighters, US legal advisers asserted "neither the Geneva Conventions nor the WCA [War Crimes Act] regulate the detention of al Qaeda prisoners captured during the Afghanistan conflict"[155] and that "the President has more than ample grounds to find that our treaty obligations under Geneva III toward Afghanistan were suspended during the period of the conflict."[156] It was mistakenly thought that a presidential determination of the non-applicability of the Conventions could nullify the need for an Article 5 tribunal.[157] Ultimately, the asserted inapplicability of even the most basic provisions of the Conventions – Common Article 3 – was rejected by the US Supreme Court.[158]

b. Treatment of POWs

The rights accorded to POWs can be divided into the following five major categories:

1. Fundamental guarantees such as humane treatment
2. General provisions regarding treatment during captivity, including matters like quarters, food, clothing, hygiene and medical care, morale, and labour, including conditions, wages and types of employment
3. Relations with the exterior, including correspondence and relief shipments and relief agencies
4. Penal and disciplinary action, including judicial guarantees
5. Termination of captivity, including repatriation during/after hostilities.

i. Rights of POWs

One of the first provisions in the POW Convention (GC III) is that POWs have the right to humane treatment and respect for their person.[159] This right is given

---

[153] Solis, *The Law of Armed Conflict*, p. 230.   [154] Ibid., pp. 230–1.
[155] John Yoo and Robert Delahunty, Memorandum 9 January 2002, in Greenberg and Dratel, *The Torture Papers*, p. 38.
[156] Memorandum for Alberto Gonzalez, Counsel to the President and William J. Haynes II, General Counsel of the Department of Defense from US Department of Justice, Office of Legal Counsel, 22 January 2002, in Greenberg and Dratel, *The Torture Papers*, p. 81.
[157] Ibid.   [158] In *Hamdan* v. *Rumsfeld*, 548 US 557 (2006).   [159] GC III, art. 13(1).

effect through the enumeration of certain prohibited acts. These include any unlawful act or omission causing death or seriously endangering the health of a prisoner of war, including physical mutilations, medical or scientific experiments which are not justified, and removal of tissue or organs for transplantation;[160] acts of violence on the part of civilians or military persons;[161] prolonged questioning, whether or not accompanied by acts of brutality, with the intent of extracting information;[162] omission of medical care to the wounded and sick;[163] prolonged deprivation of sanitary facilities;[164] prolonged deprivation of physical, intellectual and recreational pursuits;[165] inadequate conditions of food,[166] quarters[167] and clothing[168] extended over any length of time; keeping prisoners in a danger zone;[169] and making prisoners undertake labour of a dangerous nature or work that does not take into account the prisoner's physical aptitude or professional qualifications.[170]

Humane treatment also comprises respect for prisoners, which includes respect for their person or honour[171] and protection against public curiosity.[172] For example, when Saddam Hussein was captured in December 2003, footage of Hussein's medical examination by US troops was broadcast,[173] and photos of Hussein in his underwear were later published in the UK tabloid *The Sun*.[174] Both acts were denounced as violations of the GC III obligation to protect POWs from public curiosity.[175]

Also prohibited are forcing POWs to undertake degrading or humiliating labour or labour directly connected with war operations,[176] failing to provide separate quarters for women and men,[177] insulting a prisoner's person, flag, country, religion or beliefs,[178] forcing prisoners to wear their enemy's uniform[179] and measures of reprisal against prisoners of war.[180] As a final overarching protection, POWs are prohibited from renouncing their rights under the Conventions and Protocol I.[181] The intent behind this provision is to protect POWs from any agreements made under duress between their State/Power of origin and the Detaining Power.[182]

---

[160] Ibid., art.13(1); AP I, arts. 11(1) and 11(4).   [161] GC III, art. 13(2).   [162] Ibid., art. 17(4).

[163] Ibid., arts. 15 and 30.   [164] Ibid., art. 29. See also arts. 30–31.   [165] Ibid., art. 38.

[166] Ibid., arts. 15 and 26.   [167] Ibid., arts. 15 and 25.   [168] Ibid., arts. 15 and 27.   [169] Ibid., art. 19(1).

[170] Ibid., arts. 49 and 52.   [171] Ibid., art. 14(1).   [172] Ibid., art. 13(2).

[173] "Saddam Hussein Captured", *The Guardian*, 15 December 2003, www.theguardian.com/world/2003/dec/14/iraq.iraq1.

[174] "Saddam Underwear Photo Angers the US", *BBC News*, 20 May 2005, news.bbc.co.uk/2/hi/middle_east/4565505.stm.

[175] "Pentagon Vows to Probe Saddam Photos", CNN, 21 May 2005, edition.cnn.com/2005/WORLD/meast/05/20/saddam.photos/.

[176] GC III, arts. 50 and 52.   [177] Ibid., art. 25(4).   [178] Ibid., art.13(2).   [179] Ibid., art.18.

[180] Ibid., art.13(3).   [181] Ibid., art. 7; cf. art. 6.

[182] This provision was adopted in response to experiences during WWII, where some POWs were stripped of some essential rights as a result of special agreements adopted between belligerents under Article 83 of the 1929 Convention. See GC III Commentary, pp. 87–92.

ii. Rules on conditions of captivity

It is the responsibility of the Detaining Power to protect and care for the POWs in its care.[183] The Detaining Power must evacuate POWs from the field of engagement as soon as possible after capture;[184] furthermore, POW camps are not to be located in or near active hostilities.[185] In caring for POWs, the Detaining Power must observe basic standards regarding quarters, clothing, food and medical attention.[186] For example, during the Ethiopia–Eritrea conflict, both sides attempted to provide adequate conditions for POWs in their custody,[187] with attempts to ensure humane evacuation conditions[188] and some attempts to provide appropriate (if not adequate) food supplies.[189] However, violations of the law were also found, with examples of detainees being denied footwear before evacuation marches,[190] and Eritrean POWs being subjected to programmes of forced indoctrination.[191]

Prisoners are entitled to keep personal effects and articles.[192] POWs should also have access to recreational facilities, including sports, games and study[193] and be allowed to exercise their religious beliefs.[194] When the detention facility at Guantanamo Bay was first being prepared for the arrival of captured Taliban and al-Qaeda fighters, those in command of the facility took steps to involve the ICRC in those preparations, inviting them to visit the facility and ensure that they were complying with the Geneva Conventions, and also sought to acquire Korans and provide Halal food for detainees.[195] Non-compliance with the Conventions at Guantanamo was later officially excused by the Bush administration as unnecessary, as the determination had been made that Taliban and al-Qaeda operatives were not POWs under the Conventions, and thus not entitled to any protections of the Conventions.[196]

POWs may be put to work by the Detaining Power;[197] however, such work is subject to a number of conditions including limits on place and type of work.[198] POWs should also be given a monthly wage.[199] Equality of treatment of POWs must be observed, with no adverse distinction based on race, colour, language, belief, political or other opinion, nation or social origin, wealth, birth, or any other status or criteria.[200] However, special treatment is accorded to officers,[201] sick POWs,[202]

---

[183] GC III, art. 12(1), arts. 129 and 130; and AP I, arts. 11, 86–9.   [184] GC III, art. 19.

[185] Ibid., arts. 21–3.   [186] Ibid., art. 15; see also arts. 21–3 and arts. 25–8.

[187] See Ethiopia–Eritrea Claims Commission – Eritrea's Claim 17 and Ethiopia's Claim 4, Permanent Court of Arbitration, www.pca-cpa.org/showpage.asp?pag_id=1151.

[188] Ethiopia–Eritrea Claims Commission, Partial Award, Permanent Court of Arbitration, Ethiopia's Claim 4, p. 16 para. 74; Eritrea's Claim 17, p. 16, para. 68, www.pca-cpa.org/showpage.asp?pag_id=1151.

[189] Ibid., Eritrea's Claim 17, p. 26, para. 109.

[190] Ibid., Eritrea's Claim 17, p. 16, para. 68; Ethiopia's Claim 4, p. 17, para. 74.

[191] Ibid., Eritrea's Claim 17, p. 21, para. 86.   [192] GC III, art. 18.   [193] Ibid., art. 38.   [194] Ibid., art. 34.

[195] Karen Greenberg, *The Least Worst Place: Guantanamo's First 100 Days*, (Oxford / New York: Oxford University Press, 2009), p. 57. However, other GC provisions were not complied with – see ibid., p. 80.

[196] See above, pp. 102–5 on "unlawful combatants".   [197] GC III, art. 49.   [198] Ibid., arts. 49–55.

[199] Ibid., art. 60.   [200] Ibid., art. 16; AP I, art. 75.   [201] GC III, arts. 49 and 60.

[202] Ibid., arts. 30 and 109.

and women,[203] with consideration to be given to a POW's age or professional qualifications.[204]

iii. Rules on penal and disciplinary proceedings

In matters of discipline, POWs are to be treated in the same manner as the armed forces of the Detaining Power.[205] Orders are to be given in a language which the POW will understand.[206] Restrictions exist on the types of discipline that may be employed against POWs.[207] POWs may be tried only by a military court offering guarantees of independence and impartiality.[208] The accused must be afforded the rights and means of defence,[209] with the entitlement to choose their own counsel, to call witnesses and to obtain the services of a competent interpreter.[210] No coercion is to be used against a POW to induce a confession regarding the crime of which they are accused.[211] POWs retain the right to appeal or petition.[212] Furthermore, the accused captive is entitled to have a representative of the Protecting Power present at their trial, and is permitted to receive assistance from the Protecting Power.[213] If the death penalty is pronounced on the POW, the sentence can only be carried out after a six-month waiting period.[214]

iv. Obligations for detaining authorities regarding transmission of information, monitoring by Protecting Powers and the ICRC, and repatriation of prisoners of war

Convention III safeguards POW relations with the exterior. Section V of the Convention provides for POWs to be able to contact family members, as well as the Central Prisoners of War Agency.[215] Section V provides that POWs are entitled to remain in correspondence with family on a regular basis;[216] POWs are also entitled to receive relief and care packages, both from family and relief agencies.[217] All Parties to the conflict must establish an official Information Bureau for POWs,[218] responsible for the management of all information regarding POWs, such as transfers, releases, repatriations, escapes, admissions to hospital and deaths.[219] The Bureaux are also responsible for dealing with any inquiries regarding POWs currently within their State's power.[220] With regards to relief agencies, Convention III also provides that representatives of the Protecting Power and the ICRC have the right to visit POWs in places of internment, imprisonment and labour, and to interview POWs regarding the conditions of their captivity.[221]

---

[203] Ibid., arts. 25 and 29.   [204] Ibid., art. 16.   [205] Ibid., art. 82.   [206] Ibid., art. 41.
[207] Ibid., arts. 42, 89, 90, and 98.   [208] Ibid., art. 84.   [209] Ibid., art. 99.   [210] Ibid., art. 105.
[211] Ibid., art. 99(2).   [212] Ibid., art. 106.   [213] Ibid., art. 105.   [214] Ibid., art.101.
[215] Ibid., art. 70; the Central Prisoners of War Agency is provided for in art. 123.   [216] Ibid., art. 71.
[217] Ibid., arts. 72–5.   [218] Ibid., art. 122.   [219] Ibid., art. 122.   [220] Ibid., art. 122.
[221] Ibid., art. 126.

Finally, POWs retain the right to be repatriated at the end of the hostilities,[222] unless they are seriously wounded or sick, in which case they are entitled to be repatriated as soon as they are fit to travel.[223] Violations of these provisions were seen during and following the Iran–Iraq War, with both sides delaying repatriation of POWs, allowing only small numbers of sick or wounded POWs to be repatriated during the conflict[224] and holding over 100,000 POWs nearly a year after the cessation of hostilities.[225] The UN Security Council called for the return of POWs, urging "that prisoners-of-war be released and repatriated without delay after the cessation of active hostilities in accordance with the Third Geneva Convention".[226]

The rationale behind the repatriation requirement is connected to the fundamental rationale underlying POW captivity on the whole – that such captivity is not punishment but rather a means to prevent combatants from returning to active participation in the hostilities. Thus, as noted in the Commentary to Convention III, "in time of war, the internment of captives is justified by a legitimate concern – to prevent military personnel from taking up arms once more against the captor State. That reason no longer exists once the fighting is over."[227]

7. CONCLUSION

The question of determining who is and is not authorised to take direct part in hostilities is one of the most complex and controversial parts of the law of armed conflict. Correctly identifying persons as civilians or combatants is a central part of IHL for parties to a conflict, and remains one of the most complex and challenging parts of the law.

SUGGESTED READING

Akande, Dapo, "Clearing the Fog of War? The ICRC's Interpretive Guidance on Direct Participation in Hostilities" (2010) 59 *ICLQ* 190.

Baxter, Richard, "So-Called 'Unprivileged Belligerency': Spies, Guerrillas and Saboteurs" (1951) 28 *BYBIL* 323.

Cameron, Lindsay and Vincent Chetail, *Privatizing War: Private Military and Security Companies under Public International Law* (Cambridge University Press, 2013)

Crawford, Emily, *The Treatment of Combatants and Insurgents under the Law of Armed Conflict* (Oxford University Press, 2010)

---

[222] Ibid., art. 118.   [223] Ibid., arts. 109–10.

[224] John Quigley, "Iran and Iraq and the Obligations to Release and Repatriate Prisoners Of War After the Close of Hostilities" (1989) 5 *American University International Law Review* 73 at 73.

[225] "Red Cross Seeks to Interview All POW's in the Gulf War", *The New York Times,* 8 November 1988, at A8.

[226] UN Security Council, S/RES/598, 20 July 1987.   [227] GC III Commentary, pp. 546–7.

Perrin, Benjamin (ed.), *Modern Warfare: Armed Groups, Private Militaries, Humanitarian Organisations and the Law* (Vancouver: University of British Columbia Press, 2012)

Scheipers, Sibylle (ed.), *Prisoners in War* (Oxford University Press, 2010)

DISCUSSION QUESTIONS

1. Following the determination by the US that the Geneva Conventions did not apply in their conflict with the Taliban and al-Qaeda, a US administration official defended the decision by stating that some of the provisions of the Conventions were "quaint" and "obsolete"[228] – do you agree? What kinds of provisions do you think the official was referencing and how/why should these provisions be altered to reflect a more contemporary outlook?

2. Some publicists have argued that combatant status should be extended to all persons who participate in armed conflict,[229] and that the law has developed to the point that POW status and treatment could be extended to all persons under the law of armed conflict.[230] What are some of the practical and conceptual benefits of such an approach? What are the practical and conceptual problems with these arguments?

3. Following his capture, deposed Iraqi leader Saddam Hussein was given a medical examination by US personnel, who videoed the footage and then released the footage worldwide. Was this a violation of the laws of armed conflict? Why/why not?

4. The Geneva Conventions require that POWs be repatriated at the cessation of hostilities (or earlier if medical needs warrant earlier repatriation). However, there have been instances of delays in repatriation, such as following the Iran/Iraq War. What is the time frame for repatriation? Can a Detaining Power force a POW to return home if they don't want to go? What if a POW returns home and then re-enlists? Is this a violation of the laws of armed conflict?

5. Which interpretation of DPH do you prefer and why – the Israeli Supreme Court approach or the ICRC Interpretive Guidance?

6. Should spies be included in the categories of combatant? Why or why not?

---

[228] Memorandum for Alberto Gonzalez, 22 January 2002, in Greenberg and Dratel, *The Torture Papers*, p. 81.

[229] See Geoffrey Corn, "Thinking the Unthinkable: Has the Time Come to Offer Combatant Immunity to Non-State Actors?" (2011) 22 Stanford LPR 253.

[230] See generally, Jinks, "Protective Parity and the Laws of War".

5 Protection of the wounded, sick and shipwrecked

1. INTRODUCTION

One of the fundamental principles of the law of armed conflict is the notion that those *hors de combat* – persons who do not or no longer take active part in the hostilities – are to be protected "from the horrors of war".[1] This can only be achieved if those *hors de combat*, as well as the personnel and equipment needed to care for and protect them, are respected and protected, and not subject to attack. This chapter will examine the rules regarding the protection of a specific category of the *hors de combat* – the wounded, sick and shipwrecked, as well as the rules regarding the personnel and equipment involved in the protection and care of the wounded, sick and shipwrecked. This chapter will also examine the rules regarding the dead and missing, and look at the emblems designed to protect medical and relief personnel and equipment – the Red Cross, Red Crescent and Red Crystal.

2. THE ORIGINS OF THE PROTECTION OF THE *HORS DE COMBAT* IN ARMED CONFLICT

The origins of the 1864 Geneva Convention were described in Chapter 1. The fundamental principle of this first Geneva Convention was the idea of "the neutrality of wounded soldiers and of all those looking after them."[2] The Convention was specifically aimed at protecting ambulances, hospitals and all relevant medical

---

[1] Laurie Blank and Gregory Noone, *International Law and Armed Conflict: Fundamental Principles and Contemporary Challenges in the Law of War* (New York: Wolters Kluwer, 2013), p. 7.

[2] François Bugnion, "Birth of an Idea: The Founding of the International Committee of the Red Cross and of the International Red Cross and Red Crescent Movement: From Solferino to the original Geneva Convention (1859–1864)" (2012) 94 IRRC 1299, 1324-5, citing Guillaume-Henri Dufour, Gustave Moynier and Samuel

personnel including civilians assisting in relief efforts, from being objects of attack. In addition, the Convention laid down the principle that "wounded or sick combatants, to whatever nation they may belong, shall be collected and cared for".[3] The principle of collection and protection of the wounded and sick originally covered only armed forces on land. The rules were later expanded to include shipwrecked personnel (in the Hague Conventions)[4] and were expanded further again in the 1906 Geneva Conventions to include "other persons officially attached to the armed forces" (and reaffirmed in the 1949 Conventions, which replaced the 1906 and 1929 Conventions). The broadest scope of application came with the adoption of Protocol I in 1977, which provides for the protection of all wounded, sick and shipwrecked, whether military or civilian.

3. THE RULES REGARDING RESPECT FOR AND CARE OF THE WOUNDED, SICK AND SHIPWRECKED

As with much of the treaty law of armed conflict, the provisions that relate to care of the wounded, sick and shipwrecked in international armed conflict are more comprehensive than those in non-international armed conflict. This next section will look at these rules regarding the respect for and care of the wounded, sick and shipwrecked, and examine the differing scope of those rules as they apply in international and non-international armed conflicts. For the most part, the substance of the rules as they apply in international and non-international armed conflicts is similar if not identical, but more detailed.

a. In international armed conflicts

Under the law of armed conflict, parties to a conflict are obliged to respect and care for the wounded, sick and shipwrecked. Article 12 of GC I states that "members of the armed forces and other persons" who are protected under the Conventions:

... shall be treated humanely and cared for by the Party to the conflict in whose power they may be, without any adverse distinction founded on sex, race, nationality, religion, political opinions, or any other similar criteria. Any attempts upon their lives, or violence to their persons, shall be strictly prohibited; in particular, they shall not be murdered or exterminated, subjected to torture or to biological experiments; they shall not wilfully be left without

---

Lehmann, *Le Congrès de Genève: Rapport adressé au Conseil fédèral par MM. Dufour, Moynier et Lehmann, Plénipotentiaires de la Suisse* (Geneva: Imprimerie Fick, 1864), p. 3.

[3] Convention for the Amelioration of the Condition of the Wounded in Armies in the Field, Geneva, 22 August 1864, in force 22 June 1865, 129 CTS 361, art. 6.

[4] Hague III 1899; Convention (X) for the Adaptation to Maritime War of the Principles of the Geneva Convention, The Hague, 18 October 1907, in force 26 January 1910, 205 CTS 359.

medical assistance and care, nor shall conditions exposing them to contagion or infection be created.

This provision applies to all persons wounded, sick and shipwrecked. The only distinctions that may be drawn regarding the treatment of the wounded, sick and shipwrecked are medical ones: the Convention affirms that "only urgent medical reasons will authorise priority in the order of treatment to be administered."[5] Thus, parties to the conflict may not give preferential treatment to their own personnel if personnel of the adverse party under their control require more urgent medical attention.[6] If it becomes necessary for a party to the conflict to abandon the wounded and sick then the party must "as far as military considerations permit, leave with [the wounded and sick] a part of its medical personnel and material to assist in their care."[7]

These provisions are reaffirmed, almost verbatim, in Article 12 of Geneva Convention II with regards to shipwrecked personnel; logically excluded is reference to leaving medical personnel with "abandoned" wounded and sick.

The Conventions do not define the parameters of "wounded and sick"; the Commentary to the Conventions states:

No attempt has ever been made in the Geneva Convention to define what is meant by a "wounded or sick" combatant; nor has there ever been any definition of the degree of severity of a wound or a sickness entitling the wounded or sick combatant to respect. That is as well; for any definition would necessarily be restrictive in character, and would thereby open the door to every kind of misinterpretation and abuse. The meaning of the words "wounded and sick" is a matter of common sense and good faith.[8]

The Commentary goes on to state that this "common sense and good faith" approach is meant to cover "combatants who have fallen by reason of a wound or sickness of any kind, or who have ceased to fight and laid down their arms as a consequence of what they themselves think about their health."[9] As such, it is made clear that that illness (or wound, injury or act of being shipwrecked) is not the determinative factor in marking someone as *hors de combat*; rather "it is the fact of falling or laying down of arms which constitutes the claim to protection".[10] Thus, it is the sickness or wounding, as determined by the person suffering the debilitation, in conjunction with the act of laying down their arms, which combine to create the protected status of the wounded, sick and shipwrecked.

When the Protocols were debated during the 1970s, the question of whether to define the parameters of "wounded, sick and shipwrecked" arose. Ultimately, an

---

[5] GC I, art. 12; GC II, art. 12.
[6] This is known as triage – the process of determining the priority given to patients based on the severity of their illness of injuries. The term derives from the French verb *trier*, meaning to separate, sift or select.
[7] GC I, art. 12.   [8] GC I Commentary, p. 136.   [9] Ibid.   [10] Ibid.

entire article dedicated to terminology and definitions was included in Article 8 of AP I, which defined the wounded, sick and shipwrecked as follows:

(a) "wounded" and "sick" mean persons, whether military or civilian, who, because of trauma, disease or other physical or mental disorder or disability, are in need of medical assistance or care and who refrain from any act of hostility. These terms also cover maternity cases, new-born babies and other persons who may be in need of immediate medical assistance or care, such as the infirm or expectant mothers, and who refrain from any act of hostility;

(b) "shipwrecked" means persons, whether military or civilian, who are in peril at sea or in other waters as a result of misfortune affecting them or the vessel or aircraft carrying them and who refrain from any act of hostility. . . .[11]

At the Conference of Government Experts in both 1971 and 1972, delegates discussed the need for certain terms to be better defined;[12] however, there is nothing in the records to indicate why it was felt that defining "wounded, sick and shipwrecked" was necessary in the 1970s, when it had been considered problematic in 1949.

As with the 1949 Conventions, the element of "refraining from any act of hostility" is crucial to categorisation as "wounded, sick or shipwrecked". Persons who are in need of medical attention or who are imperilled at sea must not commit any act of hostility, in order to be afforded the immunity attaching to "wounded, sick or shipwrecked" status. Failure to refrain from hostile acts will render such a person liable to attack, regardless of their medical condition. Article 8 of Protocol I does not explain what amounts to an act of hostility. However, Kleffner notes the possibility of drawing analogies from other relevant sections of Protocol I, specifically from Article 51(3) relating to civilians and direct participation in hostilities. According to Kleffner, hostile acts must be considered any acts:

which by their nature and purpose are intended to cause actual harm to the personnel and equipment of the opposing armed forces … the rule of thumb is, in short, that persons commit "hostile acts" when they (continue to) perform functions inherent to being combatants … conversely, as soon as a person in need of medical attention or in peril at sea or in other waters ceases to commit "hostile acts", that person is entitled to protection as a wounded, sick or shipwrecked.[13]

Reprisals against the wounded, sick and shipwrecked are prohibited under the Conventions[14] and Protocol I.[15] Acts of violence committed against the wounded, sick or shipwrecked, whether in reprisal or not, are grave breaches under the

---

[11] AP I, art. 8(a)–(b).

[12] See CE 1971, Report, p. 24, para. 46; CE 1972, Report, vol. I, p. 33, para. 1.11 and p. 209, para. 5.48.

[13] Jann Kleffner, "Protection of the Wounded, Sick, and Shipwrecked", in Dieter Fleck (ed.), *The Handbook of Humanitarian Law in Armed Conflicts* 3rd edn (Oxford University Press, 2013), p. 325.

[14] GC I, art. 46; GC II, art. 47.   [15] AP I, art. 20.

Conventions[16] and Protocol I[17] and prosecutable as war crimes under the Statute of the ICC.[18]

b. In non-international armed conflicts

The wounded, sick and shipwrecked are protected under the law of non-international armed conflicts, in Common Article 3 of the Conventions,[19] which protects all persons who have been rendered *hors de combat*, due to factors including "sickness, wounds, detention, or any other cause". Common Article 3 provides that all persons rendered *hors de combat* are to be protected, and that prohibited "at all times and in any place whatsoever"[20] are the following acts:

(a) violence to life and person, in particular murder of all kinds, mutilation, cruel treatment and torture;
(b) taking of hostages;
(c) outrages upon personal dignity, in particular humiliating and degrading treatment;
(d) the passing of sentences and the carrying out of executions without previous judgment pronounced by a regularly constituted court, affording all the judicial guarantees which are recognized as indispensable by civilized peoples.

Common Article 3 also affirms that the "wounded and sick shall be collected and cared for". More detailed provision regarding the wounded and sick is contained in Protocol II. Article 7 of Protocol II provides that:

(1) All the wounded, sick and shipwrecked, whether or not they have taken part in the armed conflict, shall be respected and protected.

(2) In all circumstances they shall be treated humanely and shall receive, to the fullest extent practicable and with the least possible delay, the medical care and attention required by their condition. There shall be no distinction among them founded on any grounds other than medical ones.

Acts of violence against such persons in non-international armed conflicts are also criminalised as war crimes under the ICC Statute, in Article 8(2)(c).[21]

The protected status of wounded, sick and shipwrecked is retained by the *hors de combat*, until another status – such as prisoner of war – is acquired. At that stage, the rules relating to POWs supplant the rules on the wounded, sick and shipwrecked.[22] Likewise, if someone *hors de combat* recovers from their wounds or illness, or is rescued from a shipwreck, and returns to active duty as a combatant

---

[16] GC I, art. 50; GC II, art. 51.   [17] AP I, art. 85.   [18] Rome Statute, art. 8(2)(a).
[19] See Chapter 3 on Common Article 3 Non-International Armed Conflicts.   [20] Common Article 3.
[21] Which criminalises violations of Common Article 3.   [22] See Chapter 4 on POWs.

or direct participant, they lose their protected status and are subject to targeting rules.[23]

As entrenched as the protections for the wounded, sick and shipwrecked are, violence against these protected persons still occurs. In November 1991, a hospital in the Croatian town of Vukovar was raided, and nearly 300 patients and relatives forced onto buses.[24] Most were executed, their bodies found in a mass grave near the city; over fifty are still identified as missing.[25] Eventually, seven people would be indicted by the ICTY for their involvement in the war crime.[26] The ICRC calls the Vukovar massacre one of the worst cases of deliberate attacks on the wounded and sick.[27] However, despite such atrocities, there are, equally, cases which highlight the respect these provisions command: during the 2003 Iraq War, US television reported on an insurgent who was brought to a US military base for medical treatment. The insurgent had been shot while attempting to plant a roadside improvised explosive device (IED), and was losing blood. The doctors at the base put out a call for donors; dozens of soldiers responded and donated blood to save the life of a person who had been trying to kill them. When interviewed, one of the soldiers replied "a human life is a human life".[28]

4. PROVISIONS ON THE DEAD AND MISSING

One of the key provisions of the law of armed conflict is the requirement for parties to a conflict to undertake certain acts regarding the dead and missing. The intent behind these provisions is not so much to protect the dead and missing, but to ensure "the right of families to know the fate of their relatives".[29] To that end, IHL obliges parties to the conflict to ensure that the dead are searched for, collected and identified. The dead are also to be protected from being despoiled – of being stripped of their belongings and valuables.[30] This obligation is considered customary international law, applicable in international and non-international armed conflicts

---

[23] See Chapter 7 on targeting.

[24] See press reports Gabriel Partos, "Vukovar Massacre: What happened", *BBC News*, 13 June 2003, news.bbc. co.uk/2/hi/europe/2988304.stm and Alexandra Hudson, "UN tribunal to rule in Vukovar massacre case" *Reuters*, 25 September, 2007, www.reuters.com/article/2007/09/25/us-warcrimes-vukovar-idUSL2579742920070925

[25] See Amnesty International, *Behind a Wall of Silence: Prosecution of War Crimes in Croatia*, (London: Amnesty International Publications, 2010), p. 9, www.amnesty.eu/content/assets/doc2010/croatia_behind wallofsilence.pdf. See further the ICRC campaign "Health Care in Danger", www.icrc.org/eng/what-we-do/safeguarding-health-care/solution/2013-04-26-hcid-health-care-in-danger-project.htm.

[26] See www.icty.org/sid/7397.   [27] ICRC, "Health Care in Danger", p. 10.

[28] *NBC Nightly News*, 2 March 2007, reported in Blank and Noone, *International Law and Armed Conflict*, p. 249.

[29] AP I, art. 32.

[30] GC I, arts. 15(1) and 16; GC II, arts. 18–19; GC IV, art. 16(2); AP I, art. 33(4); AP II, art. 8. The obligation to search for and collect the dead was first included in Article 3 of the 1929 Geneva Conventions.

alike.[31] The obligation, as worded in Convention I and echoed in Additional Protocol II, is multi-layered, and attempts to balance military necessity with humanitarian consideration.

The obligation to search for the dead is strict – it "shall"[32] be undertaken at all times, "whenever circumstances permit, and particularly after an engagement".[33] However, the Conventions and Protocols recognise that the exigencies of military operations may make the immediate search for the dead impracticable; thus, the obligation in the treaties is worded as "all possible measures",[34] which allows for some leeway regarding when the search for the fallen takes place. The rule applies to all the dead, without distinction; that is to say, the obligation is that the dead are to be collected regardless of the party to which they belong, and regardless of whether they directly participated in hostilities.

The dead are also to be protected from despoliation. First codified in Article 16 of Hague Convention X, the obligation in current IHL provides that parties to the conflict must ensure that dead bodies are not mutilated, mistreated or plundered. This provision has a long pedigree: the *Pohl* case at the US Military Tribunal at Nuremberg stated that robbing the dead "is and always has been a crime".[35] Mutilation of dead bodies, in either international or non-international armed conflicts, is a war crime under the Rome Statute of the ICC, as outlined in the Elements of Crimes for the ICC, regarding the definition of "committing outrages upon personal dignity".[36]

However, despite the powerful sanctions against the mistreatment of the dead, violations continue in practice. The wars in Iraq and Afghanistan have been marked by numerous examples of troops mistreating the dead. Australian troops came under investigation for cutting the hands off suspected insurgents in Zabul Province in Afghanistan in April 2013;[37] a "rogue" group of US soldiers were charged with, among other charges, taking the body parts of Afghan civilians as trophies;[38] UK troops were investigated for allegedly mutilating the corpses of Iraqis following the "Battle of Danny Boy".[39] That investigations and prosecutions have been pursued in these situations is, at the very least, demonstrative of the seriousness with which

---

[31] ICRC CIHL Study, r. 112 regarding searching for and collecting the dead and Rule 113, regarding preventing the dead from being despoiled.

[32] AP II, art. 8.   [33] Ibid.   [34] Ibid.

[35] *United States* v. *Oswald Pohl et al.*, US Military Tribunal, Nuremburg V TWC 195 (3 November 1947).

[36] Rome Statute, art. 8(2)(b)(xxi), regarding war crimes in international armed conflicts; Rome Statute, art. 8(2)(c)(ii), regarding war crimes in non-international armed conflicts. See International Criminal Court, *Elements of Crimes*, 2011, ICC-ASP/1/3(part II-B), footnotes 49 and 57.

[37] Michael Brissenden, "Australian Special Forces Troops under Investigation for Cutting Off Hands of Dead Afghan Insurgent", *ABC News*, 30 August 2013, www.abc.net.au/news/2013-08-30/claims-sas-troops-cut-hands-off-afghan-insurgent/4924694.

[38] See further Seymour Hersh, "The 'Kill Team' Photographs", *The New Yorker*, 22 March 2011, www.newyorker.com/online/blogs/newsdesk/2011/03/the-kill-team-photographs.html#slide_ss_0=1.

[39] See further the Al-Sweady Public Inquiry, which has been tasked to "investigate allegations made in Judicial Review proceedings that the human rights of a number of Iraqi nationals were abused by British troops in the aftermath of a firefight in 2004 near Majar al Kabir", www.alsweadyinquiry.org/.

such allegations are treated by States, and indicative of the importance many States place on the need to repress violations of IHL.

The law of armed conflict also obliges parties to the conflict to bury the dead, or otherwise dispose of them in an appropriate manner – for example, if cremation is required for religious reasons or compelling hygiene demands.[40] The dead should be "honourably interred, if possible according to the rites of the religion to which they belonged".[41] However, burial or cremation may only take place once a careful examination – preferably a medical examination – has occurred to confirm death, establish the identity of the deceased, and for a report to be made. Any "dog tags" or other identifying objects should remain with the body, unless they are in duplicate, in which case one tag may be taken for official records.[42] Parties to the conflict are obliged to ensure that war graves are properly maintained and marked, and that, where possible, graves are grouped according to the nationality of the deceased.

In order to facilitate the fulfilment of these obligations, IHL provides that parties to an international armed conflict establish, at the commencement of hostilities, certain organisations, such as an official Information Bureau for Prisoners of War[43] and an Official Graves Registration Service. The Official Graves Registration Service, as provided for in Article 17 of GC I, has as its main task facilitating the exhumation and identification of bodies or other remains, and the transportation of such remains to the country of origin. This work is complemented by the Information Bureau, which must be informed, as soon as possible, of the exact location and markings of the graves, as well as the particulars of the dead interred there.[44] These obligations are supplemented by Additional Protocol I, which provides that parties to the armed conflict "shall conclude agreements"[45] on the protection and mainten-ance of war graves, to allow access to graves by relatives; and to facilitate the return of the remains of the dead, as well as any personal belongings.

With regards to persons killed at sea, the provisions laid down in Convention I regarding war dead in the field are essentially mirrored in Convention II regarding war dead at sea. Article 20 of Convention II allows for burial at sea, provided the requirements of examination and identification are carried out. If the deceased are landed – i.e. taken ashore – the provisions of GC I apply. Warships sunk with their crews are considered as war graves, and are to be protected as such.[46] With regards to the missing in armed conflict, parties to the conflict are obliged to search for missing persons as soon as possible.[47] In order to ensure that all persons are accounted for during times of armed conflict, parties to an armed conflict must

---

[40] GC I, art. 17(3); GC III, art. 120(4); GC IV, art. 130(1); AP I, art. 34; AP II, art. 8.   [41] GC I, art. 17.

[42] Ibid.   [43] See Chapter 4 on POWs.

[44] GC I, art. 17; cf. GC I, art. 16, regarding the transmission of information on the dead to the Information Bureau.

[45] AP I, art. 34(2).

[46] D. P. O'Connell, *The International Law of the Sea*, 2 vols., (Oxford: Clarendon Press, 1982–4), vol. II, p. 912.

[47] AP I, art. 33.

record the personal details of any person held in captivity for longer than two weeks. Any information collected must be transmitted to the Central Tracing Agency of the International Committee of the Red Cross.[48]

5. MEDICAL PERSONNEL AND THE PROTECTION OF MEDICAL GOODS AND OBJECTS, INCLUDING HOSPITALS, AMBULANCES AND HOSPITAL SHIPS

The Conventions and Protocols are designed to ensure that persons *hors de combat* are respected and protected when they are at their most vulnerable. However, this protection and care could not be assured if those providing the care – medical and religious personnel, as well as the requisite medical transports and installations – were also vulnerable to attack. As Sassòli *et al.* state, "the necessary care [for the wounded, sick and shipwrecked] can often only be given … if the people who provide it are not attacked. On the battlefield this will only work if they constitute a separate category, never participating in hostilities and caring for all the wounded without discrimination, and if they are identifiable by an emblem."[49] With this in mind, this next section examines the protection of medical and relief personnel, and the transports and other installations and objects used to provide that relief – such as ambulances, hospitals and hospital ships.

a. Medical and religious personnel

IHL makes considerable provision for the protection of medical personnel, medical installations and medical transports. Under the Conventions and Protocols, medical personnel, administrative support staff and religious personnel are to be protected and cared for;[50] they are immune from being targeted and attacked, and must be allowed to carry out their medical or religious duties.[51] Any medical or religious personnel who fall into the hands of an adverse party may not be taken as prisoners of war, but may be retained by the adverse party if needed to provide care or religious instruction for prisoners of war.[52]

Protection exists also for civilians engaged in the care of the sick and wounded, whether they are combatants or civilians. Article 18 of GC I provides:

---

[48] Ibid.

[49] Marco Sassòli, Antoine Bouvier and Anne Quintin, *How Does Law Protect in War? Cases, Documents and Teaching Materials on Contemporary Practice in International Humanitarian Law* 3rd edn (Geneva: ICRC, 2011), p. 195.

[50] GC I, arts. 24–5; GC II, art. 36.   [51] GC I, arts. 24–7; GC II, arts. 36–7; AP I, arts. 15–20; AP II, art. 9.

[52] GC I, arts. 28 and 30; GC II, art. 37; GC III, art. 33.

The military authorities may appeal to the charity of the inhabitants voluntarily to collect and care for, under their direction, the wounded and sick, granting persons who have responded to this appeal the necessary protection and facilities. Should the adverse Party take or retake control of the area, it shall likewise grant these persons the same protection and the same facilities.

The military authorities shall permit the inhabitants and relief societies, even in invaded or occupied areas, spontaneously to collect and care for wounded or sick of whatever nationality. The civilian population shall respect these wounded and sick, and in particular abstain from offering them violence.

No one may ever be molested or convicted for having nursed the wounded or sick.

The provisions of the present Article do not relieve the occupying Power of its obligation to give both physical and moral care to the wounded and sick.

Similar provision is made in Article 20(1) of GC IV and Article 10 of Protocol II. Protocol I further expands the categories of protected persons to include all those who carry out medical or religious functions – whether they fulfil such duties on a permanent or temporary basis, and regardless of whether they are military or civilian in character.[53]

Recognised national aid societies, such as national Red Cross Societies, are also protected under the Conventions.[54] These protections exist so long as protected medical and religious personnel do not take direct part in hostilities.[55] While medical and religious personnel may be armed, they may only carry light arms, which may be used only for their own defence, or for the defence of the wounded and sick in their care.[56] Most State military manuals reaffirm this provision – for example, the US Army Field Manual 2007 states that "when engaging in medical evacuation operations, medical personnel are entitled to defend themselves and their patients. They are only permitted to use individual small arms",[57] and that "medical personnel are only permitted to fire in their personal defense and for the protection of the wounded and sick in their charge against marauders and other persons violating the Law of War".[58] Finally, medical personnel must ensure that they are properly identified as such, by the wearing of the distinctive emblem.[59]

b. Medical goods and objects, including hospitals, ambulances and hospital ships

Comprehensive protections exist for medical goods and objects, including medical units and transports. Buildings and material are protected under Articles 33 and 34

---

[53] AP I, art. 8(c)–(d).   [54] GC I, arts. 26–7; GC II, arts. 25 and 36; AP I, art. 9(2).
[55] ICRC CIHL Study, r. 25.   [56] GC I, art. 22.
[57] US Department of the Army, Army Field Manual No. 4-02.2, 8 May 2007, para. A-11, Appendix A, rdl. train.army.mil/catalog/view/100.ATSC/6C060374-ABDA-4CD9-B47D-49BA83700FCF-1308726831675/ 4–02.2/appa.htm.
[58] Ibid., para. A-13.   [59] See below on the distinctive emblem.

of GC I which provide that the buildings, material and stores of fixed medical establishments of the armed forces must not be intentionally destroyed, and must be reserved for the care of the wounded and sick. This applies also to mobile medical units which may fall into the hands of the enemy – they are to be used for the welfare of the wounded and sick.

Medical transports, such as ambulances, are also to be protected and respected in accordance with the laws of armed conflict. If they are captured, proper care and respect as provided for under the law of armed conflict is to be extended to any wounded and sick persons carried in such transports.[60] Other kinds of medical transports, such as medical aircraft used exclusively for the transport of wounded and sick, and of medical personnel and equipment, are also immune from attack.[61] In carrying out their duties, medical aircraft must fly according to strictly designated flight paths, avoid flying over enemy or enemy-occupied territory, and must obey orders to land.[62]

Hospital ships are specially protected in Chapter III of Convention II.[63] Hospital ships are immune from being targeted or attacked, and may not be captured.[64] Personnel aboard hospital ships are to be respected and protected.[65] Private ships,[66] converted merchant vessels,[67] coastal rescue craft,[68] and any other water-borne vessel[69] used by relief societies or used for the purposes of tending to the wounded, sick and shipwrecked, are also protected. Sick bays of warships are likewise to be respected and spared as far as possible should hostilities occur on a warship.[70]

The protection afforded to medical installations, mobile medical units and medical ships ceases only if such installations are used to commit, outside their humanitarian duties, acts that are harmful to the enemy.[71] Protection for such units and installations will only cease after a warning has been given, a reasonable time-limit for the cessation of the harmful acts is provided, and after the warning has remained unheeded. What constitutes a "harmful" act is not defined in the Conventions, although both Conventions I and II and Protocol I outline certain conditions that are *not* to be "considered as depriving [the protected objects] of the protection due to them";[72] these include, for example, the fact that the hospital or hospital ship is tending to wounded, sick and shipwrecked civilians; or the presence of small arms or ammunition taken from the wounded, sick and shipwrecked and not yet handed in to the proper authorities.

The Commentaries to the Conventions provide some guidance as to what constitutes "acts harmful to the enemy":

---

[60] GC I, art. 35; AP I, art. 21; AP II, art. 11.   [61] GC I, art. 36; GC II, arts. 39–40.
[62] GC I, arts. 36–7; AP I, art. 24–31.
[63] See also AP I, arts. 22–3; AP II, art. 11 (which more generally protects medical transports).
[64] GC II, art. 22.   [65] Ibid., arts. 36–7.   [66] Ibid., art. 24.   [67] Ibid., art. 33.   [68] Ibid., art. 27.
[69] Ibid., art. 25.   [70] Ibid., art. 28.   [71] GC I, art. 21; GC II, art. 34; AP I, art. 12(1).
[72] GC I, art. 22; GC II, art. 35; AP I, art. 13.

In 1949, as in 1929, it was considered unnecessary to define "acts harmful to the enemy" – an expression whose meaning is self-evident and which must remain quite general. While the International Committee of the Red Cross shared this view, it had prepared an alternative wording expressing the same idea in case the Conference should wish to be more explicit. We quote it here, as we think it may throw light on the meaning to be attached to the words "acts harmful to the enemy". It reads as follows: "acts the purpose or effect of which is to harm the adverse Party, by facilitating or impeding military operations". Such harmful acts would, for example, include the use of a hospital as a shelter for able-bodied combatants or fugitives, as an arms or ammunition dump, or as a military observation post; another instance would be the deliberate siting of a medical unit in a position where it would impede an enemy attack. The sense will become still clearer when we consider Article 22 which quotes a series of conditions which are not to be regarded as being harmful to the enemy.[73]

The war in Gaza in 2009 illustrates how misuse of medical facilities and disregard for the laws relating to the protection of medical personnel and facilities are still a common occurrence in armed conflict. In January 2009, Israeli planes hit the A-Raeiya Medical Centre and its mobile clinics. The centre was clearly marked as a medical facility, and furthermore was located in the middle of a residential area, with no government or military facilities nearby.[74] There was no indication that the centre was being used in a way that would have rendered the facility a military objective. But at the time, testimony from the local Gazan population and from Israeli Defence Force soldiers was that Hamas operatives had donned medical uniforms and commandeered ambulances for military transportation.[75] Similar misuse of medical facilities was seen during the 2003 Iraq War, when Iraqi insurgent forces were often reported as using hospitals and mosques for launching military attacks.[76]

---

[73] GC I Commentary, pp. 200–1. The Commentaries make it clear that the harmful acts must be done "outside their humanitarian duties" so as to differentiate them from acts that might be considered harmful to the enemy, but which are nonetheless vital to their humanitarian purpose. As noted in the GC I Commentary, "[i]t is possible for a humane act to be harmful to the enemy, or for it to be wrongly interpreted as so being by an enemy lacking in generosity. Thus the presence or activities of a medical unit might interfere with tactical operations; so might its lights at night. It was stated, for example, at the Conference, that the waves given off by an X-ray apparatus could interfere with the transmission or reception of wireless messages by a military set, or with the working of a radar unit" (p. 201); such incidental effects do not constitute "acts harmful to the enemy".

[74] Report by the International Federation of Health and Human Rights Organisations, "Israeli Attacks and the Right to Health", 9 January 2009, reliefweb.int/report/occupied-palestinian-territory/optgaza-strip-israeli-attacks-and-right-health.

[75] Jason Koutsoukis, "Hamas Tried to Hijack Ambulances during Gaza War", *The Sydney Morning Herald*, 26 January 2009, www.smh.com.au/news/world/hamas-tried-to-hijack-ambulances-during-war/2009/01/25/1232818246374.html; Steven Erlanger, "Weighing Crimes and Ethics in the Fog of Urban Warfare", *The New York Times*, 16 January 2009, www.nytimes.com/2009/01/17/world/middleeast/17israel.html?_r=2&pagewanted=all&. For an overview of the threat to health care providers in time of violence and armed conflict, see further ICRC, "Health Care in Danger".

[76] See Antonio Castaneda, "US Marines Take Over Iraq Hospital", *Associated Press*, 6 July 2006, www.globalpolicy.org/component/content/article/168/36346.html.

That medical personnel and facilities find themselves subject to attack, contrary to the laws of armed conflict, is unfortunately a commonplace occurrence – indeed, the need to protect medical personnel and facilities has been the focus of a campaign by the ICRC. Entitled "Health Care in Danger", the project ran from 2011 to 2015, and aimed to "address the widespread and severe impact of illegal and sometimes violent acts that obstruct the delivery of health care, damage or destroy facilities and vehicles, and injure or kill health-care workers and patients, in armed conflicts and other emergencies".[77]

The misuse of the emblem, as a means to secure immunity from attack, is also commonplace.[78] It is an unfortunate side-effect of the respect engendered by the now-universal symbol of health care and relief – the Red Cross. This next section will examine how and why the Red Cross has become such an iconic and important symbol, and how IHL protects the emblem under international and domestic law.

6. THE PROTECTIVE EMBLEMS: THE RED CROSS, RED CRESCENT AND RED CRYSTAL

a. Background to the adoption of the emblems: the Red Cross

The origins of the symbol of the Red Cross can be traced to the conflicts of the nineteenth century. During the Crimean War, at the siege of Sebastopol, French military surgeon Lucien Baudens observed that medical personnel attempting to aid fallen soldiers often found themselves subject to artillery and gun fire, sometimes deliberately. Following the end of the conflict, Baudens published an article in *Revue des Deux Mondes*, in which he suggested that a distinctive sign, worn by medical personnel in wartime, could prevent medical personnel from being targeted while carrying out their duties. Baudens wrote of one particular battery of Russian artillery:

... which had sadly distinguished themselves after the battle of Traktir by firing on the doctors and nurses who were tending and evacuating Russian casualties. The same thing had happened after the battle of Inkerman ... such mistakes would not be possible if, by common accord among nations, doctors and nursing staff wore a distinctive sign – the same for all armies and all countries – that made them easily recognizable by the two sides.[79]

Baudens died shortly after the publication of his paper, and his suggestion of a distinctive emblem may have died with him, were it not for Henri Dunant and his

---

[77] ICRC, "Health Care in Danger".   [78] Ibid., p. 4.

[79] Lucien Baudens, "Une mission médicale à l'Armée d'Orient", *Revue des Deux Mondes*, XXVIIth year, February 1857, pp. 881–2. Baudens also wrote a book regarding his experience in the Crimea, *La Guerre de Crimée: Les Campements, Les Abris, Les Ambulances, Les Hopitaux etc.* (Paris: Michel Lévy Frères, 1857).

visit to Solferino in 1859. As noted in Chapter 1, Dunant, in both his book *A Memory of Solferino*, and as a member of the International Committee for Aid to Wounded Soldiers, proposed the adoption of an international convention for the protection of the wounded on the battlefield, which would also serve to protect those who come to the aid of the wounded. In order to identify members of aid societies and ensure their protection from attack, the International Committee, in their first meeting on 17 February 1863, prioritised the adoption of "a badge, uniform or armlet ... so that the bearers of such distinctive and universally adopted insignia would be given due recognition."[80]

When the International Committee submitted a draft convention to the 1863 Conference of European States, Article 9 of that convention stated that "voluntary nurses in all countries shall wear a distinctive and identical uniform or sign ... they shall be inviolable and military commanders shall give them protection."[81] While the suggestion of a uniform was not adopted, the distinctive sign was, in the form of a "white armlet [which] would bear a red cross".[82] Also recommended during the 1863 conference was:

... that a uniform distinctive sign be recognised for the Medical Corps of all armies, or at least for all persons of the same army belonging to this Service, and that a uniform flag also be adopted in all countries for ambulances and hospitals.[83]

When the European States reconvened in 1864 to debate and adopt the recommendations of the 1863 Conference, Article 7 of the 1864 Geneva Convention was thus adopted, giving force to the recommendations of Dunant and Baudens:

A distinctive and uniform flag shall be adopted for hospitals, ambulances and evacuation parties. ... An armlet may also be worn by personnel enjoying neutrality but its issue shall be left to the military authorities. Both flag and armlet shall bear a red cross on a white ground.

The Red Cross emblem described above is shown in Figure 5.1.

Figure 5.1 The Red Cross emblem

---

[80] "Unpublished Documents relative to the Founding of the Red Cross: Minutes of the Committee of Five" (1949) 2 IRRC 127 at 127.

[81] François Bugnion, *Red Cross, Red Crescent, Red Crystal* (Geneva: ICRC, 2007) p. 6, citing *Report on the International Conference held in Geneva on 26–29 October 1863 to Examine Ways of Remedying Shortcomings in the Medical Services of Armies in the Field* (Geneva: Imprimerie Fick, 1863), p. 16.

[82] Ibid., p. 119.   [83] Ibid., p. 149.

b. The Red Crescent

The extant documentation surrounding the 1863 and 1864 Conferences makes no mention as to the rationale for adopting the symbol of a cross. There are a number of hypotheses, including that the cross was a symbol of humanity and divinity and that it reaffirmed Christian charity by recalling Christ's crucifix.[84] However, others have argued that the Red Cross symbol bears no intentionally explicit religious connotations and was merely a reversing of the Swiss federal colours – a white cross on a red background. This argument draws on Switzerland's permanent neutral status[85] and reaffirms the principle of neutrality embodied by the emblem of the Red Cross, and the movement itself. As noted by Bugnion:

There is nothing in the preparatory documents to suggest that the October 1863 Conference had the slightest intention of conferring any religious significance whatsoever on the distinctive sign for volunteer nurses and military medical services, nor that it was at all aware that any religious significance could be attached to the emblem, since the aim of the founders of Red Cross was precisely to set up an institution which would transcend national borders and religious differences.[86]

Indeed, during the Conference that adopted the Geneva Convention of 1906, it was explicitly affirmed that the Red Cross had been adopted "out of respect to Switzerland... [and] formed by the reversal of the Federal colours".[87]

However, as noted by Bugnion, "nineteenth-century Europe saw itself as the centre of the world, and those who devised the emblem had no idea that the red cross might meet with opposition when the situation extended beyond the bounds of the old continent."[88] This opposition was quick to manifest. The Russo-Turkish War of 1876–8 demonstrated that non-Christian and non-European States had significant reservations regarding the use of the Red Cross. The Ottoman Empire, which had acceded to the 1864 Geneva Convention in 1865, found that the existence of the Red Cross emblem "prevented Turkey from exercising its rights under the Convention, because it gave offence to Muslim soldiers".[89] A stop-gap

---

[84] François Bugnion, *Red Cross, Red Crescent, Red Crystal* (Geneva: ICRC, 2007), p. 8: "the sign of the cross . . . is generally considered to be a symbol of the human being and his place in the world, the horizontal bar symbolizing arms extended towards the cardinal points (relationship to the world) and the vertical axis symbolizing the relationship with the divinity."

[85] Confirmed in the Treaties of Vienna and Paris of 1815 which ended the Napoleonic Wars; see further Gordon Sherman, "The Neutrality of Switzerland" (1918) 12 AJIL 462; see also the Swiss Federal Department of Foreign Affairs website www.eda.admin.ch/eda/en/fdfa/foreign-policy/international-law/neutrality.html.

[86] Bugnion, *Red Cross, Red Crescent, Red Crystal*, p. 9.   [87] GC 1906, art. 18.

[88] Bugnion, *Red Cross, Red Crescent, Red Crystal*, p. 9.

[89] Dispatch from the Sublime Porte of the Ottoman Empire to the Federal Council of the Swiss Government, 16 November 1876, *Bulletin international des Sociétés de Secours aux Militaires blessés*, No. 29, January 1877 at 36.

measure adopted during the conflict was the unilateral employment, by the Ottoman Empire, of a Red Crescent on a white background.[90]

By the time the international community met for the Peace Conferences in The Hague in 1899, the question of adopting additional emblems was squarely on the agenda. Indeed, in the years between the Russo-Turkish wars and the 1899 Convention, a number of parties to the 1864 Convention had begun advocating the introduction of additional emblems for use on ambulances and hospital ships.[91] By the 1899 and 1907 Hague Conferences, and the 1906 Geneva conference, States parties were allowed to submit reservations to the respective Conventions, regarding the use of the alternative emblems of the Red Crescent and the Red Lion and Sun.

It was not until the 1929 Conference, at which the 1864 Geneva Convention was revised, that official recognition was given to these alternative emblems. Under Article 19 of the Geneva Convention for the Amelioration of the Condition of the Wounded and Sick in Armies in the Field of 27 July 1929:

As a compliment to Switzerland, the heraldic emblem of the red cross on a white ground, formed by reversing the Federal colours, is retained as the emblem and distinctive sign of the medical service of armed forces. Nevertheless, in case of countries which already use, in place of the red cross, the red crescent or the red lion and sun on a white ground as a distinctive sign, these emblems are also recognised by the terms of the present Convention.

The Red Crescent and the Red Lion and Sun are depicted in Figures 5.2 and 5.3 respectively.

Figure 5.2 The Red Crescent

Figure 5.3 The Red Lion and Sun

---

[90] Dispatch from the Swiss Federal Council to the Ottoman Sublime Porte of 2 June 1877, in *Bulletin international des Sociétés de Secours aux Militaires blesses*, No. 31, July 1877 at 90–1.

[91] In addition to the Ottoman Red Crescent, Persia requested adoption of a Red Lion and Sun; and Siam requested a Red Flame.

The Red Lion and Sun is no longer in common use; in 1980, the newly proclaimed Islamic Republic of Iran declared that they would use the Red Crescent as their emblem.[92] However, Iran has reserved the right to take up the Red Lion and Sun in the future.[93] It therefore continues to be an internationally recognised and protected emblem – this was most recently affirmed on the adoption of the Red Crystal in 2005.[94]

c. The Red Shield of David

As the international community was debating the Geneva Conventions in 1949, the newly created state of Israel came to the diplomatic conference with a proposal for the adoption of an additional distinctive emblem – the Red Shield of David (see Figure 5.4). The Red Shield had been adopted as the distinctive emblem of the Israeli national society, known as the Magen David Adom (MDA) in 1930;[95] however the MDA was not recognised as a national society by the ICRC nor admitted as a member of the International Federation of Red Cross and Red Crescent Societies.[96] At the Geneva Conference, the Israeli delegate argued for the addition of the Red Shield as a distinctive emblem, noting its use by the Israeli armed forces medical services during the recent Palestine conflict. It was argued that, if the Geneva

Figure 5.4 The Red Shield of David

[92] ICRC, "Adoption of the Red Crescent by the Islamic Republic of Iran" (1980) 219 IRRC 316 at 316–17. See also Bugnion, *Red Cross, Red Crescent, Red Crystal,* pp. 16–17.

[93] ICRC, "Adoption of the Red Crescent by the Islamic Republic of Iran", 316–17.

[94] Protocol (III) additional to the Geneva Conventions of 12 August 1949, and relating to the Adoption of an Additional Distinctive Emblem, Geneva, 8 December 2005, in force 14 July 2007, 2404 UNTS 261 ("AP III"), art. 2 "recognizes an additional distinctive emblem in addition to, and for the same purposes as, the distinctive emblems of the Geneva Conventions" – the Red Lion and Sun is not removed from the schema of distinctive emblems with AP III. See below on the Red Crystal.

[95] See the Israeli National Society website at www.mdais.org; for a comprehensive analysis of the origins and development of the Red Shield of David, see Shabtai Rosenne, "The Red Cross, Red Crescent, Red Lion and Sun, and the Red Shield of David" (1975) 5 IYBHR 9.

[96] The Statutes of the Movement of National Societies require that a National Society must use the name and emblem of either the Red Cross or Red Crescent, in conformity with the Geneva Conventions. See art. 4, "Statutes of the International Red Cross and Red Crescent Movement, adopted by the 25th International Conference of the Red Cross, Geneva, October 1986" (1987) 256 IRRC 25, and art. 6 of the Constitution of the International Federation of Red Cross and Red Crescent Societies of 26 November 1987, www.ifrc.org/Global/Governance/Statutory/120500-statutory-texts-en.pdf. The Movement of National Societies is comprised of the recognised National Red Cross and Red Crescent Societies, the International Federation of Red Cross and Red Crescent Societies, and the ICRC.

Conventions recognised the Red Crescent, surely the Red Shield should be likewise recognised.[97]

The proposal came up against significant resistance. Part of the resistance was due to anti-Israeli sentiment, motivated in part by contemporary Israeli foreign policy.[98] However, significant resistance crystallised around the argument forwarded by ICRC President Paul Ruegger regarding the proliferation of protective emblems.[99] As noted by Bugnion:

> The number of votes against the Israeli draft amendment far exceeded the number of States in conflict with Israel. It therefore seemed that the determining factor was fear of opening the way to a constant increase in the number of protective emblems, at a time when cracks were appearing in the colonial empires and a large number of countries were on the brink of achieving independence.[100]

The idea of adopting the Red Shield was thus rejected in Geneva in 1949; Israel signed then ratified the Conventions subject to its reservation that, while it would respect the inviolability of the distinctive emblems in the Conventions, it would continue to use the Red Shield as its own distinctive emblem.[101]

The possibility of a Jewish distinctive emblem was raised again in 1977, during the Diplomatic Conferences that adopted the Additional Protocols.[102] The proposal was again unsuccessful – although this time, the Israeli delegation withdrew the proposal before it could go to a vote.[103]

The proliferation of distinctive emblems, and the calls for additional emblems to be recognised, were the driving force behind a suggestion, first put forward at Geneva in 1949, that a single "neutral" emblem be adopted, in place of the Red Cross and Red Crescent.[104] While the proposal was rejected out of hand at the 1949 conference, the idea of a "neutral" emblem (i.e., an emblem with no overt or perceived religious connotation) retained its currency, and would culminate in the adoption of the Red Crystal in 2005.

d. The Red Crystal

The renewed campaign for an additional distinctive emblem came in 1992, when ICRC president Cornelio Sommaruga stated:

---

[97] Final Record 1949, vol. II-B, p. 534.
[98] At the time, Israel had recently been, or was still engaged in, armed conflict with its neighbours Iraq, Egypt, Syria, Jordan and Lebanon.
[99] See Final Record 1949, vol. II-B, p. 223.   [100] Bugnion, *Red Cross, Red Crescent, Red Crystal,* p. 15.
[101] Final Record 1949, vol. I, p. 348.   [102] Official Records, vol. III, p. 14.   [103] Ibid., vol. IX, pp. 462–7
[104] As informally proposed by the Netherlands at the Geneva Conference in 1949; see Final Record 1949 vol. II-A, p. 89. The proposal by the Netherlands was that the new emblem – an inverted red triangle on a white background – would replace the Red Cross, Red Crescent and Red Lion and Sun and serve as the only protective distinctive emblem. For more on the debate during the Conference, see ibid., pp. 89–92.

Figure 5.5 The Red Crystal

we cannot ignore the historical events which led to the choice of the red cross as the protective emblem and then to the admission of the red crescent . . . the coexistence of the two emblems has had the effect of accentuating their religious connotations in public opinion, for there can be no doubt that this identification with a religious group has to some extent affected the victims of conflicts in which each of the adversaries uses a different emblem. . . . if the emblem loses its neutrality, there is a great danger of its becoming a target.[105]

Sommaruga acknowledged that the existing emblems could not be done away with, nor could there be a return to the Red Cross as the sole distinctive emblem. Instead, he argued for the creation of a "graphically simple" emblem, "devoid of any religious, political, ethnic or other connotation".[106] To that end, a working group comprising governments, national societies, the ICRC, the International Federation, and other interested stakeholders, met over the course of several years with the aim of devising a new additional distinctive emblem; these meetings culminated in 2000 with the creation of the Red Crystal (see Figure 5.5). The new emblem was finally taken to a diplomatic conference in 2005,[107] where the Third Protocol Additional to the Geneva Conventions of 12 August 1949, and relating to the Adoption of an Additional Distinctive Emblem was adopted.[108]

The Red Crystal was designed so as to allow States and national societies to include their own indicative emblem within the Crystal emblem itself.

e. Substance of the international law on the distinctive emblems

These emblems, designed to serve as identifiers of persons, objects or installations serving relief purposes, are symbols that are protected under the Geneva Conventions from being misused.[109] All parties to the Conventions – every State in the world as of December 2014[110] – must implement domestic legislation that prohibits the emblem from being used outside the strict confines set by the Conventions. There are two

---

[105] Cornelio Sommaruga, "Unity and Plurality of the Emblems" (1992) 289 IRRC 333 at 334–5.

[106] Ibid., p. 337.

[107] For an overview of the process leading up to the adoption of the Red Crystal, see further Gerrit Jan Pulles, "Crystallising an Emblem: On the Adoption of the Third Additional Protocol to the Geneva Conventions" (2005) 8 YBIHL 296.

[108] AP III.   [109] GC I, art. 38; GC II, art. 41, AP I, art. 8(1); AP II, art. 12, and AP III, art. 2(2).

[110] Following the accession of Palestine, the total number of parties to the Conventions now stands at 196.

kinds of permissible use of the emblems. The first, and primary, purpose for the emblems is known as "protective" usage[111] – where the symbol is used during times of armed conflict to denote the protection granted to medical personnel and medical objects under the Conventions and Protocols. The emblem is to be used, in its protective capacity, on flags, armlets and on all equipment employed by the medical service;[112] personnel who wear the armlet must also carry a special identity card bearing the distinctive emblem.[113]

Hospitals and hospital ships must be marked with the emblem;[114] civilian hospitals and staff in occupied territories are also permitted to use the emblem[115] as are convoys of vehicles, trains or aircraft being used to transport wounded and sick civilians.[116] States parties to the Conventions are obliged to enact domestic legislation regulating the use of the emblem and to repress any misuse of the emblem in peacetime;[117] misuse of the emblem during times of armed conflict may, in some circumstances, amount to a war crime.[118]

The other form of permitted usage is known as "indicative" use[119] – the means by which the distinctive emblems may be used for certain purposes in peacetime, such as blood donation drives, fundraising, civil emergency and disaster relief. These activities are usually undertaken by domestic Red Cross and Red Crescent societies and do not denote the kinds of protections envisaged by the Conventions and Protocols. Any misuse of the emblem beyond these strict rules – say, for instance, the use of a red cross to advertise a pharmacy or doctor's office – is liable to criminal sanction.[120] It is often the case however, that misuse of the emblem, negligent or intentional, goes without sanction. For example, in Australia, while misuse of the emblem is a "strict liability offence" occasioning a fine of AU $1,000, there have been, to date, no prosecutions of persons misusing the emblem. Businesses found to be misusing the emblem, such as doctors' surgeries or pharmacies, are contacted by the Australian Red Cross and asked to replace the red cross with a green or blue cross, or requested to remove the signage altogether.[121]

7. CONCLUSION

Protecting the wounded and sick in times of armed conflict was the foundational principle behind the creation of the ICRC, and the eventual development of modern

---

[111] Sassòli et al., *How Does Law Protect in War?*, p. 203.   [112] E.g., GC II, art. 41.   [113] Ibid., art. 42.

[114] GC I, art. 42; GC II, art. 43.   [115] GC IV, arts. 18 and 20.   [116] Ibid., arts. 21 and 22.

[117] GC I, art. 54.   [118] AP I, arts. 37(1) and 85(30(f). See also Rome Statute, art. 8(2)(b)(vii).

[119] Sassòli, *et al.*, *How Does Law Protect in War?*, p. 203.

[120] E.g., in Australia, under s. 15 of the Geneva Conventions Act 1957 (Cth), use of any of the protected emblems "without the consent in writing of the Minister or of a person authorized in writing by the Minister" is a strict liability offence occasioning a fine of AU $1000.

[121] For an example of the Australian work regarding misuse of the emblem, see Australian Red Cross, *Guide to Emblem Use*, www.redcross.org.au/guide-to-emblem-use.aspx.

IHL. The provisions contained in the treaties ensure the utmost respect and care for one of the most vulnerable categories of persons in armed conflict – those rendered *hors de combat*, and those who care for the *hors de combat*. The next chapter of this book examines another distinct category of persons in need of protection from the deleterious effects of the armed conflict – civilians.

SUGGESTED READING

Bugnion, François, *Red Cross, Red Crescent, Red Crystal* (Geneva: ICRC, 2007).

Solf, Waldemar, "Development of the Protection of the Wounded, Sick and Shipwrecked under the Protocols Additional to the 1949 Geneva Conventions" in Christophe Swinarski (ed.), *Studies and Essays on International Humanitarian Law and Red Cross Principles in Honour of Jean Pictet* (Geneva: ICRC, 1984).

Toebes, Birgit, "Doctors in Arms: Exploring the Legal and Ethical Position of Military Medical Personnel in Armed Conflicts", in Mariëlle Matthee, Brigit Toebes, and Marcel Brus (eds.), *Armed Conflict and International Law: In search of the Human Face: Liber Amicorum in Memory of Avril McDonald,* (The Hague: TMC Asser, 2013).

DISCUSSION QUESTIONS

1. Why is it important to protect the emblem from misuse, even in times of peace?

2. On 12 July 2007, during the Iraq War, two United States Apache helicopter crews engaged in a series of air strikes against a number of people on the ground in the neighbourhood of Al-Amin al-Thaniyah in Baghdad. Some of the men on the ground were armed with rocket-propelled grenades (RPGs). Also in the group were two Reuters journalists – Saeed Chmagh and Namir Noor-Eldeen – who were carrying their cameras and other equipment. The Apache crews mistook the journalists for armed insurgents, and misidentified their cameras as RPGs; when Noor-Eldeen crouched to take a photo, the Apache crew believed he was preparing to "fire the RPG". The Apaches opened fire on the group – eight men were killed during the first strike, including Noor-Eldeen. When a wounded Chmagh and two other unarmed men came to the aid of the wounded and dead, and attempted to move them to a van, the Apaches fired on the van, killing the three men and wounding two children inside the van.[122]

---

[122] For a complete detailing of the incident, see the *Investigation Into Civilian Casualties Resulting From An Engagement On 12 July 2007 In The New Baghdad District Of Baghdad, Iraq,* undertaken by US Department of Defense, www2.centcom.mil/sites/foia/rr/CENTCOM%20Regulation%20CCR%2025210/ Death%20of%20Reuters%20Journalists/6–2nd%20Brigade%20Combat%20Team%2015–6%20Investiga tion.pdf.

Information about this attack was revealed by the website Wikileaks in 2010.[123] Discuss this example, drawing on the relevant rules of the law of armed conflict relating to targeting and protected objects. Did the US troops commit a war crime in firing on the wounded and those who came to their aid? Or was this an example of honest mistaken belief?

3. Should the Red Shield of David have been accepted as an internationally recognised emblem, along with the Red Cross and Red Crescent, instead of the Red Crystal?

5. If an insurgent is *hors de combat*, or feigns death, only to attack an enemy soldier, would the soldier be committing a war crime if they shot the insurgent? Would it be a violation of the laws of armed conflict if a unilateral policy of "double-tapping" (pre-emptively "shooting wounded or apparently dead enemy fighters to ensure that they are dead and not feigning death"[124]) were implemented by a party to the conflict?

---

[123] See Wikileaks, *Collateral Murder*, wikileaks.org/wiki/Collateral_Murder,_5_Apr_2010.

[124] Blank and Noone, *International Law and Armed Conflict,* p. 250.

6 The law of occupation and the protection of civilians

1. INTRODUCTION

The law of armed conflict contains many measures that are designed to protect the civilian population – found in the general provisions on distinction, proportionality and discrimination,[1] but also in more specific rules on targeting, such as the prohibitions on targeting civilian objects[2] or objects indispensable to the survival of the civilian population.[3] These rules can be categorised as "rules providing protection of the civilian population against the direct effects of military operations and other acts of hostility".[4]

However, there is an additional body of rules in the Conventions that aim to protect civilians from other effects of the armed conflict, and specifically those who find themselves in the hands of an adverse party to the conflict. This is most commonly seen in situations of belligerent occupation, where the rules are designed to protect civilians from arbitrary treatment or any acts of violence perpetrated against them by the Occupying Power (OP). This chapter will examine the rules on belligerent occupation in international armed conflicts, as well as some of the general rules that exist to protect civilians from arbitrary treatment when they find themselves in the hands of an adverse party.

2. GENERAL PROTECTIONS FOR CIVILIANS

Geneva Convention IV and Additional Protocol I contain general rules for the protection of all civilian inhabitants of any territory. The ICTY in *Tadić* described

---

[1] See generally Chapter 2 on fundamental principles.   [2] AP I, art. 52.
[3] AP I, art. 54. For more on these rules, see Chapter 7 on targeting.
[4] Hans-Peter Gasser and Knut Dörmann, "Protection of the Civilian Population" in Dieter Fleck (ed.), *The Handbook of Humanitarian Law in Armed Conflicts*, 3rd edn (Oxford University Press, 2013), p. 231.

GC IV as intending to protect "civilians (in enemy territory, occupied territory or the combat zone) who do not have the nationality of the belligerent in whose hands they find themselves, or who are stateless persons".[5] As outlined in Article 51(2) of Protocol I, the fundamental rule relating to civilians is that they are immune from attack. No definition of the term "civilian" exists in either the Hague Regulations or Geneva Conventions, but is contained in Article 50 of Protocol I which defines civilians thus:

1. A civilian is any person who does not belong to one of the categories of persons referred to in Article 4A(1), (2), (3) and (6) of the Third Convention and in Article 43 of this Protocol. In case of doubt whether a person is a civilian, that person shall be considered to be a civilian.
2. The civilian population comprises all persons who are civilians.
3. The presence within the civilian population of individuals who do not come within the definition of civilians does not deprive the population of its civilian character.[6]

Civilians are defined in contrast to combatants – any person who does not qualify as a combatant is considered a civilian. Furthermore, Article 50(1) makes it clear that where there is any doubt as to whether a person is a civilian, the presumption is in favour of civilian status. Civilians enjoy their immunity both individually and collectively, as part of the civilian population; as such, the presence within the civilian population of combatants or other persons taking direct part in hostilities does not deprive the civilians within that population of their immunity from attack. This was affirmed by the ICTY in the *Blaškić* case.[7]

Beyond immunity from direct attack, civilians are also protected from the effects of the hostilities in a number of ways. In Geneva Convention IV, these are found in Articles 13–26, which detail rules on the establishment of hospital and safety zones;[8] rules on protecting the wounded and sick,[9] and those evacuating from besieged or encircled areas;[10] rules on protecting hospitals[11] and hospital staff,[12] as well as any land[13] and air[14] transport used for the removal of the wounded and sick civilians, the infirm and maternity cases, and for the transport of medical personnel and equipment. Consignments of medical supplies, food and clothing are also to be permitted through occupied territory.[15] Families[16] and children[17] are accorded special protection, to ensure that children under the age of fifteen orphaned or separated from their families as a result of the conflict are not to be "left to their own resources";[18] parties to the conflict are to help facilitate family

---

[5] *Prosecutor* v. *Dusko Tadić* , IT-94-1-A, Appeals Judgment, 15 July 1999, ("*Tadić Appeal Judgment*"), 164.
[6] AP I, art. 50.   [7] *Prosecutor* v. *Blaškić*, Case No. IT-95–14-A, Appeals Judgment, 29 July 2004, para 113.
[8] GC IV, art. 14.   [9] Ibid., art. 16.   [10] Ibid., art. 17.   [11] Ibid., art. 19.   [12] Ibid., art. 20.
[13] Ibid., art. 21.   [14] Ibid., art. 22.   [15] Ibid., art. 23.   [16] Ibid., arts. 25–6.   [17] Ibid., art. 24.
[18] Ibid.

reunions[19] and the transmission of family news[20] amongst those dispersed or separated from their family as a result of the conflict.

In addition to these rules, supplemental protection is found in Article 75 of Protocol I, which is designed to protect all persons who "are in the power of a Party to the conflict and who do not benefit from more favourable treatment under the Conventions or under this Protocol". Article 75 outlines a wide range of protections such as humane treatment, non-discrimination, respect for one's "person, honour, convictions and religious practices", protection from acts of "violence to … life, health, or physical or mental well-being" including prohibitions on murder, torture, corporal punishment, mutilation, outrages upon personal dignity, in particular humiliating and degrading treatment, enforced prostitution and any form of indecent assault, hostage-taking and collective punishment.[21]

Article 75 also contains comprehensive fair trial and due process protections for any person arrested, detained or interned in relation to the armed conflict, including the right to be informed of the reasons for the arrest or detention, the right to a fair trial, upholding the principles of individual (rather than collective) criminal responsibility and *nullum crimen sine lege*,[22] and respecting fundamental due process rights including the right to be informed of the charges, the presumption of innocence, protections against self-incrimination, the rule on double jeopardy and rights of appeal against judgment and sentence.[23] Article 75 also contains provisions for the special protection of women whose liberty has been restricted.[24] Article 75 thus acts as a comprehensive outline of the fundamental provisions of the Conventions and Protocols in their entirety, ensuring that any person who may not be able to avail themselves of the special protections of Conventions I, II or III will still be covered by thorough protections relating to rights to due process and fair trial, as well as protection from, among other things, acts of violence, murder, torture and mutilation.

In addition to these general civilian protections contained in GC IV and Protocol I, GC IV provides a régime of additional protection for certain categories of civilians who warrant special treatment, known as "protected persons". Protected persons are discussed in more detail in this next section on belligerent occupation.

3. THE HISTORICAL DEVELOPMENT AND PHILOSOPHICAL UNDERPINNINGS OF THE MODERN LAW OF OCCUPATION

Traditionally, invasion and belligerent occupation of foreign territory during wartime was a precursor to annexation. An adverse party would invade a country,

---

[19] Ibid., art. 26.   [20] Ibid., art. 25.   [21] AP I, art. 75(2).

[22] "No crime without a law" – the principle that no person can be charged with a crime that did not exist in law at the time the alleged offence was committed.

[23] Ibid., art.75(4).   [24] Ibid., art.75(5).

annex it and claim the territory and its population as its own.[25] German inter-national lawyer Georg Friedrich von Martens,[26] writing in 1789, stated that in situations of occupation "the enemy is not obliged to conserve the constitution of the conquered country. Nor is it obliged to leave to that country the rights and privileges that its Sovereign has accorded".[27] However, by the time of the Congress of Vienna (1814–15), the notion began to emerge that in situations of occupation a "conservationist"[28] approach should be taken: that "occupation was merely the form of temporary control that suspended the exercise of sovereign rights of the occupied state, without bringing about the transfer of sovereignty as such."[29] This was reflected in the writings of the time,[30] and was eventually incorporated in the Lieber Code[31] and the Oxford Manual,[32] finding ultimate expression in the Hague Regulations of 1899 and 1907.[33]

The Hague Regulations provided some general rules on occupation, outlining in Article 43 the "conservationist" principle of the modern law of occupation: "[t]he authority of the legitimate power having in fact passed into the hands of the occupant, the latter shall take all the measures in his power to restore, and ensure, as far as possible, public order and safety, while respecting, unless absolutely prevented, the laws in force in the country."

Articles 43–56 of the Hague Regulations also provided some general rules regarding the administration of occupied territory, including specific rules for the protection of civilians in occupied territory, by prohibiting pillage[34] and collective punishments,[35] protecting civilians from forced conscription into the armies of the adverse power or OP,[36] and obliging parties to the Regulations to respect "family honour and rights, the lives of persons, and private property, as well as religious convictions and practice".[37]

However, the atrocities committed against civilians in occupied territory during the Second World War highlighted the shortcomings of the Hague Regulations in this respect. There were widespread abuses perpetrated against civilian populations in occupied Europe, including deportation, internment, forced labour and extermin-ation.[38] The Axis powers and the USSR all "engaged in a practice of occupation that

---

[25] Leslie Green, *The Contemporary Law of Armed Conflict*, 3rd edn (Manchester University Press, 2008), p. 284.

[26] As mentioned in Chapter 1, von Martens is to be distinguished from the Russian international lawyer, Fyodor Fyodorovich Martens, author of the Martens clause.

[27] Von Martens, *Précis du droit des gens modernes de l'Europe* (1789), translated by and cited in Yutaka Arai-Takahashi, "Preoccupied with Occupation: Critical Examinations of the Historical Development of the Law of Occupation" (2012) 94 IRRC 51, 57.

[28] Ibid., 56.   [29] Ibid., 57.

[30] August Wilhelm Heffter, *Das Europäische Völkerrecht der Gegenwart* (Berlin: Schroeder, 1844).

[31] In art. 37; see also art. 3.

[32] Oxford Manual, art. 6 – note however that the Oxford Manual does not preclude the possibility that at the end of hostilities, the territory under occupation may well be ceded to the occupying State.

[33] Hague II 1899 and Hague IV 1907, art. 43.   [34] Hague IV 1907, art. 47.   [35] Ibid., art. 50.

[36] Ibid., art. 44.   [37] Ibid., art. 46.

[38] For a general overview of the devastating effects that occupation had on Europe during the Second World War, see Mark Mazower, *Hitler's Empire: Nazi Rule in Occupied Europe* (London: Allen Lane, 2008);

completely disregarded and rejected the fundamental tenets of the law of occupation".[39] Additionally, civilians not in occupied territory, but nonetheless in the hands of an adverse power, were also subject to persecution: it was common practice in Allied States like the US, UK and Australia to intern so-called "enemy aliens" – persons who were residents (some were even nationals) of Allied states but who might also have been of German, Italian or Japanese heritage or nationality. The justification for internment was that of "national security". For example, in Australia, Australian authorities interned over twelve thousand people during the course of the Second World War, including 1,500 who were naturalised British citizens.[40] The internment of these people was explained as "a precautionary measure to prevent residents from assisting the enemy, to appease public opinion, and to accommodate people interned overseas and brought to Australia for the duration of the war."[41] Similar internment policies existed in the United States in relation to Japanese nationals and those of Japanese ancestry.[42]

It was these acts that contributed to the adoption of Geneva Convention IV Relative to the Protection of Civilian Persons in Time of War, also known as the Civilians Convention, which introduced comprehensive rules outlining the permissible acts of an OP, and rules for protecting civilians in occupied territory or otherwise in the hands of an adverse power. These protections were expanded with the adoption of Protocol I in 1977. In conjunction with the prohibition on the use of force in the UN Charter, the modern law of occupation enshrines the fundamental principle that occupation is a temporary state of affairs, and entails no licence to use force to alter the sovereignty of territory under occupation.[43]

4. BEGINNING OF OCCUPATION

Article 42 of the Hague Regulations states that "territory is considered occupied when it is actually placed under the authority of the hostile army";[44] however, "occupation extends only to the territory where such authority has been established

William Hitchcock, *The Bitter Road to Freedom: The Human Cost of Allied Victory in World War II Europe* (New York: Free Press, 2008); Martin Gilbert, *The Holocaust: A History of the Jews of Europe during the Second World War* (New York: Henry Holt, 1985).

[39] Arai-Takahashi, "Preoccupied with Occupation", 64; see also Eyal Benvenisti, *The International Law of Occupation*, 2nd edn (Princeton University Press, 2004), pp. 60–72.

[40] Klaus Neumann, *In the Interest of National Security: Civilian Internment in Australia During World War II* (Canberra: National Archives of Australia, 2006), p. 7.

[41] Ibid. The legal basis for the Australian internment policy was the National Security Act 1939, which empowered the authorities to intern residents and impose restrictions on employment, travel, residential location and possessions – for instance, enemy aliens were often prohibited from owning guns, cars, radios or cameras.

[42] See generally Brian Masaru Hayashi, *Democratizing the Enemy: the Japanese American Internment* (Princeton University Press, 2004).

[43] GC IV, art. 47.   [44] Hague IV 1907, art. 42(1).

and can be exercised".[45] Active hostilities are not required for the law on belligerent occupation to come into effect – Common Article 2 to the Geneva Conventions makes it clear that the Conventions "apply to all cases of partial or total occupation of the territory of a High Contracting Party, even if the said occupation meets with no armed resistance".[46] Determining the commencement of occupation has been examined by international courts, most notably in the ICJ decision on *Armed Activities on the Territory of the Congo*, where it was held that Uganda was the occupying power in parts of the Democratic Republic of the Congo (DRC) as it had "established and exercised authority in Ituri [a region in north-eastern DRC] as an occupying power".[47]

a. Protected persons

In situations of occupation, certain categories of person are specially protected under the Conventions – these are known as "protected persons", who are defined in GC IV as "those who, at a given moment and in any manner whatsoever, find themselves, in case of a conflict or occupation, in the hands of a Party to the conflict or Occupying Power of which they are not nationals."[48]

Why do these civilians warrant special protections above those outlined in Articles 13–26? The idea behind these special civilian protections is that persons who find themselves in the hands of a belligerent or enemy occupation force are particularly vulnerable, as they are under the control of "the enemy"; thus such persons should be additionally protected under international law. As Kolb and Hyde note, GC IV applies to so-called "enemy civilians" "because they are thought to be in need of protection on account of their adverse allegiance, and due to the fact that they cannot be protected by the normal mechanism of diplomatic representation as these ties are severed on account of the situation of armed conflict between the belligerents".[49]

However, Article 4 raises a number of issues – first, what does it mean to be "in the hands of a party to the conflict" for the purposes of claiming "protected person" status and, second, how is "nationality" defined under the law of armed conflict? The question of the scope of the concept of "in the hands of a party" was addressed by the ICTY in *Rajić*, where the Court stated that "in the hands of a party" should not be limited to having actual physical control over the person in question but should be understood in a more general sense. The Court stated that "the protected person

---

[45] Ibid., art. 42(2).   [46] Common Article 2 to the Four Geneva Conventions.

[47] *Armed Activities on the Territory of the Congo (Democratic Republic of the Congo v. Uganda)*, Judgment ICJ Rep. 2005, p. 116, para. 176.

[48] GC IV, art. 4.

[49] Robert Kolb and Richard Hyde, *An Introduction to the International Law of Armed Conflicts* (Oxford: Hart, 2008), p. 222.

requirement should be interpreted to provide broad coverage ... the expression 'in the hands of' is used in an extremely general sense".[50] In making this determination, the Court cited the ICRC *GC IV Commentary*, which states that, "it is not merely a question of being in enemy hands directly, as a prisoner is ... the expression 'in the hands of' need not necessarily be understood in the physical sense; it simply means that the person is in territory under the control of the Power in question".[51] As such, "in the hands of" should be given a broad interpretation, to include anyone under the effective power and control of an authority.

With regards to nationality, the situation is more complex. What happens if one finds oneself in the hands of "the enemy", but that enemy happens to also share your nationality? This is best illustrated with examples from the Second World War. Prior to and in the early stages of the war, some German Jews fled Germany and relocated to France; however, upon invasion of the Nazis in 1940, these German Jews found themselves in the hands of people they considered the enemy, but who held the same nationality as they did. Under a strict reading of the law of occupation, no special protection would extend to such refugees.

However, as was outlined in the *Tadić* judgement, the law of occupation takes a more nuanced approach:

the Convention intends to protect civilians (in enemy territory, occupied territory or the combat zone) who do not have the nationality of the belligerent in whose hands they find themselves, or who are stateless persons. In addition, as is apparent from the preparatory work ... the Convention also intends to protect those civilians in occupied territory who, while having the nationality of the Party to the conflict in whose hands they find themselves, are refugees and thus no longer owe allegiance to this Party and no longer enjoy its diplomatic protection ... Thus already in 1949 the legal bond of nationality was not regarded as crucial and allowance was made for special cases. In the aforementioned case of refugees, the lack of both allegiance to a State and diplomatic protection by this State was regarded as more important than the formal link of nationality.[52]

The position has therefore developed to look at "substantial relations more than ... formal bonds"[53] and factors additional to nationality, such as ethnicity, may become the substantive grounds for protection under GC IV. Indeed, as noted in *Tadić*:

[in] present-day international armed conflicts ... new States are often created during the conflict and ethnicity rather than nationality may become the grounds for allegiance. Or, put another way, ethnicity may become determinative of national allegiance. Under these

---

[50] *Prosecutor* v. *Rajić*, IT-95-12-S, Review of the Indictment Pursuant to Rule 61 of the Rules of Procedure and Evidence, 13 September 1996, p. 36.

[51] GC IV Commentary, p. 47.

[52] *Prosecutor* v. *Dusko Tadić*, Judgment, IT-94-1-T, 7 May 2997, ("*Tadić Trial Judgment*"), 164–5.

[53] Ibid., 166.

conditions, the requirement of nationality is even less adequate to define protected persons. In such conflicts, not only the text and the drafting history of the Convention but also, and more importantly, the Convention's object and purpose suggest that allegiance to a Party to the conflict and, correspondingly, control by this Party over persons in a given territory, may be regarded as the crucial test.[54]

The determination of nationality is important because a number of other categories of persons are excluded from the protections of GC IV. These include anyone already protected by Geneva Conventions I–III,[55] as they already have extensive protections enshrined in those instruments. Certain nationals of other States are also excluded from the ambit of GC IV:

Nationals of a State which is not bound by the Convention are not protected by it. Nationals of a neutral State, who find themselves in the territory of a belligerent State, and nationals of a co-belligerent State, shall not be regarded as protected persons while the State of which they are nationals has normal diplomatic representation in the State in whose hands they are.[56]

Thus, nationals of a State not involved in the conflict, or who have the nationality of the belligerent or co-belligerent State when the State in question comes under occupation, are not specifically protected by GC IV. This is because it is understood that normal diplomatic relations still exist between neutral and co-belligerent States and the OP, and that the individual's own State will therefore be able to protect them; thus, there will be no need to ensure special protections for the nationals of such States.[57]

b. Administration of occupied territory

Once territory is deemed occupied, the OP is under an obligation to "take all the measures in his power to restore and ensure, as far as possible, public order and safety, while respecting, unless absolutely prevented, the laws in force in the country".[58] This is supplemented by the obligation under Article 64 of GC IV, which provides that:

The penal laws of the occupied territory shall remain in force, with the exception that they may be repealed or suspended by the Occupying Power in cases where they constitute a threat to its security or an obstacle to the application of the present Convention.

Subject to the latter consideration and to the necessity for ensuring the effective administration of justice, the tribunals of the occupied territory shall continue to function in respect of all offences covered by the said laws.

---

[54] Ibid.   [55] Ibid.   [56] Ibid.   [57] Gasser and Dörmann, "Protection of the Civilian Population", p. 266.
[58] Hague IV 1907, art. 43.

The Occupying Power may, however, subject the population of the occupied territory to provisions which are essential to enable the Occupying Power to fulfil its obligations under the present Convention, to maintain the orderly government of the territory, and to ensure the security of the Occupying Power, of the members and property of the occupying forces or administration, and likewise of the establishments and lines of communication used by them.

While Article 64 only explicitly mentions the criminal law of the occupied territory, the GC IV Commentary[59] makes it clear that "the entire legal system of the occupied territories is actually meant by this rule".[60] Thus, the OP must observe the law in place in the occupied territory, and not alter the law except in two situations: where the application of the national law would directly prejudice the security of the OP, and where provisions of the national law would hinder the OP's application of IHL. While the OP may establish its own administrative bodies if needed in order to maintain public order or if military necessity so requires, the OP may not alter the status of judges or public officials, or apply any sanctions of measures of coercion or discrimination against them, if such officials chose to abstain from performing their role on grounds of conscience.[61]

The OP may collect taxes, tariffs and any other dues, for the purpose of defraying the costs of the administration of the occupied territory.[62] The OP is also permitted to take movable government property which may be used for military purposes,[63] such as modes of transport, weapons and medical and food supplies. However, food and medical supplies may only be taken for military purposes *after* the needs of the civilian population are met.[64] Civilian hospitals may only be requisitioned temporarily, and only in cases of urgent necessity.[65] Movable private property and immovable government property may only be requisitioned and not confiscated;[66] title to such property does not pass to the OP, and any items seized or real estate used is to be restored to the original owners.[67] For example, during the Iraq occupation in 2003, both the occupying authority and the UN Security Council agreed that any Iraqi oil collected during the occupation would only be used for the benefit of the Iraqi people.[68]

Any real or personal property belonging individually or collectively to private persons may not be destroyed, except where such destruction is rendered absolutely necessary due to military operations.[69] However, it is forbidden to requisition, destroy or damage cultural property.[70]

---

[59] GC IV Commentary, p. 335.   [60] Gasser and Dörmann, "Protection of the Civilian Population", p. 284.
[61] GC IV, art. 54.   [62] Hague IV 1907, art. 48.   [63] Ibid., art. 53(1).   [64] GC IV, art. 55; AP I, art. 69.
[65] GC IV, art. 57.   [66] Hague IV 1907, arts. 53 and 55.   [67] Ibid., art. 46.
[68] Letter addressed to the Security Council from the Permanent Representatives to the UN of the UK and USA, May 2003, UN Doc. S/2003/538, see also UN Security Council, S/RES/1483, 22 May 2003, para. 20.
[69] GC IV, art. 53.
[70] Hague IV 1907, art. 56, and Convention for the Protection of Cultural Property in the Event of Armed Conflict, The Hague, 14 May 1954, in force 7 August 1956, 249 UNTS 240, arts. 4(3) and 5.

c. Rules on protected persons and persons deprived of their liberty

The remainder of the substantive rules in GC IV relate specifically to the protection of protected persons, and to protections for persons who may be detained for security reasons in relation to the occupation.

i. Protected persons

Part III of GC IV relates to the treatment of protected persons. Article 27 provides that

Protected persons are entitled, in all circumstances, to respect for their persons, their honour, their family rights, their religious convictions and practices, and their manners and customs. They shall at all times be humanely treated, and shall be protected especially against all acts of violence or threats thereof and against insults and public curiosity.

Women shall be especially protected against any attack on their honour, in particular against rape, enforced prostitution, or any form of indecent assault.

Without prejudice to the provisions relating to their state of health, age and sex, all protected persons shall be treated with the same consideration by the Party to the conflict in whose power they are, without any adverse distinction based, in particular, on race, religion or political opinion.

However, the Parties to the conflict may take such measures of control and security in regard to protected persons as may be necessary as a result of the war.

Reprisals against civilians and their property are prohibited,[71] as is pillage,[72] collective penalties,[73] any measures of intimidation or terrorism[74] and the taking of hostages.[75] It is the responsibility of the OP to retain and forward any information it possesses regarding protected persons in its power[76] to a National Information Bureau (NIB), which is to be established at the beginning of hostilities and in all cases of belligerent occupation.[77] The NIB is to cooperate with the Central Tracing Agency of the ICRC.[78] Protected persons are entitled to receive religious and spiritual assistance,[79] as well as individual[80] and collective relief.[81]

Convention IV also provides for the protection of civilians in the form of the "Protecting Power". Article 9 of GC IV states that the Convention "shall be applied with the cooperation and under the scrutiny of the Protecting Powers whose duty it is to safeguard the interests of the Parties to the conflict."[82] The Protecting Power is a Third State, neutral in the context of the conflict, tasked with ensuring that IHL is respected and implemented by the parties to the conflict.[83] The Protecting Power is

---

[71] GC IV, art. 33; AP I, arts. 20 and 51(6).   [72] GC IV, art. 33.   [73] Ibid.   [74] Ibid.   [75] Ibid., art. 34.
[76] Ibid., art. 136.   [77] Ibid., arts. 136–41.   [78] Ibid., art. 140.   [79] Ibid., art. 58.   [80] Ibid., art. 62.
[81] Ibid., art. 59. See also arts. 60–3.   [82] Ibid., art. 9. See also AP I, art. 5.
[83] The full extent of the role of the Protecting Power is dealt with in more detail in Chapter 9.

referred to frequently in the Conventions and Protocol I,[84] regarding its tasks and responsibilities, including the right to inspect POW camps,[85] to assist in judicial proceedings[86] and to "render their good offices" to the parties to the conflict, in order to help resolve disputes.[87] The task of the Protecting Power is to serve as a diplomatic aid between the parties to the conflict, due to the fact that the normal diplomatic relations between the warring sides will have naturally, as a result of the conflict, broken down or been suspended.[88] The Protecting Power thus functions to protect the interests of all civilians who find themselves in the hands of an adverse party, either due to occupation or any other reason.

GC IV makes it clear that occupation in no way alters the legal status of the population of the occupied territory; no agreement between the authorities of the occupied territory and the OP can be undertaken to alter the legal status of the population.[89] Annexation of the whole or part of the territory occupied "is not recognised by international law. Such annexation would be invalid".[90] GC IV contains a number of rules to ensure that protected persons retain their rights under international law and protected persons are not able to renounce their rights under the Convention.[91] If, at the outbreak of hostilities, a protected person wishes to leave the territory of the adverse party in which they find themselves, they are entitled to do so, unless the State considers it contrary to national security interests to allow such a departure.[92] Refusal to leave may be challenged before an appropriate court or administrative board, and reasons for refusal are to be provided.[93]

Protected persons may seek gainful employment[94] and may only be compelled to work "to the same extent as nationals of the Party to the conflict in whose territory they are".[95] Protected persons of enemy nationality may only be compelled to do work normally necessary for ensuring basic civil functions – i.e., any civil society work not directly related to the conduct of military operations.[96] If put to work, all protected persons are entitled to the same benefits, working conditions and safeguards that national workers would enjoy in similar professions, including in relation to rates of pay, hours of labour, work clothes and equipment, as well as training and compensation for work-related tasks.[97] However, the OP may not compel protected persons to serve in its armed forces,[98] or otherwise take part in any military operations against their own country.[99] Any pressure or propaganda aimed at securing voluntary enlistment is prohibited.[100]

---

[84] See for instance, GC I, art. 8; GC III, art. 126; GC IV, art. 143; AP I, art. 5.   [85] GC IV, art. 143.
[86] Ibid., art. 74.   [87] Ibid., art. 12.
[88] See further Hans-Joachim Heintze, "Protecting Power", in the *Max Planck Encyclopaedia of Public International Law* (2009).
[89] GC IV, art. 47.   [90] Gasser and Dörmann, "Protection of the Civilian Population", p. 281.
[91] GC IV, art. 8; cf. GC IV, art. 47.   [92] Ibid., art. 35.   [93] Ibid.   [94] Ibid., art. 39.   [95] Ibid., art. 40.
[96] Ibid.   [97] Ibid. See also arts. 51 and 52.   [98] Ibid., art. 51.   [99] Hague IV 1907, art. 52.   [100] Ibid.

Individual or mass forcible transfers, as well as deportations of protected persons from occupied territory to the territory of the OP (or to that of another State) are prohibited.[101] While the OP is entitled to evacuate, in whole or in part, the population of a given area "if the security of the population or imperative military reasons so demand",[102] such evacuations must be temporary and persons thus evacuated must be returned to their homes as soon as hostilities in the area have ceased. Any persons subject to transfer or evacuation must be provided with sufficient accommodation and supplies, and the conditions of hygiene, safety, health and nutrition must be satisfactory.[103] Protected persons are not to be transferred to a Power which is not party to GC IV (except in cases of repatriation);[104] protected persons are not to be transferred to a country where he or she may have reason to fear persecution on the grounds of political or religious beliefs and opinions.[105] Furthermore, the OP is not to transfer or deport parts of its own civilian population into the territory it occupies – this has become a particularly contentious issue in the Israel–Palestine conflict, and will be discussed in more detail later in this chapter.

As noted above, Article 64 of GC IV provides that the penal laws of the occupied territory are to remain in force. In addition, the OP is obliged to observe additional rules regarding penal laws in occupied territory. If the OP needs to introduce laws (or repeal existing laws) to ensure the maintenance of security and order in the occupied territory, such changes must be publicised[106] and may not be retroactive.[107] Protected persons who commit an offence against the OP:

which does not constitute an attempt on the life or limb of members of the occupying forces or administration, nor a grave collective danger, nor seriously damage the property of the occupying forces or administration or the installations used by them, shall be liable to internment or simple imprisonment, provided the duration of such internment or imprisonment is proportionate to the offence committed. Furthermore, internment or imprisonment shall, for such offences, be the only measure adopted for depriving protected persons of liberty.[108]

No protected person may be prosecuted for offences committed prior to the territory having been occupied, unless the offence amounts to a breach of IHL.[109] If a protected person is brought to trial in occupied territory, they are entitled to a wide spectrum of fair trial rights including the right to be informed of the charges against them;[110] the right to present evidence in their defence, including the right to legal counsel and the right to call witnesses;[111] the right to an interpreter;[112] the right to appeal;[113] and the right to seek assistance from the Protecting Power.[114] Anyone subject to the death penalty is entitled to petition for pardon or reprieve.[115]

---

[101] GC IV, art. 49.   [102] Ibid.   [103] Ibid.   [104] Ibid., art. 45.   [105] Ibid.   [106] Ibid., art. 65.
[107] Ibid.   [108] Ibid., art. 68.   [109] Ibid., art. 70.   [110] Ibid., art. 71.   [111] Ibid., art. 72.   [112] Ibid.
[113] Ibid., art. 73.   [114] Ibid., art. 74.   [115] Ibid., art. 75.

ii. Persons deprived of their liberty

The OP is entitled to subject individual civilians to assigned residence or internment, if imperative security reasons exist.[116] As a general rule, except when in accordance with Articles 41–3, 68 and 78, protected persons are not to be interned.[117] Internment is a "drastic restriction of personal freedom"[118] and must not be implemented if less severe measures, such as assigned residence, or registration with the police, could instead be used.[119] Internment cannot be used as a form of punishment. As noted by the Israeli Supreme Court in *Salame* v. *IDF Commander of Judea and Samaria*, "administrative detention is designed to thwart a future danger to the security of the State or public safety. Administrative detention is not a punitive measure for what has happened in the past nor is it a substitute for criminal proceedings."[120]

What amounts to "imperative security reasons" is not defined in the Convention; however, the ICTY stated in *Delalić* that:

the mere fact that a person is a national of, or aligned with, an enemy party cannot be considered as threatening the security of the opposing party where he is living and is not, therefore a valid reason for interning him . . . to justify recourse to such measures, the party must have good reason to think that the person concerned, by his activities, knowledge or qualifications, represents a real threat to its present or future security.[121]

If a person is interned, there are considerable protections provided in GC IV. Internees retain their full civil rights[122] and their maintenance while interned is to be provided by the Detaining Power (DP).[123] Internees should be detained with persons of the same nationality, language and customs[124] and are to be housed in safe[125] and hygienic facilities,[126] providing protection from the climate, and adequate health facilities, such as showers, baths and laundry facilities,[127] food,[128] clothing,[129] and medical attention.[130] Internees must be able to access religious, intellectual and physical activities.[131] If put to work, they are to enjoy appropriate working standards with regards to wages and working conditions,[132] but are not to be put to work in conditions which are degrading, humiliating, or, if forced on protected persons not in internment, would constitute a breach of Articles 40 or 51 of GC IV.[133] Internees are entitled to retain personal property and monies;[134] any objects taken from them by the DP during internment must be registered and returned at the cessation of internment.[135]

---

[116] Ibid., art. 78; cf. arts. 41–3 re: internment of protected persons.   [117] Ibid., art. 79.

[118] Gasser and Dörmann, "Protection of the Civilian Population", p. 316.

[119] Ibid. See also Yoram Dinstein, *The International Law of Belligerent Occupation* (Cambridge University Press, 2009), pp. 172–6.

[120] *Salame et al.* v. *IDF Commander of Judea and Samaria et al.*, HCJ 5784/03, 57(6) PD 721, 33(1) 471, 726.

[121] *Prosecutor* v. *Delalić et al.*, IT-96-21-T, Judgment, 16 November 1998, para. 577.   [122] GC IV, art. 79.

[123] Ibid., art. 81.   [124] Ibid., art. 82.   [125] Ibid., arts. 83–4, 88.   [126] Ibid., art. 85.   [127] Ibid.

[128] Ibid., arts. 87 and 89.   [129] Ibid., art. 90.   [130] Ibid., arts. 91–2.   [131] Ibid., arts. 86, 93–4.

[132] Ibid., art. 95.   [133] Ibid.   [134] Ibid., art. 97.   [135] Ibid.

Any interment facility must be run under the authority of a responsible officer of the DP,[136] who is bound by rules regarding general discipline,[137] including affording the right of complaint and petition by internees.[138] To that end, internees are entitled to form committees to serve their interests.[139] Internees are also entitled to maintain relations with the exterior, including being able to correspond with relatives[140] and receive collective and individual relief shipments.[141]

If any internee is subject to penal or disciplinary sanctions, GC IV contains comprehensive rules on permissible punishments.[142] Any internee who faces judicial proceedings is entitled to the same judicial guarantees afforded to protected persons in Articles 71–6 of GC IV. Internees are to be released by the DP when the "reasons which necessitated his internment no longer exist".[143] Internees are entitled to challenge the grounds of their detention at its commencement, and then subsequently every six months.[144]

d. End of occupation

Belligerent occupation continues for as long as the OP continues to exercise effective control in an occupied territory. Article 6 of GC IV outlines that the Convention will cease to apply on the general close of military operations, but that in the case of occupied territory, the Convention will only cease operation one year after the general close of military operations, by which point the OP must have relinquished actual control to the original sovereign.

e. Problems regarding long-term occupation

What the long list of comprehensive protections outlined above is designed to achieve is the short-term administration of territory until the cessation of hostilities and the resumption of normal diplomatic relations between former adversaries. This is achieved through the numerous provisions that highlight the temporary nature of belligerent occupation, and the presumption that the current situation of occupation will eventually end. The rules on occupation make it clear that occupation is only ever considered a temporary state of affairs. As noted by President of the ICRC, Peter Maurer, IHL "does not allow military endeavours that aim to make permanent changes to occupied territory; to force people to leave their homes; or to unlawfully seize land and resources from communities."[145]

---

[136] Ibid., art. 99.   [137] Ibid., art. 100.   [138] Ibid., art. 101.   [139] Ibid., arts. 102–104.
[140] Ibid., art. 107.   [141] Ibid., arts. 108–10; cf arts. 111–16.   [142] Ibid., art. 117–26.
[143] Ibid., art. 132.   [144] Ibid., art. 78.
[145] Peter Maurer, "Challenges to International Humanitarian Law: Israel's Occupation Policy" (2012) 94 IRRC 1503 at1505.

So what happens when occupation is not a short-term event? How does the current law deal with occupiers who must, through necessity or legal obligation, alter the domestic law of the occupied territory? How is the law as it stands and the law as it is implemented to be reconciled, when occupation lasts years, even decades? In this instance, a case study of Israel's occupation of the West Bank and the Gaza Strip is instructive, as it highlights some of the problems that arise when occupation is protracted.

Israel has exercised "actual authority"[146] over the West Bank and Gaza Strip for nearly fifty years, following the Six Day War in 1967.[147] While the mechanics of the on-going Israel–Palestine conflict will not be explored in any detail in this chapter, it is useful to think about some of the problems raised by the protracted occupation of the Palestinian territories by the Israelis. Article 64 of GC IV provides that the OP must, as far as possible, respect the existing penal laws of the occupied territory; the GC IV Commentary makes it clear that this provision relates to *all* the laws in place in the territory.[148] What is the outcome when an OP establishes a quasi-judicial body to help settle labour disputes? This was at issue in the case *Christian Society for the Holy Places* v. *Minister for Defence.*[149] In this case, the petitioners were objecting to the establishment of an administrative body to settle labour disputes. Their argument was that Jordanian laws relating to the settlement of labour disputes had never been implemented, as the Jordanian government had established no such body prior to the occupation of the West Bank in 1967. In this case, the Court ruled against the petitioners, stating that the prolonged nature of the occupation warranted changing the laws in order to meet the changing needs of the situation.[150]

This case thus highlights one of the problems raised by protracted occupation: if, as the Geneva Convention states, no major changes to the legal order of the occupied territory are to be enacted, how then does an occupier deal with changing social norms and needs? As noted by Dinstein:

the Occupying Power . . . may regard it as a necessity to alter the laws in force in the occupied territory, in order to ensure the continuation of normal life under an "orderly government". . . [however] it goes without saying that any concern shown by the Occupying Power for the welfare of the population in the occupied territory is not above suspicion. Professed humanitarian motives of the Occupying Power may serve as a ruse for a hidden agenda.[151]

---

[146] As defined under Hague IV 1907, art. 42.

[147] See K. A. Cavanaugh, "Rewriting Law: The Case of Israel and the Occupied Territory", in David Wippman and Matthew Evangelista (eds.), *New Wars, New Laws? Applying Laws of War in 21st Century Conflicts* (Dordrecht: Martinus Nijhoff, 2005), p. 233.

[148] GC IV Commentary, p. 335; see also Gasser and Dörmann, "Protection of the Civilian Population", p. 284.

[149] *Christian Society for the Holy Places* v. *Minister of Defence*, HC 337/71 (1971), 26 [1] PD 574.

[150] See Yoram Dinstein, "The Dilemmas Relating to Legislation under Article 43 of the Hague Regulations and Peace-Building", Background Paper prepared for the Informal High-Level Expert Meeting on Current Challenges to International Humanitarian Law, Cambridge 25–27 June, 2004, www.hpcrresearch.org/sites/default/files/publications/dinstein.pdf.

[151] Ibid., p. 8. See also Allan Gerson, "War, Conquered Territory, and Military Occupation in the Contemporary International Legal System" (1976–7) 18 Harv Int'l L J 525 at 538.

However, even in situations where there is no ostensible "hidden agenda", no attempt to change the social, cultural or political landscape of the occupied territory, how are prolonged occupations, the laws of occupation and the progression of time to be reconciled? With no end in sight to the Israeli occupation of Palestinian territory, how can the Israelis (or indeed, any Occupying Power in a situation of prolonged occupation) respect the laws in place in the occupied territory, while at the same time ensuring that the laws do not ossify, and fail to adequately reflect the contemporary social, cultural and political climate of the territory and population they govern?[152]

Dinstein has proposed a "test" for distinguishing between "legitimate and illegitimate concern for the welfare of the civilian population"[153] as depending on whether the OP "shows similar concern for the welfare of its own population . . . if the Occupying Power enacts a law . . . the crux of the issue is whether a parallel (not necessarily identical) law exists back home. If the answer is negative, the ostensible concern for the welfare of the civilian population deserves being disbelieved."[154] While this seems a reasonable approach, Dinstein's test is problematic when one considers that the OP may have draconian laws in its own territory. Thus, the introduction of similarly restrictive laws might not be justifiable on the grounds of similarity with the domestic law of the OP. While Dinstein reminds us that "the legislation of the Occupying Power in the occupied territory is temporary and its effects and will normally expire at the end of the occupation",[155] where the occupation looks to be without end, the situation is less than clear.

Also problematic in the context of protracted occupation are the activities undertaken by the OP regarding security concerns. As noted above, Article 49 of GC IV provides that the OP may not engage in forcible mass or individual transfers of protected persons from the occupied territory to the territory of the OP (or any other territory) but that total or partial evacuations of a given area may be undertaken if the security of the population or imperative military reasons so demand. Likewise, Articles 42 and 78 permit internment of civilians for imperative reasons of security. What happens in situations where the security concerns are, like the occupation connected to it, protracted and on-going? This was highlighted in the case of *Ajuri v. IDF Commander in the West Bank*,[156] where the Israeli policy of "assigned residence" was challenged. In that case, the petitioners, residents of Judaea and Samaria, had been subject to an "order assigning place of residence", relocating them to the Gaza Strip. The Israeli government justification was that the petitioners needed to be relocated in order to counter the active participation of the petitioners and other family members in the terrorist activities of their relatives. In finding

---

[152] For examination of the problems faced in regards to long-term occupation, see further Gregory Fox, "Transformative Occupation and the Unilateralist Impulse" (2012) 94 IRRC 237, and Adam Roberts, "Transformative Military Occupation: Applying the Laws of War and Human Rights" (2006) 100 AJIL 580.

[153] Dinstein, "Dilemmas", p. 9.   [154] Ibid.   [155] Ibid.

[156] *Ajuri et al.* v. *IDF Commander in the West Bank et al.*, HCJ 7015/02, [2002] IsrLR 1, translation at 62.90.71.124/mishpat/html/en/system/index.html.

against the petitioners in two of the three counts brought, the Court stated that it was permissible for an OP to assign residence as it:

strikes a proper balance between the essential condition that the person himself presents a danger – which assigned residence is designed to prevent – and the essential need to protect the security of the territory. It is entirely consistent with the approach of the Fourth Geneva Convention, which regards assigned residence as a legitimate mechanism for protecting the security of the territory. It is required by the harsh reality in which the State of Israel and the territory are situated, in that they are exposed to an inhuman phenomenon of "human bombs" that is engulfing the area.[157]

Again, this would seem to raise problems regarding the supposed temporary nature of "assigned residence" – if the security risk is on-going because the occupation is long-term and indefinite, how then can such assigned resident be truly temporary?

The Israeli construction of the security barrier also demonstrates some of the problems presented by protracted occupation. Starting in 1996, the Israeli government considered plans to build a barrier to prevent people moving into Israel from the West Bank; by 2003, the Israel Ministry of Defence approved a full barrier along the West Bank, totalling 720 kilometres. Parts of the barrier were built in Palestinian territory, with deviations from the "Green Line"[158] in places up to twenty-two kilometres into Palestinian territory.[159] As a result of the barrier, parts of Palestinian territory were enclosed, resulting in some Palestinians effectively being contained in enclaves. The Israeli government justified the building of the barrier on the grounds of military necessity and the need to ensure the safety of the Israeli defence forces – "to improve and strengthen operational capability in the framework of fighting terror, and to prevent the penetration of terrorists from the area of Judea and Samaria into Israel".[160] Israel argued that it was taking steps to secure the safety of its population, and that the construction of a barrier was the only means feasible to achieve this. However, while Israel was, and is, entitled to build a barrier on its side of the Green Line, it is problematic, to say the least, that it built the barrier in part in Palestinian territory, not least because the construction of such a wall would seem contrary to the temporary nature of the law of occupation.[161] Indeed, a number of acts undertaken by the Israelis seem prejudicial to the transitory nature of occupation, such as the building of Israeli-inhabited settlements in the Occupied Territories, which are incompatible with the prohibition in Article 49 of GC IV on the

---

[157] Ibid., para. 16.

[158] The 1949 Armistice Line between Israel and Jordan, also encompassing the Gaza Strip – see further Dinstein, *The International Law of Belligerent Occupation*, pp. 13–16.

[159] See Report of the Secretary-General Prepared Pursuant to General Assembly Resolution ES-10/13, UN Doc. No. A/ES-10/248, 24 November 2003, pp. 2–6 for a detailed description of the route of the barrier, as well as its construction.

[160] The Ministers' Committee for National Security, cited in *Beit Sourik Village Council* v. *The Government of Israel and the Commander of the IDF Forces in the West Bank*, HCJ 2056/04, para. 3.

[161] Dinstein, *The International Law of Belligerent Occupation*, p. 248.

deportation or transfer of parts of the OP's own civilian population into territory it occupies.[162]

Problems relating to protracted occupation are evident also in the context of detaining civilians who present a continuing security threat. If the conflict lasts for years, problems arise regarding the length of such administrative detention.[163] Even though civilian detainees retain the right to challenge their detention every six months,[164] there may be no hope of release from detention if the OP considers that imperative security measures demand such long-term detention. This has been demonstrated in the Israeli context in the 2000 case of *Anon* v. *Minister of Defence*,[165] which looked at the legality of the fourteen-year detention of the Lebanese petitioners by the Israelis following Israeli occupation of Lebanon;[166] problems with prolonged administrative detention have also been aptly demonstrated in the context of the seemingly indefinite US detention of persons in Guantanamo Bay.[167]

5. RULES ON THE TREATMENT OF CIVILIANS IN NON-INTERNATIONAL ARMED CONFLICTS

Finally, brief mention should be made regarding the protection of civilian detainees in the context of non-international armed conflict. The law of armed conflict does not contemplate the possibility of "occupation" in non-international armed conflict – logically, one's own territory cannot be occupied in the way envisaged by the law, though territorial control of part of the State may fall to organised armed groups.

However, the laws relating to non-international armed conflict do contemplate that civilians may be detained in such a conflict. Common Article 3 refers to persons *hors de combat* due to detention; Additional Protocol II also outlines protections for persons who have been detained.[168] As such, certain fundamental rules apply to detention situations in non-international armed conflict.

---

[162] For more on the settlements issue, see Ibid., pp. 240–247; William Mallison, "A Juridical Analysis of the Israeli Settlements in the Occupied Territories" (1998–9) 10 Pal YB Int'l L 1; Yoram Dinstein, "The Israel Supreme Court and the Law of Belligerent Occupation: Deportations" (1993) 23 IYBHR 1.

[163] See further Chapter 4, specifically the section on unlawful combatants, and the Israeli Detention of Unlawful Combatants Law.

[164] GC IV, arts. 43 and 78.

[165] Further Hearing [F.H.] 7048197 *Anonymous* v. *Minister of Defence*, Crim FH 7048/97, 54(l) PD 721.

[166] See also Ashley Deeks, "Administrative Detention in Armed Conflict" (2009) 40 Case W Res J Int'l L 403; and Emanuel Gross, "Human Rights, Terrorism and the Problem of Administrative Detention in Israel: Does a Democracy Have the Right to Hold Terrorists as Bargaining Chips?" (2001) 18 Ariz J Int'l & Comp L 721.

[167] See further Chris Jenks and Eric Talbot Jensen, "Indefinite Detention Under the Laws of War" (2011) 22 Stanford LPR 41.

[168] AP II, art. 5.

Common Article 3 outlines certain basic protections for persons detained in non-international armed conflicts, including prohibitions on murder and other forms of violence to life, including mutilation, cruel treatment and torture, outrages upon personal dignity and the taking of hostages, and enshrines fundamental due process guarantees for detainees. Additionally, the ICRC is entitled to offer its services to parties to the conflict to provide humanitarian aid.[169]

Protocol II is more comprehensive. In Article 4, all persons who do not or have ceased to take direct part in hostilities (whether or not their liberty has been restricted) are entitled to a wide range of protections including respect for their person, honour and religious practices, and humane treatment without any adverse distinction.[170] Article 4 expands on the Common Article 3 prohibitions and includes prohibitions on collective punishments, corporal punishment, rape, indecent assault and enforced prostitution, pillage and acts of terrorism.[171] For persons whose liberty has been restricted, additional protections apply, including being allowed to receive individual or collective relief, to be housed in safe and hygienic detention facilities with access to food and drinking water, to practise their religious beliefs, to have certain labour protections, to have contact with the exterior, to have access to medical treatment and to have certain due process and fair trial rights.[172] The rules outlined in Common Article 3 and Protocol II are supplemented by the soft law ICRC Procedural Principles and Safeguards for Internment/Administrative Detention in Armed Conflict and other Situations of Violence.[173]

Examples of States and non-State armed groups respecting or agreeing to abide by the provisions regarding persons detained in the context of non-international armed conflicts can be found in a number of instances. For example, during the conflict with Biafran separatists, the Head of the Nigerian Federal Military Government, Major General Gowon, issued the 1967 Operational Code of Conduct for the Nigerian Armed Forces. The Code specifically stated that Nigerian troops were "in honour bound to observe the rules of the Geneva Convention [sic]".[174] Nigeria thus agreed to apply the GC rules designed to protect civilians in the hands of the enemy[175] and also allowed regular ICRC

---

[169] Common Article 3 to the Four Geneva Conventions.   [170] AP II, art. 4.   [171] Ibid., art. 4(2).

[172] Ibid., arts. 5, 6.

[173] Annex 1, ICRC, *Report on International Humanitarian Law and the Challenges of Contemporary Armed Conflicts*, 87 IRRC 375 (2005). See also the "Expert Meeting on Procedural Safeguards For Security Detention In Non-International Armed Conflict", Chatham House and International Committee of the Red Cross, London, 22–3 September 2008, 91 IRRC 859 (2009).

[174] Directive to all Officers and Men of the Armed Forces of the Federal Republic of Nigeria on conduct of Military Operations, para. 3; www.dawodu.com/codec.htm.

[175] The ICRC had managed to obtain assurances from both the Nigerian government and the Biafran separatists that they would observe the rules of the Geneva Conventions. See the ICRC *Annual Report 1967* p. 36, and ICRC, "External Activities: Nigeria" (1967) 79 IRRC 535.

visits to detainees.[176] An independent observer team comprising delegates from Canada, Poland, Sweden, the UK, the UN Secretary-General and the OAU was invited by Nigeria to observe and report on Nigerian compliance with IHL. The Observer Team reported that, in large part, Nigerian forces were aware of the rules of the Code of Conduct and were fulfilling their obligations under the Code.[177]

Additional Protocol II and Common Article 3 make no mention of the grounds upon which a person may be interned or detained, or whether such detention may be challenged or reviewed. Nonetheless these two instruments ensure that certain fundamental rights exist and are to be observed.

6. CONCLUSION

The Civilians Convention was ground-breaking in terms of enshrining protections for civilians in occupied territory, or for persons who may otherwise find themselves in the hands of an adverse party. However, these protections form only part of the vast array of rules that seek to protect all civilians from the deleterious effects of the conflict. The other part of these rules can be found in the law on targeting, which forms the basis of the next chapter.

SUGGESTED READING

Arai-Takahashi, Yutaka, *The Law of Occupation: Continuity and Change of International Humanitarian Law, and its Interaction with International Human Rights Law* (Leiden: Martinus Nijhoff, 2009).

Benvenisti, Eyal, *The International Law of Occupation* (Princeton University Press, 2004).

Dinstein, Yoram, *The Law of Belligerent Occupation* (Cambridge University Press, 2009).

Lovell, David and Igor Primoratz (eds.), *Protecting Civilians During Violent Conflict: Theoretical and Practical Issues for the 21st Century* (Farnham: Ashgate, 2012).

Playfair, Emma (ed.), *International Law and the Administration of Occupied Territories: Two Decades of Israeli Occupation of the West Bank and Gaza Strip* (Oxford: Clarendon, 1992).

---

[176] See ICRC reports entitled "Help to War Victims in Nigeria" (1968) 92 IRRC 571, (1969) 94 IRRC 3, (1969) 95 IRRC 81 and (1969) 96 IRRC 119. See also Michael Bothe, "Article 3 and Protocol II: Case Studies of Nigeria and El Salvador" (1982) 31 AULR 899 and Pius Nwogugu, "The Nigerian Civil War: A Case Study in the Law of War" (1974) 14 IJIL 13.

[177] See *Report of the Observer Team to Nigeria*, 24 September to 23 November 1968, Presented to Parliament by the Secretary of State for Foreign and Commonwealth Affairs by Command of Her Majesty (London: HMSO, 1969) pp. 31–4.

DISCUSSION QUESTIONS

1. Should there be additional criteria when considering "affiliation" under GC IV – beyond just nationality or ethnicity?

2. Following the invasion of Iraq in 2003, the occupying authorities undertook what has been called by some to be "transformative occupation"[178] whereby many of the laws in existence in Iraq were altered or discarded in favour of new laws enshrining democratic government and respect for international human rights norms. How could you argue that such acts were in keeping with the conservationist approach of the law of occupation?

3. How does one account for the Israeli policy of bulldozing the homes of those who have attacked Israel? What principles of the law on belligerent occupation are relevant?

4. Should all civilians in occupied territory benefit from the Civilians Convention, even if they are not "in the hands of the enemy"?

---

[178] For an overview of this line of argument, see further Gregory Fox, "Transformative Occupation and the Utilitarian Impulse" (2012) 94 IRRC 237, 238–41.

7 Targeting

1. INTRODUCTION

The law of targeting is, as Michael Schmitt puts it, "the *sine qua non* of warfare. Reduced to its essence, war is about attacking the enemy. The law of targeting consequently lies at the very heart of the law of war."[1] The law of targeting comprises complex and detailed rules regarding when objects may be lawfully targeted by parties to a conflict, and when such objects are immune from targeting. In addition to these rules, IHL also places limits on the kinds of attacks that can be launched, and the means and methods that may be employed in such attacks,[2] and outlines additional precautions that parties to a conflict must take before attacking a target.

The first part of the chapter examines the general rules on targeting, including the provisions in Article 52 regarding defining a lawful target. The second part of the chapter examines the more specific rules that have developed regarding certain types of objects, and the permissible targeting of such objects, such as cultural property, the environment, and objects necessary for the survival of the civilian population. Finally, the chapter will look at the contentious issue of objects which have been called "dual-use"[3] – objects which have both military and civilian use, complicating targeting assessments, and the law of targeting as it applies to non-international armed conflicts.

---

[1] Michael Schmitt, "Foreword", in William Boothby, *The Law of Targeting* (Oxford University Press, 2012), p. vii.

[2] See Chapter 8 on means and methods.

[3] Gary Solis, *The Law of Armed Conflict: International Humanitarian Law in War*, (Cambridge University Press, 2010), p. 534.

2. THE PHILOSOPHICAL UNDERPINNINGS OF THE LAW OF TARGETING

[margin note: war is limited]

The fundamental principles that underpin the modern law of targeting are drawn from the fundamental principles that underpin *all* the laws of armed conflict: that the means and methods of warfare available to parties to the conflict are not unlimited; that a distinction must be made between military and civilian persons and objects; that the only legitimate military act is that which is aimed at bringing about the submission of the adverse party through the weakening of their military potential. These principles – distinction, military necessity, proportionality, humanity – all speak to the notion of there being restraint in war.[4]

[margin note: restraint in war]

However, the idea that "even wars have limits"[5] is not an approach that has always been unequivocally supported – theorists from Cicero[6] to Clausewitz were sceptical, if not outright dismissive of the possibility that warfare could be regulated and limited. In his famous work, *On War*, Clausewitz argued that war "is an act of violence to compel our opponent to fulfil our will. ... Self-imposed restrictions, almost imperceptible and hardly worth mentioning, termed usages of International Law, accompany it without essentially impairing its power" and that:

philanthropists may easily imagine there is a skilful method of disarming and overcoming an enemy without causing great bloodshed, and that this is the proper tendency of the art of War. However plausible this may appear, still it is an error which must be extirpated; for in such dangerous things as war, the errors which proceed from a spirit of benevolence are just the worst.[7]

Indeed, the increased involvement of civilians in the war effort throughout the early twentieth century prompted some States to focus their attentions on the civilian population, in the belief that only through targeting the civilian population could one hope to achieve absolute victory. The First World War demonstrated the importance of the home front on the general war effort, and the benefit that could accrue from a more liberal targeting strategy. As Chickering and Förster point out, in twentieth century warfare:

---

[4] See further Chapter 2 on the general principles of the law of armed conflict.

[5] The phrase "even wars have limits" is the title of a short film created by the ICRC, to commemorate the fiftieth anniversary of the adoption of the Geneva Conventions: ICRC, *People on War: Even Wars have Limits*, 1998, www.icrc.org/eng/resources/documents/film/f00392.htm.

[6] Cicero's famous maxim was "*silent enim leges inter arma*" (for the laws are silent amid the clash of arms) – that in times of warfare, the law was, justifiably, mute, and that the need to prosecute the war was more important than the need to abide by the rule of law. See Marcus Tullius Cicero, *Oratio pro Tito Annio Milone*, trans. John Smyth Purton (Cambridge University Press, 1853), p. 48.

[7] Carl von Clausewitz, *On War*, 1832, trans. J. J. Graham 1873 (London: Penguin Classics, 1982), Book I, Chapter. I, ss. 2–3.

civilians were critical to the supply of weapons, munitions, and the other essential materials of combat, and they provided the moral backing without which the war could not be sustained. However, civilians were also more vulnerable to both subversion and military attack, for they were less acclimated to the terrors, deprivations, and demoralization of war. ... The German military leadership genuinely believed that the moral collapse of the home front in 1918 has wrecked what would otherwise have been a victorious military campaign. They concluded that in a future war the civilian front would again constitute the weakest dimension of any belligerent's war effort, hence the most vulnerable and inviting target of an enemy's attentions.[8]

However, when the Geneva Conventions were adopted in 1949, the idea that all parts of a State, including its civilian population, were targetable was rejected as a guiding principle.[9] This was likely due in no small part to the devastation experienced by all parties to the Second World War, where the practice of targeting the civilian population was frequently the norm, rather than the exception.[10] When the Additional Protocols were adopted, the modern law of armed conflict rejected outright total war,[11] with express prohibitions on the deliberate targeting of civilian persons and objects, and prohibitions on attacks which might be expected to cause disproportionate damage to the civilian population. The modern law of armed conflict permits only military objectives to be targeted. However, making the distinction between objects that can be targeted and those that cannot is not always straightforward and requires a complex series of evaluations. It is these evaluations that will be explored in this next section.

3. THE BASIC RULE: ARTICLE 48 OF ADDITIONAL PROTOCOL I

In any targeting assessment, the first step is to comply with the fundamental principle of distinction, as outlined in Article 48 of Protocol I:

In order to ensure respect for and protection of the civilian population and civilian objects, the parties to the conflict shall at all times distinguish between the civilian population and combatants and between civilian objects and military objectives and accordingly shall direct their operations only against military objectives.

---

[8] Roger Chickering and Stig Förster, "Are We There Yet? World War II and the Theory of Total War", in Roger Chickering, Stig Förster and Bernd Greiner (eds.), *A World at Total War: Global Conflict and the Politics of Destruction, 1937–1945* (Cambridge University Press, 2005), p. 11.

[9] The Geneva Conventions did not include specific rules on targeting; however the Conventions did prohibit the targeting of persons *hors de combat* in, e.g., Common Article 3. See further Chapters 4, 5 and 6.

[10] Dresden, London, Hiroshima, Nagasaki, Darwin and Coventry were just a few of the cities that were subject to large-scale bombardment during the Second World War, resulting in significant civilian casualties; see generally Geoffrey Best, *Humanity in Warfare: The Modern History of the International Law of Armed Conflicts* (London: Methuen, 1983), pp. 262–85.

[11] Laurie Blank and Gregory Noone, *International Law and Armed Conflict: Fundamental Principles and Contemporary Challenges in the Law of War* (New York: Wolters Kluwer, 2013), p. 396.

For all binding

Article 48 is considered customary international law,[12] and is reinforced by Article 57(2) of Protocol I, which states that in the planning of an attack, parties to a conflict must "do everything feasible to verify that the objectives to be attacked are neither civilians nor civilian objects".

Article 48 contains a number of terms which require definition – civilian, combatant, military objectives. The terms "civilian" and "combatant" are explored in detail in the chapters in this book on those areas of the law;[13] this chapter will now look at how to define a military objective.

4. MILITARY OBJECTS AND OBJECTIVES

The starting point for determining the scope of the term "military objective" is Article 52(2) of Protocol I, which provides:

Attacks shall be limited strictly to military objectives. In so far as objects are concerned, military objectives are limited to those objects which by their nature, location, purpose or use make an effective contribution to military action and whose total or partial destruction, capture or neutralization, in the circumstances ruling at the time, offers a definite military advantage.

Article 52(2) does not contain examples of what constitutes a military objective, despite early attempts by the ICRC to outline a list of such examples.[14] This reflects the mutable nature of modern warfare; civilian objects can be militarised through use or location, while certain military objects may not offer any definite military advantage, and thus may not be worth attacking.

There are a number of key concepts contained in Article 52(2). First of these is the distinction between military objects and military objectives. Under the law of targeting, a military object might not, in and of itself, be a lawful military objective.[15] Second, Article 52(2) mentions "nature, location, purpose or use" as determinative factors in ascertaining whether something can be a lawful military objective. This suggests that certain objects may have a variable status, which, depending on a variety of factors, might make the object immune from targeting on one day, but targetable the following day. Third, the element of "circumstances ruling at the time" implies that any *post hoc* assessment of the lawfulness of targeting decisions must look at those decisions in context – that is to say, the decision must be viewed in light of the circumstances surrounding the targeting

---

[12] ICRC CIHL Study, r. 1.   [13] Chapter 4 on combatants and Chapter 6 on civilians.

[14] See the Annex to the Draft Rules for the Limitation of Dangers incurred by the Civilian Population in Time of War, reprinted in AP Commentary, p. 631, n. 3.

[15] Indeed, this interpretation is held out when one looks at the rules on precautions in attacks and prohibited attacks, discussed in more detail later in this chapter.

decision at the time the decision was made, rather than with hindsight or informed by later intelligence. Finally, the idea of "definite military advantage" warrants investigation: how can one quantify "definite advantage"? Does this necessarily preclude the legality of an "indefinite advantage"? These issues will be explored in this next section.

criteria

a. "Objects" and "objectives"

As noted earlier in this section, the law of armed conflict makes the distinction between military objects and military objectives. An object which is military in nature might not be lawfully targetable because it fails to meet the criteria for a military objective – for instance, if its destruction, neutralisation or capture fails to offer a definite military advantage. Furthermore, additional rules on permissible attacks under the law of armed conflict, such as those on proportionality and indiscriminate attacks, may also prevent an attack on a military object. Thus, for example, a military barracks, which houses low-level administrative facilities, but happens to be located in a densely populated civilian area, may not be a lawful military objective, even though its nature and use is military.[16] The destruction of such a facility could violate the principle of proportionality and thus the attack would be illegal.

proportionality / indiscriminate attack / prevent attack on military obj

A Side Note: Are people lawful military objectives?

as principle of proportionality is key

Article 52(2) does not make explicit reference to combatants (or persons taking direct part in hostilities) as being lawful military objectives. Read in conjunction with the basic rule in Article 48, which allows only for targeting of military objectives, it would seem that only objects, and not persons, may be lawfully targeted. A superficial reading of Article 52(2) would seem to place participants in an armed conflict in the untenable situation of being able to target military objectives, but only if there were no people in, on, or near the objective. A *only if no ppl around*

However, as the Bothe Commentary to the Additional Protocols notes, "it would, of course, be manifestly absurd to conclude from this somewhat imprecise drafting, that combatants are not a legitimate object of attack."[17] This seeming anomaly in the law can be attributed to misgivings held by delegates during the Diplomatic Conferences for the Additional Protocols, who were concerned that "affirmatively suggesting violence even against combatants is not appropriate in a humanitarian

[16] As noted by Colonel Charles Garraway, "I would suggest that the USS *Constitution* in Boston Harbor is a military object, but not necessarily a military objective": "Discussion: Reasonable Military Commanders and Reasonable Civilians", in Andru E. Wall (ed.), *International Law Studies – Volume 78: Legal and Ethical Lessons of NATO's Kosovo Campaign*, (Newport, RI: US Naval War College, 2002), p. 215.

[17] Michael Bothe, Karl Partsch and Waldemar Solf (eds.), *New Rules for Victims of Armed Conflicts: Commentary on the Two 1977 Protocols Additional to the Geneva Conventions of 1949* (The Hague/Boston/London: Martinus Nijhoff, 1982), p. 325.

Combatants are still legit target

[handwritten: more harm than good?]

instrument".[18] However, a reading of a number of Articles in Protocol I – such as Articles 37, 41, 42, 43(2), 44(3), 51(3) and 52(2) – supports an interpretation of military objectives as including combatants.

[handwritten: military objs includes combatants]

b. Nature, location, purpose, use

[handwritten: changeable nature lol]

Article 52(2) recognises the changeable nature of objects in times of armed conflict, and how different objects may be put to different uses according to the dictates of military necessity. The "nature, location, purpose or use" categories can affect one another; for example, an object's use may fundamentally alter its nature or purpose, thus changing its status from targetable to immune (or vice versa).

i. Nature

[handwritten: what's it being used for → if military can be attacked]

An object's "nature" is its essential character – its inherent and intrinsic qualities. A warship, an army barracks, a tank: all of these objects are military in nature, without need for further consideration of their use. However, *prima facie* non-military objects can also become military in nature, if their use makes it so. Thus, a commercial car manufacturer, which starts manufacturing exclusively military vehicles at the start of an armed conflict, has changed the nature of the facility from civilian to military.

ii. Location

[handwritten: locations useful to military]

"Location" refers to the military importance that attaches to the physical locale of a specific object – for example, an airfield, or a bridge. Capturing, destroying or otherwise denying the enemy access to that location thus carries military significance and makes such locations military objectives. As such, the object need not be military in nature. Indeed, as noted by US Colonel Charles Garraway, "a civilian house, which may not be being used by the military in any way but may be interrupting a tank advance, can by its location be a military objective".[19] Solis clarifies this further by stating that "if military necessity dictates that a civilian house be seized or destroyed to clear a field of fire or block an enemy avenue of approach . . . the house ceases to be a civilian object and may be considered a military object."[20]

iii. Purpose

The "purpose" of an object refers to its "intended future use, or possible use".[21] "Purpose" is employed both in contradistinction to and interconnection with "use";

---

[18] Ibid.; see also Official Records XV, p. 235, para. 17.
[19] Garraway, "Discussion: Reasonable Commanders and Civilians", p. 215.
[20] Solis, *The Law of Armed Conflict*, p. 522.   [21] Ibid., p. 525.

where "use" relates to how something is actually being utilised, while "purpose" relates to possible future uses of an object. Thus, a recently built but as yet unopened or uninhabited military base has a military purpose, even if it has not been used as such. This applies even to civilian objects and installations; if intelligence indicates that a civilian factory is preparing to build tanks, then the "purpose" requirement would be satisfied, and the factory would become a lawful target.[22]

iv. Use

An object's use can also render it a military objective. This is the case even if the object is *prima facie* immune from targeting, such as a school or hospital. These objects, traditionally immune from targeting,[23] lose their immunity if used for military purposes.[24] However, such determinations must be made in light of the obligation outlined in Article 52(3) of Additional Protocol I, which states that "in case of doubt whether an object which is normally dedicated to civilian purposes, such as a place of worship, a house or other dwelling or a school, is being used to make an effective contribution to military action, it shall be presumed not to be so used". For example, during the US advance on the Iraqi city of Najaf in 2003, Iraqi armed forces were allegedly using a mosque as a military base.[25] Such usage rendered the mosque targetable.[26]

c. Destruction, capture or neutralisation

Article 52(2) covers a spectrum of attacks – from total or partial destruction, to capture or neutralisation. The terms "neutralisation or capture" were not originally found in the draft protocol submitted by the ICRC; a committee added the terms during the Diplomatic Conferences.[27] The Article thus makes it clear that lawful targeting may involve both the partial or total destruction of an objective, as well as capturing, disabling or neutralising the objective. As such, endeavours to disable or neutralise an object are still covered by the law on targeting, as much as outright destructive attacks.[28]

---

[22] See also William Boothby, *The Law of Targeting* (Oxford University Press, 2012), pp. 103–4.

[23] Hague IV 1907, art. 27; GC IV, art. 18; AP I, art. 52(3).

[24] For the rules on loss of immunity for objects, see Hague IV 1907, art. 27; GC IV, art. 19; AP I, arts. 13(1) and 52(3); AP II, art. 11(2).

[25] "US Accuses Iraq of Using Mosque as Military Base", *PBS Newshour*, 2 April 2003, www.pbs.org/newshour/updates/middle_east/jan-june03/najaf_04–02.html.

[26] Yoram Dinstein, "Legitimate Military Objects Under the Current Jus in Bello: The Principle of Distinction and Military Objectives", in Andru E. Wall (ed.), *International Law Studies – Volume 78: Legal and Ethical Lessons of NATO's Kosovo Campaign* (Newport, RI: US Naval War College, 2002), p. 150. Ultimately, in the Najaf case, US troops were ordered not to fire on the mosque, due to its cultural and religious significance (ibid.).

[27] Committee III: Bothe *et al.*, *New Rules*, p. 367.   [28] Ibid.

This part of Article 52(2) builds on the "military objective" test; that is to say, "not only must a military objective make an effective contribution to the adverse Party's military action, its destruction, capture, or neutralisation must also offer a definite military advantage to the attacker."[29] Thus, there is an interaction between the military significance that attaches to the object *per se*, and the military significance that attaches to the destruction/capture/neutralisation of that object. If one of these factors is missing, the object may not be lawfully targeted.

d. Circumstances ruling at the time

Any targeting, when assessed for its legality, must be evaluated in light of the circumstances ruling at the time. Put another way, an attack against an objective which all intelligence suggests is military in nature, purpose, location or use, and which fulfils all other targeting obligations, is lawful. The attack will remain lawful, even if *ex post facto*, intelligence suggests that the target was not a military objective.

A good example of how this works in practice can be seen regarding the targeting of the Al Firdos bunker during the 1991 Gulf War. Intelligence gathered by the US on the bunker indicated that it was being used by Ba'ath secret police, and by Iraqi armed forces as a military command and control centre. Information on its usage came from highly placed intelligence operatives working in the Hussein government, as well as signals and satellite intelligence and air force reconnaissance sorties.[30] Given such information, the bunker was added to the US target list, and bombed in February 1991. After the attack, it was discovered that the bunker was being used by family members of the Ba'ath secret police.[31] As a result, 204 people, mainly civilian women and children, were killed.

While the US came in for criticism in the aftermath of the attack,[32] any assessment of the attack must take into account the "circumstances ruling at the time" the targeting decision was made. If the US genuinely had not known the facility was housing civilians, then as noted by Geoff Corn, "although the attack may have resulted in unfortunate civilian deaths, there was no law of war violation because the attackers acted in good faith based upon the information

---

[29] Ibid., p. 366.

[30] Human Rights Watch, *Needless Deaths in the Gulf War: Civilian Casualties During the Air Campaign and Violations of the Laws of War* (June 1991), www.hrw.org/reports/pdfs/u/us/us.91o/us910full.pdf, pp. 126–34.

[31] However, Human Rights Watch claims that the bunker had long been used as a civilian shelter, both during the Iran–Iraq War, and in the early stages of the 1991 War, and that the US "should have taken steps to ensure that what at least previously was known to be a civilian defense shelter was no longer considered a safe haven by the civilian population": Ibid., pp. 126, 129–31.

[32] Ibid., pp. 126–43. For an overview of the event see Michael W. Lewis, "The Law of Aerial Bombardment in the 1991 Gulf War" (2003) 97 AJIL 481 at 502–4.

reasonably available at the time the decision to attack was made."[33] For these reasons, the attack was lawful.

e. Definite military advantage

For an attack to be lawful, it must offer a "definite military advantage". The ICRC Commentary states that "military advantage can only consist in ground gained and in annihilating or weakening the enemy armed forces".[34] More guidance can be gleaned from additional sources of law, such as the St Petersburg Declaration, which states that "the only legitimate object which States should endeavour to accomplish during war is to weaken the military forces of the enemy".[35]

However, the idea of a "definite" military advantage is a complicated concept to unravel – what amounts to a "definite" advantage and what is only an "indefinite" advantage? The Working Group of Committee III at the 1974–7 Diplomatic Conferences, tasked with debating this provision, rejected a number of synonymous adjectives, such as "distinct", "clear", "immediate", "obvious", "specific" and "substantial".[36] However, neither the Official Records, the Rapporteur for the Working Group, nor the Bothe or ICRC Commentaries can provide any indication of why these terms were rejected in favour of "definite".[37] In interpreting "definite", the Bothe Commentary states that the destruction of the target or objective must offer "a concrete and perceptible military advantage rather than a hypothetical and speculative one".[38] The ICRC Commentary states that "it is not legitimate to launch an attack which only offers potential or indeterminate advantages".[39] Thus, a specified and defined outcome must result from the attack. For example, if the destruction of a bridge might only *potentially* hinder the advance of the enemy (if, say, the bridge was not the only way to traverse a river) its destruction may not meet the threshold of Article 52(2).

The requirement of an attack having a "definite" military advantage is the reason that attacks designed solely to achieve propaganda or political aims are unlawful. As Bothe notes, "air attacks have a definite impact on the morale of the entire population and, thus, on political and military decision-makers . . . [but] this type of 'advantage' is political, not military. The morale of the population and of political decision-makers is not a contribution to 'military action'. Thus [it] cannot be used as a legitimation for any targeting decision."[40]

---

[33] Geoffrey Corn, "Hamdan, Lebanon, and the Regulation of Hostilities: The Need to Recognize a Hybrid Category of Armed Conflict" (2007) 40 Vand. J. Transnat'l L 295 at 352. See also Solis, *The Law of Armed Conflict*, pp. 257–8.

[34] AP Commentary, p. 685, para. 2218.   [35] St Petersburg Declaration, Preamble.

[36] Official Records IV, p. 332.

[37] See further Bothe *et al*, *New Rules*, p. 367; Official Records IV, p. 332; AP Commentary, pp. 636–7, paras. 2024–8.

[38] Bothe *et al*, *New Rules*, p. 326.   [39] AP Commentary, p. 636, para. 2024.   [40] Bothe, *Targeting*, p. 116.

However, some states have argued that purely economic targets may be lawful targets,[41] and that a State's economic capabilities form a crucial part of their war effort. Therefore, a definite military advantage is gained in targeting the economic infrastructure of a State. Indeed, the Report on US Practice makes reference to the "enemy's war-fighting or war-sustaining capability",[42] evidencing a broad interpretation of lawful targets as including "war-supporting economic facilities".[43] Some publicists have rightly pointed out that such a broad approach could not support attacking most economic targets, as one must still fulfil the requirement of a definite military advantage to justify targeting, and that the causal link may be too tenuous to make out. As argued by Rogers:

if a country relies almost entirely on, say, the export of coffee beans or bananas for its income and even if this income is used to great extent to support its war efforts ... it would not be legitimate to attack banana or coffee bean plantations or warehouses. The reason for this is that such plants would not make an *effective* contribution to *military* action nor would their destruction offer a *definite* military advantage.[44]

As such, attacks on purely economic targets are likely illegal under the current law.

5. ADDITIONAL RULES ON TARGETING MILITARY OBJECTIVES

In addition to the Article 48 and Article 52 rules on lawful objectives, targeting decisions must also comply with a number of additional rules, including the rule on proportionality and the prohibition on indiscriminate attacks.

must be distinct

a. Indiscriminate attacks

Under Article 51(4) of AP I, indiscriminate attacks are prohibited. Indiscriminate attacks are:

(a) those which are not directed at a specific military objective;
(b) those which employ a method or means of combat which cannot be directed at a specific military objective; or
(c) those which employ a method or means of combat the effects of which cannot be limited as required by this Protocol;

---

[41] See Solis, *The Law of Armed Conflict*, p. 522.
[42] US Naval Handbook (1995) §8.1.1, cited in ICRC CIHL Study, Practice Relating to Rule 8, www.icrc.org/customary-ihl/eng/docs/v2_cou_us_rule8.
[43] ICRC CIHL Study, r. 8.
[44] A. P. V. Rogers, *Law on the Battlefield*, 3rd edn (Manchester/New York: Manchester University Press, 2012), pp. 109–10 (emphasis in original).

and consequently, in each such case, are of a nature to strike military objectives and civilians or civilian objects without distinction.

The connection to the principles of distinction (in subparagraphs (a) and (b)) and the principle of proportionality in attack (in subparagraph (c)) are evident – any attack which violates either the principle of distinction or the principle of proportionality is an indiscriminate attack.

Article 51(5) provides further clarification as to what constitutes an indiscriminate attack, including:

(a) an attack by bombardment by any methods or means which treats as a single military objective a number of clearly separated and distinct military objectives located in a city, town, village or other area containing a similar concentration of civilians or civilian objects; and

(b) an attack which may be expected to cause incidental loss of civilian life, injury to civilians, damage to civilian objects, or a combination thereof, which would be excessive in relation to the concrete and direct military advantage anticipated.

The rule against indiscriminate attacks is considered customary international law, in both international and non-international armed conflicts.[45] There is, however, no explicit rule on indiscriminate attacks in either Common Article 3 or AP II.

The rule on indiscriminate attacks seeks to prevent such attacks by prohibiting a number of different kinds of behaviour. The first kind of indiscriminate attack involves a failure to identify a specific military target as the objective; an example of such behaviour would be the act of not aiming the chosen weapon – for instance, "carpet bombing", or "blind firing" at, a particular target. While this may not breach the rule on indiscriminate attacks if the target was a single military objective located in the middle of an otherwise empty desert, more care must be taken when the more likely scenario is encountered – the placement of a military objective in close proximity to civilians and civilian objects.[46] Thus, the kinds of aerial attacks that were common prior to and during the Second World War would be unlawful under the modern IHL.[47] The carpet bombing of the cities of London[48] and

---

[45] ICRC CIHL Study, r. 11.

[46] See the UK Ministry of Defence, *The Manual of the Law of Armed Conflict* (Oxford University Press, 2004), p. 69, para. 5.23.3: "if the military objective consists of scattered enemy tank formations in an unpopulated desert, it would be permissible to use weapons having a wider area of effect than would be possible if the target were a single communications site in the middle of a heavily populated area".

[47] See AP Commentary, p. 619, para. 1946, which notes that art. 51(4) "confirms the unlawful character of certain regrettable practices during the Second World War and subsequent armed conflicts. Too often the purpose of attacks was to destroy all life in a particular area or to raze a town to the ground without this resulting ... in any substantial military advantages".

[48] See, generally, Ronald Schaffer, "The Bombing Campaigns in World War II: The European Theater", in Yuki Tanaka and Marilyn Young (eds.), *Bombing Civilians: A Twentieth Century History* (New York/London: The New Press, 2009), pp. 31–4; see also Timothy McCormack and Helen Durham, "Aerial Bombardment of

Dresden[49] are examples of such indiscriminate attacks; the Iraqi practice of launching SCUD missiles indiscriminately at Saudi Arabia and Israel during the 1991 Gulf War is also an example.[50]

A second kind of indiscriminate act is the use of a weapon that lacks the capability of being directed at a military objective. The use of non-guided weapons such as certain kinds of cluster munitions, or other weapons that cannot be controlled once released, such as certain chemical or biological weapons like mustard gas, would fall within this provision.[51] Indeed, the ICTY in the *Martić* case held that the firing of unguided missiles containing cluster munitions was an indiscriminate attack.[52]

Indiscriminate attacks are to be distinguished from a violation of the principle of distinction. A person launching an indiscriminate attack does not intentionally seek out civilians to target, but rather does not consider whether civilians might be injured or killed in an attack.[53]

b. Proportionality

Article 51(5)(b), on indiscriminate attacks, also refers to a type of attack which connects to another fundamental principle of IHL: the principle of proportionality.[54] Article 51(5)(b) prohibits as indiscriminate attacks:

an attack which may be expected to cause incidental loss of civilian life, injury to civilians, damage to civilian objects, or a combination thereof, which would be excessive in relation to the concrete and direct military advantage anticipated.

These kinds of attacks are also known as disproportionate attacks. Though there is no explicit treaty rule on proportionality in non-international armed conflicts, the rule on proportionality is considered customary international law in both international and non-international armed conflicts.[55] Violation of the rule on proportionality in attack is a war crime, for example under the Rome Statute.[56]

The Article 51(5)(b) rule on proportionality is supplemented by Article 57(2)(a)(iii) of AP I, which states that those who plan or decide upon an attack shall "refrain from deciding to launch any attack which may be expected to cause incidental loss of civilian life, injury to civilians, damage to civilian objects, or a combination

Civilians: The Current International Legal Framework" in Tanaka and Young (eds.), *Bombing Civilians*, pp. 228–30.

[49] Schaffer, "The Bombing Campaigns", pp. 40–5.

[50] US Department of Defense, "Final Report to Congress on the Conduct of the Persian Gulf War – Appendix O: The Role of the Law of War" (1992) 31 ILM 615 at 635.

[51] See further Chapter 8.   [52] *Prosecutor* v. *Martić*, IT-95-11, Judgment, 12 June 2007, para. 462.

[53] Solis, *The Law of Armed Conflict*, p. 537.   [54] See Chapter 2.   [55] ICRC CIHL Study, r. 14.

[56] Rome Statute, art. 8(2)(b)(iv).

thereof, which would be excessive in relation to the concrete and direct military advantage anticipated".[57]

Proportionality assessments impact on all stages of the targeting process – the selection of the target, the choice of weapon, and the overall execution of the attack.[58] An attack in which civilians are killed is not, *prima facie*, disproportionate. Rather, the rule on proportionality in attack is instead a balancing test,[59] whereby the anticipated direct military gain to be achieved is balanced against the antici-pated loss of civilian life and damage to civilian objects. Only when the scale tips towards the civilian damage being excessive in relation to the military benefit, does the attack become disproportionate. Much like the general rules on targeting in relation to "circumstances ruling at the time", so too must proportionality assess-ments be weighed in context. As Boothby notes, the rule on proportionality:

recognises that in modern warfare ... the judgment that is made in advance of the attack must of necessity concern itself with the military advantage that is "anticipated" and with the civilian injury and damage "which may be expected". The decision-maker is not therefore dealing in certainties. On the other hand, "concrete and direct military advantage" cannot be based on mere hope or speculation. The decision-maker is making his assessment on the basis of available information ... more may well be known after the event, but it is the information available to him at the time which matters.[60]

c. Precautions in attack and defence

Parties to an armed conflict must also abide by certain other general guidelines when undertaking targeting assessments, including taking certain precautionary measures, from both an offensive and a defensive perspective. For those planning and directing the attacks, these precautions are outlined in Article 57 of AP I. For those defending against attacks, the precautions are outlined in Article 58.[61]

i. Precautions in attack

Article 57 begins by outlining that "[i]n the conduct of military operations, constant care shall be taken to spare the civilian population, civilians and civilian

---

[57] AP I, art. 57(2)(a)(iii).

[58] See further Judith Gardam, "Proportionality and Force in International Law" (1993) 87 AJIL 391 at 407.

[59] See Enzo Cannizzaro, who states that "proportionality is not a rule of conduct but a rule which requires a balancing of antagonistic values, such as the interest of a belligerent in carrying out a military action on the one hand, and the interest of civilians who, although extraneous to the conduct of the hostilities, might be victimised by that action": "Contextualising Proportionality: *Jus ad Bellum* and *Jus in Bello* in the Lebanese War" (2000) 864 IRRC 779 at 787.

[60] Boothby, *Targeting*, pp. 94–5.

[61] Articles 57 and 58 are considered customary international law applicable in both international and non-international armed conflicts: see further ICRC CIHL Study, rr. 14–24.

objects". The Article goes on to state that those who plan or decide upon an attack shall:

> do everything feasible to verify that the objectives to be attacked are neither civilians nor civilian objects and are not subject to special protection but are military objectives within the meaning of paragraph 2 of Article 52 and that it is not prohibited by the provisions of this Protocol to attack them.[62]

Para 2. article 52

The remainder of Article 57(2)(a) deals with proportionality, and is discussed above.

In addition, a targeting decision must be cancelled or suspended if "it becomes apparent that the objective is not a military one or is subject to special protection or that the attack may be expected to cause incidental loss of civilian life, injury to civilians, damage to civilian objects, or a combination thereof, which would be excessive in relation to the concrete and direct military advantage anticipated";[63] this requirement builds further on the principles of distinction and proportionality.

Article 57(2)(c) obliges parties to the conflict to give "effective advance warning . . . of attacks which may affect the civilian population, unless circumstances do not permit." Thus, prior to launching an attack which may impact the civilian population, an attacker must, unless circumstances preclude, warn the civilian population of the impending attack. This can take the form of transmitting radio broadcasts or the dropping of leaflets – the Israeli Defence Force (IDF), for example, has used leaflet drops,[64] television, radio and other forms of telecommunications such as SMS text messages to mobile/cellular phones[65] to warn the civilians of Gaza of impending attacks.

The key term in Article 57(2)(c) is "effective", which implies the need for the warning to be understandable to those most directly affected by the attack, and delivered in such a way as to reach those most likely to be directly affected. In looking at the scope of the word "effective", the Goldstone Report stated that for a warning to be effective

> it must reach those who are likely to be in danger from the planned attack, it must give them sufficient time to react to the warning, it must clearly explain what they should do to avoid harm and it must be a credible warning. The warning also has to be clear so that the civilians are not in doubt that it is indeed addressed to them. As far as possible, warnings should state the location to be affected and where the civilians should seek safety. A credible warning

---

[62] AP I, art. 57(2)(a)(i).   [63] Ibid., art. 57(2)(b).

[64] See American–Israeli Cooperative Enterprise, *Operation Cast Lead: Examples of IDF Warnings to Gaza Civilians,* www.jewishvirtuallibrary.org/jsource/Peace/warnings.html for an example of the kinds and scope of warning to civilians by the IDF.

[65] Noah Shachtman, "Israel Calls Gazans Before Bombing", *Wired*, 2 January 2009, www.wired.com/2009/01/israel-calls-th/.

means that civilians should be in no doubt that it is intended to be acted upon, as a false alarm of hoax may undermine future warnings, putting civilians at risk.[66]

However, some publicists, such as Boothby, have criticised the Goldstone "test" for effective warning, arguing that it "puts forward an ideal which may for a variety of reasons be unachievable".[67] Indeed, the need for secrecy in the planning of certain attacks against lawful targets is taken into consideration in Article 57, which obliges parties to warn "unless circumstances do not permit". As Boothby notes, "the circumstances that may legitimately preclude the giving of a warning include military ones. Accordingly, if for example the attack is intended to take the adversary by surprise this may be a valid reason for giving no warning".[68]

The remainder of Article 57 obliges parties to the conflict to choose objectives that pose the least danger to civilians. Article 57(3) states that "[w]hen a choice is possible between several military objectives for obtaining a similar military advantage, the objective to be selected shall be that the attack on which may be expected to cause the least danger to civilian lives and to civilian objects".[69] Thus, if given the choice between an army barracks located near a major city and an army base in a remote or sparsely inhabited area, the remote base would be the objective most compliant with Article 57(3). This laudable provision is, however, dependent on the equivalency of the potential targets in terms of the military advantage offered; the provision is also dependent on there being a choice of targets in the first instance.[70]

The final provisions of Article 57 reiterate that "in the conduct of military operations at sea or in the air", parties to the conflict must "take all reasonable precautions to avoid losses of civilian lives and damage to civilian objects".[71] The Commentary to the Protocols notes that this provision relates to any attacks launched from the air or sea that might conceivably endanger the civilian population also inhabiting that battle-space – i.e., civilian aircraft and watercraft.[72] Article 49(4) of AP I already confirms the applicability of the Protocol regarding "the protection of civilians and civilian objects on land, at sea or in the air"; thus, this part of Article 57 seems superfluous. The Bothe Commentary to the Protocols clarifies the situation, stating that the provision was included during the Diplomatic Conferences in 1977 "to satisfy those delegations which felt uneasy about the limitation of the scope of this Section of Protocol I to the effects of attacks on objectives on land."[73]

---

[66] Human Rights Council, Human Rights in Palestine and other Occupied Arab Territories: Report of the United Nations Fact-Finding Mission on the Gaza Conflict, UN Doc. A/HRC/12/48, 25 September 2009 ("Goldstone Report"), para. 530.

[67] Boothby, *Targeting*, p. 128.

[68] Ibid., pp. 128–9. See also Ian Henderson, *The Contemporary Law of Targeting: Military Objectives, Proportionality and Precautions in Attack under Additional Protocol I*, (Leiden/Boston: Martinus Nijhoff, 2009), pp. 185–9.

[69] AP I, art. 57(3).   [70] See Henderson, *The Contemporary Law of Targeting*, pp. 189–92.

[71] AP I, art. 57(4).   [72] AP Commentary, pp. 687–8, para. 2230.   [73] Bothe *et al.*, *New Rules*, p. 411.

Finally, Article 57 reaffirms that "no provision of this Article may be construed as authorizing any attacks against the civilian population, civilians or civilian objects".[74]

ii. Precautions in defence

Article 58 of Protocol I obliges parties, "to the maximum extent feasible",[75] to undertake a number of acts to assist in the protection of the civilian population. The first of these is contained in Article 58(a) which obliges parties to "endeavour to remove the civilian population, individual civilians and civilian objects under their control from the vicinity of military objectives". The qualification here is that such relocation must be compliant with Article 49 of Geneva Convention IV, which states that "individual or mass forcible transfers, as well as deportations of protected persons from occupied territory to the territory of the Occupying Power or to that of any other country, occupied or not, are prohibited, regardless of their motive".[76] However, Article 49 also provides that "total or partial evacuation of a given area if the security of the population or imperative military reasons so demand"[77] may be undertaken.

A number of issues arise with regards to this provision. First, Article 49 applies only in situations of occupied territory, and only to those persons protected by GC IV.[78] However, Article 58 applies to both occupied and non-occupied territory and to all civilians "under the control" of the party to the conflict taking the steps outlined in Article 58. Thus the two articles have differing scopes of application.

Of additional concern is the idea of relocating the civilian population from the vicinity of "military objectives". As noted earlier in this chapter, the definition of "military objective" is not fixed, and can change according to an object's location, purpose or use. It seems unfeasible that a party to the conflict would be able to ensure that the civilian population was not located near a military objective, if it is not possible to always know what is going to be a military objective. Furthermore, in densely populated small States, it may be physically impossible to ensure that the civilian population is moved away from military objectives during times of armed conflict. In such instances, regard must be had to the phrase "to the maximum extent feasible".

Connected to the obligation in Article 58(a) is the obligation in Article 58(b) which provides that parties to the conflict shall, to the maximum extent feasible, "avoid locating military objectives within or near densely populated areas". This builds on Article 28 of Geneva Convention IV, which prohibits the use of individual protected persons as human shields. Article 58 extends that rule to the entire civilian

---

[74] AP I, art. 57(5).   [75] Ibid., art. 58.   [76] GC IV, art. 49.   [77] Ibid.
[78] For more detail regarding the scope of application of GC IV, see Chapter 6.

population.[79] This provision prohibits the use of the civilian population or civilian objects as shields for military objectives. As with Article 58(a), this provision may create problems for highly urbanised and densely populated States, where there is little physical space and little choice but to locate military facilities in proximity to civilian populations. Many countries would certainly seem to run afoul of a strict reading of Article 58(a). The passage of time, growing populations and urban sprawl would likely also result in certain military objectives, initially built far from urban centres, becoming part of metropolitan areas.

Finally, Article 58(c) is a more generally worded provision, obliging parties to the conflict to "take the other necessary precautions to protect the civilian population, individual civilians and civilian objects under their control against the dangers resulting from military operations".

6. SPECIFIC RULES ON TARGETING CERTAIN TYPES OF OBJECTS

In addition to the general rules on targeting, specific rules exist to protect certain kinds of objects. These rules cover cultural property, the natural environment, hospitals and other aid and relief facilities, and certain civilian installations that are necessary for the survival of the civilian population.

a. Cultural property

The idea that cultural property should be spared from attack is not a new one; during the eighteenth century, Vattel argued:

for whatever cause a country is ravaged, we ought to spare those edifices which do honour to human society, and do not contribute to increase the enemy's strength, such as temples, tombs, public buildings, and all works of remarkable beauty. What advantage is obtained by destroying them?[80]

Early treaties on the law of armed conflict reflected this position: both the Lieber Code[81] and the 1907 Hague Regulations[82] included provisions regarding the protection of cultural property.[83] However, despite these rules, the plunder and destruction

---

[79] The question of human shields is dealt with in more detail in Chapter 8.

[80] Emmer de Vattel, *The Law Of Nations, Or, Principles of the Law of Nature, Applied to the Conduct and Affairs of Nations and Sovereigns, with Three Early Essays on the Origin and Nature of Natural Law and on Luxury*, 1797, trans. Thomas Nugent 2008 (Indianapolis, IN: Liberty Fund, 2008), p. 571.

[81] Lieber Code, art. 35.   [82] Hague IV 1907, arts. 27, 56.

[83] Rules on the protection of cultural property were also included in the Draft Rules concerning the Control of Wireless Telegraphy in Time of War 1922–1923, The Hague, www.icrc.org/ihl/INTRO/275?OpenDocument ("Hague Rules of Air Warfare 1923") and the regional instrument of the Treaty on the Protection of Artistic

of cultural property was commonplace in both the First and Second World Wars; countless works of art were looted throughout occupied Europe[84] and many cities of cultural importance were severely damaged.[85] In the aftermath of the conflict, and in the wake of the war crimes trials that saw prosecutions for the looting and destruction of cultural property,[86] impetus developed to adopt an international instrument for the protection of cultural property in times of armed conflict. This eventually led to the adoption, in 1954, of the Hague Convention for Protection of Cultural Property.

The Convention, along with its two protocols,[87] aims to protect:

movable or immovable property of great importance to the cultural heritage of every people, such as monuments of architecture, art or history, whether religious or secular; archaeological sites; groups of buildings which, as a whole, are of historical or artistic interest; works of art; manuscripts, books and other objects of artistic, historical or archaeological interest; as well as scientific collections and important collections of books or archives or of reproductions of the property defined above . . .[88]

The Convention was innovative in that it proposed the protection of both movable and immovable cultural property; additional innovation came with the specific mention of architecture as well as archaeological sites, manuscripts and scientific collections. The scope of protected objects and installations in the Convention is comprehensive, and far more encompassing than any previous attempts at protecting cultural property.[89]

As a general rule, under Article 4(1) of the Convention:

The High Contracting Parties undertake to respect cultural property situated within their own territory as well as within the territory of other High Contracting Parties by refraining from any use of the property and its immediate surroundings or of the appliances in use for its

---

and Scientific Institutions and Historic Monuments (Roerich Pact), Washington, 16 December 1933, in force 15 April 1935, 167 LNTS 290. The Pact was only applicable in the American States. See further Boothby, *Targeting*, pp. 217–18.

[84] See generally Roger O'Keefe, *The Protection of Cultural Property in Armed Conflict* (Cambridge University Press, 2006), pp. 80–6; and Matthew Lippmann, "Art and Ideology in the Third Reich: The Protection of Cultural Property and the Humanitarian Law of War" (1998–9) 17 Dick. J. Int'l L. 1 at 14–25.

[85] The bombing of Dresden is one of the best known examples; see generally Tami Davis Biddle, "Dresden 1945: Reality, History, and Memory" (2008) 72 *The Journal of Military History* 413.

[86] See IMT, *Judgement of the International Military Tribunal: Judgment against Alfred Rosenberg*, 1 October 1946. See also French Permanent Military Tribunal at Metz, "Trial of Karl Lingenfelder: Judgment delivered on 11 March 1947" in UN War Crimes Commission, *Law Reports of Trials of War Criminals* (London: HM Stationery Office, 1949), vol. IX.

[87] Protocol to the Hague Convention for the Protection of Cultural Property in the Event of Armed Conflict 1954, The Hague, 14 May 1954, in force 7 August 1956, 249 UNTS 358; Second Protocol to the Hague Convention of 1954 for the Protection of Cultural Property in the Event of Armed Conflict 1999, 26 March 1999, in force 9 March 2004, 2253 UNTS 212.

[88] Hague Convention on Cultural Property in the Event of Armed Conflict 1954, art. 1(a).

[89] Boothby, *Targeting*, p. 219.

protection for purposes which are likely to expose it to destruction or damage in the event of armed conflict; and by refraining from any act of hostility directed against such property.

Thus, parties to the Convention must not target cultural property and must refrain from using cultural property in such a way as to render it liable to targeting. This provision is tempered by Article 4(2), which provides that the obligation to protect and respect cultural property may be waived in cases "where military necessity imperatively requires such a waiver".[90]

The Convention also includes a régime for registering certain cultural property for "special protection", obliging parties to the conflict to refrain from any act of hostility directed against that property and the use of such property or its surroundings for military purposes.[91] However, the strict nature of the Article 9 special protection régime has meant that few objects have been registered – Vatican City is one example.[92] An "enhanced protection" régime was introduced in the Second Protocol to the Cultural Property Convention, designed to protect property that is "cultural heritage of the greatest importance for humanity."[93]

As with the basic protection régime, special and enhanced protection can be waived. Special protection can be waived in "exceptional cases of unavoidable military necessity";[94] however, such a decision can only be made by an officer commanding a force equivalent in size to a division or larger.[95] Enhanced protection may be waived "if, and for as long as, the property has, by its use, become a military objective" and the attack may only be approved by the "highest operational level of command".[96]

In order to identify property containing cultural property, such objects and installations are marked with an emblem of blue and white shields (depicted in Figure 7.1).

Specially protected property under the Article 9 special protection regime is marked with a triple-shield (see Figure 7.2).

The Hague Convention is applicable in all armed conflicts, both international and non-international; the protection of cultural property is considered a customary international law obligation.[97] Intentional attacks against cultural property that is not a military objective is a war crime under Article 8(2)(b)(ix) of the Rome Statute.

AP I also contains rules on the protection of cultural property, in Article 53, which provides:

---

[90] Hague Convention on Cultural Property 1954, art. 4(2).   [91] Ibid., arts. 8 and 9.

[92] See UN Educational, Scientific and Cultural Organisation, *International Register of Cultural Property under Special Protection: Coordination of Implementation of Conventions Protecting the Cultural Heritage,* UN Doc. WHC.94/CONF.003/INF.12, 16 November 1994.

[93] Second Protocol to The Hague Convention on Cultural Property 1954, art. 10.

[94] Hague Convention on Cultural Property 1954, art. 11(2).

[95] E.g., in the Australian Army, a division would usually made up of between 10,000 and 20,000 persons, and is commanded by a Major General – see Australian War Memorial, *Army: Structure,* www.awm.gov.au/atwar/structure/army-structure/.

[96] Second Protocol to The Hague Convention on Cultural Property 1954, art. 13.

[97] ICRC CIHL Study, r. 38. See also *Tadić Jurisdiction,* para. 127.

Fig 7.1 Cultural property emblem

Fig 7.2 Special protection emblem

Without prejudice to the provisions of the Hague Convention for the Protection of Cultural Property in the Event of Armed Conflict of 14 May 1954, and of other relevant international instruments, it is prohibited:

(a) to commit any acts of hostility directed against the historic monuments, works of art or places of worship which constitute the cultural or spiritual heritage of peoples;

(b) to use such objects in support of the military effort;

(c) to make such objects the object of reprisals.

AP I is slightly broader in scope than the 1954 Cultural Property Convention, in that it includes "places of worship" amongst those items protected from attack.[98] As with the Convention, AP I provides that cultural property may not be made the object of reprisals.[99]

---

[98] AP I, art. 53(a).   [99] The Hague Convention on Cultural Property 1954, art. 4(4); AP I, art. 53(c).

Unfortunately, despite the provisions of the Cultural Property Convention, and AP I, and the customary status of the rules on the protection of cultural property, culturally significant property continues to be targeted in armed conflict. During the conflicts following the break-up of the former Yugoslav republic, attacks against cultural property occurred in places like Dubrovnik and Mostar, and were found in post-war trials in the ICTY to be unjustifiable on the grounds of military necessity.[100] US forces in Iraq used a 1,200 year old minaret as a sniper observation post, resulting in insurgent attacks on the tower, and leading to allegations that the US was improperly using protected cultural property.[101]

However, it does not always follow that a culturally significant site will be attacked if there is some military gain to be made. During the 1991 Gulf War, the US did not launch bombing attacks against Iraqi fighter jets that were located adjacent to the Ziggurat of Ur, a Sumerian temple built in the twenty-first century BC.[102] However, the refusal to target the Ziggurat, though partially due to its cultural significance, was more likely due to the lack of military significance that attached to the Iraqi jets – two small fighter craft that were not capable of being armed or launched, as they had neither servicing equipment nor a usable runway.[103]

b. The environment

The idea that the environment should also be protected from targeting in times of armed conflict is comparatively recent. US practice in the Vietnam War, which included the widespread use of defoliants,[104] was partial impetus for the international community to debate the adoption of an international instrument regarding the environment and armed conflict.[105] The first of these, the 1976 UN Convention on the Prohibition of Military or any other Use of Environmental Modification Techniques (ENMOD),[106] prohibited the use of environmental modification techniques as a weapon of warfare. This convention provides that States parties shall not engage in "military or any other hostile use of environmental

---

[100] For the attacks on Dubrovnik, see *Prosecutor* v. *Strugar*, IT-01–42-T, Judgment, 31 January 2005; for the attack on the old bridge at Mostar, see *Prosecutor* v. *Prlić et al.*, IT-04–74-T, Judgment, 23 May 2013.

[101] For an overview of the event and debates around the use of the minaret, see Geoffrey Corn, "Snipers in the Minaret – What Is the Rule? The Law of War and the Protection of Cultural Property: A Complex Equation" (July 2005) *The Army Lawyer* 28.

[102] Contrast this with the failure of US troops to prevent the looting of the Iraqi National Museum during the 2003 invasion of Iraq – which, though not a violation of the law of targeting, was nonetheless a violation of the rules on the protection of cultural property more generally. At the time, however, the US was not party to the Hague Convention 1954 (it acceded in 2009) or AP I; see generally Sasha Paroff, "Another Victim of the War in Iraq: The Looting of the National Museum in Baghdad and the Inadequacies of International Protection of Cultural Property" (2004) 53 *Emory Law Review* 2021.

[103] See Michael W. Lewis, "The Law of Aerial Bombardment in the 1991 Gulf War" (2003) 97 *AJIL*, 487–8.

[104] See generally Alvin Young, "Vietnam and Agent Orange Revisited" (2002) 9 *Environmental Science and Pollution Research* 158.

[105] Boothby, *Targeting*, p. 199.   [106] Geneva, 18 May 1977, in force 10 December 1976, 1108 UNTS 151.

modification techniques having wide-spread, long-lasting or severe effects as the means of destruction, damage or injury to any other State Party."[107] As such, ENMOD is not strictly related to protecting the natural environment from being targeted; rather, it prohibits manipulation of the natural environment for use as a weapon of war. However, ENMOD does touch on targeting issues, in that ENMOD "prohibits direct and intentional destruction of any element of the environment with the explicit purpose of using that destruction as a way of causing destruction, damage, or injury to another State that is a party to the treaty."[108]

It was only with AP I that specific rules regarding the targeting of the natural environment were adopted, in Articles 35 and 55. Article 35(3) provides that "it is prohibited to employ methods or means of warfare which are intended, or may be expected, to cause widespread, long-term and severe damage to the natural environment".[109] This is reaffirmed in Article 55, which provides that:

Care shall be taken in warfare to protect the natural environment against widespread, long-term and severe damage. This protection includes a prohibition of the use of methods or means of warfare which are intended or may be expected to cause such damage to the natural environment and thereby to prejudice the health or survival of the population.

Attacks against the natural environment by way of reprisals are prohibited.

The term "the natural environment" is not defined in the Protocol. The Commentary to the Protocols asserts that the term should be interpreted as widely as possible:

to cover the biological environment in which a population is living. It does not consist merely of the objects indispensable to survival mentioned in Article 54 ... foodstuffs, agricultural areas, drinking water, livestock – but also includes forests and other vegetation mentioned in the Convention of 10 October 1980 on Prohibitions or Restrictions on the Use of Certain Conventional Weapons, as well as fauna, flora and other biological or climatic elements.[110]

The test outlined in Article 55 is cumulative – the damage to the environment must be "widespread, long-lasting and severe". Thus, short-term or otherwise limited but severe damage would not fall within the scope of Article 55. However, the drafters seemed reluctant to attach a specific timeframe to the terminology, even though some delegates suggested that the test for "long-term" be measured in decades, with some commenting that twenty years would be the minimum.[111] However, as noted by the Rapporteur to Committee III in relation to Article 35:

it is impossible to say with certainty what period of time might be involved. It appeared to be a widely shared assumption that battlefield damage incidental to conventional warfare would not normally be proscribed by this provision. What the article is primarily directed

---

[107] ENMOD, art. 1(1).   [108] Boothby, *Targeting*, p. 201.   [109] AP I, art. 35(3).
[110] AP Commentary, p. 662, para. 2126.   [111] See Official Records XV, pp. 268–9, para. 27.

to is thus such damage as would be likely to prejudice, over a long term, the continued survival of the civilian population or would risk causing it major health problems.[112]

Examples of environmental damage in armed conflict include actions taken by the retreating Iraqi army as they withdrew from Kuwait in 1991. Hundreds of oil wells were deliberately set alight, and millions of litres of oil were dumped in the Persian Gulf.[113] The result of these actions included damage to the marine and land environment, damage to agricultural capabilities, and decrease in air quality, due to pollution by hazardous gases released by the fires.[114] However, despite the catastrophic environmental damage, it is likely that the environmental damage wrought by the fires would not have been significant enough to trigger Articles 35 and 55 of AP I, even if Iraq had been party to the Protocol in 1991.[115] The test of "widespread, long-lasting and severe" was likely not met as early fears that the environmental damage would be "long-term" were not realised. This conclusion was reached by scholars and the US government alike.[116]

The importance of protecting the natural environment was affirmed by the ICJ in the *Nuclear Weapons Advisory Opinion*, where the Court stated that "the environment is not an abstraction but represents the living space, the quality of life and the very health of human beings, including generations unborn".[117] The rules on the protection of the natural environment are considered customary international law in both international and non-international armed conflicts – despite the law of non-international armed conflict containing no specific provision regarding protection of the natural environment.[118]

c. Medical facilities

The immunity of medical facilities and transports and other related relief organisations like the ICRC is covered in Chapter 5 of this book.

d. Works and installations containing dangerous forces

Certain installations are not to be targeted, due to the deleterious impact upon the civilian population that would likely follow the destruction of such objects. Article 56 of AP I provides:

---

[112] Ibid., p. 268, para. 27; see also AP Commentary, pp. 416–17, paras. 1453–4.

[113] See Ali Mohamed Al-Damkhi, "Kuwait's Oil Well Fires, 1991: Environmental Crime and War" (2007) **64** *International Journal of Environmental Studies* 31 at 32–3.

[114] See Frederick Warner, "The Environmental Consequences of the Gulf War" (1991) **33** *Environment* 6.

[115] Iraq ratified AP I in 2010 – see ICRC, www.icrc.org/applic/ihl/ihl.nsf/States.xsp?xp_viewStates=XPages_NORMStatesParties&txp_treatySelected=470.

[116] See Rogers, *Law on the Battlefield*, pp. 230–1; Dinstein, *The Conduct of Hostilities*, pp. 214–15; US, Department of Defense, "Report on the Persian Gulf War", pp. 636–7.

[117] *Nuclear Weapons*, para. 242.   [118] ICRC CIHL Study, rr. 43–5.

Fig 7.3 Emblem for works and installations containing dangerous forces

Works or installations containing dangerous forces, namely dams, dykes and nuclear electrical generating stations, shall not be made the object of attack, even where these objects are military objectives, if such attack may cause the release of dangerous forces and consequent severe losses among the civilian population. Other military objectives located at or in the vicinity of these works or installations shall not be made the object of attack if such attack may cause the release of dangerous forces from the works or installations and consequent severe losses among the civilian population.

As the article states, this is directed at prohibiting attacks on installations such as dams and nuclear power stations, which if damaged might release destructive amounts of water and radiation, respectively. This rule is applicable in non-international armed conflicts also, as outlined in Article 15 of Protocol II,[119] and is considered customary international law in both international and non-international armed conflicts.[120] Works and installations containing dangerous forces should be marked with the distinctive symbol (depicted in Figure 7.3) of three orange circles on a white background.[121]

Special protections against attack cease in certain circumstances, as outlined in Article 56(2); attacks may be authorised:

(a) for a dam or a dyke only if it is used for other than its normal function and in regular, significant and direct support of military operations and if such attack is the only feasible way to terminate such support;

(b) for a nuclear electrical generating station only if it provides electric power in regular, significant and direct support of military operations and if such attack is the only feasible way to terminate such support;

(c) for other military objectives located at or in the vicinity of these works or installations only if they are used in regular, significant and direct support of military operations and if such attack is the only feasible way to terminate such support.

---

[119] AP II, art. 15.

[120] ICRC CIHL Study, r. 42. Note however that Dinstein and Solis question the customary status of the protection of works and installations containing dangerous forces, challenging the methodology and cited practice behind the ICRC study; see Dinstein, *The Conduct of Hostilities*, p. 194; Solis, *The Law of Armed Conflict*, p. 530.

[121] AP I, art. 56(7).

The protections for these works and installations are therefore not absolute, which some publicists find problematic;[122] equally, other publicists have queried the immunity that attaches to these objects "even when they glaringly constitute military objectives".[123] The targeting of these objects thus presents a complex problem when making targeting decisions – the potential civilian damage must be weighed against the military benefit that attaches to the destruction of the installation.

e. Objects necessary for the survival of the civilian population

Additional protection for the civilian population is found in Article 54 of AP I, which prohibits starvation of civilians as a method of warfare, and states that:

It is prohibited to attack, destroy, remove or render useless objects indispensable to the survival of the civilian population, such as foodstuffs, agricultural areas for the production of foodstuffs, crops, livestock, drinking water installations and supplies and irrigation works, for the specific purpose of denying them for their sustenance value to the civilian population or to the adverse Party, whatever the motive, whether in order to starve out civilians, to cause them to move away, or for any other motive.[124]

The objects named in Article 54 are given as examples but are not meant to be an exhaustive list.[125] Objects indispensable to the survival of the civilian population are prohibited from being the subject of reprisals.[126] The prohibition on attacks against these objects is part of the law of non-international armed conflict contained in Article 14 of Additional Protocol II.[127] The prohibition on attacks on these objects is considered customary international law in both international and non-international armed conflicts.[128]

The prohibition on attacking such items under Article 54(2) is modified by Article 54(3) and 54(5); Article 54(3) states:

The prohibitions in paragraph 2 shall not apply to such of the objects covered by it as are used by an adverse Party:

(a) as sustenance solely for the members of its armed forces; or
(b) if not as sustenance, then in direct support of military action, provided, however, that in no event shall actions against these objects be taken which may be expected to leave the civilian population with such inadequate food or water as to cause its starvation or force its movement.

---

[122] See Frits Kalshoven, *Reflections on the Law of War: Collected Essays* (Leiden: Martinus Nijhoff, 2007), p. 235.
[123] Dinstein, *The Conduct of Hostilities*, p. 194.   [124] AP I, art. 54(2).   [125] Boothby, *Targeting*, p. 110.
[126] AP I, art. 54(4).   [127] AP II, art. 14.   [128] ICRC CIHL Study, r. 54.

Article 54(5) provides:

In recognition of the vital requirements of any Party to the conflict in the defence of its national territory against invasion, derogation from the prohibitions contained in paragraph 2 may be made by a Party to the conflict within such territory under its own control where required by imperative military necessity.

Thus, the prohibition on attacking such objects is not absolute, and can be overridden in certain situations if required by imperative military necessity – i.e., to prevent or slow the invasion of one's own territory (or the territory within a party's control) by an adverse party. However, such "scorched earth" actions – like the deliberate flooding of land or destruction by fire – may only be undertaken when evacuating or retreating from one's own territory "prior to its occupation by the enemy … [a party] may not resort to such a policy when seeking to expel the enemy or reoccupy its own territory."[129]

f. Civil defence, non-defended localities and demilitarised zones

The law of armed conflict also prohibits targeting certain areas such as "non-defended localities". Under Article 59 of AP I, parties to the conflict may unilaterally declare an area a non-defended locality as:

any inhabited place near or in a zone where armed forces are in contact which is open for occupation by an adverse Party. Such a locality shall fulfil the following conditions:

(a) all combatants, as well as mobile weapons and mobile military equipment must have been evacuated;
(b) no hostile use shall be made of fixed military installations or establishments;
(c) no acts of hostility shall be committed by the authorities or by the population; and
(d) no activities in support of military operations shall be undertaken.

3. The presence, in this locality, of persons specially protected under the Conventions and this Protocol, and of police forces retained for the sole purpose of maintaining law and order, is not contrary to the conditions laid down in paragraph 2.
4. The declaration made under paragraph 2 shall be addressed to the adverse Party and shall define and describe, as precisely as possible, the limits of the non-defended locality. The Party to the conflict to which the declaration is addressed shall acknowledge its receipt and shall treat the locality as a non-defended locality unless the conditions laid down in paragraph 2 are not in fact fulfilled, in which event it shall immediately so inform the Party making the declaration. Even if the conditions laid down in paragraph 2 are not fulfilled, the locality shall continue to enjoy the protection provided by the other provisions of this Protocol and the other rules of international law applicable in armed conflict.

---

[129] Green, *The Contemporary Law of Armed Conflict*, p. 169.

5. The Parties to the conflict may agree on the establishment of non-defended localities even if such localities do not fulfil the conditions laid down in paragraph 2. The agreement should define and describe, as precisely as possible, the limits of the non-defended locality; if necessary, it may lay down the methods of supervision.

6. The Party which is in control of a locality governed by such an agreement shall mark it, so far as possible, by such signs as may be agreed upon with the other Party, which shall be displayed where they are clearly visible, especially on its perimeter and limits and on highways.

7. A locality loses its status as a non-defended locality when it ceases to fulfil the conditions laid down in paragraph 2 or in the agreement referred to in paragraph 5. In such an eventuality, the locality shall continue to enjoy the protection provided by the other provisions of this Protocol and the other rules of international law applicable in armed conflict.

Article 59(1) "confirms and codifies customary law",[130] and is directed at a situation where a town or other locality is declared undefended, and open to occupation by the adversary, in order to protect it from what would otherwise be an imminent and inevitable attack as enemy forces advanced.

Article 60 of AP I also prohibits the conduct of active hostilities in agreed demilitarised zones (DMZ). Demilitarised zones are distinguished from non-defended localities, in that all parties to the conflict must agree on the existence of a DMZ; however, similar to non-defended localities, a DMZ must fulfil the following conditions:

(a) all combatants, as well as mobile weapons and mobile military equipment, must have been evacuated;

(b) no hostile use shall be made of fixed military installations or establishments;

(c) no acts of hostility shall be committed by the authorities or by the population; and

(d) any activity linked to the military effort must have ceased.

The Parties to the conflict shall agree upon the interpretation to be given to the condition laid down in sub-paragraph (d) and upon persons to be admitted to the demilitarized zone other than those mentioned in paragraph 4.

4. The presence, in this zone, of persons specially protected under the Conventions and this Protocol, and of police forces retained for the sole purpose of maintaining law and order, is not contrary to the conditions laid down in paragraph 3.[131]

Finally, Articles 61 and 62 provide for protection for civil defence personnel and organisations. Civil defence is outlined in Article 61 as:

---

[130] AP Commentary, p. 700, para. 2263.   [131] AP I, art. 60(3)–(4).

the performance of some or all of the undermentioned humanitarian tasks intended to protect the civilian population against the dangers, and to help it to recover from the immediate effects, of hostilities or disasters and also to provide the conditions necessary for its survival. These tasks are:

   (i) warning;
   (ii) evacuation;
   (iii) management of shelters;
   (iv) management of blackout measures;
   (v) rescue;
   (vi) medical services, including first aid, and religious assistance;
   (vii) fire-fighting;
   (viii) detection and marking of danger areas;
   (ix) decontamination and similar protective measures;
   (x) provision of emergency accommodation and supplies;
   (xi) emergency assistance in the restoration and maintenance of order in distressed areas;
   (xii) emergency repair of indispensable public utilities;
   (xiii) emergency disposal of the dead;
   (xiv) assistance in the preservation of objects essential for survival;
   (xv) complementary activities necessary to carry out any of the tasks mentioned above, including, but not limited to, planning and organization;

Article 62 of AP I provides that civilian civil defence organisations and their personnel must be respected and protected; activities undertaken in civil defence should not be considered harmful to the enemy, even if they are carried out under the direction or control of military authorities, in cooperation with military personnel, or if the work of civil defence personnel incidentally benefits military personnel – for instance, those who are *hors de combat.*[132] In order to ensure protection for persons carrying out civil defence activities, civil defence personnel, organisations, buildings, materiel and shelters should be identified as such through use of a distinctive emblem, of a blue triangle on a yellow circle (see Figure 7.4):

Fig 7.4 Civil defence emblem

---

[132] Ibid., art. 65(1)–(2).

7. DUAL USE OBJECTS – A NEW CATEGORY IN THE LAW OF TARGETING?

One of the issues that arises for military planners in targeting decisions is the question of so-called "dual use" objects. While the term is not used in IHL treaties, the phrase has emerged in the literature to describe objects that do not easily fit within the definitions of military or civilian[133] – objects that serve both a military and civilian function, such that destruction of the military element of the object would necessarily entail destruction of the civilian element.[134] This includes objects such as electrical power grids, telecommunications systems, highways or bridges.

Perhaps one of the best examples of the targeting of an alleged "dual-use" object was the NATO bombing of the Serbian radio and television station RTS in Belgrade, which took place during the 1999 Operation Allied Force. A number of civilians were killed in the attack[135] and the issue was brought to the ICTY for investigation. A committee of experts was convened to investigate the legality of the bombing. In its final report, the committee commented on NATO's justification for the attacking, highlighting that:

... NATO stressed the dual-use to which such communications were put, describing civilian television as "heavily dependent on the military command and control system and military traffic is also routed through the civilian system" ... NATO claimed that the RTS facilities were being used "as radio relay stations and transmitters to support the activities of the FRY military and special police forces, and therefore they represent legitimate military targets".[136]

Ultimately, the ICTY decided against further investigation into the bombing of RTS. However, it must be queried whether the phrase "dual use" serves as a merely descriptive function, and one that perhaps obfuscates the already complex questions that arise in targeting. Surely if, as NATO argued regarding RTS, a targeting decision complies with the rules on proportionality and discrimination, and if the general and specific rules on targeting are complied with, then a target is a lawful military objective.[137] Thus, the idea of something being "dual use" adds nothing new or helpful to the debate. Indeed, as Rogers comments, "legally, there is no intermediate

---

[133] See Marco Sassòli and Lindsey Cameron, "The Protection of Civilian Objects – Current State of the Law and Issues de lege ferenda", in Natalino Ronzitti and Gabriella Venturini (eds.), *The Law of Air Warfare* (Utrecht: Eleven Publishing, 2006), pp. 35, 57; Solis, *The Law of Armed Conflict*, pp. 534–6.

[134] Rogers, *Law on the Battlefield*, p. 110.

[135] A definite number has not been established – reports place the casualties at between ten and seventeen. See ICTY, *Final Report to the Prosecutor by the Committee Established to Review the NATO Bombing Campaign Against the Federal Republic of Yugoslavia*, (ICTY, June 2000), www.icty.org/sid/10052, para. 71.

[136] Ibid., paras. 72–4.

[137] See Christopher Greenwood, "Customary International Law and the First Geneva Protocol of 1977 in the Gulf Conflict", in Christopher Greenwood (ed.), *Essays on War in International Law* (London: Cameron May, 2006), p. 73.

category of dual-use objects: 'either something is a military objective or it's not'.[138] As such, it is 'not possible to state that there is a distinct category of "dual use" under the law of armed conflict; rather, these objects must be carefully assessed in line with the existing targeting rules, as explored in this chapter.'

8. A NOTE ON THE LAW OF TARGETING IN NON-INTERNATIONAL ARMED CONFLICTS

Finally, a closing note for this chapter on the law of targeting in the context of non-international armed conflicts. A number of sources, such as the ICTY,[139] the ICRC[140] and many publicists,[141] have noted that the gap between the laws of international and non-international armed conflict is narrowing, and more of the general laws governing international armed conflict are applicable in times of non-international armed conflict.

With regards to the law of targeting, many of the rules on the law of targeting are applicable to both international and non-international armed conflicts, including those on distinction and proportionality, on discrimination and precautions in attack, on protecting the civilian population, and on protecting the numerous works and installations that are vital to the survival of the civilian population, including hospitals, cultural objects and places of worship, works and installations containing dangerous forces, and objects that provide food and water supplies.[142] Violations of many of these rules are considered war crimes under Article 8(2)(e) of the Rome Statute, such as:

(i)   Intentionally directing attacks against the civilian population as such or against individual civilians not taking direct part in hostilities;

(ii) Intentionally directing attacks against buildings, material, medical units and transport and personnel using the distinctive emblems of the Geneva Conventions in conformity with international law;

(iii) Intentionally directing attacks against personnel, installations, material, units or vehicles involved in a humanitarian assistance or peacekeeping mission in accordance with the Charter of the United Nations, as long as they are entitled

---

[138] Rogers, *Law on the Battlefield*, p. 111, n. 120.   [139] In *Tadić Jurisdiction*.

[140] In the ICRC CIHL Study.

[141] Including Lindsey Moir, "Towards the Unification of International Humanitarian Law?", in Richard Burchill, Nigel White and Justin Morris (eds.), *International Conflict and Security Law: Essays in Memory of Hilaire McCoubrey* (Cambridge University Press, 2005); Emily Crawford, "Unequal Before the Law: The Case for the Elimination of the Distinction Between International and Non-International Armed Conflict" (2007) 20 *LJIL* 441; Marco Sassòli, Antoine Bouvier and Anne Quintin, *How Does Law Protect in War? Cases, Documents and Teaching Materials on Contemporary Practice in International Humanitarian Law* 3rd edn (Geneva: ICRC, 2011), pp. 324–5.

[142] See Sassòli *et al*, *How Does Law Protect in War?*, pp. 324–5, for a more detailed analysis of the convergence of the laws.

to the protection given to civilians or civilian objects under the international law of armed conflict;

(iv) Intentionally directing attacks against buildings dedicated to religion, education, art, science or charitable purposes, historic monuments, hospitals and places where the sick and wounded are collected, provided they are not military objectives;

(v) Pillaging a town or place, even when taken by assault;

. . .

(viii) Ordering the displacement of the civilian population for reasons related to the conflict, unless the security of the civilians involved or imperative military reasons so demand;

. . .

(xii) Destroying or seizing the property of an adversary unless such destruction or seizure be imperatively demanded by the necessities of the conflict . . . .

Thus, while the scope and breadth of the laws on targeting in international armed conflicts may not be duplicated verbatim in the law of non-international armed conflict, the fundamental principles are applicable.

9. CONCLUSION

Targeting decisions entail complex processes whereby the manifold obligations on parties to the conflict are weighed against the military benefits that result from attacking certain objects.[143] However, targeting decisions are only one half of the equation; how such decisions are put into effect, that is to say, what means and methods of combat are employed to give kinetic effect to a targeting decision, forms the second part. It is this topic that is analysed in the next chapter, on permissible means and methods of warfare.

SUGGESTED READING

Boothby, William, *The Law of Targeting* (Oxford University Press, 2012)

Downes, Alexander, *Targeting Civilians in War* (Ithaca, NY: Cornell University Press, 2008)

Gardam, Judith, *Necessity, Proportionality and the Use of Force by States* (Cambridge University Press, 2004)

Grunawalt, Richard, John King and Ronald McClain (eds.), *Protection of the Environment During Armed Conflict* (Newport, RI: Naval War College, 1996)

---

[143] See further Solis, *The Law of Armed Conflict*, pp. 530–4 for a detailed explanation of the general US process involved in targeting decisions.

Henderson, Ian, *The Contemporary Law of Targeting: Military Objectives, Proportionality and Precautions in Attack under Additional Protocol I* (Leiden: Martinus Nijhoff, 2009)

O'Keefe, Roger, *The Protection of Cultural Property in Armed Conflict* (Cambridge University Press, 2006)

DISCUSSION QUESTIONS

1. Should there be specific rules developed to deal with "dual-use" objects?
2. Some publicists have argued that there should be a "fifth Geneva Convention" that protects the natural environment in times of armed conflict (see for example Glen Plant, *Environmental Protection and the Law of War: A "Fifth Geneva" Convention on the Protection of the Environment in Time of Armed Conflict* (London: Belhaven Press, 1992)). Do you agree?
3. Discuss the looting and destruction that occurred in the Iraqi national museum following the US invasion in 2003. Did the failure of US troops to prevent such destruction amount to a violation of the laws of war?
4. Some publicists have criticised the lack of an absolute prohibition on targeting works and installations containing dangerous forces. Should there be an absolute prohibition, or is it better that there is some flexibility in the provisions?
5. Jean Pictet once commented "[i]f we can put a soldier out of action by capturing him, we should not wound him; if we can obtain the same result by wounding him, we must not kill him. If there are two means to achieve the same military advantage, we must choose the one which causes the lesser evil." (*Development and Principles of International Humanitarian Law*, (Dordrecht: Martinus Nijhoff, 1985), p. 75.) Should targeting decisions be informed by Pictet's philosophy, or is this too strict?

8 Means and methods of warfare

1. INTRODUCTION

In order to give practical effect to the fundamental principles of IHL, there are numerous treaties and treaty provisions that prohibit certain kinds of weapons, regulate the use of certain kinds of weapons, or prohibit or otherwise limit certain kinds of military strategy or conduct. These provisions are generally referred to as rules on "means and methods", where "means" relates to all types of weapons and weapons systems, and "methods" relates to the way in which such weapons are used, as well as "any specific, tactical or strategic, ways of conducting hostilities that are not particularly related to weapons".[1]

2. THE GENERAL RULES – THE PROHIBITIONS ON CAUSING UNNECESSARY SUFFERING AND SUPERFLUOUS INJURY, AND ON INDISCRIMINATE MEANS AND METHODS

The law on means and methods of warfare is first governed by the "basic rule" outlined in Article 35 of AP I:

In any armed conflict, the right of the Parties to the conflict to choose methods or means of warfare is not unlimited.

It is prohibited to employ weapons, projectiles and material and methods of warfare of a nature to cause superfluous injury or unnecessary suffering.[2]

---

[1] Marco Sassòli, Antoine Bouvier and Anne Quintin, *How Does Law Protect in War? Cases, Documents and Teaching Materials on Contemporary Practice in International Humanitarian Law,* 3rd edn (Geneva: ICRC, 2011), p. 280.

[2] AP I, art. 35.

This basic rule stems from the St Petersburg Declaration, which stated that "the only legitimate object which States should endeavour to accomplish during war is to weaken the military forces of the enemy . . . [and] that this object would be exceeded by the employment of arms which uselessly aggravate the sufferings of disabled men, or render their death inevitable."[3] This was reaffirmed in the 1907 Hague Regulations, which forbade the employment of "arms, projectiles, or material calculated to cause unnecessary suffering".[4] Article 35 is considered customary international law in both international and non-international armed conflicts;[5] using weapons of a nature to cause superfluous injury or unnecessary suffering is a war crime under Article 8 of the Rome Statute.[6] The ICJ acknowledged the primacy of the principle in the *Nuclear Weapons Advisory Opinion*:

> The cardinal principles contained in the texts constituting the fabric of humanitarian law are the following . . . it is prohibited to cause unnecessary suffering to combatants: it is accordingly prohibited to use weapons causing them such harm or uselessly aggravating their suffering . . . States do not have unlimited freedom of choice of means in the weapons they use . . . In conformity with the aforementioned principles, humanitarian law, at a very early stage, prohibited certain types of weapons either because of their indiscriminate effect on combatants and civilians or because of the unnecessary suffering caused to combatants, that is to say, a harm greater than that unavoidable to achieve legitimate military objectives . . . these fundamental rules are to be observed by all States . . . because they constitute intransgressible principles of international customary law.[7]

The first part of Article 35 affirms a fundamental principle of IHL – that of balancing humanity and military necessity, rejecting the maxim "*Kriegsraison geht vor Kriegsmanier*" (the necessities of war take precedence over the rules of war).[8] This philosophy, that "the commander on the battlefield can decide in every case whether the rules will be respected or ignored, depending on the demands of the military situation at the time",[9] would be obviously detrimental to all parties involved in armed conflicts: "if combatants were to have the authority to violate the laws of armed conflict every time they consider this violation to be necessary for the success of an operation, the law would cease to exist."[10]

The second part of Article 35 enunciates another fundamental principle of IHL – the prohibition on causing superfluous injury and unnecessary suffering. This

---

[3] St Petersburg Declaration, Preamble; see also Lieber Code, arts. 14 and 16, which state that "[m]ilitary necessity, as understood by modern civilized nations, consists in the necessity of those measures which are indispensable for securing the ends of the war, and which are lawful according to the modern law and usages of war" (art. 14) and that "military necessity does not admit of cruelty – that is, the infliction of suffering for the sake of suffering or for revenge, nor of maiming or wounding except in fight, nor of torture to extort confessions. It does not admit of the use of poison in any way, nor of the wanton devastation of a district" (art. 16).
[4] Hague IV 1907, art. 23(e).   [5] ICRC CIHL Study, r. 70.   [6] Rome Statute, art. 8(2)(b)(xx).
[7] *Nuclear Weapons*, paras. 78–9.   [8] AP Commentary, p. 391, para. 1386.   [9] Ibid.
[10] Ibid. See also Morris Greenspan, *The Modern Law of Land Warfare* (Berkeley/Los Angeles, CA: UCLA Press, 1959), p. 314.

prohibition lies at the heart of the numerous weapons treaties in the law of armed conflict, and, as such, requires some analysis – what exactly is superfluous injury and unnecessary suffering?

The rule on superfluous injury and unnecessary suffering "is intended to restrain the suffering inflicted on opposing combatants, rather than civilians".[11] Moreover, superfluous injury and unnecessary suffering are not assessed in IHL from a purely medical point of view.[12] When an informal working group of medical experts were called upon to deliver their expert opinion to the Conference of Government Experts on the Use of Certain Conventional Weapons, the working group stated that:

> from a strictly medical standpoint it seems impossible at the present stage of medical knowledge to objectively define suffering or to give absolute values permitting comparisons between human individuals. Pain, for instance, which is but one of many components of suffering, is subject to enormous individual variations. Not only does the pain threshold vary between human beings: at different times it varies in the same persons, depending upon circumstances.[13]

The ICRCs own perspective on superfluous injury and unnecessary suffering is that "[i]t is forbidden to employ weapons, projectiles, substances, methods and means which uselessly aggravate the sufferings of disabled adversaries or render their death inevitable in all circumstances".[14] This approach seems to correlate with the position later espoused by a number of States during the Diplomatic Conferences, who "understood the injuries covered by that phrase to be limited to those which were more severe than would be necessary to render an adversary *hors de combat.*"[15]

The prohibition on causing unnecessary suffering or superfluous injury is not a prohibition on causing *any* injury; as Dinstein notes, a weapon "is not banned on the ground of 'superfluous injury or unnecessary suffering' merely because it causes 'great' or even 'horrendous' suffering or injury. The effects of . . . certain weapons may be repulsive, but that is not, in and of itself, enough to render these weapons illegal."[16] Rather, it is that these injuries are excessive in relation to the military advantage achieved, or, as Solis puts it, banned weapons are banned because they

---

[11] Gary Solis, *The Law of Armed Conflict: International Humanitarian Law in War* (Cambridge University Press, 2010), p. 270.

[12] Ibid.

[13] ICRC, "Statement Concerning Unnecessary Suffering Presented by the Informal Working Group of Medical Experts", in *Report on the Second Session of the Conference of Government Experts on the Use of Certain Conventional Weapons* (ICRC, January-February 1976), www.loc.gov/rr/frd/Military_Law/pdf/RC-conf-experts-1976.pdf, p. 140 (*"Lugano Report"*).

[14] ICRC, "Article 33: Prohibition of Unnecessary Injury", in *Draft Additional Protocols to the Geneva Conventions of August 12, 1949: Commentary* (Geneva: ICRC, 1973), p. 41.

[15] Official Records XV, p. 267, para. 21.

[16] Yoram Dinstein, *The Conduct of Hostilities under the Law of International Armed Conflict,* 2nd edn (Cambridge University Press, 2010), p. 59.

"increase suffering without increasing military advantage".[17] Indeed, this interpretation has been confirmed by the ICJ, which defined unnecessary suffering as "a harm greater than that avoidable to achieve legitimate military objectives".[18] In terms of the "quantum" of harm necessary for a weapon to breach the prohibition, State practice suggests that the "degree of 'superfluous' injury must be clearly disproportionate . . . the suffering must outweigh substantially the military necessity for the weapon."[19]

The second basic rule in relation to means and methods of warfare is the Article 51(4) prohibition on the employment of means or methods of warfare that are indiscriminate.[20] Article 51(4) of AP I states:

Indiscriminate attacks are prohibited. Indiscriminate attacks are:

(a) those which are not directed at a specific military objective;
(b) those which employ a method or means of combat which cannot be directed at a specific military objective; or
(c) those which employ a method or means of combat the effects of which cannot be limited as required by this Protocol; and consequently, in each such case, are of a nature to strike military objectives and civilians or civilian objects without distinction.

The prohibition on means and methods that are deemed indiscriminate is considered customary international law in both international and non-international armed conflicts.[21] Breach of the prohibition is a war crime under the Rome Statute of the ICC.[22] The ICJ confirmed the importance of the rule on indiscriminate means and methods, stating in the *Nuclear Weapons Advisory Opinion* that parties to a conflict may not "use weapons that are incapable of distinguishing between civilian and military targets".[23]

It should be noted that potentially *all* weapons can be indiscriminate – as Blank and Noone point out "there is little doubt that any weapon can be used in an indiscriminate way during conflict, such as spraying automatic weapons fire into a crowd with no regard for the presence of civilians or others *hors de combat*".[24] Rather, the prohibition on indiscriminate means and methods ensures that fundamentally indiscriminate means and methods of warfare are pre-emptively banned – such as missiles which have no aiming system. Moreover, lawful means and methods must not be employed in indiscriminate ways. The prohibition is thus two-fold.

---

[17] Solis, *The Law of Armed Conflict*, p. 270.   [18] *Nuclear Weapons*, para. 78.
[19] W. Hays Parks, "Joint Service Combat Shotgun Program" (1997) *The Army Lawyer* 16, at 18.
[20] See also Chapter 7 on indiscriminate attacks.   [21] ICRC CIHL Study, r. 71.
[22] Rome Statute, art. 8(2)(b)(xx).   [23] *Nuclear Weapons*, para. 257.
[24] Laurie Blank and Gregory Noone, *International Law and Armed Conflict: Fundamental Principles and Contemporary Challenges in the Law of War* (New York: Wolters Kluwer, 2013), p. 512.

3. THE OBLIGATION TO ASSESS THE LEGALITY OF NEW MEANS AND METHODS OF WARFARE

Article 36 of Protocol I obliges parties to the Protocol to review the legality of any newly-developed weapons prior to their employment:

In the study, development, acquisition or adoption of a new weapon, means or method of warfare, a High Contracting Party is under an obligation to determine whether its employment would, in some or all circumstances, be prohibited by this Protocol or by any other rule of international law applicable to the High Contracting Party.[25]

Thus, any new weapons must be assessed in line with AP I and IHL more generally, as well as any other relevant international law treaty. Article 36 does not, however, oblige parties to prohibit a weapon because it *might* be used in an indiscriminate or disproportionate manner. The determination of the legality of a particular weapon "is to be made on the basis of normal use of the weapon as anticipated at the time of evaluation";[26] States are "not required to foresee or analyse all possible misuses of a weapon, for almost any weapon can be misused in ways that would be prohibited".[27] Article 36 acts as an important "stop-gap" in the law – to ensure that parties to AP I do not attempt to justify the use of new weaponry by claiming that there is no specific prohibition on the weapon in particular, thus permitting its usage.

As mentioned, Article 36 obliges State parties to undertake reviews of weaponry prior to their use. For example, the United States' review process involves the relevant Judge Advocate (i.e., drawn from the service proposing to use the weapon, such as the Air Force Judge Advocate, or Navy Judge Advocate) reviewing the proposed weapon at a number of stages, including prior to the award of the engineering and development contract, and again before the production of the weapon.[28] Any review assesses the weapon in light of whether the injury caused by the weapon would be superfluous, cause unnecessary suffering, or be generally considered "grossly disproportionate"[29] to any advantage gained. In reviewing the combat shotgun for US armed forces, the history and development of the combat shotgun was examined, focusing specifically on its legality in light of other treaties, such as those on expanding bullets[30] as well as whether a weapon capable of inflicting multiple wounds upon a single enemy combatant would be considered as inflicting superfluous injury or unnecessary suffering.[31]

---

[25] AP I, art. 36.   [26] AP Commentary, p. 423, para. 1466.
[27] Comments by the Rapporteur of Committee III, in Official Records XV, p. 269, para. 31.
[28] See Blank and Noone, *International Law and Armed Conflict*, p. 513.   [29] Ibid.
[30] Hays Parks, "Joint Service Combat Shotgun Program", 21–24.   [31] Ibid., 18.

4. SPECIFICALLY PROHIBITED WEAPONS AND RESTRICTED WEAPONS

In addition to these general rules regarding weapons, a number of treaties specifically prohibit particular weapons.

a. Explosive and dum-dum bullets

Some of the first IHL treaties related to projectiles – specifically, exploding and expanding bullets. The first of these was the 1868 St Petersburg Declaration, which bans the use, in both land and naval warfare, of projectiles that weigh less than 400 grammes and that are either explosive or charged with fulminating or inflammable substances. The limit of 400 grammes was, according to publicists, essentially arbitrary[32] and became obsolete fairly soon after its adoption. While the Brussels Declaration affirmed the prohibition,[33] the Hague Rules of Air Warfare 1923 did not prohibit the use of explosive projectiles when used by or against aircraft, even when such projectiles are used against ground troops.[34] Indeed, the ICRC CIHL Study affirms that State practice since the adoption of the Declaration has modified the obligations it contains,[35] such that anti-personnel use of the bullets is prohibited in both international and non-international armed conflicts, but that the use of the bullets in an anti-materiel capacity is not prohibited.[36]

The Hague Declaration (IV, 3) of 1899 bans the use of bullets "which expand or flatten easily in the human body, such as bullets with a hard envelope which does not entirely cover the core or is pierced with incisions".[37] The examples given in the Declaration are indicative only; the Declaration's prohibition applies to any bullets designed to expand or flatten easily in the human body.[38] Such projectiles, often called dum-dum bullets,[39] are designed to flatten upon hitting soft tissue, causing a larger radial wound which creates significant damage to tissue and bone and, frequently, fails to exit the body.[40] The use of such expanding bullets is a war crime

---

[32] Frits Kalshoven, "Arms, Armaments and International Law" (1985) 191 RCADI 183 at 207.

[33] Brussels Declaration 1874, art. 13(e).

[34] Hague Rules of Air Warfare 1923, art. 18. See also Dinstein, *The Conduct of Hostilities*, p. 69.

[35] ICRC CIHL Study, r. 78.

[36] See William Boothby, *Weapons and the Law of Armed Conflict* (Oxford University Press, 2009), p. 142.

[37] Hague IV 1899, Declaration III.   [38] Boothby, *Weapons and the Law of Armed Conflict*, p. 145.

[39] Reportedly so-called because they were first manufactured by British soldiers stationed at Dum-Dum in India: Dinstein, *The Conduct of Hostilities*, p. 69. See also R. A. Steindler, "The Case of the Mysterious Dum-Dum Bullet" (1983) 4 *American Journal of Forensic Medicine and Pathology* 205.

[40] David Andrew, "Over a Century of Service: The .303 Projectile and its Wounding Capabilities – An Historical Profile" (2003) 12 *Australian Military Medicine* 144 at 145. See also A. Keith and H. M. Rigby, "Modern Military Bullets: A Study of Their Destructive Effects", *The Lancet*, 2 December 1899, pp. 1499–1507.

under the Rome Statute,[41] and is considered unlawful under the customary law of both international and non-international armed conflicts.[42] However, a number of States continue to use expanding bullets in law enforcement operations.[43] The ICRC[44] and some publicists[45] claim such usage is lawful, as the use of expanding projectiles in situations not amounting to armed conflict does not conflict with the prohibition on use in armed conflicts.[46]

b. Mines and booby-traps

Landmines – explosive devices that are engineered to detonate when a person or object is in contact with or proximity to the device – have an ancient pedigree; military historians trace the use of explosive devices placed underneath the ground to the 1400s.[47] Mines as we know them now have become common means by which an advance by an enemy force can be blocked, delayed or diverted.[48] However, landmines are essentially indiscriminate – they detonate regardless of whether the person triggered them is a combatant or a civilian. The widespread use of landmines in the Korean and Vietnam Wars, as well as in States beset by internal conflicts such as Afghanistan, Angola and Cambodia, resulted in numerous injuries and fatalities, often mainly within the civilian population.[49] In response, organisations like the ICRC[50] routinely called for a prohibition on the use of such devices. The Additional Protocol I prohibition on indiscriminate means and methods[51] of warfare further solidified the campaign, which resulted in the adoption in 1980 of the Conventional Weapons Convention (CCW), which, in its Protocol II, banned certain landmines and booby-traps.[52]

---

[41] Rome Statute, art. 8(2)(b)(xvii).

[42] ICRC CIHL Study, r. 77. Note however that a number of States consider the prohibition to apply only to international armed conflicts – see, e.g., UK Ministry of Defence, *The Manual of the Law of Armed Conflict* (Oxford University Press, 2004), para. 6.9.

[43] See further Kenneth Watkin, "Chemical Agents and Expanding Bullets: Limited Law Enforcement Exceptions or Unwarranted Handcuffs?" (2006) 36 IYBHR 43.

[44] ICRC CIHL Study, r. 77.   [45] Dinstein, *The Conduct of Hostilities*, p. 70.

[46] For more on the debate regarding the legality of expanding bullets in all situations of violence, see William Boothby, *Weapons and the Law of Armed Conflict* (Oxford University Press, 2009), pp. 146–50.

[47] William Schneck, "The Origins of Military Mines", *Engineer Bulletin*, July 1998, www.fas.org/man/dod-101/sys/land/docs/980700-schneck.htm.

[48] Boothby, *Weapons and the Law of Armed Conflict*, p. 155.   [49] Ibid.

[50] See Draft Rules for the Protection of the Civilian Population from the Dangers of Indiscriminate Warfare 1955, Geneva, art. 10(3), and Draft Rules for the Limitation of the Dangers Incurred by the Civilian Population in Time of War 1956, Geneva, www.icrc.org/ihl/INTRO/420?OpenDocument, art. 15. See also Stuart Maslen, *Commentaries on Arms Control Treaties, Volume I: The Convention on the Prohibition of the Use, Stockpiling, Production, and Transfer of Anti-Personnel Mines and on their Destruction* (Oxford University Press, 2004), pp. 3–6.

[51] AP I, art. 51(4).

[52] Protocol (II) on Prohibitions or Restrictions on the Use of Mines, Booby Traps and Other Devices 1980, Geneva, 10 October 1980, in force 2 December 1983, 1342 UNTS 168 ("Protocol (II) CCW").

i. Booby-traps

Protocol II of the CCW prohibits the use of booby-traps, defined in Article 2(2) as "any device or material which is designed, constructed or adapted to kill or injure and which functions unexpectedly when a person disturbs or approaches an apparently harmless object or performs an apparently safe act".[53] The Protocol reaffirms the prohibition of indiscriminate means and methods of armed conflict,[54] and seeks to achieve this aim by outlining an expansive list of objects that are prohibited from being booby-trapped, such as protective emblems (like the Red Cross or Red Crescent); sick, wounded or dead persons; burial or cremation sites; medical facilities, equipment, supplies or transportation; children's toys and other portable objects specially connected to children such as objects for feeding, health, hygiene, clothing or education; food or drink; kitchen utensils and appliances (excluding those in military installations); animals or animal carcasses; and objects of religious, historical or cultural significance.[55] Article 6 also provides that it is prohibited to use any booby-trap designed to cause superfluous injury or unnecessary suffering.[56] The Protocol also bans the use of booby-traps, either directly or indiscriminately, against civilians.[57]

The rules on booby-traps are primarily designed to protect civilians; however, some protections extend to combatants also.[58] Thus, while it is permissible to booby-trap kitchen utensils or appliances in military installations, the booby-trapping of food or drink is not permitted.[59] The rules on booby-traps are considered customary international law, in both international and non-international armed conflicts.[60]

ii. Landmines

In addition to booby-traps, certain types of landmines are banned under Protocol II to the CCW. Article 2 of Protocol II to the CCW defines mines as:

any munition placed under, on or near the ground or other surface area and designed to be detonated or exploded by the presence, proximity or contact of a person or vehicle, and "remotely delivered mine" means any mine so defined delivered by artillery, rocket, mortar or similar means or dropped from an aircraft[61]

Article 4 of the Protocol outlines the bulk of the prohibitions relating to mines, stating that:

---

[53] Ibid., art. 2(2).   [54] Ibid., art. 3(3).   [55] Ibid., art. 6(1)(b).   [56] Ibid., art. 6(2).   [57] Ibid., art. 3.
[58] Frits Kalshoven, "Arms, Armaments and International Law" (1985) 191 RCADI 183,, 255; Dinstein, *The Conduct of Hostilities*, p. 71.
[59] See A. P. V. Rogers, "A Commentary on the Protocol on Prohibitions or Restrictions on the Use of Mines, Booby Traps and Other Devices" (1987) 26 RDMDG 185, 199.
[60] ICRC CIHL Study, r. 80.   [61] Protocol (II) CCW, art. 2(1).

It is prohibited to use weapons to which this Article applies in any city, town, village or other area containing a similar concentration of civilians in which combat between ground forces is not taking place or does not appear to be imminent, unless either:

(a) they are placed on or in the close vicinity of a military objective belonging to or under the control of an adverse party; or

(b) measures are taken to protect civilians from their effects, for example, the posting of warning signs, the posting of sentries, the issue of warnings or the provision of fence.

Anti-ship mines are not included in the Protocol.[62] Remotely delivered mines – mines whose location cannot be recorded in a designated minefield – are also restricted, under Article 5:

1. The use of remotely delivered mines is prohibited unless such mines are only used within an area which is itself a military objective or which contains military objectives, and unless:

(a) their location can be accurately recorded in accordance with Article 7(1)(a); or

(b) an effective neutralizing mechanism is used on each such mine, that is to say, a self-actuating mechanism which is designed to render a mine harmless or cause it to destroy itself when it is anticipated that the mine will no longer serve the military purpose for which it was placed in position, or a remotely-controlled mechanism which is designed to render harmless or destroy a mine when the mine no longer serves the military purpose for which it was placed in position.

2. Effective advance warning shall be given of any delivery or dropping of remotely delivered mines which may affect the civilian population, unless circumstances do not permit.

While Protocol II went some way to limiting the damage caused by mines, the continued loss of life and limb experienced around the world prompted a push for an outright ban on anti-personnel mines. To that end, Amended Protocol II[63] was adopted in 1996, which extended the scope of Protocol II to include non-international armed conflicts.[64] The Amended Protocol prohibited the use of land-mines which "employ a mechanism or device specifically designed to detonate the munition by the presence of commonly available mine detectors as a result of their magnetic or other non-contact influence during normal use in detection oper-ations";[65] which are "equipped with an anti-handling device that is designed in such a manner that the anti-handling device is capable of functioning after the mine has ceased to be capable of functioning";[66] which are indiscriminately used or

---

[62] Ibid., art. 1.
[63] Protocol on Prohibitions or Restrictions on the Use of Mines, Booby-Traps and Other Devices 1996, Geneva, as amended on 3 May 1996, in force 3 December 1998, 2048 UNTS 93 ("Amended Protocol (II) CCW").
[64] Ibid., art. 1(2).   [65] Ibid., art. 3(3).   [66] Ibid., art. 3(6).

located;[67] which cause unnecessary suffering or superfluous injury;[68] or which are otherwise undetectable.[69] The Amended Protocol obliges State parties to ensure the recording of locations of minefields,[70] and the clearing of mined areas following the cessation of hostilities.[71]

However, the Amended Protocol "fell far short of common expectations".[72] Failing to ban landmines outright, its provisions were "widely considered to be overly complex and insufficiently stringent to deal with the extent of the humanitarian crisis".[73] The Canadian government initiated a review process of landmines in 1996, consulting with NGOs like the International Campaign to Ban Landmines, the ICRC, and with numerous States also keen to ban landmines outright. The result of this process was the International Strategy Conference: Towards a Global Ban on Anti-Personnel Mines (the Ottawa Conference),[74] which led to the negotiation and adoption, in 1997, of the Convention on the Prohibition of the Use, Stockpiling, Production and Transfer of Anti-Personnel Mines and on their Destruction, also known as the Ottawa Convention.[75]

The Ottawa Convention prohibits outright the use, stockpiling, production and transfer of anti-personnel mines, and obliges States parties to the Convention to engage in measures to destroy their own stockpiles. Anti-vehicle mines are not prohibited under the Convention. The Ottawa Convention applies in both international and non-international armed conflicts, and the general provisions of the Convention relating to placement, removal, and neutralisation of landmines are considered customary international law in both international and non-international armed conflicts.[76]

It is interesting to note that, during the Ottawa Process, debate emerged as to whether non-State actors should be allowed to attend the diplomatic conferences, participate in debates, and eventually sign the final document.[77] That idea was rejected during the negotiations of the Ottawa Convention; however, an alternate, parallel document – the Deed of Commitment – was created by the non-governmental organisation Geneva Call,[78] for the express purpose of allowing armed opposition groups to publicly express their intent to abide by the rules of the Ottawa Convention. As of January 2015, the "Deed of Commitment for Adherence to a Total Ban on Anti-Personnel Mines and for Cooperation in Mine Action"[79]

---

[67] Ibid., art. 3(8).   [68] Ibid., art. 3(3).   [69] Ibid., art. 4.   [70] Ibid., art. 9.   [71] Ibid., art. 10.

[72] Dinstein, *The Conduct of Hostilities*, p. 73. See also Stuart Maslen and Peter Herby, "An International Ban on Anti-Personnel Mines: History and Negotiations of the 'Ottawa Treaty'" (1998) 38 IRRC 693.

[73] Maslen, *Commentaries on Arms Control Treaties*, pp. 21–2.

[74] For a more detailed discussion of the so-called "Ottawa Process" that led to the adoption of the Ottawa Convention banning landmines, see further ibid., pp. 26–44.

[75] Oslo, 18 September 1997, in force 1 March 1999, 2056 UNTS 211 ("Ottawa Convention").

[76] ICRC CIHL Study, rr. 81–3.   [77] See Maslen, *Commentaries on Arms Control Treaties*, pp. 53, 64, 74–5.

[78] Geneva Call, *Geneva Call*, www.genevacall.org/.

[79] Geneva Call, *Deed of Commitment under Geneva Call for Adherence to a Total Ban on Anti-Personnel Mines and for Cooperation in Mine Action*, 2000, www.genevacall.org/wp-content/uploads/dlm_uploads/2013/12/DoC-Banning-anti-personnel-mines.pdf.

has been signed by forty-eight armed groups around the world.[80] The Deed has had a significant impact, with a number of non-State actors destroying mine stockpiles; for instance, in 2006, a stockpile of over 3,000 anti-personnel and 140 anti-vehicle mines was destroyed by the Polisario Front armed group in the Western Sahara region.[81]

c. Incendiary weapons

Also restricted by the CCW are certain incendiary weapons – that is, weapons designed to injure or kill persons, and damage or destroy property, through fire. Protocol III to the CCW[82] does not prohibit the use of incendiary devices – such as flame-throwers or napalm – outright, but rather prohibits their use against civilians or civilian objects.[83] Protocol III also prohibits the use of air-delivered incendiary weapons, and limits non-air-delivered incendiary attacks, against a military objective if such objective is located within a concentration of civilians.[84] The Protocol does not explicitly prohibit the use of incendiary weapons against combatants. However, the ICRC has claimed that the anti-personnel use of incendiaries is contrary to customary international law in both international and non-international armed conflicts.[85]

d. Non-detectable fragments

Protocol I to the CCW[86] prohibits the use of weapons that injure primarily through use of fragments that cannot be detected through X-ray, such as plastic or glass. The prohibition on such weapons is considered customary international law in both international and non-international armed conflicts.[87] These weapons are prohibited because the fragments in the weapons are undetectable to conventional medical scans, rendering effective medical treatment almost impossible. As such, they cause unnecessary suffering. The Protocol is a blanket prohibition, protecting both combatants and civilians.[88] However, the prohibition on such weapons applies only to those weapons whose *primary* method of injury is through non-detectable

---

[80] Geneva Call, *Armed Non-State Actors*, www.genevacall.org/how-we-work/armed-non-state-actors/.

[81] See Andrew Clapham, *Human Rights Obligations of Non-State Actors* (Oxford University Press, 2005), pp. 291–9.

[82] Protocol (III) on Prohibitions or Restrictions on the Use of Incendiary Weapons 1980, Geneva, 10 October 1980, in force 2 December 1983, 1342 UNTS 137 ("Protocol (III) CCW").

[83] Ibid., art. 2(1).   [84] Ibid., art. 2(2), 2(3).   [85] ICRC CIHL Study, r. 85.

[86] Protocol (I) on Non-Detectable Fragments 1980, Geneva, 10 October 1980, in force 2 December 1983, 1342 UNTS 168.

[87] ICRC CIHL Study, r. 79.

[88] Boothby, *Weapons and the Law of Armed Conflict*, p. 196; Kalshoven, "Arms, Armaments and International Law", p. 252.

fragments. It is not illegal to, for example, use plastic casing on a grenade, as it is the explosives within the grenade, and not the plastic used to house the explosives, that is the primary method of causing injury.[89]

e. Blinding laser weapons

The use of weapons of which the sole combat function is to cause permanent blindness is prohibited under Protocol IV to the CCW.[90] Protocol IV, adopted in 1995, is a rarity in the law of armed conflict, in that it marks the first time a weapon has been prohibited before it has "actually been deployed in a battle situation".[91] While blinding laser weapons had been developed by some States, the Protocol was debated and adopted prior to the weapons being used in the field.[92]

Protocol IV prohibits any weapons that "as their sole combat function or as one of their combat functions . . . cause permanent blindness to unenhanced vision, that is to the naked eye or to the eye with corrective eyesight device".[93] It is also prohibited to transfer such weapons to any other State or non-State entity. The Protocol only prohibits the use of weapons with the sole function of causing permanent blindness; weapons that might incidentally blind (e.g., that are equipped with lasers as a range finder or targeting device) are not prohibited.[94] Weapons that cause temporary blindness – such as "flash-bang" grenades[95] – are permitted, as the weapon is not designed to cause permanent blindness as its combat function.[96] The ICRC states that the prohibition on blinding laser weapons is customary in both international and non-international armed conflicts.[97]

---

[89] Boothby, *Weapons and the Law of Armed Conflict*, p. 197.
[90] Protocol (IV) on Blinding Laser Weapons 1995, Vienna, 13 October 1995, in force 30 July 1998, 1380 UNTS 370 ("Protocol (IV) CCW")
[91] Boothby, *Weapons and the Law of Armed Conflict*, p. 209.
[92] ICRC, *The Vienna Review Conference: Success on Blinding Laser Weapons but Deadlock on Landmines* (ICRC, December 1995), www.icrc.org/eng/resources/documents/misc/57jmt3.htm; see also generally Burrus Carnahan and Marjorie Robertson, "The Protocol on Blinding Laser Weapons: A New Direction for International Humanitarian Law" (1996) 90 AJIL 484.
[93] Protocol (IV) CCW, art. 1.
[94] Boothby, *Weapons and the Law of Armed Conflict*, p. 211. See also Christopher Greenwood, "The Law of Weaponry at the Start of the New Millennium", in Leslie Green and Michael Schmitt (eds.), *International Law Studies – Volume 71: The Law of Armed Conflict: Into the Next Millennium* (Newport, RI: US Naval War College, 1998), p. 207.
[95] Stun grenades, also called "flash-bangs", are grenades which emit a loud noise and a bright burst of light, temporarily disorienting anyone in proximity to the explosion. They are non-lethal and have no permanent effects on hearing or sight. See further "Stun Grenade", in *Oxford Essential Dictionary of the US Military* (Oxford University Press, 2002), www.oxfordreference.com/view/10.1093/acref/9780199891580.001.0001/acref-9780199891580-e-7984?rskey=dr0jC6&result=7707.
[96] Boothby, *Weapons and the Law of Armed Conflict*, p. 211.
[97] ICRC CIHL Study, r. 86. However, see further Boothby, *Weapons and the Law of Armed Conflict*, pp. 213–14, who challenges the contention that "a rule adopted as a matter of conventional law for the first time in 1995 and ratified by a little less than half the states in the world is, some ten years later, described as a customary norm". See also Steven Haines, 'Weapons, Means and Methods of Warfare', in Elizabeth Wilmshurst and Susan Breau (eds.), *Perspectives on the ICRC Study on Customary International Humanitarian Law* (Cambridge University Press, 2007), p. 277, n. 17.

f. Explosive remnants of war

The final protocol to the CCW, Protocol V,[98] obliges States parties to clear their territory of explosive remnants of war (ERW), such as cluster munitions, landmines and other unexploded ordnance. The Protocol does not ban the use of such weapons, but rather seeks to limit the damage that is caused by unexploded and abandoned ordnance, damage which is usually disproportionately felt by the civilian population.[99] Under the Protocol, parties are obliged to take pre- and post-conflict measures to secure and remove ERW[100] from their territory, as well as to assist other States in their own clearance, removal and destruction activities.[101]

g. Cluster munitions

Cluster munitions are best described as "a canister-type device dispenser containing sub-munitions, or bomblets, that disperse in the air after the dispenser opens. The bomblets, in general, arm after dispersal and detonate upon impact".[102] They are designed to spread their sub-munitions over a wide space, and are effective for attacking large or dispersed targets.

However, cluster munitions have historically caused significant casualties in civilian populations, in part due to the technological short-comings of the weapons. The scattering dispersal of bomblets was, until recently, unable to be limited in scope – a single cluster munition would spread dozens or hundreds of bomblets across a wide area.[103] Furthermore, bomblets were not generally equipped with self-destruct or deactivation mechanisms; if bomblets landed without detonation, they would become *de facto* mines.[104] Indeed, the "dud" rate of bomblets – the percentage of bomblets in a cluster bomb that failed to detonate on impact – could be as high as 25 or 30 per cent.[105] The impact on the civilian population of cluster munitions has been notably disproportionate, with the effects of the weapons frequently felt years, if not decades, following the cessation of hostilities. For instance, Cambodia was

---

[98] Protocol (V) on Explosive Remnants of War 2003, Geneva, 28 November 2003, in force 12 November 2006, 2399 UNTS 100 ("Protocol (V) CCW").

[99] See Louis Maresca, "A New Protocol on Explosive Remnants of War: The History and Negotiation of Protocol V to the 1980 Convention on Certain Conventional Weapons" (2004) 86 IRRC 815 at 815–17 on the civilian toll of ERW.

[100] Protocol (V) CCW, art. 3.   [101] Ibid., arts. 7–8.

[102] T. S. Tudor, J. K. Walker and N. S. Richards (eds.), *Air Force Operations and the Law: A Guide for Air and Space Forces* (USAF Judge Advocate General's Department, 2002), p. 296.

[103] See Human Rights Watch, *Meeting the Challenge: Protecting Civilians through the Convention on Cluster Munitions* (Human Rights Watch, November 2010), www.hrw.org/sites/default/files/reports/armsclusters1110webwcover.pdf, p. 2.

[104] Andrew Feickert and Paul K. Kerr, *Cluster Munitions: Background and Issues for Congress* (US Congressional Research Service, 29 April 2014), www.fas.org/sgp/crs/weapons/RS22907.pdf, p. 2

[105] See Human Rights Watch, *Ticking Time Bombs: NATO's Use of Cluster Munitions in Yugoslavia* (Human Rights Watch, June 1999), www.hrw.org/reports/1999/nato2/nato995-01.htm#P77_13303.

subject to numerous cluster-munition attacks during the Vietnam War, with US estimates of 9,500 sorties delivering up to 87,000 air-dropped cluster munitions;[106] nearly forty years after the conflict, contamination from unexploded ordnance is estimated to span 900 km².[107]

Cluster munitions were initially discussed during the original Conventional Weapons Conference in 1977–80, as well as at subsequent review conferences in 2001 and 2006. Protocol V went some way to addressing the humanitarian concern raised by cluster munitions, but a (limited) ban on the weapons did not eventuate until 2008. The 2008 Convention on Cluster Munitions[108] bans the use, development, stockpiling, production, retention or transfer to a third party of cluster munitions.[109] No State party to the Convention may assist, encourage or induce any State to engage in the use of cluster munitions,[110] and States parties are obliged to destroy any existing stocks of the weapons.[111] The Convention also obliges States parties to assist other States in removing and destroying stockpiles of cluster munitions,[112] and to provide victim assistance for persons affected by the weapons.[113]

While the seemingly expansive ban on the use, development, stockpiling, production, retention or transfer of cluster munitions is laudable, only certain kinds of cluster munitions are covered by the Convention. The Convention defines cluster munitions as:

a conventional munition that is designed to disperse or release explosive submunitions each weighing less than 20 kilograms, and includes those explosive submunitions. It does not mean the following:

(a) A munition or submunition designed to dispense flares, smoke, pyrotechnics or chaff; or a munition designed exclusively for an air defence role;
(b) A munition or submunition designed to produce electrical or electronic effects;
(c) A munition that, in order to avoid indiscriminate area effects and the risks posed by unexploded submunitions, has all of the following characteristics:
   (i) Each munition contains fewer than ten explosive submunitions;
   (ii) Each explosive submunition weighs more than four kilograms;
   (iii) Each explosive submunition is designed to detect and engage a single target object;
   (iv) Each explosive submunition is equipped with an electronic self-destruction mechanism;
   (v) Each explosive submunition is equipped with an electronic self-deactivating feature.[114]

Only those cluster munitions defined in the Convention are covered by the ban.

---

[106] Cluster Munition Coalition, *A Timeline of Cluster Bomb Use*, www.stopclustermunitions.org/en-gb/cluster-bombs/use-of-cluster-bombs/a-timeline-of-cluster-bomb-use.aspx.
[107] Landmine and Cluster Munition Monitor, *Contamination and Clearance*, 2013, www.the-monitor.org/index.php/publications/display?url=cmm/2013/CMM_Contamination_And_Clearance_2013.html.
[108] Oslo, 3 December 2008, in force 1 August 2010, 2688 UNTS 39.   [109] Ibid., art. 1(b)–(c).
[110] Ibid., art. 1(c).   [111] Ibid., art. 3.   [112] Ibid., art. 4.   [113] Ibid., art. 5.   [114] Ibid., art. 2(2).

h. Chemical weapons and poison

Among some of the earliest weapons treaties were those relating to the use of poison and other chemicals. The 1899 Hague Declaration Concerning Asphyxiating Gases[115] obliged parties to the Hague Regulations to "abstain from the use of projectiles the sole object of which is the diffusion of asphyxiating or deleterious gases";[116] the use of poison was prohibited in Article 23(a) of the Hague Regulations.[117]

The use of chemical weapons – in the form of deleterious gases – was more comprehensively regulated in the 1925 Protocol for the Prohibition of the Use in War of Asphyxiating, Poisonous or Other Gases, and of Bacteriological Methods of Warfare,[118] also known as the Geneva Gas Protocol. That instrument prohibited "the use in war of asphyxiating, poisonous or other gases, and of all analogous liquids materials or devices" and also prohibited the employment of "bacteriological methods of warfare".[119] The adoption of the Geneva Gas Protocol was prompted by the widespread use of chemical weapons during the First World War, and the horrific injuries they caused – for example German armed forces released 160 tons of chlorine gas along the trenches in Ypres on 22 April 1915, resulting in the deaths of five thousand French soldiers and the wounding of 100,000 in only one day.[120]

Despite the absolute injunction against the use of chemical weapons in the Geneva Gas Protocol, chemical weapons continued to be used by participants in armed conflicts throughout the twentieth century.[121] The US and Soviet Union did not ratify the Geneva Gas Protocol until 1975;[122] widespread use of chemical weapons on both sides of the Iran–Iraq War of the 1980s resulted in thousands of deaths.[123] It was only in 1993 that an outright ban on chemical weapons was adopted, in the form of the Convention on the Prohibition of the Development, Production, Stockpiling and Use of Chemical Weapons and on their Destruction 1993 ("Chemical Weapons Convention" or "CWC").[124] The CWC bans chemical weapons outright; State parties to the Convention:

---

[115] Hague IV 1899, Declaration II.   [116] Ibid.   [117] Hague IV 1907, art. 23(a).

[118] Geneva, 17 June 1925, in force 8 February 1928, 94 LNTS 65 ("Geneva Gas Protocol").   [119] Ibid.

[120] Gerald Fitzgerald, "Chemical Warfare and Medical Response During World War I" (2008) 98 Am J Public Health 631, 631–2. By war's end, chlorine, mustard and phosgene gas were believed to have caused over 90,000 deaths and over one million casualties – see Seymour Hersh, *Chemical and Biological Warfare: America's Hidden Arsenal* (Indianapolis, in: Bobbs Merrill, 1968), pp. 4–5.

[121] See further Corey Hilmas, Jeffrey Smart and Benjamin Hill, "History of Chemical Warfare", in Martha Lenhart (ed.), *Medical Aspects of Chemical Warfare* (Washington DC: Borden Institute/US Department of the Army, Office of the Surgeon General, 2008).

[122] Dinstein, *The Conduct of Hostilities*, p. 81; Blank and Noone, *International Law and Armed Conflict*, p. 520.

[123] See UN SC, Report of the Specialists Appointed by the Secretary-General to Investigate Allegations by the Islamic Republic of Iran Concerning the Use of Chemical Weapons: Note by the Secretary-General, UN Doc. S/16433, 26 March 1984; see also Tim McCormack, "International Law and the Use of Chemical Weapons in the Gulf War" (1990–1) 21 Cal W Int'l L J 1 at 10–17.

[124] Paris, 13 January 1993, in force 29 April 1997, 1974 UNTS 45.

[undertake] never under any circumstances:

(a) To develop, produce, otherwise acquire, stockpile or retain chemical weapons, or transfer, directly or indirectly, chemical weapons to anyone;

(b) To use chemical weapons;

(c) To engage in any military preparations to use chemical weapons;

(d) To assist, encourage or induce, in any way, anyone to engage in any activity prohibited to a State Party under this Convention.

2. Each State Party undertakes to destroy chemical weapons it owns or possesses, or that are located in any place under its jurisdiction or control, in accordance with the provisions of this Convention.

3. Each State Party undertakes to destroy all chemical weapons it abandoned on the territory of another State Party, in accordance with the provisions of this Convention.

4. Each State Party undertakes to destroy any chemical weapons production facilities it owns or possesses, or that are located in any place under its jurisdiction or control, in accordance with the provisions of this Convention.

5. Each State Party undertakes not to use riot control agents as a method of warfare.[125]

Article 1(5) prohibits the use of riot-control agents, such as tear gas, in warfare; however, the use of such agents in domestic disturbances and internal tensions not amounting to warfare is not illegal.[126] The use of chemical weapons is prohibited in both international armed conflicts and non-international armed conflicts,[127] and is considered customary international law.[128] The use of chemical weapons is a war crime.[129]

i. Biological and bacteriological weapons

The 1925 Geneva Gas Protocol also banned the use of bacteriological agents in warfare; however, as Dinstein notes, "over the years, it was felt necessary to address the issue of biological weapons head-on, delinked from gas warfare".[130] In 1972, the international community adopted the Convention on the Prohibition of the Development, Production and Stockpiling of Bacteriological (Biological) and Toxin Weapons and on Their Destruction (Biological Weapons Convention or BWC).[131] The BWC bans the use of biological weapons outright, and obliges parties to the treaty to undertake "never in any circumstances to develop, produce, stockpile or otherwise acquire or retain"[132] any "microbial or other biological agents, or toxins

---

[125] Ibid., art. 1.   [126] See Blank and Noone, *International Law and Armed Conflict*, p. 521.
[127] Chemical Weapons Convention, art. 1.   [128] ICRC CIHL Study, r. 74.
[129] Rome Statute, art. 8(b)(2)(xviii).   [130] Dinstein, *The Conduct of Hostilities*, p. 82.
[131] London/Moscow/Washington, 10 April 1972, in force 26 March 1975, 1015 UNTS 163.
[132] Biological Weapons Convention, art. 1.

whatever their origin or method of production, of types and in quantities that have no justification for prophylactic, protective or other peaceful purposes"[133] as well as any "weapons, equipment or means of delivery designed to use such agents or toxins for hostile purposes or in armed conflict."[134]

The BWC does not explicitly prohibit the "use" of biological weapons – only their development, stockpiling, production, retention or acquisition. However, as Dinstein notes, "the Preamble of the BWC gives vent to a flat abnegation of biological weapons"[135] by stating that one of the aims of the BWC is "to exclude the possibility of bacteriological (biological) agents and toxins being used as weapons".[136] The prohibition on the use of biological weapons therefore seems a reasonable inference. Indeed, the ICRC claims that the prohibition on the use, development, stockpiling, production, retention or acquisition of biological weapons is considered customary international law.[137] The use of bio-weapons is, however, not included in the Rome Statute of the ICC.[138]

5. PROHIBITED METHODS OF WARFARE

In addition to prohibited and restricted weapons, IHL prohibits or restricts certain methods of warfare. As with means, there are general rules regarding methods of warfare. Under Article 57(2) of AP I:

(a) those who plan or decide upon an attack shall:
  (i) do everything feasible to verify that the objectives to be attacked are neither civilians nor civilian objects and are not subject to special protection but are military objectives within the meaning of paragraph 2 of Article 52 and that it is not prohibited by the provisions of this Protocol to attack them;
  (ii) take all feasible precautions in the choice of means and methods of attack with a view to avoiding, and in any event to minimizing, incidental loss of civilian life, injury to civilians and damage to civilian objects;
  (iii) refrain from deciding to launch any attack which may be expected to cause incidental loss of civilian life, injury to civilians, damage to civilian objects, or a combination thereof, which would be excessive in relation to the concrete and direct military advantage anticipated;
(b) an attack shall be cancelled or suspended if it becomes apparent that the objective is not a military one or is subject to special protection or that the attack may be expected to cause incidental loss of civilian life, injury to civilians, damage to civilian objects, or a combination thereof, which would

---

[133] Ibid., art. 1(1).   [134] Ibid., art. 1(2).   [135] Dinstein, *The Conduct of Hostilities*, p. 83.
[136] Chemical Weapons Convention, Preamble.   [137] ICRC CIHL Study, r. 73.
[138] See Robert Cryer, *Prosecuting International Crimes: Selectivity and the International Criminal Law Regime* (Cambridge University Press, 2005), pp. 279–80, on the absence of bio-weapons in the Rome Statute.

be excessive in relation to the concrete and direct military advantage anticipated;

(c) effective advance warning shall be given of attacks which may affect the civilian population, unless circumstances do not permit.

3. When a choice is possible between several military objectives for obtaining a similar military advantage, the objective to be selected shall be that the attack on which may be expected to cause the least danger to civilian lives and to civilian objects.

In addition to these general principles, there are certain specific rules regarding permitted and prohibited methods of warfare, as described below.

a. Orders of "no quarter"

It is prohibited in all types of armed conflict to order or threaten that "no quarter" will be given; i.e., that there will be no survivors and that no prisoners will be taken. This was first prohibited in Article 23(d) of the Hague Regulations,[139] and is reaffirmed in Article 40 of AP I.[140] The prohibition on such orders is also included in AP II, in Article 4.[141] The prohibition on orders of no quarter is considered customary international law in both international and non-international armed conflicts,[142] and declaring no quarter is a war crime under the Rome Statute of the ICC.[143] Though a well-established rule of the law of armed conflict, examples where such prohibited orders have been made still exist. For instance, during the 1990 invasion of Kuwait, instructions were given to Iraqi armed forces ordering "the execution of every Kuwaiti military man should he fail to surrender to Iraqi forces"; Kuwaiti authorities condemned the orders as "savage practices".[144]

b. Perfidy

Perfidy is an act that invites "the confidence of an adversary to lead him to believe that he is entitled to, or is obliged to accord, protection under the rules of international law applicable in armed conflict, with intent to betray that confidence".[145] The essence of perfidy is the intentional misuse of a protected or particular status to invite or encourage an adversary to believe that the person acting perfidiously is immune from attack. Examples of acts that are prohibited as perfidious include feigning an intent to negotiate under a flag of truce or surrender; feigning an

---

[139] Hague IV 1907, art. 23(d).   [140] AP I, art. 40.   [141] AP II, art. 4.   [142] ICRC CIHL Study, r. 46.
[143] Rome Statute, art. 8(2)(b)(xii).
[144] Letter from Kuwait, dated 24 September 1990, to the UN Secretary-General, UN Doc. S/21815, 24 September 1990.
[145] AP I, art. 37(1).

incapacitation by wounds or sickness; feigning civilian, non-combatant status; and feigning protected status by the use of signs, emblems or uniforms of the United Nations or of neutral or other States not parties to the conflict.[146] Article 37(1) of AP I states that it is prohibited to kill, injure or capture an adversary by resort to perfidy.[147] The rules on perfidy are considered customary in both international and non-international armed conflicts.[148]

Article 8(2)(b)(xi) of the Rome Statute of the ICC makes perfidy a war crime; however, the terminology used in Article 8(2)(b)(xi) refers only to killing or wounding "treacherously individuals belonging to the hostile nation or army".[149] This terminology is drawn from Article 23(b) of the Hague Regulations, which prohibits the treacherous wounding or killing of an adversary.[150] Are treachery and perfidy synonymous? The Elements of Crimes of the Rome Statute employ the Article 37(1) definition of perfidy,[151] and the Commentary to the Rome Statute states that treachery and perfidy can be considered coterminous.[152] In 2009 perfidious activity was alleged to have taken place during Operation Cast Lead, when local Gazans as well as IDF soldiers reported seeing Hamas operatives putting on medical uniforms and attempting to commandeer ambulances.[153]

Perfidy must be distinguished from ruses of war, such as faking retreat or camouflaging troops, which are not considered perfidy and thus not prohibited. As outlined in Article 37(2):

Ruses of war are not prohibited. Such ruses are acts which are intended to mislead an adversary or to induce him to act recklessly but which infringe no rule of international law applicable in armed conflict and which are not perfidious because they do not invite the confidence of an adversary with respect to protection under that law. The following are examples of such ruses: the use of camouflage, decoys, mock operations and misinformation.[154]

---

[146] Ibid. See further Chapter 5 on misuse of the protected emblems.   [147] Ibid.

[148] ICRC CIHL Study, rr. 58–61, 64; Rules 62 and 63 on the improper use of flags, military emblems, insignia or uniforms of the enemy (r. 62) and the use of military emblems, insignia or uniforms of neutral or other States not party to the conflict (r. 63) are considered customary in international armed conflicts only. The ICRC argues that the customary prohibition is emerging, if not yet crystallising into an obligation, in non-international armed conflicts.

[149] Rome Statute, art. 8(2)(b)(xi).   [150] Hague IV 1907, art. 23(6).

[151] See Elements of Crimes, Official Records of the Assembly of States Parties to the Rome Statute, 1st sess., New York, 3–10 September 2002, www.icc-cpi.int/nr/rdonlyres/336923d8-a6ad-40ec-ad7b-45bf9de73d56/0/elementsofcrimeseng.pdf, p. 24; see also Knut Dörmann, *Elements of War Crimes under the Rome Statute of the International Criminal Court: Sources and Commentary* (Geneva: ICRC, 2003), p. 240.

[152] Michael Cottier, "Article 8(2)(b)(xi)", in Otto Triffterer (ed.), *Commentary on the Rome Statute of the International Criminal Court*, 2nd edn (Oxford: Hart, 2002), p. 386.

[153] Jason Koutsoukis, "Hamas Tried to Hijack Ambulances During Gaza War", *The Sydney Morning Herald*, 26 January 2009, www.smh.com.au/news/world/hamas-tried-to-hijack-ambulances-during-war/2009/01/25/1232818246374.html. However, the Goldstone Report did not find any evidence that such events occurred, though they could not categorically say that no attempts to use ambulances for military purposes were ever made: see Goldstone Report, pp. 118–19.

[154] AP I, art. 37(2).

Indeed, during the Second World War, allied forces engaged in numerous ruses in order to trick the Axis powers into thinking that the invasion of Europe would occur at the Pas-de-Calais, rather than the Contentin Peninsula in Normandy; the plans were termed Operation Bodyguard and Operation Fortitude.[155] Ruses employed included using decoy machinery and equipment, such as inflatable and papier-mâché trucks and tanks, mock airfields with wooden "airplanes", and a fake oil dock at Dover – constructed by stagehands from the British film industry.[156]

c. Siege warfare and starvation of civilians

Siege warfare is the practice of "encircling an enemy military concentration, a strategic fortress or any other location defended by the enemy, cutting it off from channels of support and supply".[157] Siege warfare is not prohibited outright, but there are limitations on the practice. Under Article 17 of GC IV:

The Parties to the conflict shall endeavour to conclude local agreements for the removal from besieged or encircled areas, of wounded, sick, infirm, and aged persons, children and maternity cases, and for the passage of ministers of all religions, medical personnel and medical equipment on their way to such areas.[158]

Article 54 of AP I further provides that:

1. Starvation of civilians as a method of warfare is prohibited.
2. It is prohibited to attack, destroy, remove or render useless objects indispensable to the survival of the civilian population, such as foodstuffs, agricultural areas for the production of foodstuffs, crops, livestock, drinking water installations and supplies and irrigation works, for the specific purpose of denying them for their sustenance value to the civilian population or to the adverse Party, whatever the motive, whether in order to starve out civilians, to cause them to move away, or for any other motive.
3. The prohibitions in paragraph 2 shall not apply to such of the objects covered by it as are used by an adverse Party:
   (a) as sustenance solely for the members of its armed forces; or
   (b) if not as sustenance, then in direct support of military action, provided, however, that in no event shall actions against these objects be taken which may be expected to leave the civilian population with such inadequate food or water as to cause its starvation or force its movement.
4. These objects shall not be made the object of reprisals.

---

[155] Dan van der Vat, *D-Day: The Greatest Invasion – A People's History* (Sydney: Allen and Unwin, 2003), pp. 34–6.
[156] See Stephen Ambrose, *D-Day June 6, 1944: The Climactic Battle of World War II* (New York: Touchstone, 1994), pp. 80–3.
[157] Dinstein, *The Conduct of Hostilities*, p. 220.   [158] GC IV, art. 17.

Thus, an absolute siege of a military installation is permissible. However, where civilians are affected (i.e., if the locality under siege has both civilian and military populations), then some of the key elements of siege warfare – cutting off supplies, destroying foodstuffs and water supplies – *are* prohibited. This prohibition has led some publicists to question "how can a siege be a siege if it is disallowed to destroy foodstuffs and drinking water installations sustaining the civilian population in a besieged, defended, town?"[159] Essentially, what the Protocol I rules on siege warfare have meant is that sieges "in the old meaning and function of the term"[160] are prohibited. However, what this new prohibition fails to recognise, according to publicists like Dinstein, is the:

> purpose of siege as a method of warfare, which is not to kill civilians with hunger and thirst, but to induce the encircled defended locality to surrender. The text of Article 54 fails to take into account the inherent nature of siege: starvation within the invested site continues only because the besieged garrison persists in waging warfare. Once the garrison surrenders, foodstuffs and drinking water must certainly be made available to all.[161]

Given the premium placed on the protection of civilians by IHL it seems unlikely that an interpretation of the law on siege warfare favouring a broad application of military necessity is sustainable. Article 8(2)(b)(xxv) of the Rome Statute criminalises the starvation of civilians as a method of warfare;[162] the ICRC CIHL Study also considers the prohibition on the starvation of civilians as customary international law in both international and non-international armed conflicts.[163] This was confirmed by the Ethiopia–Eritrea Claims Commission, which stated that the provisions of the Article 54 prohibition on attacking drinking water installations and other supplies indispensable to the survival of the civilian population had become part of customary IHL by 1999.[164]

d. Pillage

The prohibition on pillage is long-established in IHL, having been part of most of the major laws of armed conflict since the Lieber Code.[165] None of the IHL treaties defines pillage, and it is often equated with plunder or looting; the essence is the unlawful taking of property – public or private – without the owner's consent,

---

[159] Dinstein, *The Conduct of Hostilities*, p. 222.
[160] Ingrid Detter, *The Law of War*, 3rd edn (Oxford: Ashgate, 2013), p. 327.
[161] Dinstein, *The Conduct of Hostilities*, p. 223. See also G. A. Mudge, "Starvation as a Means of Warfare" (1969–70) 4 Int'l Lawyer 228 at 246.
[162] Rome Statute, art. 8(2)(b)(xxv).   [163] ICRC CIHL Study, r. 53.
[164] Eritrea-Ethiopia Claims Commission, *Partial Award: Western Front, Aerial Bombardments and Related Claims, Eritrea's Claims, 1, 3, 5, 9-13, 14, 21, 25, and 26*, 19 December 2005, 45 ILM 396, p. 416.
[165] Lieber Code, art. 44.

during an armed conflict.[166] It is a war crime in both international and non-international armed conflict under the Rome Statute, and the ICC's Elements of Crime emphasise the requirement that the taking be for personal or private use or gain – in contrast to a lawful military requisition.[167] In 2014 the ICC convicted Congolese warlord Germain Katanga of pillage committed by his militia, who had raided a village and removed housing materials, domestic goods and livestock.[168]

Pillage of individuals and/or locations is prohibited in a number of contexts. Pillage of military wounded and sick is prohibited under Article 15 of GC I[169] and Article 18 of GC II.[170] Pillage of civilian wounded and sick is prohibited under Article 16 of GC IV.[171] Pillage of towns and other locations is prohibited under the Hague Regulations[172] and Article 4(2)(g) of AP II.[173] The prohibition on pillage is considered customary international law in both international and non-international armed conflicts.[174]

Unfortunately, as demonstrated in the *Katanga* case, pillage in times of armed conflict remains prevalent. Numerous cases at the ICTY have also dealt with the question of pillage,[175] and the ICTR[176] as well as the Special Court for Sierra Leone (SCSL)[177] have examined allegations of pillage.

e. Other rules relating to methods of warfare

i. Belligerent reprisals

Belligerent reprisals are actions which would normally be contrary to the laws of war but which are justified because they are taken by one party to an armed conflict against another party, in response to the latter's violation of the law of armed conflict. Reprisals are thus a "self-help LOAC enforcement action; the purpose of a reprisal is to sanction the enemy for its violations and compel the enemy to comply with the LOAC in the future".[178] As summarised by Dinstein, the customary international law rules on belligerent reprisals comprise five conditions:

---

[166] The UK Manual, for example, defines pillage as "the obtaining of property against the owner's will and with the intent of unjustified gain": UK Ministry of Defence, *Manual of the Law of Armed Conflict*, para. 5.35.1.

[167] Rome Statute, arts. 8(2)(b)(xvi), 8(2)(e)(v); ICC, Elements of Crimes, arts. 8(2)(b)(xvi), 8(2)(e)(v).

[168] *Prosecutor* v. *Katanga*, ICC-01/04–01/07, *Judgment*, 8 March 2014, paras. 949–57.   [169] GC I, art. 15.

[170] GC II, art. 18.   [171] GC IV, art. 16.   [172] Hague IV 1907, arts. 28, 47.   [173] AP II, art. 4(2)(g).

[174] ICRC CIHL Study, r. 52.

[175] See, e.g., *Prosecutor* v. *Jelisić*, IT-95-10-T, Judgment, 14 December 1999, paras. 48–9; *Prosecutor* v. *Delalić et al.*, IT-96-21-T, Judgment, 16 November 1998, paras. 590–1; *Prosecutor* v. *Blaškić*, IT-95-14-T, Judgment, 3 March 2000, para. 184; *Prosecutor* v. *Kordić and Čerkez*, IT-95-14/2-A, Appeals Judgment, 17 December 2004, para. 84; *Prosecutor* v. *Hadžihasanović*,. IT-01-47-T, Judgment, 15 March 2006, paras. 49–56; *Prosecutor* v. *Martić*, IT-95-11, Judgment, 12 June 2007, paras. 101–4.

[176] *Prosecutor* v. *Bisengimana*, ICTR-00-60-T, Judgment, 13 April 2006, paras. 7, 12, 19, 25 and 203.

[177] *Prosecutor* v. *Fofana and Kondewa*, SCSL-04-14-T, Judgment, 2 August 2007, paras. 157–66; *Prosecutor* v. *Brima et al.*, SCSL-04-16-T, Judgment, 20 June 2007, paras. 751–8.

[178] Geoffrey Corn *et al.*, *The Law of Armed Conflict: An Operational Approach* (New York: Wolters Kluwer, 2012), p. 226.

(i) protests or other attempts to secure compliance of the enemy with LOIAC [law of international armed conflict] must be undertaken first (unless the fruitlessness of such steps "is apparent from the outset");

(ii) a warning must generally be issued before resort to belligerent reprisals;

(iii) the decision to launch belligerent reprisals cannot be taken by an individual combatant, and must be left to higher authority;

(iv) most significantly, belligerent reprisals must always be proportionate to the original breach of LOIAC;

(v) once the enemy desists from its breach of LOIAC, belligerent reprisals must be terminated.[179]

In addition to these rules, there are certain persons and objects against which belligerent reprisals may never be launched – including the wounded, sick and shipwrecked,[180] POWs,[181] civilians and the civilian population,[182] certain civilian objects,[183] cultural property,[184] the natural environment,[185] works and installations containing dangerous forces[186] and objects indispensable to the survival of the civilian population.[187] The extensive number of prohibitions on permissible belligerent reprisals has thus led to a significant diminution in the practice of belligerent reprisals.[188] As noted by Corn *et al.*, the practical effect of these extensive limitations "is to eliminate reprisals as viable options to respond to enemy non-compliance with the LOAC. In essence, compliance with AP I would limit reprisals to enemy armed forces, their facilities, and equipment – an outcome that seems illogical as all of these targets are always subject to lawful attack."[189]

Indeed, though the ICRC claims that certain kinds of belligerent reprisals are prohibited under customary law in both international and non-international armed conflict,[190] they nonetheless acknowledge that:

Because of existing contrary practice, albeit very limited, it is difficult to conclude that there has yet crystallized a customary rule specifically prohibiting reprisals against civilians during the conduct of hostilities. Nevertheless, it is also difficult to assert that a right to resort to such reprisals continues to exist on the strength of the practice of only a limited number of States, some of which is also ambiguous. Hence, there appears, at a minimum, to exist a trend in favour of prohibiting such reprisals.[191]

---

[179] Dinstein, *The Conduct of Hostilities*, p. 255.   [180] GC I, art. 46; GC II, art. 46.   [181] GC III, art. 13(3).

[182] GC IV, art. 33(3); AP I, art. 51(6).   [183] AP I, art. 52.

[184] Ibid., art. 53(c); Hague Convention on Cultural Property, art. 4(4).   [185] AP I, art. 55.

[186] Ibid., art. 56.   [187] Ibid., art. 54.

[188] See Christopher Greenwood, "Twilight of the Law of Belligerent Reprisals" (1989) 20 Netherlands YB Int'l L 35.

[189] Corn *et al.*, *The Law of Armed Conflict*, p. 227.   [190] ICRC CIHL Study, rr. 145–8.   [191] Ibid., r. 146.

The ICRC points to the ICTY cases of *Martić*[192] and *Kupreškić*[193] as evidence of the emerging prohibition on reprisals against civilians, with the Tribunal stating in *Kupreškić*:

It should be added that while reprisals could have had a modicum of justification in the past, when they constituted practically the only effective means of compelling the enemy to abandon unlawful acts of warfare and to comply in future with international law, at present they can no longer be justified in this manner. ... Due to the pressure exerted by the requirements of humanity and the dictates of public conscience, a customary rule of international law has emerged on the matter under discussion.[194]

However, some publicists, such as Dinstein, have argued that "this extravagant claim is far from convincing".[195] Indeed, the ICTY itself essentially acknowledged the legality of reprisals in the 2007 case of *Martić*, stating that reprisals may be permitted provided they meet the strict conditions established under customary international law.[196]

ii. Mercenaries

The use of mercenaries in armed conflicts is prohibited under Article 47 of AP I; see further Chapter 4 of this book.

iii. Parachutists in distress

Under Article 42(1) of AP I, no-one "parachuting from an aircraft in distress shall be made the object of attack during his descent".[197] This provision was based on Article 20 of the Hague Rules of Air Warfare 1923, which provides: "[i]n the event of an aircraft being disabled, the persons trying to escape by means of parachutes must not be attacked during their descent."[198] As Dinstein notes, "during their descent parachutists in distress are assimilated to *hors de combat*"[199] much like those who are shipwrecked and, as such, must be protected from direct attack. This provision in Article 42 only applies to parachutists (aircrews and passengers) who are bailing out of aircraft in distress. Airborne troops – like paratroopers – are excluded from this provision, even if they themselves are bailing out of a distressed aircraft.[200]

The prohibition on attacking such persons applies only for as long as they are in descent; once they have reached the ground, Article 42(2) applies, which states that "upon reaching the ground in territory controlled by an adverse Party, a person who

---

[192] *Prosecutor v. Martić*, IT-95-11, Judgment, 12 June 2007, paras. 15–17.

[193] *Prosecutor v. Kupreškić*, IT-95-16-T, Judgment, 14 January 2000, paras. 527–31.

[194] Ibid., paras. 530–1.   [195] Dinstein, *The Conduct of Hostilities*, p. 260.

[196] *Prosecutor v. Martić*, IT-95-11, Judgment, 12 June 2007, para. 465.   [197] AP I, art. 42(1).

[198] Hague Rules of Air Warfare 1923, art. 20.   [199] Dinstein, *The Conduct of Hostilities*, p. 162.

[200] AP I, art. 42(3).

has parachuted from an aircraft in distress shall be given an opportunity to surrender before being made the object of attack, unless it is apparent that he is engaging in a hostile act".[201] The rule in Article 42 is considered customary international law, in both international and non-international armed conflicts.[202] During the Iran–Iraq War, both parties to the conflict respected the prohibition on attacking persons bailing out of aircraft in distress,[203] even though neither Iran nor Iraq was a party to Protocol I at the time.[204]

iv. Espionage

Espionage is defined in AP I as the act of gathering or attempting to gather information of military value within enemy territory "through an act of false pretences or deliberately in a clandestine manner".[205] The Hague Regulations define espionage in more detail:

A person can only be considered a spy when, acting clandestinely or on false pretences, he obtains or endeavours to obtain information in the zone of operations of a belligerent, with the intention of communicating it to the hostile party.

Thus, soldiers not wearing a disguise who have penetrated into the zone of operations of the hostile army, for the purpose of obtaining information, are not considered spies. Similarly, the following are not considered spies: Soldiers and civilians, carrying out their mission openly, entrusted with the delivery of despatches intended either for their own army or for the enemy's army. To this class belong likewise persons sent in balloons for the purpose of carrying despatches and, generally, of maintaining communications between the different parts of an army or a territory.[206]

Espionage is thus a lawful method of warfare; however, persons who are caught while engaging in espionage, under either the Hague or Geneva formulations, are not entitled to combatant or POW status[207] and will be liable for domestic prosecution on capture.[208] However, soldiers who wear distinctive insignia (or uniforms) while engaged in espionage will not be considered spies and will retain their combatant immunity.[209] Likewise, if a person engages in espionage while out of uniform (or devoid of any identifying marks) but manages to return to their own lines without capture, they will "regain" their combatant/POW immunities – that is to say, if they are "later captured as a lawful combatant, the former spy cannot be tried for past espionage".[210] Thus in summary:

---

[201] Ibid., art. 42(2).   [202] ICRC CIHL Study, r. 48.   [203] See ibid., Practice Relating to Rule 48.
[204] Iraq became party to AP I in 2010; Iran is not a party as of this writing: ICRC, *Treaties and State Parties to Such Treaties*, www.icrc.org/IHL.
[205] AP I, art. 46(3).   [206] Hague IV 1907, art. 29.   [207] See Chapter 4 on Combatants.
[208] Corn *et al.*, *The Law of Armed Conflict*, p. 226.   [209] Hague IV 1907, art. 29; AP I, art. 46(2).
[210] AP I, art. 46(4). See Chapter 4.

- a soldier engaged in espionage while in uniform is not a spy and has POW status if and whenever captured
- a person captured while engaging in espionage, and not in uniform, is a spy and does not have POW status, and
- a person who has engaged in espionage while not in uniform but manages to return to his own forces before capture does have POW status.

6. MEANS AND METHODS OF WARFARE OF INDETERMINATE OR CONTESTED STATUS

The last part of this chapter examines certain means and methods of warfare that have an indeterminate or contested status – that is, they are not *prima facie* illegal, in that there is no specific prohibition on their use or employment, but the employment of such means and methods is disputed among States and publicists as potentially being contrary to the general principles of IHL.

a. Depleted uranium

Depleted uranium (DU) is a by-product of the process by which uranium ore is turned into enriched uranium.[211] As the name implies, depleted uranium is less radioactive than uranium proper.[212] Munitions constructed with DU are notably stronger and more durable – the density of DU is 1.7 times that of lead;[213] as a result, DU munitions have remarkable armour-piercing capabilities.

The military utility of armour-piercing DU munitions, coupled with DU's lower radioactivity, has led to DU weapons being widely used in the armed forces of the US and UK,[214] with their first widespread use by those States in the First Gulf War (Operation Desert Storm) in 1991,[215] and then in the former Yugoslavia during the conflict in the 1990s.[216] However, following these conflicts, there were reports of

---

[211] OECD Nuclear Energy Agency and the International Atomic Energy Agency, Management of Depleted Uranium (OECD Publications Service, 2001), www.oecd-nea.org/ndd/pubs/2001/3035-management-depleted-uranium.pdf, p. 9.

[212] DU is around 40 per cent less radioactive than naturally occurring uranium. See further Naomi H. Harley *et al.*, *A Review of the Scientific Literature as it Pertains to Gulf War Illnesses* (Washington DC: National Defense Research Institute/RAND, 1999), p. 57; Owen Thomas Gibbons, "Uses and Effects of Depleted Uranium Munitions: Towards a Moratorium on Use" (2004) 7 YBIHL 191 at 194–8.

[213] Harley *et al.*, *Gulf War Illnesses*, p. 6.   [214] Boothby, *Weapons and the Law of Armed Conflict*, p. 243.

[215] Ministry of Defence, *DU in the Gulf War (90–91)*, 2003, webarchive.nationalarchives.gov.uk/20051219115252/http://mod.uk/issues/depleted_uranium/gulf_1.htm.

[216] See United National Environmental Programme (UNEP), *Depleted Uranium in Bosnia and Herzegovina: Post Conflict Environmental Assessment* (UNEP, 2003) postconflict.unep.ch/publications/BiH_DU_report.pdf; UNEP, *Depleted Uranium in Serbia and Montenegro: Post-Conflict Environmental Assessment in the Federal Republic of Yugoslavia* (UNEP, 2002), postconflict.unep.ch/publications/duserbiamont.pdf.

significant increases in cancer rates in Iraq,[217] as well as veterans presenting with a debilitating series of symptoms and maladies eventually dubbed "Gulf War Syndrome"[218] and "Balkans Syndrome".[219] Such medical problems led to calls to prohibit the use of DU munitions, due to the impact that DU may have on human health and the environment.[220]

DU weapons are not currently prohibited under the law of armed conflict.[221] The USAF Judge Advocate General's Department has stated that "there is no significant radiation hazard from depleted uranium".[222] Despite the presence of uranium, DU weapons are not classified as nuclear weapons[223] nor, according to the USAF Judge Advocate General's Department, does DU warrant classification as a poison weapon.[224] According to such reasoning, the use of DU munitions is lawful under the law of armed conflict.[225]

The potential health and environmental damage caused by DU weapons is disputed; as such, there do not appear to be grounds for prohibiting the weapons under IHL as it currently exists.[226]

b. White phosphorus

White phosphorus (WP) is an incendiary chemical which is "highly lipophilic [easily dissolves in lipids, ie fat] and penetrates tissues readily. White phosphorus combusts

---

[217] See Dahr Jamail, "Iraq: War's Legacy of Cancer", *Al-Jazeera*, 15 March 2013, www.aljazeera.com/indepth/features/2013/03/2013315171951838638.html; Alexander Smoltczyk, "Mystery in Iraq: Are US Munitions to Blame for Basra Birth Defects?", *Der Spiegel*, 18 December 2012, www.spiegel.de/international/world/researchers-studying-high-rates-of-cancer-and-birth-defects-in-iraq-a-873225.html.

[218] See US Department of Veterans Affairs Research Advisory Committee on Gulf War Veterans' Illnesses, *Gulf War Illness and the Health of Gulf War Veterans: Scientific Findings and Recommendations* (US Government Printing Office, November 2008) www.va.gov/rac-gwvi/docs/committee_documents/gwiandhealthofgwveterans_rac-gwvireport_2008.pdf.

[219] See Asaf Duraković, "On Depleted Uranium: Gulf War and Balkan Syndrome" (2001) 42 *Croatian Medical Journal* 130; Ian Fairlie, "The Health Hazards of Depleted Uranium" (2008) 3 *Disarmament Forum* 3.

[220] See generally Gibbons, "Use and Effects of Depleted Uranium". See also the statement made by the European Parliament on 22 May 2008, when the Parliament issued a resolution calling on "all EU Member States and NATO countries to impose a moratorium on the use of depleted uranium weapons and to redouble efforts towards a global ban" (approved by 491 votes in favour, 18 against and 12 abstentions): European Parliament, *European Parliament resolution of 22 May 2008 on (depleted) uranium weapons and their effect on human health and the environment – towards a global ban on the use of such weapons*, Doc. P6_TA(2008)0233, 22 May 2008.

[221] See generally Avril McDonald, "Depleted Uranium Weapons: The Next Target for Disarmament?" (2008) 3 *Disarmament Forum* 17.

[222] USAF Judge Advocate General, Air Force Operations and the Law, p. 37.

[223] Owen Thomas Gibbons, "Uses and Effects of Depleted Uranium Munitions", 195. See below for the legality of nuclear weapons under IHL.

[224] Boothby, *Weapons and the Law of Armed Conflict*, p. 243.

[225] Corn *et al.*, *The Law of Armed Conflict*, p. 219.

[226] See Lesley Wexler, "'Limiting the Precautionary Principle' Weapons Regulation in the Face of Scientific Uncertainty" (2006) 39 UC Davis LR 459 at 470–5, 495–505, for an overview of the conflicting evidence regarding the impact of DU weapons.

spontaneously when exposed to ambient oxygen."[227] Due to its highly combustible nature, WP is used as an incendiary munition to ignite fuel or ammunition depots. WP also produces copious smoke, which provides effective screening for firing positions or other military activities.[228] WP is most commonly deployed in shells, which explode in mid-air, releasing WP-coated material (like wool felt) which scatters over a wide area. For example, a 155mm artillery shell will typically release nearly six kilogrammes of WP in 116 WP coated felt wedges which, when deployed, cover an area of up to 250 metres in diameter.[229]

Due to its chemical structure, WP burns on human tissue can be extensive – WP will burn through human tissue until the ambient oxygen supply is exhausted.[230] Some research contends that WP also poisons internal organs: a report for the Israeli Ministry of Health states that:

in addition to its "usual" burn effects, white phosphorus is poisonous, and has serious consequences that intensify the effects of the injury. Many laboratory studies have shown that burns covering a relatively small area of the body – 12–15% in laboratory animals and less than 10% in humans – may be fatal because of their effects on the liver, heart and kidneys. Additional effects include serious hypocalcaemia and delayed healing of wounds and burns.[231]

Given such debilitating and deleterious effects, the anti-personnel use of WP has been prohibited by some States in their military manuals – for instance, the UK Manual of the Law of Armed Conflict states that WP "should not be used directly against personnel".[232] However, the use of WP "for marking or illuminating targets, creating smoke screens to cover military manoeuvres and incendiary purposes"[233] (i.e., not directed at personnel) is not illegal under IHL.[234] There is no specific treaty that regulates its use, and WP is therefore governed only by the general principles of IHL.[235]

[227] Johnathan Conner and Vikhyat Bebarta, "White Phosphorus Dermal Burns" (2007) 357 *The New England Journal of Medicine* 1530 at 1530.

[228] Blank and Noone, *International Law and Armed Conflict*, pp. 530–1.

[229] Human Rights Watch, *Rain of Fire: Israel's Unlawful Use of White Phosphorus in Gaza* (Human Rights Watch, March 2009), www.hrw.org/node/81760, p. 11.

[230] US Department of Defense, "Part I: Types of Wounds and Injuries, Chapter III, Burn Injury – Chemical Burns and White Phosphorus Injury" in *Emergency War Surgery: NATO Handbook* (US Government Printing Office, November 2000), www.rexresearch.com/survival/NATOemergsurgery.pdf.

[231] Israeli Ministry of Health, *Exposure to White Phosphorus* (Israel Ministry of Health War Room, 15 January 2009, Ref. Cast Lead SH9 01393109), cited in Human Rights Watch, *Rain of Fire*, p. 12.

[232] UK Ministry of Defence, *Manual of the Law of Armed Conflict*, para. 6.12.6.

[233] David Fidler, "The Use of White Phosphorus Munitions by US Forces in Iraq" (2005) 9 *ASIL Insights*, www.asil.org/insights/volume/9/issue/37/use-white-phosphorus-munitions-us-military-forces-iraq.

[234] Boothby, *Weapons and the Law of Armed Conflict*, p. 244.

[235] See also Fidler, "The Use of White Phosphorus Munitions", who argues that WP cannot be classified as a chemical weapon (and thus prohibited under the Chemical Weapons Convention) because its function is permitted under the CWC as it is used for "military purposes not connected with the use of chemical weapons and not dependent on the use of the toxic properties of chemicals as a method of warfare". Anti-materiel use of incendiaries is also permitted under the Conventional Weapons Convention.

Where the controversy arises is whether the injuries caused by the use of WP, even when not intentionally directed at civilians or personnel, are justifiable under the general IHL principles: do WP injuries amount to superfluous injury or unnecessary suffering? There is compelling evidence to suggest that the use of WP would violate the prohibition on weapons causing unnecessary suffering and superfluous injury, as well as the prohibition on weapons which have an indiscriminate effect. For instance, during Operation Cast Lead in Gaza in 2009, civilians were presenting with "relatively small burn injuries, which ought to be survivable, [but] were dying unexpectedly".[236] The comparatively high toxicity of WP, coupled with the seemingly indiscriminate manner in which the WP-laden wedges deploy, would seem to make a strong case for their potential illegality under the law of armed conflict. However, weapons are illegal for how they are *intended* to be used, rather than how they are actually used. As such, it is not possible to say that WP is currently illegal under IHL.

c. Nuclear weapons

For a generation that grew up during the Cold War, the spectre of nuclear war, and the devastation caused by nuclear warfare, was a shared experience – popular culture was rife with representations of impending nuclear holocausts,[237] and the images of the devastation caused by the only wartime use of nuclear weapons in Japan in 1945[238] were well-known. Seventy years later the threat of the use of nuclear weapons remains a potent concern.[239] States such as Iran continue to strive for nuclear power,[240] and concerns about unsecured nuclear materials falling into

---

[236] Rory McCarthy, "Gaza Doctors Struggle to Treat Deadly Burns Consistent with White Phosphorus", *The Guardian*, 21 January 2009, www.theguardian.com/world/2009/jan/21/gaza-phosphorus-israel.

[237] Films and television programmes such as *Fail-Safe* (1964), *La Jetée* (1960) and *The Day After* (1983), and books like George Orwell's *Nineteen Eighty-Four* (London: Secker & Warburg, 1949), Nevil Shute's *On the Beach* (Melbourne: Heinemann, 1957) and Ray Bradbury's *Fahrenheit 451* (New York: Ballantine Books, 1953) all drew on the collective fear of nuclear war, and the devastation that would follow a nuclear strike.

[238] With the bombing of Hiroshima and Nagasaki in August 1945, see François Bugnion, "The International Committee of the Red Cross and Nuclear Weapons" (2005) 859 IRRC 511 at 512–15.

[239] Currently nine States possess nuclear weapons capabilities – the US, UK, Russia, China, France, India, Pakistan, North Korea and Israel. However, India, Pakistan and Israel are not party to the Treaty on the Non-Proliferation of Nuclear Weapons 1968, New York, 1 July 1968, in force 5 March 1970, 729 UNTS 161, and are, as such, considered "non-declared" nuclear States. See further Stockholm International Peace Research Institute, *SIPRI Yearbook 2013*, www.sipri.org/yearbook/2013/06. South Africa had a nuclear weapons arsenal, which they relinquished, and a number of other States have also abandoned nuclear weapons programmes – see further Paul Davis, *Giving Up The Bomb: Motivations And Incentives* (The Nuclear Energy Futures Project, Centre for International Governance Innovation, Waterloo and the Canadian Centre for Treaty Compliance, Carleton University, 2009), icnnd.org/Documents/Davis_Giving_Up_NW.doc.

[240] See the information available on the website of the International Atomic Energy Agency on Iran (International Atomic Energy Agency, *Monitoring and Verification in Iran*, www.iaea.org/newscenter/focus/iaeairan/index.shtml).

the hands of armed non-State groups continue to be raised by international bodies like the UN.[241]

In order to better understand the legal situation regarding nuclear weapons, it is useful to know a little of the destructive effects of the weapons. Nuclear weapons are exploding weapons, which operate by either atomic fission[242] or atomic fusion,[243] and create a "very large and extremely rapid energy release"[244] resulting in damage from four direct effects – blast/shock, thermal radiation, electromagnetic pulse (EMP), and nuclear radiation.[245] The blast or shock from a nuclear weapon is felt as a high-pressure wave that moves out at supersonic speed from the epicentre of the explosion (known as Ground Zero). Nuclear weapons cause significant injuries and damage due to blast waves, a combination of the high pressure and long duration of the blast; most buildings in proximity to the blast will be demolished or heavily damaged, and high casualties result from "injuries resulting from impact of penetrating and non-penetrating missiles on the body or as the consequences of displacement of the body as a whole".[246]

The thermal effects of a nuclear weapon include the flash that results from the heat energy and visible light that travels from the centre of the explosion – the flash can cause permanent blindness if a person happens to be looking in the direction of the explosion when it occurs. The other thermal effect of a nuclear explosion is the heat pulse, which is comprised of both the heat felt in the initial fireball after the explosion, and the radiating heat that accompanies the shock front as its radiates outwards from Ground Zero.[247] The EMP results in disruption to electronic devices, due to the ionisation of the atmosphere that can occur when a nuclear explosion at high altitude causes electrons to be ejected from atoms in the air.[248]

Nuclear radiation in the form of neutrons and gamma rays can damage or destroy brain and muscle cells, as well as bone marrow and the lining of the intestines. Low-level radiation exposure can result in short-term nausea and vomiting, with

---

[241] See UN Security Council Resolution 1373 which "notes with concern the close connection between international terrorism and the illegal movement of nuclear materials" (UN Doc. S/Res/1373, 28 September 2001) and UN Security Council Resolution 1540 which "obliges all States to adopt and enforce appropriate effective laws which prohibit non-State actors to manufacture, acquire, possess, develop, transport, transfer or use nuclear weapons, in particular for terrorist purposes, and to establish domestic controls to prevent the proliferation of nuclear weapons, including the establishment of appropriate controls over related material" (UN Doc. S/Res/1540, 28 April 2004).

[242] "A process which disintegrates the atomic nucleus of a heavy metal such as uranium or plutonium": Bugnion, "The International Committee of the Red Cross and Nuclear Weapons", 518.

[243] "Thermonuclear weapons operate by atomic fusion, that is the combination of two light atoms, deuterium and tritium, which are both isotopes of hydrogen": ibid.

[244] Erik Koppe, *The Use of Nuclear Weapons and the Protection of the Environment during International Armed Conflict* (Portland, OR: Hart, 2008), p. 68.

[245] Ibid.

[246] Samuel Glasstone and Philip Dolan (eds.), *The Effects of Nuclear Weapons* (Washington: United States Department of Defense and the Energy Research and Development Administration, 1977), p. 548.

[247] L. W. McNaught, *Nuclear Weapons and Their Effects* (London: Brassey's Defence Publishers, 1984), pp. 37–49.

[248] Ibid., p. 30.

immediate high-level exposure (defined as radiation emitted within one minute of a nuclear blast) resulting in death, while residual exposure to radiation (all exposure after the first minute) can lead to birth defects, cancer and general "life-shortening".[249]

It is undisputed that IHL applies to nuclear weapons. This was acknowledged by the ICJ in the *Nuclear Weapons Advisory Opinion*, where the Court stated "in the view of the vast majority of States as well as writers there can be no doubt as to the applicability of humanitarian law to nuclear weapons. The Court shares that view."[250] Given the devastating effects of nuclear weapons on people and property, and given the general principles that regulate armed conflict, it would seem impossible that nuclear weapons could be considered lawful. As with all weapons, nuclear weapons are subject to the same customary and treaty norms that govern the conduct of hostilities more generally – the principles of distinction and discrimination, the rules on military necessity, the dictates of humanity and the prohibition on causing unnecessary suffering and superfluous injury.

However, nuclear weapons are not currently subject to any IHL treaty specifically prohibiting or regulating their use. Despite the applicability of general principles of IHL to nuclear weapons, there is also no customary prohibition on the use of such weapons either. This was affirmed by the ICJ in the *Nuclear Weapons Advisory Opinion*, where the Court held that "there is in neither customary nor conventional international law any comprehensive and universal prohibition of the threat or use of nuclear weapons as such".[251] The Court explained the status of nuclear weapons under the current law of armed conflict, stating that it could not:

make a determination on the validity of the view that the recourse to nuclear weapons would be illegal in any circumstance owing to their inherent and total incompatibility with the law applicable in armed conflict. Certainly, as the Court has already indicated, the principles and rules of law applicable in armed conflict – at the heart of which is the overriding consideration of humanity – make the conduct of armed hostilities subject to a number of strict requirements. Thus, methods and means of warfare, which would preclude any distinction between civilian and military targets, or which would result in unnecessary suffering to combatants, are prohibited. In view of the unique characteristics of nuclear weapons ... the use of such weapons in fact seems scarcely reconcilable with respect for such requirements. Nevertheless, the Court considers that it does not have sufficient elements to enable it to conclude with certainty that the use of nuclear weapons would necessarily be at variance with the principles and rules of law applicable in armed conflict in any circumstance.[252]

The Court went on to state that it could not rule out the legality of the use of nuclear weapons in self-defence in situations where the very existence of the State was under threat.[253] The decision of the ICJ was met with criticism by some publicists, such as Tim McCormack, who dismissed the ICJ's *non liquet* as, in effect, privileging

---

[249] Koppe, *The Use of Nuclear Weapons*, pp. 86–101.   [250] *Nuclear Weapons*, paras. 85–6.
[251] Ibid., para. 105(2)(B).   [252] Ibid., para. 95.   [253] Ibid.

the law on the use of force over that of the law of armed conflict.[254] Others, such as Christopher Greenwood, have argued that the entire endeavour of seeking an advisory opinion was "misconceived and the Court should not have been expected to answer such a question",[255] stating that there was simply not enough evidence to warrant the Court proclaiming an absolute prohibition on nuclear weapons: "for the Court to have done so ... would have been wholly unwarranted and a departure from the judicial function. Whatever views there may be about the direction in which the law should go, the job of the Court is to apply the law as it is."[256]

Thus despite the *potential* for nuclear weapons to violate the principles of distinction, humanity, proportionality, discrimination and the prohibitions on unnecessary suffering and superfluous injury, there is still the possibility that certain tactical nuclear weapons may be employed in such a way as to not violate those principles. Therefore, their use would not violate IHL, in the absence of any new treaty prohibiting their use.[257]

d. Cyber warfare

Cyber warfare has emerged as the so-called "fifth domain"[258] of warfare (after land, air, sea and space), where the "mouse and the keyboard"[259] rather than the tank and the rifle are the weapons of choice. Politicians and policy-makers have routinely spoken of an impending "cyber Pearl Harbor",[260] where cyber-attacks "as destructive as the terrorist attack on 9/11 ... virtually paralyze the nation".[261] Warnings of cyber-attacks against vulnerable systems predict near apocalyptic outcomes: "oil refineries and pipelines explode; air-traffic-control systems collapse; freight and metro trains derail; financial data are scrambled; the electrical grid goes down in the eastern United States; orbiting satellites spin out of control. Society soon breaks down as food becomes scarce and money runs out."[262]

---

[254] Tim McCormack, "A *Non Liquet* on Nuclear Weapons – The ICJ Avoids the Application of General Principles of International Humanitarian Law" (1997) 316 IRRC 76, at 88.

[255] Christopher Greenwood, "The Advisory Opinion on Nuclear Weapons and the Contribution of the International Court to International Humanitarian Law" (1997) 316 IRRC 65, at 65–6.

[256] Ibid., 75.

[257] As of this writing, the International Federation of the Red Cross and Red Crescent Societies, in conjunction with the ICRC, are engaged in an international campaign to prohibit the use, development, production, and stockpiling of nuclear weapons, in the form of a multilateral treaty. The first Conference on the Humanitarian Impact of Nuclear Weapons was held in 2013, with the second held in 2014. See further ICRC, *Nuclear Weapons*, www.icrc.org/eng/war-and-law/weapons/nuclear-weapons/index.jsp.

[258] "War in the Fifth Domain", *The Economist*, 1 July 2010, www.economist.com/node/16478792.

[259] Ibid.

[260] Leon E. Panetta, "Remarks by US Secretary of Defense Leon Panetta on Cybersecurity to the Business Executives for National Security", New York City, 11 October 2012, www.defense.gov/transcripts/transcript.aspx?transcriptid=5136.

[261] Ibid.

[262] Richard Clarke and Robert Knake, *Cyber War: The Next Threat to National Security and What To Do About It* (New York: Ecco, 2010), cited in "War in the Fifth Domain: Are the Mouse and Keyboard the New Weapons of Conflict", *The Economist*, 1 July 2010, www.economist.com/node/16478792.

It would be easy to dismiss such statements as hyperbole; however, States have not done so, and most major military powers now consider cyber war a genuine threat, establishing strategic command centres to deal with the question of cyber warfare. One of the first to do so was the US, which in 2009 established US Cyber Command (CYBERCOM) within the Department of Defense.[263] The US has tasked departments like CYBERCOM with readying the US for computer network operations (CNO), operations which comprise offensive actions such as computer network attack (CNA) and computer network exploitation (CNE), and defensive actions like computer network defence (CND) – all forming part of a broader concept of electronic warfare (EW):[264]

CNO is one of the latest capabilities developed in support of military operations. CNO stems from the increasing use of networked computers and supporting IT infrastructure systems by military and civilian organizations. CNO, along with EW, is used to attack, deceive, degrade, disrupt, deny, exploit, and defend electronic information and infrastructure. For the purpose of military operations, CNO are divided into CNA, CND, and related computer network exploitation (CNE) enabling operations. CNA consists of actions taken through the use of computer networks to disrupt, deny, degrade, or destroy information resident in computers and computer networks, or the computers and networks themselves. CND involves actions taken through the use of computer networks to protect, monitor, analyze, detect, and respond to unauthorized activity within DOD [Department of Defense] information systems and computer networks. CND actions not only protect DOD systems from an external adversary but also from exploitation from within, and are now a necessary function in all military operations. CNE is enabling operations and intelligence collection capabilities conducted through the use of computer networks to gather data from target or adversary automated information systems or networks.[265]

The US is just one of nearly thirty States or international organisations known to be engaged in developing offensive and defensive cyber capabilities.[266]

Is cyber warfare truly war, for the purposes of the applicability of IHL? States that have been subject to so-called cyber wars have indeed suffered disruptions. During the Russian–Georgian conflict in 2008, Georgian government and media websites were inaccessible, with some sites defaced with pro-Russian propaganda.[267] The Georgian Ministry of Defence website was subject to extensive cyber attacks,

---

[263] US Army Cyber Command, *Army Cyber,* www.arcyber.army.mil/org-uscc.html.

[264] US Joint Chiefs of Staff, *Joint Publication 3–13: Information Operations*, 13 February 2006, www.globalsecurity.org/intell/library/policy/dod/joint/jp3_13_2006.pdf, pp. II-4-II-5.

[265] Ibid.

[266] See further Jeffrey Carr, *Inside Cyber Warfare* (Sebastopol, CA: O'Reilly, 2012), pp. 243–61, for an overview of the cyber war capabilities of States (as of 2012).

[267] Independent International Fact Finding Mission on the Conflict in Georgia, *Report: Volume II*, September 2009, rt.com/files/politics/georgia-started-ossetian-war/iiffmcg-volume-ii.pdf, p. 217; "Russian Hackers Attack Georgia in Cyberspace", *Fox News*, 13 August 2008, www.foxnews.com/story/0,2933,402406,00.html ("hackers took over the Web site of Georgia's parliament and replaced it with an image that drew parallels between Georgian president Mikhail Saakashvili and Adolf Hitler").

resulting in loss of functionality.[268] The Independent Fact-Finding Mission on the Conflict in Georgia reported that "some experts believe that these attacks may have reduced Georgian decision-making capability, as well as its ability to communicate with allies, thereby possibly impairing the operational flexibility of Georgian forces."[269] The Fact-Finding Mission stated that, if the attacks could be attributed to Russia, then it was "likely that this form of warfare was used for the first time in an inter-state armed conflict".[270]

But are such "disruptions" enough to warrant the application of IHL? While cyber weaponry is not yet at the stage where it can cause the kinds of damage to persons and property that more conventional kinetic weapons can accomplish, such weapons may yet be developed. Consequently, the question of whether cyber war can be considered armed conflict, thus triggering the application of IHL, seems logically answerable in the affirmative, especially when one considers the statement made by the ICJ in the *Nuclear Weapons Advisory Opinion*: that international law applies to "any use of force, regardless of the weapons employed".[271]

Indeed, organisations like the ICRC have affirmed that IHL does indeed apply to cyber operations;[272] this position has been confirmed with the production of the *Tallinn Manual on the International Law Applicable to Cyber Warfare*.[273] The Manual is the work of an international group of experts drawn from government, the military and academia, who have drafted a list of the rules of international law, relating to both the use of force and armed conflict, which are applicable to cyber warfare. The Manual affirms that:

[even though t]here are no treaty provisions that directly deal with "cyber warfare" …. [t]his uncertainty does not mean cyber operations exist in a normative void. The International Group of Experts was unanimous in its estimation that both the *jus ad bellum* and *jus in bello* apply to cyber operations.[274]

The Manual defines a cyber attack as "a cyber operation, whether offensive or defensive, that is reasonably expected to cause injury or death to persons or damage or destruction to objects".[275] The Manual reaffirms the applicability of the general principles of the law of armed conflict to cyber operations – such as distinction,[276] proportionality,[277] discrimination,[278] the prohibition on causing superfluous injury or unnecessary suffering,[279] as well as the general rules on the protection of those

---

[268] Fact Finding Mission on the Conflict in Georgia, Report, p. 217.   [269] Ibid., pp. 217–18.   [270] Ibid.
[271] *Nuclear Weapons*, para. 39.
[272] See ICRC, *What limits does the law of war impose on cyber attacks?*, 28 June 2013, www.icrc.org/eng/resources/documents/faq/130628-cyber-warfare-q-and-a-eng.htm.
[273] *Tallinn Manual on the International Law Applicable to Cyber Warfare*, (Cambridge University Press, 2013), r. 20.
[274] Ibid., p. 5.   [275] Ibid., r. 30.   [276] Ibid., rr. 31–2.   [277] Ibid., r. 51.   [278] Ibid., rr. 43, 49.
[279] Ibid., r. 42.

hors de combat,[280] medical and religious personnel,[281] cultural property[282] and the natural environment.[283]

However, the Manual leaves unresolved the question of whether purely "cyber-on-cyber" attacks which cause damage only to digital resources (i.e., data) can be considered attacks under international law. The Manual states that such attacks will only trigger the law of armed conflict if they result "in the injury or death of individuals or damage or destruction of physical objects".[284] This would seem to preclude attacks that destroy or damage only "virtual" assets or property, something which may become a genuine issue as the technology develops. As McCormack and Liivoja have argued:

> Permanent destruction of data can have significant ramifications, even though falling short of physical violence. For example, wiping out the data in the entire State's banking system or patent database by means of a computer virus may have far more deleterious consequences than the physical destruction of a single data centre. Yet, under the Manual, the former would be an attack only if it can be demonstrated that some physical injury occurred, whereas the second is undoubtedly an attack.[285]

The Tallinn Manual is non-binding; however it is a valuable affirmation of the how cyber warfare can be governed by international law, and will likely only grow in importance as technological developments make cyber warfare more reality than theory.

e. Targeted killing and drone warfare

Targeted killing as a contemporary wartime tactic has become part of the conventional military and counter-terrorism strategy of a number of States in their operations against terrorist suspects, with Israel and the US the most notable practitioners.[286] There is no specific international legal definition of the term "targeted killing",[287] but a useful working definition has been proposed by the former UN Special Rapporteur on Extrajudicial, Summary or Arbitrary Executions, Philip Alston, who defined targeted killing as "the intentional, premeditated and deliberate use of lethal force, by States or their agents acting under colour of law, or by an organized armed group in armed conflict, against a specific individual who is not in the physical custody of the perpetrator".[288] The US is known for carrying out targeted killings with unmanned aerial vehicles (UAVs), also known as drones.

---

[280] Ibid., r. 32, 75.   [281] Ibid., r. 70.   [282] Ibid., r. 82.   [283] Ibid., r. 83.
[284] Ibid., Commentary to Rule 30, p. 108.
[285] Rain Liivoja and Tim McCormack, "Law in the Virtual Battlespace: The Tallinn Manual and the *Jus in Bello*" (2013) 15 YBIHL 45, 53.
[286] Philip Alston, *Study on Targeted Killings: Report of the Special Rapporteur on Extrajudicial, Summary or Arbitrary Executions*, UN Doc. A/HRC/14/24/Add.6, 28 May 2010, pp. 5–9.
[287] Solis, *The Law of Armed Conflict*, p. 538.   [288] Alston, *Study on Targeted Killings*, p. 3.

These armed aircraft are able to fire missiles at targets from a high altitude, while being piloted from thousands of miles away from the site of the strike.

One of the arguments used to justify targeted killing of terrorist suspects has been that such persons are taking direct part in hostilities against the targeting State, and under IHL they are subject to targeting for such participation.[289] A targeted killing will indeed be lawful if the target can be considered either a combatant (in international armed conflict) or a person who is deemed to be taking direct part in hostilities (DPH) (in international or non-international conflicts).[290] However, controversy has arisen regarding how States are making those targeting determinations, and what criteria they use to assess possible DPH. For instance, a report in the *New York Times* in 2012 revealed some of the details regarding the Obama administration policy on drone strikes and selection of targets, suggesting very broad targeting criteria, designating "all military-age males in a strike zone"[291] as lawful targets. When challenged on this issue, an administration source dismissed concerns that the targeting scope was too wide, suggesting that people in an area of known terrorist activity, or found with a senior al-Qaeda operative, are probably engaged in activities that would inevitably render them liable for targeting.[292]

Concerns have also been raised regarding the targeting of individuals beyond the scope of "active" hostilities. Some have argued that IHL only applies in very specific areas – i.e., where there are active armed hostilities.[293] Thus, beyond the scope of such hostilities, the law of armed conflict does not apply.[294] Critics of the drone wars as conducted by the US have stated that the practice of targeting persons anywhere they may be located has rendered the entire world a battlefield.[295]

---

[289] For example, see comments made by Colonel Daniel Reisner, IDF Legal Division in Israel Ministry of Foreign Affairs, "Press Briefing by Colonel Daniel Reisner – Head of the International Law Branch of the IDF Legal Division", 15 November 2000, mfa.gov.il/MFA/PressRoom/2000/Pages/Press%20Briefing%20by %20Colonel%20Daniel%20Reisner-%20Head%20of.aspx.

[290] See Chapter 4 on classification of combatants and the determination of persons taking direct part in hostilities.

[291] Jo Becker and Scott Shane, "Secret 'Kill List' Proves a Test of Obama's Principles and Will", *The New York Times*, 29 May 2012, www.nytimes.com/2012/05/29/world/obamas-leadership-in-war-on-al-qaeda.html? pagewanted=all.

[292] Ibid.

[293] See, e.g., the arguments forwarded by the plaintiff in *Al-Aulaqi* v. *Obama*, 727 F Supp 2d 1, 9 (DDC 2010): because Anwar al-Aulaqi was located in Yemen he was "outside the context of armed conflict". This argument has been made by Mary Ellen O'Connell in "Combatants and the Combat Zone" (2009) 43 U Rich L Rev 845, at 860; and by American Civil Liberties Union lawyer Hina Shamsi following the April 2014 dismissal of the *Al-Aulaqi* v. *Obama* case; Shamsi made reference to incongruence of a government that "claims to be at war, even far from any battlefield" (quoted in "Drone Killings Case Thrown Out in US", *The Guardian*, 7 April 2014).

[294] Christopher Greenwood, "Scope of Application of International Humanitarian Law", in Dieter Fleck (ed.), *The Handbook of International Humanitarian Law*, 2nd edn (Oxford University Press, 2008), pp. 61–2.

[295] See, e.g., Jeremy Scahill, *Dirty Wars: The World is a Battlefield* (London: Serpent's Tail, 2013).

However, the existing case law suggests that one should not prescribe an overly narrow approach to the geographical demarcations of the battlefield. In this respect, guidance can be found in the *Tadić* decision,[296] where the Chamber stated that:

[i]nternational humanitarian law applies from the initiation of such armed conflicts and extends beyond the cessation of hostilities until a general conclusion of peace is reached; or, in the case of internal conflicts, a peaceful settlement is achieved. Until that moment, international humanitarian law continued to apply in the whole territory of the warring States or, in the case of internal conflicts, the whole territory under the control of a party, whether or not actual combat takes place there.[297]

Concerns have also been raised regarding the use of drones to carry out targeted killings. Some have criticised drones as unlawful weapons, in that they are inherently indiscriminate, due to the collateral casualties and deaths that have resulted from their use.[298] While it is true that there have been significant civilian casualties as a result of drone strikes,[299] this has, arguably, more to do with the targeting criteria employed in the strike, than the use of the drone itself. As Alston has pointed out, "a missile fired from a drone is no different from any other commonly used weapon, including a gun fired by a soldier or a helicopter or gunship that fires missiles. The critical legal question is the same for each weapon: whether its specific use complies with IHL."[300]

Another criticism levelled at the use of drones is that the remote-piloted vehicles somehow "sterilise" the act of killing, and "that because they make it easier to kill without risk to a State's forces, policy makers and commanders will be tempted to interpret the legal limitations on who can be killed, and under what circumstances, too expansively".[301] Connected to this concern is fear of the so-called "PlayStation Effect" – "because operators are based thousands of miles away from the battlefield, and undertake operations entirely through computer screens and remote audiofeed, there is a risk of developing a 'Playstation' mentality to killing".[302] Proponents of this argument believe that operators may treat their targets more like fictional

---

[296] Jens David Ohlin, "The Duty to Capture" (2013) 97 *Minnesota Law Review* 1268, at 1290.

[297] *Prosecutor* v. *DuskoTadić*, IT-94-1-AR72, Decision on the Defence Motion for Interlocutory Appeal on Jurisdiction, 2 October 1995, para. 70.

[298] "US Drone Strike Killings in Pakistan and Yemen 'Unlawful'", *BBC News*, 22 October 2013, www.bbc.com/news/world-us-canada-24618701.

[299] See, e.g., work undertaken by the Bureau of Investigative Journalism (*Get the Data: Drone Wars*, www.thebureauinvestigates.com/category/projects/drones/drones-graphs/); *The Long War Journal*, a project of the Foundation for Defence of Democracies, (Bill Roggio, "Charting the Data for US Airstrikes in Pakistan, 2004–2012", *The Long War Journal*, 4 January 2015, www.longwarjournal.org/pakistan-strikes.php); and the Jamestown Foundation, (Bryan Glyn Williams, Matthew Fricker and Avery Plaw, "New Light on the Accuracy of the CIA's Predator Drone Campaign in Pakistan", *Terrorism Monitor*, 11 November 2010, www.jamestown.org/programs/tm/single/?tx_ttnews%5Btt_news%5D=37165&tx_ttnews%5BbackPid%5D=457&no_cache=1#.UyZRxE3xvxM).

[300] Alston, *Study on Targeted Killings*, p. 24.   [301] Ibid.   [302] Ibid., p. 25.

figures in a computer game, rather than real-life human beings with rights under international law.[303]

These are plausible concerns, but they are concerns which can, arguably, be refuted by recourse to the same rationale that underpins IHL more generally – the principles of humanity, proportionality, distinction and discrimination. The remoteness of the drone operator and the additional distance of the computer screen *could* lead to an operator developing a "PlayStation" approach to his or her activities. However, this is arguably no different to a sniper in the field perceiving their target as part of a computer game. A lawful weapon can always be used unlawfully, depending on the targeting criteria and training given to the person operating the weapon. Indeed, there is some emerging evidence to suggest that drone pilots are in fact acutely aware that they are watching and targeting human beings – the spike in the numbers of drone pilots presenting with post-traumatic stress disorder suggests that the opposite of the PlayStation effect is in play.[304]

However, one major concern that has been raised about the US drone programme *is* valid – the use of the Central Intelligence Agency (CIA) in the execution of targeted killings. It has been reported that the CIA has been overseeing drone strikes.[305] This raises concerns regarding US compliance with IHL because most CIA personnel are civilians. Any CIA operative conducting or otherwise participating in a drone strike may be considered as taking direct part in hostilities. A number of legal consequences attach to such DPH. First, as stated by Alston:

... intelligence personnel do not have immunity from prosecution under domestic law for their conduct. They are thus unlike state armed forces which would generally be immune from prosecution for the same conduct ... thus, CIA personnel could be prosecuted for murder under the domestic law of any country in which they conduct targeted drone killings, and could also be prosecuted for violations of applicable US law.[306]

Furthermore, if "they are 'directly participating in hostilities' by conducting targeted killings, intelligence personnel may themselves be targeted and killed" in keeping with the law of armed conflict.[307] Alston is not alone in this assessment of the status of CIA drone pilots. As Solis has argued:

---

[303] Philip Alston and Hina Shamsi, "A Killer Above the Law", *The Guardian*, 8 February 2010, www. theguardian.com/commentisfree/2010/feb/08/afghanistan-drones-defence-killing; Chris Cole, Mary Dobbing and Amy Hailwood, *Convenient Killing: Armed Drones and the "Playstation" Mentality* (Fellowship of Reconciliation, 2010), dronewarsuk.files.wordpress.com/2010/10/conv-killing-final.pdf.

[304] See Denise Chow, "Drone Wars: Pilots Reveal Debilitating Stress Beyond Virtual Battlefield", *LiveScience*, 5 November 2013, www.livescience.com/40959-military-drone-war-psychology.html; James Dao, "Drone Pilots Are Found to Get Stress Disorders Much as Those in Combat Do", *The New York Times*, 22 February 2013, www.nytimes.com/2013/02/23/us/drone-pilots-found-to-get-stress-disorders-much-as-those-in-combat-do.html?_r=0.

[305] Chris Woods, "CIA's Pakistan Drone Strikes Carried Out By Regular US Air Force Personnel", *The Guardian*, 14 April 2014, www.theguardian.com/world/2014/apr/14/cia-drones-pakistan-us-air-force-documentary.

[306] Alston, *Study on Targeted Killings*, p. 22.   [307] Ibid.

those CIA agents are, unlike their military counterparts but like the fighters they target, unlawful combatants. No less than their insurgent targets, they are fighters without uniforms or insignia, directly participating in hostilities, employing armed force contrary to the laws and customs of war. Even if they are sitting in Langley, the CIA pilots are civilians violating the requirement of distinction, a core concept of armed conflict, as they directly participate in hostilities. ... It makes no difference that CIA civilians are employed by, or in the service of, the US government or its armed forces. They are civilians; they wear no distinguishing uniform or sign, and if they input target data or pilot armed drones in the combat zone, they directly participate in hostilities – which means they may be lawfully targeted. ... Moreover, CIA civilian personnel who repeatedly and directly participate in hostilities may have what recent guidance from the International Committee of the Red Cross terms "a continuous combat function." That status, the ICRC guidance says, makes them legitimate targets whenever and wherever they may be found, including Langley.[308]

Furthermore, the US may be setting a bad precedent in their own use of drones. By claiming the right to target their enemies wherever they may find them, the US may be setting the stage for the same argument to be used against them in future. As noted by Alston:

Some 40 states already possess drone technology, and some already have, or are seeking, the capacity to fire missiles from them... The result is that the rules being set today are going to govern the conduct of many States tomorrow. I'm particularly concerned that the United States seems oblivious to this fact when it asserts an ever-expanding entitlement for itself to target individuals across the globe.[309]

The US has been prepared to launch attacks against particular persons even when they are in civilian locations such as family residences.[310] It is not unreasonable to suggest that civilian CIA pilots might eventually find themselves on the receiving end of similar treatment.

The use of drones in armed conflict will likely remain a contested issue, as the benefits of the technology continue to outweigh the detrimental effect of the policies in place surrounding the use of drones. It is incumbent on States who employ drones to ensure that any targeting policy behind the use of such aircraft is compliant with the law of armed conflict.

---

[308] Gary Solis, "CIA Drone Attacks Produce America's Own Unlawful Combatants", *The Washington Post*, 12 Match 2010, www.washingtonpost.com/wp-dyn/content/article/2010/03/11/AR2010031103653_pf.html.

[309] UN Human Rights Commissioner, "UN Expert Criticizes 'Illegal' Targeted Killing Policies and Calls on the US to Halt CIA Drone Killings", 2 June 2010, www.ohchr.org/EN/NewsEvents/Pages/DisplayNews.aspx?NewsID=10094&LangID=E.

[310] See, e.g., the 2009 drone attack which killed Baitullah Mehsud, a Pakistani Taliban operative, while he was at his father-in-law's house in South Waziristan province. Killed in the attack were Mehsud, his wife, her parents, Mehsud's uncle and eight others, including Mehsud's bodyguards. Mehsud was on the roof of the house in the process of being fitted with an intravenous drip. See Shane Harris, "Are Drone Strikes Murder?", *National Journal*, 9 January 2010, webspace.utexas.edu/rmc2289/LT/Shane%20Harris%20in%20NLJ%20on%20Drones.pdf.

7. CONCLUSION

Together with the law of targeting, the rules on means and methods of warfare constitute a comprehensive set of provisions which assist in achieving the aims of the law of armed conflict. However, as with all laws, IHL rules can be and have been broken. How international law deals with such violations of IHL is the subject of the final chapter of this book, which deals with the implementation, enforcement and accountability of IHL.

SUGGESTED READING

Boothby, William, *Weapons and the Law of Armed Conflict* (Oxford University Press, 2009)

Greenwood, Christopher, "The Law of Weaponry at the Start of the New Millennium" (1998) 71 *International Law Studies* 185

Melzer, Nils, *Targeted Killing in International Law* (Oxford University Press, 2008)

Oeter, Stefan, "Methods and Means of Combat", in Dieter Fleck (ed.), *The Handbook of International Humanitarian Law,* 3rd edn (Oxford University Press, 2013)

Saxon, Dan (ed.), *International Humanitarian Law and the Changing Technology of War* (Leiden: Martinus Nijhoff, 2013)

DISCUSSION QUESTIONS

1. Should white phosphorus be banned under the law of armed conflict?
2. Discuss the contrast between the illegality of riot-control agents in international armed conflicts, compared to their "legality" (or at least non-illegality) in international armed conflicts? Does this position seem compliant with the general principles of international law?
3. Do you think drones should be prohibited under the law of armed conflict? Should targeted killing be prohibited?
4. What weapon do you think should be subject to the next comprehensive ban and why?

9 Implementation, enforcement and accountability

1. INTRODUCTION

The law of armed conflict, like international law more generally, faces unique problems when it comes to the implementation and enforcement of its rules. International law, unlike domestic legal systems, has no central hierarchical system or institution that can enforce or implement its rules. Implementation, enforcement and accountability under IHL are thus decentralised, and effected through various means and methods, including domestic and international judicial, quasi-judicial, legislative and diplomatic measures, as well as through mechanisms such as public scrutiny and public education. This chapter examines the manifold ways in which the law of armed conflict is implemented and enforced, and operates to hold those who violate the law accountable.

2. COMMON ARTICLE 1: THE OBLIGATION TO ENSURE RESPECT

The starting point for implementation, enforcement and accountability is Common Article 1 of the Geneva Conventions, which outlines the general obligation under IHL that all parties to the Conventions must "undertake to respect and to ensure respect for the present Convention in all circumstances".[1] The ICJ has held that this principle is customary international law,[2] and is also applicable in non-international armed conflicts.[3]

---

[1] Common Article 1 to the Four Geneva Conventions.   [2] *Nicaragua*, paras. 115, 216, 255 and 256.
[3] *Legal Consequences of the Construction of a Wall in the Occupied Palestinian Territory*, Advisory Opinion, ICJ Rep. 2004, p. 136 *("The Wall")*, paras. 158–9.

What the Article actually means in practice is somewhat complex. The Commentaries to the Conventions explain it thus:

it would not, for example, be enough for a State to give orders or directives to a few civilian or military authorities, leaving it to them to arrange as they pleased for the details of their execution. It is for the State to supervise their execution. Furthermore, if it is to keep its solemn engagements, the State must of necessity prepare in advance, that is to say in peacetime, the legal, material or other means of loyal enforcement of the Convention as and when the occasion arises. It follows, therefore, that in the event of a Power failing to fulfil its obligations, the other Contracting Parties (neutral, allied or enemy) may, and should, endeavour to bring it back to an attitude of respect for the Convention.[4]

This explanation highlights a number of key elements regarding implementation and enforcement of IHL. First, the State must follow the rules to which it has agreed to be bound. Second, the State must ensure that those rules are followed at all times, through supervision of its organs and subsidiaries tasked with prosecuting the armed conflict. In addition, the State must ensure that a "culture of compliance" with the law exists prior to the laws ever being put into practical effect (i.e., in peacetime) through "legal, material or other means"[5] – such as programmes of education of the civilian population. Finally, States are obliged to ensure that any other parties to a conflict comply with the law of armed conflict in their own conduct. This has been affirmed by the ICTY in the *Kupreškić* decision, where the Tribunal held that:

as a consequence of their absolute character, these norms of international humanitarian law do not pose synallagmatic obligations, i.e. obligations of a State vis-à-vis another State. Rather . . . they lay down obligations towards the international community as a whole, with the conse-quence that each and every member of the international community has a "legal interest" in their observance and consequently a legal entitlement to demand respect for such obligations.[6]

How these obligations are put into effect in practice is relatively straightforward in terms of the State's own conduct; that is to say, the State must ensure that its own armed forces, as well as civil society, are cognisant of the laws and obey them at all times. How a State ensures respect by *other* States is less clear. There is nothing *prima facie* wrong with a State not party to an armed conflict publicly condemning States who violate IHL in armed conflicts. Thus, for example, when it was revealed that the Syrian régime had used chemical weapons, that act was condemned by a number of States, including Austria,[7] Indonesia[8] and

---

[4] GC I Commentary, p. 26.   [5] Ibid.

[6] ICTY, *Prosecutor* v. *Kupreškić et al.*, IT-95-16-T, Judgment, 14 January 2000, para. 517.

[7] Foreign Ministry Republic of Austria, *Spindelegger on Syria: "Use of chemical weapons would be classified as war crime": Vice-Chancellor concerned about alleged reports on the use of weapons of mass destruction*, 22 August 2013, www.bmeia.gv.at/en/foreign-ministry/news/press-releases/2013/spindelegger-zu-syrien-einsatz-von-chemiewaffen-waere-kriegsverbrechen.html.

[8] Ezra Sihite, "Indonesia Condemns Syria Chemical Weapons Attack", *Jakarta Globe*, 27 August 2013, www.thejakartaglobe.com/news/indonesia-condemns-syria-chemical-weapons-attack/.

South Korea.[9] However, whether any States are entitled to pursue additional measures to ensure respect for the IHL is unsettled.

This raises questions with regards to the law of State responsibility – specifically, Article 48 of the Draft Articles of the Responsibility of States for Internationally Wrongful Acts,[10] which provides that in any case of a breach of an obligation owed to the international community as a whole, "all states have the right to demand its cessation and, if necessary, guarantees of non-repetition, as well as reparation in the interest of the beneficiaries of the obligation breached".[11] In theory, Common Article 1 would therefore allow all States to "take all measures to ensure respect afforded under general international law, so long as they are compatible with general international law ... and not excluded by IHL".[12] However, there is little State practice to suggest that acts more aggressive than public statements or other essentially diplomatic measures (such as cessation of trade agreements or expulsion of consular and diplomatic staff) would be permissible – as Sassòli, Bouvier and Quintin note, "[s]tate practice is unfortunately not rich enough to determine the upper limits of how a State may or must 'ensure respect'".[13]

3. MEASURES TO BE TAKEN IN PEACETIME

The commentary to Common Article 1 notes that it is incumbent on States to "prepare in advance, that is to say in peacetime, the legal, material or other means of loyal enforcement of the Convention as and when the occasion arises."[14] Thus, IHL rules must be communicated to anyone who may be affected by violations of IHL if and when a conflict breaks out. Indeed, this was noted in the preface of the 1880 Oxford Manual on the Laws of War, which stated that:

[9] "S. Korea Slams Syria for Apparent Use of Chemical Weapons", *Yonhap News Agency*, 1 September 2013, english.yonhapnews.co.kr/news/2013/09/01/0200000000AEN20130901001200315.html.

[10] International Law Commission, Draft Articles on Responsibility of States for Internationally Wrongful Acts, UN Doc. A/56/10, November 2001, ch.IV.E.1, legal.un.org/ilc/texts/instruments/english/commentaries/9_6_2001.pdf.

[11] Marco Sassòli, Antoine Bouvier and Anne Quintin, *How Does the Law Protect in War ? Cases, Documents and Teaching Materials on Contemporary Practice in International Humanitarian Law*, 3rd edn (Geneva: ICRC, 2011), p. 368.

[12] Ibid., p. 369. See also Silja Vöneky, "Implementation and Enforcement of International Humanitarian Law" in Dieter Fleck (ed.), *The Handbook of International Humanitarian Law*, 3rd edn (Oxford University Press, 2013), pp. 650–1.

[13] Ibid. A more detailed investigation of the scope of Common Article 1 can be found in Carlo Focarelli, "Common Article 1 of the 1949 Geneva Conventions: A Soap Bubble?" (2010) 21 EJIL 125; and Laurence Boisson de Chazournes and Luigi Condorelli, "Common Article 1 of the Geneva Conventions Revisited: Protecting Collective Interests" (2000) 837 IRRC 67.

[14] GC I Commentary, p. 26.

it is not sufficient for sovereigns to promulgate new laws. It is essential, too, that they make these laws known among all people, so that when a war is declared, the men called upon to take up arms to defend the causes of the belligerent States may be thoroughly impregnated with the special rights and duties attached to the execution of such a command.[15]

States must therefore educate their civilian and military population on the substance of IHL, in order that all persons know the rules, and know when they have been broken. This is achieved in a number of ways, including dissemination to the armed forces (through training programmes); dissemination to civil society (through public education programmes and university instruction) and through the transformation of the relevant law of armed conflict principles into domestic legislation. The obligation to disseminate IHL is customary in both international and non-international armed conflicts.[16]

a. Dissemination to the armed forces

In all four Geneva Conventions, and in the Additional Protocols, it is provided that the parties to the Convention must:

in time of peace as in time of war ... disseminate the text of the present Convention as widely as possible in their respective countries and, in particular, to include the study thereof in their programmes of military and, if possible, civil instruction, so that the principles thereof may become known to their armed forces and to the entire population.[17]

This provision builds on equivalent rules in the Hague Conventions[18] that require all members of the armed forces be trained in the law of armed conflict. This can manifest in a number of ways – including the production of State military manuals that outline the relevant treaty and customary rules (as well as any domestic policy directives) to which the State is bound;[19] the provision, to members of the armed forces, of training sessions and training programmes conducted by military lawyers or other IHL experts;[20] the requirement to have legal advisers in the field with the

---

[15] The Oxford Manual on the Laws of War on Land: Manual Published by the Institute of International Law, 9 September 1880, reprinted in J. B. Scott (ed.), *Resolutions of the Institute of International Law, Dealing with the Law of Nations* (New York: Oxford University Press, 1916), Preface.

[16] See ICRC CIHL Study, rr. 141–3.

[17] GC I, art. 47; GC II, art. 48; GC III, art. 127; GC IV, art. 144. See also AP I, arts. 80, 83 and 87(2); AP II, art. 19.

[18] See Hague II 1899, art. 1.

[19] See, e.g., the UK Ministry of Defence, *The Manual of the Law of Armed Conflict* (Oxford University Press, 2004).

[20] See AP I, art. 6; see also Laurie Blank and Gregory Noone, *International Law and Armed Conflict: Fundamental Principles and Contemporary Challenges in the Law of War* (New York: Wolters Kluwer, 2013), pp. 552–3. National Red Cross Societies routinely deliver such instruction and training courses; one of the authors of this work, Emily Crawford, has delivered a number of training courses for the Australian Red Cross.

armed forces;[21] and the distribution of "rules of engagement" (ROE) cards to members of the armed forces – palm-sized cards which provide an abbreviated summary of the relevant rules of engagement for the deployment, including the relevant IHL principles.[22] Commanders of armed forces are under special obligations to ensure that those under his or her command comply with IHL; furthermore, a commander may, in certain circumstances, be personally liable for violations of IHL committed by his or her subordinates – this is discussed in more detail below in the section on Command Responsibility.

b. Dissemination to civil society

In addition to instructing the military, States parties to the Conventions are encouraged to disseminate IHL throughout civil society. In practice, this takes the form of courses in IHL, offered either through universities[23] or through other agencies such as national Red Cross societies.[24] Instruction to civil society can also take the form of public lectures and other events[25] that publicise the rules of IHL and highlight current issues in the field. For example, in 2011, the Australian Red Cross launched a social media campaign, calling for a multilateral treaty to ban the use of nuclear weapons. Entitled "Make Nuclear Weapons the Target", the campaign called on Australians to vote for a treaty to prohibit the use of nuclear weapons, and staged "flash mobs" and Twitter campaigns to raise awareness of the issue.[26]

c. Implementation into domestic legislation

The Geneva Conventions also require States parties to implement their IHL obligations into national domestic law[27] through binding domestic

---

[21] Article 82 of AP I states that parties "shall ensure that legal advisers are available, when necessary, to advise military commanders at the appropriate level on the application of the Conventions and this Protocols and on the appropriate instruction to be given to the armed forces on this subject". See also AP I, art. 6; Michael Kramer and Michael Schmitt, "Lawyers on Horseback? Thoughts on Judge Advocates and Civil-Military Relations" (2008) 55 UCLA L Rev 1407.

[22] See Gary Solis, *The Law of Armed Conflict: International Humanitarian Law in War* (Cambridge University Press, 2010), pp. 510–18 for examples of the information included on ROE cards, and a critique of some of the drawbacks of ROE cards.

[23] In Australia, courses in the law of armed conflict are offered by numerous universities, at both undergraduate and postgraduate levels. E.g., the University of Sydney offers an undergraduate course in "War Law" (University of Sydney, *2014 Unit of Study Descriptions: Bachelor of Laws*, September 2014, sydney.edu.au/law/cstudent/undergrad/docs_pdfs/2014_LLBUoS_descriptions.pdf) and a postgraduate course in "International Humanitarian Law" (University of Sydney, *International Humanitarian Law (LAWS6218)*, sydney.edu.au/courses/uos/LAWS6218/international-humanitarian-law).

[24] See the courses offered by the Australian Red Cross, at Australian Red Cross, *IHL training courses*, www.redcross.org.au/ihl-courses.aspx.

[25] See, e.g., a listing of speeches and articles on the Australian Red Cross website, at Australian Red Cross, *Speeches and articles*, 2014, www.redcross.org.au/speeches.aspx.

[26] See Australian Red Cross, *Make Nuclear Weapons the Target*, 2013, targetnuclearweapons.org.au/#/petition.

[27] See GC I, arts. 48, 50; GC II, arts. 49, 51; GC III, arts. 128, 130; GC IV, arts. 145, 147; AP I, arts. 11(4), 84, 85.

legislation.[28] Translation of the treaty obligations into national languages and transformation into domestic legislation makes the obligations contained in those instruments domestically enforceable. For example, in Australia the Geneva Conventions Act 1957 (Cth) and the Criminal Code 1995 (Cth) give domestic effect to the Geneva Conventions as well as Additional Protocols I and III. The 1957 Act contains sections which punish misuse of the protective emblem, and give domestic effect to the provisions contained in Articles 53–4 of GC I and Articles 43–5 of GC II.[29]

4. ROLE OF THE PROTECTING POWERS AND THE INTERNATIONAL COMMITTEE OF THE RED CROSS

As noted in Chapter 6, the Conventions and AP I make frequent mention of the role of the Protecting Power – a neutral third State which may be called on or volunteer its services to protect the interests of foreigners and others who find themselves in the hands of an adverse power.[30] Appointing Protecting Powers requires the consent of all parties to the conflict, as well as the State nominated as the Protecting Power.

Protecting Powers are empowered to ensure that the relevant provisions of the law of armed conflict are observed and implemented in times of armed conflict;[31] their duties include visiting protected persons, especially those held in detention,[32] supervision of relief missions,[33] assistance in judicial proceedings against protected persons,[34] transmission of information and documents,[35] and the provision of "good offices" to the parties to the conflict.[36]

Due to the requirement that all parties to the conflict agree to the appointment of a Protecting Power, it has frequently been the case that Protecting Powers have *not* been appointed – indeed, most reports place the number of successful Protecting Power appointments since the Second World War at only five.[37] As Pfanner has noted, the failure to successfully appoint Protecting Powers in any other of the numerous conflicts that have taken place since WWII "can be explained mainly in terms of political motives. It is rare for States to agree to submit to supervision by a third State in a situation of armed conflict."[38]

---

[28] For a database of national implementation measures, see ICRC, *National Implementation Database*, www.icrc.org/ihl-nat.

[29] *Geneva Conventions Act 1957* (Cth), s 15; see Chapter 5 on the measures to protect the emblem.

[30] AP I, art. 2(c); see also art. 5.   [31] See Article 8 Common to GC I–III; GC IV, art. 9 and AP I, art. 5.

[32] GC III, art. 126; GC IV, art. 143.   [33] GC IV, art. 59.   [34] GC III, art. 105, GC IV, art. 74.

[35] GC IV, art. 137.   [36] AP I, art. 5.

[37] These are Suez (1956), Goa (1961), the France–Tunisia conflict over Bizerte (1961), the Indo–Pakistani conflict (1971) and the Falklands War between the UK and Argentina (1982); see further François Bugnion, *The International Committee of the Red Cross and the Protection of War Victims* (Geneva: ICRC, 2003), pp. 860–901.

[38] Toni Pfanner, "Various Mechanisms and Approaches for Implementing International Humanitarian Law and Protecting and Assisting War Victims" (2009) 91 IRRC 279 at 287, n. 45.

Many of the responsibilities and rights granted to the Protecting Power are mirrored in those rights and responsibilities enjoyed by the ICRC. As Sassòli, Bouvier and Quintin note "this duplication is intended, as it should lead to increased supervision of respect for IHL".[39] Indeed, the Conventions and Protocol I acknowledge that the ICRC may take on the role of Protecting Power, "to assume the humanitarian functions performed by Protecting Powers".[40] However, the ICRC has traditionally been somewhat reluctant to take on the role of Protecting Power, in addition to its own treaty-based responsibilities. As Sassòli, Bouvier and Quintin note, this is a pragmatic decision as "the ICRC, for its part, has no interest in acting as a substitute Protecting Power, as it can fulfil most of the latter's functions in its own right, without giving the impression that it represents only one State and not all the victims."[41]

Indeed, the ICRC is perhaps best known for its provision of humanitarian assistance, the right of which is guaranteed in the Conventions and Protocols. As provided in Article 81 of Protocol I, State parties are obliged to:

grant to the International Committee of the Red Cross all facilities within their power so as to enable it to carry out the humanitarian functions assigned to it by the Conventions and this Protocol in order to ensure protection and assistance to the victims of conflicts; the International Committee of the Red Cross may also carry out any other humanitarian activities in favour of these victims...

The ICRC's key mandate is to "undertake the tasks incumbent upon it under the Geneva Conventions, to work for the faithful application of international humanitarian law applicable in armed conflicts, and to take cognizance of any complaints based on alleged breaches of that law".[42] The ICRC is a unique organisation with unique responsibilities under international law. The ICRC is a private organisation, governed by Swiss law, but with limited international personality;[43] the Committee comprises up to twenty-five co-opted members, all of whom have Swiss nationality.[44] The ICRC operates under the mandate of impartiality, neutrality and independence – it does not take the side of any State (or non-State group) in times of armed conflict; it is not partial to any political or governmental influence; its sole

---

[39] Sassòli *et al*, *How Does Law Protect in War?*, p. 366.

[40] GC I, GC II and GC III, art. 10; GC IV, art. 11; AP I, art. 5.

[41] Sassòli *et al.*, *How Does Law Protect in War?*, p. 366.

[42] Article 5, Statutes of the International Red Cross and Red Crescent Movement – the Statutes of the Movement are approved by the International Conference of the Red Cross and Red Crescent, which comprises the ICRC, the International Federation of the Red Cross and Red Crescent Societies, and the National Red Cross and Red Crescent Societies. For a more detailed examination of the differing tasks that are assigned to each of these bodies, see Christophe Lanord, "The Legal Status of National Red Cross and Red Crescent Societies" (2000) 840 IRRC 1053; Hans Haug, *Humanity for All: The International Red Cross and Red Crescent Movement* (Geneva: Henri Dunant Institute, 1993); and David Forsythe, *The Humanitarians: The International Committee of the Red Cross* (Cambridge University Press, 2005).

[43] Article 5, Statutes of the International Red Cross and Red Crescent Movement.

[44] ICRC, *Who We Are*, www.icrc.org/eng/who-we-are/overview-who-we-are.htm.

obligation is to encourage and promote adherence to the laws of armed conflict, and to assist parties to conflicts.[45] The ICRC is also considered as having a general "right of initiative" – the right to offer its services to all parties to any conflict, both international and non-international, on any matters that the ICRC considers as within its purview.[46] The ICRC achieves its mandate and mission through activities such as visiting the detained and interned,[47] carrying out its activities in occupied territories,[48] providing relief services[49] and administering the Central Tracing Agency regarding missing persons.[50]

The ICRC also takes on the role of reaffirming and developing IHL, by encouraging the adoption of new rules and treaties relating to armed conflict[51] and by monitoring observance of the rules of armed conflict. For example, if it is brought to its attention that serious violations of IHL are taking place,[52] the ICRC will attempt to stop the breach, by engaging in dialogue with the relevant authorities. This dialogue can take place at any level – the ICRC may approach the governor of a detention facility that is failing to provide adequate food and water to detainees; equally, the ICRC may engage in dialogue with higher level governmental decision-makers to ensure that the breaches of the law cease.

Key to this dialogue is the confidentiality of such communications – the ICRC will not disclose the source of such allegations of breaches of the law, but neither will they communicate the substance of the dialogue to the international community at large.[53] The idea is to stop the breach of the law, and not to engage in a "name and shame" of the perpetrators of the breach. However, the principle of confidentiality is not absolute – the ICRC has policies in place which outline when the ICRC may publicise a State's violation of the law of armed conflict. As stated in the policy document *Action by the International Committee of the Red Cross in the Event of Violations of International Humanitarian Law or of Other Fundamental Rules Protecting Persons in Situations of Violence*,[54] the ICRC will publicly name a State for breaches of the law of armed conflict if:

---

[45] ICRC, *The ICRC's Mandate and Mission*, www.icrc.org/eng/who-we-are/mandate/overview-icrc-mandate-mission.htm.

[46] Hans-Peter Gasser, "The International Committee of the Red Cross", *Max Planck Encyclopaedia of International Law* (Online, Oxford University Press) opil.ouplaw.com/view/10.1093/law:epil/9780199231690/law-9780199231690-e310#law-9780199231690-e310-div1-1.

[47] GC III, art. 126.   [48] GC IV, art. 143.   [49] Ibid., arts. 23 and 55.

[50] See further ICRC, *ICRC Central Tracing Agency: Half a Century of Restoring Family Links,* 7 April 2010, www.icrc.org/eng/resources/documents/interview/centra-tracing-agency-interview-070410.htm.

[51] Such as the adoption of a treaty to ban the use of nuclear weapons – see further the Australian Red Cross campaign, *Make Nuclear Weapons the Target,* 2013, targetnuclearweapons.org.au/#/petition.

[52] Whether through information gathered by an ICRC delegate, through media reports, or through other diplomatic channels – see Gasser, "The International Committee of the Red Cross".

[53] See Vöneky, "Implementation and Enforcement", p. 691.

[54] ICRC, "Action by the International Committee of the Red Cross in the Event of Violations of International Humanitarian Law or of Other Fundamental Rules Protecting Persons in Situations of Violence" (2005) 87 IRRC 393.

(a) the violations are serious and repeated or likely to be repeated;

(b) delegates have witnessed the violations first hand, or the existence and extent of those violations have been established on the basis of reliable and verifiable sources;

(c) bilateral confidential representations and, when attempted, humanitarian mobilisation efforts have failed to put an end to the violations;

(d) such publicity is in the interest of the persons or populations affected or threatened.[55]

Only in very rare circumstances will the ICRC publicly name a State in such a manner – one example was when the ICRC stated that Israel was in violation of IHL in failing to allow ambulances into the Zeitun neighbourhood of Gaza City in 2009.[56] While this was not an outright condemnation, the ICRC nonetheless took the unusual stance of publicly proclaiming a State to be in violation.[57]

5. THE INTERNATIONAL HUMANITARIAN FACT FINDING COMMISSION

The Geneva Conventions make provision for the creation of an *ad hoc* fact-finding commission, on the request of a party to the conflict.[58] These provisions allow for parties to a conflict to have a neutral third State, most likely the Protecting Power,[59] make enquiries into alleged breaches of the Conventions, to lend their good offices to help settle any disputes or disagreements, and to take steps to ensure that all parties to the conflict observe the relevant rules. The Commentary to the Conventions maintains that this provision is binding, stating that the wording of Article 52 "makes it clear that the holding of the enquiry is compulsory once one of the belligerents has asked for it".[60] However, there have been, as of this writing, no instances of an Article 52 enquiry being undertaken.[61]

In response to the failure of any State to take advantage of Article 52, the Diplomatic Conferences for the Additional Protocols examined the question of whether there should be a standing commission of enquiry for violations

---

[55] Ibid., p. 397.

[56] ICRC Press Release, "Gaza: ICRC Demands Urgent Access to Wounded as Israeli Army Fails to Assist Wounded Palestinians", 8 January 2009, www.icrc.org/eng/resources/documents/news-release/2009-and-earlier/palestine-news-080109.htm ("the Israeli military failed to meet its obligation under international humanitarian law to care for and evacuate the wounded").

[57] For more on the role of the ICRC in promoting compliance with the law of armed conflict, see Steven Ratner, "Law Promotion Beyond Law Talk: The Red Cross, Persuasion, and the Laws of War" (2011) 22 EJIL 459; and Jacob Kellenberger, "Speaking out or Remaining Silent in Humanitarian Work" (2004) 855 IRRC 593.

[58] GC I, art. 52; GC II, art. 53; GC III, art. 132; GC IV, art. 149.   [59] See GC I Commentary, p. 378.

[60] Ibid., p.377.   [61] See Vöneky, "Implementation and Enforcement", p. 688.

of IHL.[62] This eventually led to the adoption of Article 90 of Protocol I, which established the International Fact-Finding Commission (IFFC). The Commission is tasked with enquiring "into any facts alleged to be a grave breach as defined in the Conventions and this Protocol or other serious violations",[63] and with "facilit-[ating], through its good offices, the restoration of an attitude of respect for the Conventions and this Protocol".[64]

The Commission is made up of fifteen individuals of "high moral standing and acknowledged impartiality",[65] acting in their personal capacity. They are able to conduct investigations at the behest of parties to the conflict, provided all parties agree to the involvement of the IFFC; indeed, it is not necessary for a party to have officially accepted the competence of the Committee under Article 90, as the IFFC is able to act on an *ad hoc* basis (provided all parties approve). The Commission is also entitled to offer its services to parties to armed conflicts, but it may not independently investigate situations without the consent of the parties to the conflict. The Commission, based in Berne in Switzerland, was established in 1991, following the twentieth acceptance of its competence.[66] As of January 2015, the IFFC has not yet been called upon to undertake any investigations.[67]

6. ACCOUNTABILITY THROUGH INTERNATIONAL CRIMINAL LAW

So far, this chapter has examined the ways in which States are able to fulfil their obligations under the law of armed conflict both prior to and during an armed conflict. This compliance with the law is achieved through mechanisms such as training of the armed forces, implementation of treaty obligations into domestic legislation, and use of instrumentalities like the Protecting Powers and the ICRC. Broadly speaking, these steps can be categorised as measures of implementation and enforcement to be undertaken by the State. However an equally important limb in the framework of compliance with IHL is that of accountability for violations of IHL committed by individuals. It is incumbent on parties to an armed conflict to investigate and prosecute individuals who violate IHL, through

---

[62] See AP I Commentary, pp. 1039–41; and Official Records Vol IX, CDDH/I/SR.56, pp. 189–94. See generally Erich Kussbach, "The International Humanitarian Fact-Finding Commission" (1994) 43 ICLQ 174; Charles Garraway, "The International Humanitarian Fact-Finding Commission" (2008) 34 Comm L Bull 813; Aly Mokhtar, "Will This Mummification Saga Come to an End? The International Humanitarian Fact-Finding Commission: Article 90 of Protocol 1" (2003–4) 22 Penn St Int'l L Rev 243.
[63] AP I, art. 90(2)(c)(i).   [64] Ibid., art. 90(2)(c)(ii).   [65] Ibid., art. 90(1)(a).
[66] Ibid., art. 90(1)(b). As at January 2015, seventy-six States have accepted the competence of the IFFC.
[67] See the website of the IFFC at www.ihffc.org/index.asp?Language=EN&page=home.

civilian or military courts at either the domestic or international level; these provisions are outlined in this next section.[68]

a. Individual criminal responsibility for violations of the laws of armed conflict

It was the Nuremburg Tribunals that acknowledged that "[c]rimes against International Law are committed by men, not by abstract entities, and only by punishing individuals who commit such crimes can the provisions of International Law be enforced".[69] Indeed, international criminal law in its modern form is the direct result of the post-Second World War military tribunals, held in Nuremburg and Tokyo, which promised that the principles long enshrined in laws of The Hague and Geneva would finally be given normative force.[70] However, as noted by James Crawford, such ambitions did not come to fruition easily, and instead "the arena of international criminal law became populated by conventions largely without implementation, and state practice turned to emphasise national trials for specified treaty-defined offences such as aircraft hijacking and drug trafficking."[71] For nearly fifty years, it seemed that the "promise"[72] of Nuremburg would remain unfulfilled. However, during the 1990s, the legal landscape changed dramatically. The atrocities committed in the Former Yugoslavia and in Rwanda provided the impetus for widespread international support for establishing mechanisms to hold individuals to account for their violations of IHL. Just over twenty years later, it is possible to speak of international criminal law as a large, complex and distinct field of international law. Those parts of international criminal law that directly relate to IHL – namely, war crimes and other serious violations of IHL – are discussed in this next section.

i. War crimes and grave breaches

As Dinstein notes, there is no "single binding definition of war crimes".[73] However, it is generally accepted that war crimes are those acts considered to be serious

---

[68] International criminal law is a vast and complex area of international law – as such, only some of the basic elements that are directly tied to the law of armed conflict will be mentioned. For a more detailed examination of international criminal law, see, e.g., Antonio Cassese and Paola Gaeta, *Cassese's International Criminal Law*, 3rd edn, (Oxford University Press, 2013).

[69] Judgment of the International Military Tribunal, in *The Trial of German Major War Criminals: Proceedings of the International Military Tribunal sitting at Nuremberg, Germany*, Part 22, (London, 1950), p. 447.

[70] Calls for a standing international tribunal to investigate violations of the law of armed conflict can be traced back to at least 1872, when one of the founders of the ICRC, Gustave Moynier, advocated such a body – see Christopher Hall, "The First Proposal for a Permanent International Criminal Court" (1998) 322 IRRC 57.

[71] James Crawford, *Brownlie's Principles of Public International Law*, 8th edn (Oxford University Press, 2012), p. 671.

[72] Ibid.

[73] Yoram Dinstein, *The Conduct of Hostilities under the Law of International Armed Conflict*, 2nd edn (Cambridge University Press, 2010), p. 264.

violations of the law of armed conflict.[74] The qualifier "serious" is intentional; not all violations of IHL are war crimes.[75] Indeed, in this respect, it is useful to employ the terminology and categories used in the Rome Statute of the International Criminal Court, which divides war crimes into four categories – grave breaches, serious violations of the laws of war in international armed conflicts, serious violations of Common Article 3 and serious violations of the laws of war in non-international armed conflicts.

Grave breaches are considered the most serious violations of the law of armed conflict. As outlined in Article 8(2)(a) of the Rome Statute, they include:

- Wilful killing;
- Torture or inhuman treatment, including biological experiments;
- Wilfully causing great suffering, or serious injury to body or health;
- Extensive destruction and appropriation of property, not justified by military necessity and carried out unlawfully and wantonly;
- Compelling a prisoner of war or other protected person to serve in the forces of a hostile Power;
- Wilfully depriving a prisoner of war or other protected person of the rights of fair and regular trial;
- Unlawful deportation or transfer or unlawful confinement;
- Taking of hostages.

Article 8(2)(a) of the Rome Statute draws on the grave breaches régimes contained in the Geneva Conventions. Under the Conventions, parties to the Conventions must implement domestic legislation to provide penal sanctions for persons who commit, or who order others to commit, grave breaches. As the most serious violations of IHL, grave breaches also attract universal jurisdiction; that is to say, every State has an obligation:

to search for persons alleged to have committed, or to have ordered to be committed, such grave breaches, and shall bring such persons, regardless of their nationality, before its own courts. It may also, if it prefers, and in accordance with the provisions of its own legislation, hand such persons over for trial to another High Contracting Party concerned, provided such High Contracting Party has made out a *prima facie* case.[76]

This principle is known as *aut dedere aut judicare* – the obligation to prosecute or extradite. Any State which is able to make out a case against a person suspected of committing grave breaches is entitled to prosecute such a person, even if the traditional jurisdictional links[77] are absent – thus, for example, Australia could, in

---

[74] ICRC CIHL Study, r. 156.   [75] See further Cassese and Gaeta, *International Criminal Law*, pp. 67 et seq.
[76] GC I, arts. 49–50; GC II, arts. 50–1; GC III, arts. 129–30; GC IV, arts. 146–7.
[77] For a discussion of the traditional grounds of jurisdiction under international law, see further Crawford, *Brownlie's Principles*, pp. 456–86; and Richard Baxter, "The Municipal and International Law Basis of Jurisdiction over War Crimes" (1951) 28 BYBIL 382.

theory, prosecute a British national in the Australian courts for the commission of grave breaches that took place in Afghanistan against an Afghan national, even though none of the requisite elements of the crime took place in Australia, or was committed by an Australian or perpetrated against an Australian national.[78]

ii. Violations of the law of armed conflict not amounting to grave breaches

In addition to grave breaches, certain violations of the law of armed conflict also attract international criminal sanction. Article 8(2)(b) lists twenty-six acts that amount to war crimes, including: intentionally directing attacks against the civilian population;[79] the launching of indiscriminate or disproportionate attacks;[80] attacking those *hors de combat*;[81] attacking cultural property that is not a military objective;[82] giving orders of no quarter;[83] using certain prohibited weapons;[84] employing human shields;[85] and using child soldiers.[86]

iii. Crimes against humanity and genocide

Finally, brief mention should be made of the international crimes of genocide and crimes against humanity. The origins of these terms can be traced to the Nuremburg trials and the actions of Axis leaders in occupied Europe during the Second World War.[87] However, under the Rome Statute, crimes against humanity and genocide do not require a nexus to an armed conflict; they can occur in both peacetime and wartime.[88] Crimes against humanity are defined in Article 7 of the Rome Statute as certain acts when "committed as part of a widespread or systematic attack directed against any civilian population, with knowledge of the attack", and include murder,[89] extermination,[90] enslavement,[91] deportation or forcible transfers of populations,[92] torture,[93] sexual violence including rape, enforced prostitution, forced pregnancy or enforced sterilisation,[94] persecution of a group or collectivity

---

[78] In practice, however, most States usually seek to find some jurisdictional nexus, as prosecution on the grounds of "pure" universal jurisdiction has tended to be unsuccessful. For more on the limits of universal jurisdiction, see M. Cherif Bassiouni, "The History of Universal Jurisdiction and its Place in International Law" in Steven Macedo (ed.), *Universal Jurisdiction: National Courts and the Prosecution of Serious Crimes under International Law* (Philadelphia: University of Pennsylvania Press, 2004).

[79] Rome Statute, art. 8(2)(b)(i).   [80] Ibid., art. 8(2)(b)(iv).   [81] Ibid., art. 8(2)(b)(vi).

[82] Ibid., art. 8(2)(b)(ix).   [83] Ibid., art. 8(2)(b)(xii).   [84] Ibid., arts. 8(2)(b)(xvii)–(xx).

[85] Ibid., art. 8(2)(b)(xxiii).   [86] Ibid., art. 8(2)(b)(xxvi).

[87] For the origins of the term "genocide", see Raphael Lemkin, *Axis Rule in Occupied Europe* (Concord, NH: Rumford Press, 1944), p. 79; Lemkin coined the term "genocide" to describe the destruction of a "nation or an ethnic group"; for the origins of the term "crimes against humanity", see Article 6(c) of the Agreement for the Prosecution and Punishment of the Major War Criminals of the European Axis, and Charter of the International Military Tribunal, London, 8 August 1945, in force 8 August 1945, 82 UNTC 280, the Charter that established the Nuremburg Tribunals.

[88] Blank and Noone, *International Law and Armed Conflict*, pp. 620, 633.

[89] Rome Statute, art. 7(1)(a).   [90] Ibid., art. 7(1)(b).   [91] Ibid., art. 7(1)(c).

[92] Ibid., art. 7(1)(d).   [93] Ibid., art. 7(1)(f).   [94] Ibid., art. 7(1)(g).

on political, racial, national, ethnic, cultural, religious, or gender grounds,[95] apartheid[96] and enforced disappearances.[97] The key element in crimes against humanity is that the constituent acts must be committed as part of a widespread and systematic attack against the civilian population, pursuant to some form of defined policy.[98]

Genocide is defined under Article 6 of the Rome Statute as any of the following acts committed with intent to destroy, in whole or in part, a national, ethnical, racial or religious group, as such:

(a) Killing members of the group;
(b) Causing serious bodily or mental harm to members of the group;
(c) Deliberately inflicting on the group conditions of life calculated to bring about its physical destruction in whole or in part;
(d) Imposing measures intended to prevent births within the group;
(e) Forcibly transferring children of the group to another group.

Genocide is also prohibited under the 1948 Convention on the Prevention and Punishment of Genocide, from which the Article 6 definition is drawn.[99]

The commission of these acts – war crimes, crimes against humanity and genocide – attracts individual criminal responsibility under international law. However, it is possible for persons to be liable for violations of the law of armed conflict committed by subordinates; this is known as command responsibility.

b. Command responsibility

Command responsibility (also known as superior responsibility) operates to hold commanders accountable for the acts of their subordinates. It is outlined in Article 87 of Protocol I:

1. The High Contracting Parties and the Parties to the conflict shall require military commanders, with respect to members of the armed forces under their command and other persons under their control, to prevent and, where necessary, to suppress and to report to competent authorities breaches of the Conventions and of this Protocol.

2. In order to prevent and suppress breaches, High Contracting Parties and Parties to the conflict shall require that, commensurate with their level of responsibility,

---

[95] Ibid., art. 7(1)(h).   [96] Ibid., art. 7(1)(j).   [97] Ibid., art. 7(1)(i).

[98] Article 7(2) of the Rome Statute states that for acts to be considered crimes against humanity, they must be com mitted as part of a "course of conduct involving the multiple commission of acts referred to in paragraph 1against any civilian population, pursuant to or in furtherance of a State or organizational policy to commit such attack".

[99] Convention on the Prevention and Punishment of the Crime of Genocide, Paris, 9 December 1948, in force 12 January 1951, 78 UNTS 277.

commanders ensure that members of the armed forces under their command are aware of their obligations under the Conventions and this Protocol.

3. The High Contracting Parties and Parties to the conflict shall require any commander who is aware that subordinates or other persons under his control are going to commit or have committed a breach of the Conventions or of this Protocol, to initiate such steps as are necessary to prevent such violations of the Conventions or this Protocol, and, where appropriate, to initiate disciplinary or penal action against violators thereof.

There are two elements to command responsibility. First, a commander must not order his or her subordinates to commit violations of the law of armed conflict. Second, a commander must properly supervise and instruct his or her subordinates in IHL, to ensure that the subordinates do not violate IHL themselves. Along with their own duty to obey the law, commanders must ensure that their subordinates also obey the law; if the commander fails in this regard, or they become aware that persons under their control have committed or are going to commit a breach of the law, they must take steps to prevent and/or punish such breaches, else they will be held responsible under the doctrine of command responsibility. As such, a commander is responsible for acts of omission as well as acts of commission.[100]

The modern formulation of command responsibility has its origins in the post-Second World War trials, and affirms that command responsibility is not simply a vicarious liability by mere fact of misconduct by subordinates. For a commander to be liable under the principle of command responsibility, "there must be a personal dereliction. That can occur only where the act is directly traceable to [the commander] ... or where his failure to properly supervise his subordinates constitutes criminal negligence on his part. In the latter case, it must be a personal neglect amounting to a wanton, immoral disregard of the action of his subordinates amounting to acquiescence."[101] This has been affirmed by the ICTY in *Krnojelac*, where the Appeals Chamber stated that "where superior responsibility is concerned, an accused is not charged with the crimes of his subordinates but with his failure to carry out his duty as a superior to exercise control".[102]

The core issue to determine is one of "knowledge" – that the commander knew that violations were taking place, or ought to have known, and did nothing to prevent, repress or punish perpetrators of the breach. In the pre-trial chamber in the ICC in the *Bemba* case, the court looked at how one determines knowledge:

With respect to the suspect's actual knowledge that the forces or subordinates were committing or about to commit a crime, it is the view of the Chamber that such knowledge cannot be "presumed". Rather, the suspect's knowledge must be obtained by way of direct or

[100] See *Prosecutor* v. *Halilović*, IT-01-48-T, Judgment, 16 November 2005, para. 54.

[101] *US* v. *Von Leeb et al.* ("*the High Command* case"), US Military Tribunal Nuremburg, X-XI, TWC 1 (27 October 1948), 543.

[102] *Prosecutor* v. *Krnojelac*, IT-97-25-A, Appeals Chamber Judgment, 17 September 2003, para. 171.

circumstantial evidence. In this regard, the Chamber takes note of the relevant jurisprudence of the *ad hoc* tribunals which considered several factors or *indicia* to reach a finding on a superior's actual knowledge. These factors include the number of illegal acts, their scope, whether their occurrence is widespread, the time during which the prohibited acts took place, the type and number of forces involved, the means of available communication, the *modus operandi* of similar acts, the scope and nature of the superior's position and responsibility in the hierarchal structure, the location of the commander at the time and the geographical location of the acts. Actual knowledge may be also proven if, "*a priori*, [a military commander] is part of an organised structure with established reporting and monitoring systems".[103]

As to the test of "should have known", the court stated that the standard requires that the superior has "merely been negligent in failing to acquire knowledge"[104] of his subordinates' illegal conduct. As Dinstein notes, the formula "demands that a commander will only be culpable if he closes his eyes and ears to information, which should have alerted him to the wrongdoing of his subordinates."[105]

Command responsibility is outlined in Article 28 of the Rome Statute,[106] and provides that command responsibility will attach to persons "effectively acting as a military commander" and to crimes "committed by forces under his or her effective command and control".[107] Thus, command responsibility can attach to both members of the armed forces and civilians,[108] provided they have effective command and control over subordinates – the Commentary to the Protocols gives the example of a low-ranked soldier who takes over command in the field when the commanding officer has been rendered *hors de combat*.[109] In such a case, the soldier is effectively the commander. Thus, a commander will *not* be liable under the doctrine of command responsibility if they have no practical effective command and control of subordinates.[110]

7. THE INTERNATIONAL CRIMINAL COURT, THE INTERNATIONAL TRIBUNALS AND THE HYBRID AND INTERNATIONALISED COURTS

The law of armed conflict has benefitted greatly from the establishment of the International Criminal Court, the *ad hoc* Tribunals for the former Yugoslavia and

---

[103] *Prosecutor* v. *Bemba*, ICC-01/05-01/08, Decision on the Confirmation of Charges, 15 June 2009, paras. 430–1.

[104] Ibid., para. 432.   [105] Dinstein, *The Conduct of Hostilities*, p. 275.

[106] See also Practice Relating to Rule 153 in the ICRC CIHL Study, for a complete listing of command responsibility in the statutes of the ICTY, ICTR and in military manuals and national legislation, as well as case law from Indonesia, Australia, Canada, Iraq, the ITCR and ICTY.

[107] Rome Statute, art. 28(1).

[108] This was affirmed in the *Delalić* case, para. 668; see also James Levine, "The Doctrine of Command Responsibility and its Application to Superior Civilian Leadership: Does the International Criminal Court have the Correct Standard?", 193 Mil L Rev 52 (2007).

[109] AP Commentary, pp. 1017–19.   [110] Affirmed in *Blaškić*, para. 612.

Rwanda, and the so-called "hybrid" tribunals and courts in Sierra Leone, Lebanon, Timor-Leste, Cambodia, Bosnia and Herzegovina, and Kosovo. The jurisprudence of these bodies has helped clarify many of the rules of the law of armed conflict, especially in the case of non-international armed conflicts. For example, prior to the *Tadić* jurisprudence, the accepted position under international law was that breaches of the law of non-international armed conflict could not amount to war crimes.[111] The ICC Statute developed the law in this regard, and serious violations of both Common Article 3 and AP II are considered war crimes under international law. Jurisprudence from the ICTR has also developed the law, with the *Akayesu* case marking the first instance of prosecution of rape as a constitutive act of genocide,[112] and the *Nahimana* case's significance in convicting three radio and television executives for public incitement to genocide.[113]

It is clear that the various international criminal bodies have gone a considerable way to ensure that breaches of IHL are investigated and repressed. These tribunals and courts have also made significant contributions to our understanding of the scope of many of the rules of IHL. Whether these bodies have contributed to another of the overall aims of IHL, that of fostering a culture of compliance with the law so that such acts will not be committed at all, is less clear. As Sassòli notes:

criminal lawyers have known for a long time that criminalisation and punishment are not the only answer to socially deviant behaviour. International lawyers are sometimes so impressed by the relatively new branch of ICL and the increasing effectiveness of international criminal justice that they forget the need for prevention through other means, such as education, analysis and reduction of the root causes of violations and reparations to victims independently of any criminal trial.[114]

As such, there is concern that emphasis on punitive post-conflict measures of IHL enforcement fails to encourage a more holistic approach to IHL implementation and the creation of a peace-time culture of compliance with IHL.

The *ad hoc* tribunals, and the hybrid courts and tribunals have all come in for significant scrutiny and criticism, including denunciation of the extraordinary costs of maintaining them and the inordinate length of time many of the cases take to finalise.[115] However, a more fundamental challenge is that facing the International

---

[111] See further Theodor Meron, "International Criminalisation of Internal Atrocities" (1995) 89 AJIL 554; Payam Akhavan *et al.*, "The Contribution of the Ad Hoc Tribunals to International Humanitarian Law" (1998) 13 AUILR 1510; Marco Sassòli, 'Humanitarian Law and International Criminal Law' in Cassese (ed), *The Oxford Companion to International Criminal Justice* (Oxford University Press, 2009), pp. 114–17.

[112] *Prosecutor* v. *Akayesu*, ICTR-96–4-T, Judgement, 2 September 1998.

[113] *Prosecutor* v. *Nahimana*, ICTR-99–52-T, Judgment, 3 December 2003; and, *Prosecutor* v. *Nahimana*, ICTR-99–52-A, Appeals Judgment, 28 November 2007.

[114] Sassòli, "Humanitarian Law and International Criminal Law", p. 117

[115] Jon Silverman,"Ten Years, $900m, One Verdict: Does the ICC Cost Too Much?" *BBC News Magazine*, 14 March 2012, www.bbc.com/news/magazine-17351946; "Africa: How Close Is an African Criminal

Criminal Court. Still in its infancy, it has been accused of cultural bias because all of the situations investigated so far have concerned African countries.[116] Tensions between the Court and African States were exacerbated by the issuing of arrest warrants for two African Heads of State (Kenyatta of Kenya and Al Bashir of Sudan) despite protests that they were protected by sovereign immunity.[117] In 2013 Kenya threatened to withdraw from the Rome Statute, with support from the African Union.[118] In late 2014 in the face of the Kenya's continued refusal to cooperate, the Prosecutor withdrew the charges against Kenyatta.[119] Although there are several non-African situations being investigated, the concern is that a loss of confidence in the Court by African States would seriously undermine the credibility of the Court, and ultimately its success as an institution.[120]

8. REPARATIONS FOR VIOLATIONS OF THE LAW OF ARMED CONFLICT

Under Article 3 of Hague IV 1907 and Article 91 of Protocol I, parties to a conflict who have failed to comply with IHL are obliged to make reparations; Article 91 restates the obligation in Hague IV.[121] Reparations may take a number of forms and can include restitution – the re-establishment of the situation prior to the violation of the law; monetary compensation; rehabilitation (such as legal or social rehabilitation to remedy the effects of the wrongful act); satisfaction, such as acknowledgment of the wrongful act or an apology for the wrongful conduct; and guarantees of non-repetition. This is generally reflective of the remedies available under the law of State responsibility,[122] and is outlined in more detail

Court?" *All Africa*, 13 June 2012, www.globalpolicy.org/international-justice/general-articles-on-inter national-justice/51707-africa-how-close-is-an-african-criminal-court.html; and see generally Kirsten Ainley, "The International Criminal Court on Trial" (2011) 24 Camb Rev of Int'l Aff 309 for an overview of criticisms of the court.

[116] Currently (early 2015), these are Central African Republic, Cote d'Ivoire, Darfur, Democratic Republic of the Congo, Kenya, Libya, Mali and Uganda: see ICC, *Situations and Cases*, www.icc-cpi.int/en_menus/icc/situations%20and%20cases/Pages/situations%20and%20cases.aspx.

[117] See e.g. Paola Gaeta, "Does President Al Bashir Enjoy Immunity from Arrest?", (2009) 7(2) JICJ 315; Dire Tladi, "Cooperation, Immunities, and Article 98 of the Rome Statute: The ICC, Interpretation, and Conflicting Norms", (2012) 106 AJIL 307.

[118] Chris Keeler, "Kenya's Decision to Withdraw from Rome Statute", *Human Rights Brief*, 24 October 2013, hrbrief.org/2013/10/kenya%E2%80%99s-decision-to-withdraw-from-rome-statute/.

[119] ICC, *Situations and Cases*, www.icc-cpi.int/en_menus/icc/situations%20and%20cases/Pages/situations%20and%20cases.aspx.

[120] See further Konstantinos Magliveras and Gina Naldi, "The International Criminal Court's Involvement with Africa: Evaluation of a Fractious Relationship", (2013) 82 Nordic J Int'l L 417.

[121] The duty to make reparation for violations of the law can be found also in Article 38 of the Second Protocol to the Hague Convention of 1954 for the Protection of Cultural Property.

[122] See Articles 30–7, ILC Articles on State Responsibility.

in Principle 18 of the UN General Assembly's Basic Principles and Guidelines on the Right to Remedy and Reparations for Victims of Gross Violations of International Human Rights Law and Serious Violations of International Humanitarian Law.[123]

State responsibility for breaches of IHL, and the right of reparations have, in practice, "widely been neglected".[124] There is also no general individual right to reparation for violations of the law of armed conflict, as that right is something owed only to the State, rather than the individual.[125] Thus, under Article 6 of the Ottawa Convention on Anti-Personnel Mines, and Article 5 of the Cluster Munitions Convention, States are obliged to develop and implement assistance plans for victims of these weapons, but there is no explicit provision for individual reparations for injuries resulting from the unlawful use of these weapons.

In recent years, there have been calls for there to be a right of individual reparation for violations of IHL.[126] This push has been strengthened by work undertaken by the International Law Association, which in 2010 established a Committee on Compensation for Victims of War, responsible for issuing the "Declaration on International Law Principles on Reparation for Victims of Armed Conflict (Substantive Issues)".[127] As such, there is an emergent development of a right of individual reparation for violations of the law of armed conflict;[128] however, this is not yet considered customary international law.[129]

9. THE ROLE OF THE UNITED NATIONS AND INTERNATIONAL AND NON-GOVERNMENTAL ORGANISATIONS

The United Nations, and other international and non-governmental bodies and organisations, have also proven useful in helping States (and non-State groups)

---

[123] Adopted by General Assembly Resolution 60/147, UN Doc. A/RES/60/147, 16 December 2005.

[124] Silja Vöneky, "Implementation and Enforcement", p. 683.

[125] ICRC CIHL Study, r. 150. See generally Marco Sassòli, 'State Responsibility for Violations of International Humanitarian Law' (2002) 84 IRRC 419. However, see Rome Statute, art. 75, which provides that the ICC can order that reparations be made to individuals.

[126] See Jann Kleffner, "Improving Compliance with International Humanitarian Law Through the Establishment of an Individual Complaints Procedure" (2002) 15 Leiden J Int'l L 237; Elke Schwager, "The Right to Compensation for Victims of an Armed Conflict" (2005) 4 Chinese J Int'l L 417; Christine Evans, *The Right to Reparation in International Law for Victims of Armed Conflict* (Cambridge University Press, 2012); Emanuela-Chiara Gillard, "Reparation for Violations of International Humanitarian Law" (2003) 85 IRRC 536.

[127] See the International Law Association, *Reparation for Victims of Armed Conflict*, www.ila-hq.org/en/committees/index.cfm/cid/1018.

[128] Note also that some regional human rights treaties require individual reparation for violations of international human rights law that also amount to violations of the law of armed conflict, both in international and non-international armed conflicts. See further Pfanner, "Various Mechanisms and Approaches", 289, 310–14, and examples of State practice as cited in ICRC CIHL Study, Commentary to Rule 150.

[129] See ICRC CIHL Study, r. 150.

fulfil their obligations under the law of armed conflict. The UN General Assembly and the UN Security Council have the power to issue resolutions and declarations that remind States (and non-State groups) of their duties under the law of armed conflict; for example, the General Assembly has issued a number of resolutions calling on States to respect human rights in armed conflicts, such as Resolution 2444 (XXIII) on Respect for Human Rights in Armed Conflict.[130] Resolution 2444, unanimously adopted, recognised "the necessity of applying basic humanitarian principles in all armed conflicts" and stated that certain principles should be observed "by all governmental and other authorities responsible for action in armed conflicts", including that the right of the parties to a conflict to adopt means of injuring the enemy is not unlimited; that it is prohibited to launch attacks against the civilian population; and that distinction must be made at all times between persons taking part in the hostilities and members of the civilian population to the effect that the latter be spared as much as possible. This tendency to call for respect of the law of armed conflict and human rights in "all armed conflict" has been reiterated in a number of other UN General Assembly Resolutions, all entitled "Respect for Human Rights in Armed Conflicts".[131]

The UN Security Council has also been active in calling for observance of the law of armed conflict, for example, in resolutions on Liberia,[132] Somalia,[133] Angola,[134] Georgia[135] and Afghanistan.[136] The Security Council is also empowered to take action if the armed conflict in a certain region (either between two or more States or within a State's borders) represents a threat to international peace and security.[137] This may include ensuring humanitarian assistance, sending in peacekeepers, authorising the use of force against a State, or initiating fact-finding missions or other endeavours, such as tribunals or truth and reconciliation commissions to assist in post-conflict peace-building, reconciliation and reconstruction.

---

[130] UN Doc. A//RES/2444 (18 December 1968).

[131] See e.g. UN Docs. A/RES/2597 (16 December 1969); A/RES/2674 (9 December 1970); A/RES/2676 (9 December 1970); A/RES/2677 (9 December 1970); A/RES/2852 (20 December 1971); A/RES/2853 (20 December 1971); A/RES/3032 (18 December 1972); A/RES/3102 (12 December 1973); A/RES/3500 (15 December 1975); A/RES/31/19 (24 November 1976); A/RES/31/19 (8 December 1977).

[132] UN Docs. S/RES/788 (19 November 1992), S/RES/972 (13 January 1995), S/RES/1001 (30 June 1995) S/RES/1083 (27 November 1996). All four resolutions appealed to "all parties to the conflict and all others concerned to respect strictly the provisions of international humanitarian law".

[133] UN Docs. S/RES/794 (3 December 1992), S/RES/814 (26 March 1993), condemning breaches of international humanitarian law, including "the deliberate impeding of the delivery of food and medical supplies".

[134] UN Doc. S/RES/1213 (3 December 1998), calling upon the government of Angola and UNITA in particular to "respect international humanitarian, refugee and human rights law"; see also the statement by the UN Security Council President in 1993, condemning UNITA's attacks on a train that was carrying civilians, and urging "UNITA leaders to make sure that its forces abide by the rules of international humanitarian law" (UN Doc. S/25899, 8 June 1993).

[135] UN Doc. S/RES/993 (12 May 1993), reaffirming "the need for the parties to comply with international humanitarian law".

[136] UN Doc. S/RES/1193 (28 August 1998).   [137] Under Chapter VII of the UN Charter.

In addition to action by the Security Council, many UN human rights bodies, as well as regional human rights bodies, have increasingly played a role in situations of armed conflict. While these human rights bodies are generally only empowered to examine whether violations of international human rights law have taken place, this has not stopped such bodies from drawing on, where relevant, the law of armed conflict. For example, in the case of *Abella* v. *Argentina* (also known as the *La Tablada* case)[138] concerning an attack in 1989 by forty-two armed non-State fighters on an Argentine national forces barracks at La Tablada, the Inter-American Commission on Human Rights determined that it could apply IHL in its decision-making processes. The Commission held that where international human rights law did not assist them in deciding, for instance, how to differentiate between a civilian installation and a military one, it was appropriate to draw on the law of armed conflict for guidance.[139] This development, of recognising the inter-operability of international human rights law and IHL, has been reflected in the jurisprudence of bodies like the European Court of Human Rights and the ICJ, which have either ruled on violations of human rights in armed conflicts,[140] or stated that human rights law must be respected during times of armed conflict.[141]

Finally, non-governmental organisations and civil society organisations have become increasingly influential in holding States and non-State actors to account under IHL. The work of Geneva Call has been discussed in Chapter 8 of this book, regarding their advocacy relating to non-State groups and compliance with the Ottawa provisions on anti-personnel mines; other organisations such as Human Rights Watch, Médicins sans Frontières and Amnesty International, for example, have proven to be effective and persuasive advocates for promoting a culture of compliance and accountability for both IHL and international human rights law. These organisations, frequently independent of the kinds of policy constraints (such as confidentiality and neutrality) that might limit the activities of organisations such as the ICRC, are often able to investigate activities that may be "off-limits" to other inter-governmental or international organisations. For example, in recent years, Human Rights Watch has published a number of studies investigating and condemning current practice in areas such as drone warfare and targeted killing, as well as autonomous weapons systems.[142]

---

[138] IACHR, *Juan Carlos Abella* v. *Argentina*, Case 11.137, Report No. 55/97, IACHR, OEA/Ser.L/V/II.95 doc. 7 rev. p. 271 (1997). See also the Inter-American Court of Human Rights in *Bámaca-Velásquez* v. *Guatemala*, Series C No. 70 (2000), Judgment, 16 November 2000, paras. 205–9.

[139] *Abella* p. 44, para 161. See also S. Zegveld, "The Inter-American Commission on Human Rights and International Humanitarian Law: A Comment on the Tablada Case" (1998) 38 IRRC 505.

[140] See e.g. the European Court of Human Rights in *Al-Skeini et al.* v. *UK* (Application No 55721/07), Judgment, 7 July 2011, and *Al-Jedda* v. *UK* (Application No. 27021/08), Judgment of 7 July 2011.

[141] *The Wall*, 226, para. 25.

[142] See generally Human Rights Watch, www.hrw.org/topic/counterterrorism/targeted-killings-and-drones.

10. IMPLEMENTATION, ENFORCEMENT AND ACCOUNTABILITY IN NON-INTERNATIONAL ARMED CONFLICTS

It will have been apparent that much of the discussion in this chapter has applied as much to non-international armed conflict as to international armed conflict – the role that can be played by the UN and other organisations, for example, and the obligation on States to respect and to ensure respect for international humanitarian law.[143] This section therefore focuses on the issues particular to internal conflicts. The approach followed is to address the following questions: what law applies, to whom, and how is it implemented and enforced?

a. What law applies?

To recap the various parts of this text relating to non-international armed conflict, the applicable law comprises treaty law and customary law. Humanitarian treaty law applicable specifically to non-international armed conflict comprises Common Article 3, Additional Protocol II and other treaties such as the 1996 (amended) Mines Protocol,[144] Protocols I, III, IV and V to the 1980 Conventional Weapons Convention,[145] and the 1954 Cultural Property Convention[146] and its 1999 Protocol.[147] In addition, the Ottawa Convention banning anti-personnel landmines and the Chemical Weapons Convention also apply to NIACs since they prohibit the production and use of certain weapons "under any circumstances".[148] Customary international

---

[143] On the latter issue Fleck, for example, points out that while this obligation, as encapsulated in Common Article 1 to the 1949 Geneva Conventions, was originally intended or assumed to apply to international armed conflicts only, but has steadily been more widely accepted as applying equally to non-international armed conflict: Dieter Fleck, "The Law of Non-International Armed Conflict" in Dieter Fleck (ed.), *The Handbook of International Humanitarian Law*, 3rd edn, (Oxford University Press, 2013), pp. 607–8.

[144] Protocol (II) on Prohibitions or Restrictions on the Use of Mines, Booby-Traps and Other Devices 1996, Geneva, as amended on 3 May 1996, in force 3 December 1998, 2048 UNTS 93 ("Amended Protocol (II) CCW").

[145] Protocol (I) on Non-Detectable Fragments 1980, Geneva, 10 October 1980, in force 2 December 1983, 1342 UNTS 168; 19 ILM 1529 ("Protocol (I) CCW"); Protocol (III) on Prohibitions or Restrictions on the Use of Incendiary Weapons 1980, Geneva, 10 October 1980, in force 2 December 1983, 1342 UNTS 137 ("Protocol (III) CCW"); Protocol (IV) on Blinding Laser Weapons 1995, Vienna, 13 October 1995, in force 30 July 1998, 1380 UNTS 370 ("Protocol (IV) CCW"); Protocol (V) on Explosive Remnants of War 2003, Geneva, 28 November 2003, in force 12 November 2006, 2399 UNTS 100 ("Protocol (V) CCW").

[146] Convention for the Protection of Cultural Property in the Event of Armed Conflict, The Hague, 14 May 1954, in force 7 August 1956, 249 UNTS 240.

[147] Second Protocol to the Hague Convention of 1954 for the Protection of Cultural Property in the Event of Armed Conflict 1999, 26 March 1999, in force 9 March 2004, 2253 UNTS 212 ("Second Protocol to The Hague Convention 1954").

[148] Convention on the Prohibition of the Use, Stockpiling, Production and Transfer of Anti-Personnel Mines and on their Destruction, Oslo, 18 September 1997, in force 1 March 1999, 2056 UNTS 211

law now contains many rules that apply to both international and non-international armed conflicts, relating especially to the conduct of hostilities. The whole of Common Article 3 is now accepted as having customary status,[149] as well as many of the substantive rules in AP II such as:

- the prohibition of attacks on civilians,
- the obligation to respect and protect medical and religious personnel, medical units and transports,
- the prohibition of starvation,
- the prohibition of attacks on objects indispensable to the survival of the civilian population,
- the obligation to respect the fundamental guarantees of persons who are not taking a direct part, or who have ceased to take a direct part, in hostilities,
- the obligation to search for and respect and protect the wounded, sick and shipwrecked,
- the obligation to search for and collect the dead,
- the obligation to protect persons deprived of their liberty,
- the prohibition of the forced movement of civilians, and
- specific protection for women and children.[150]

The ICRC also considers that most, but not all, of the rules of customary international humanitarian law that it has identified apply not only to international but also non-international armed conflicts, such as the distinction between civilian objects and military objectives, the prohibition of indiscriminate attacks, the principle of proportionality, rules on protected persons and objects, and rules on particular methods of warfare.[151] The precise scope and content of this customary international humanitarian law (for both IAC and NIAC) are, as noted elsewhere, not entirely clear, and there are differing views among States and jurists. But for present purposes it suffices to be aware that there is a fairly substantial body of customary international humanitarian law applicable to non-international armed conflicts. In addition, it has been seen that international human rights law will apply to internal conflicts, as will any relevant domestic law.

It is relatively easy to state, at least in general terms, what law applies; how that law applies to the parties to a non-international armed conflict is less straightforward and is discussed in the next section.

("Ottawa Convention"), art. 1; Convention on the Prohibition of the Development, Production, Stockpiling and Use of Chemical Weapons and on their Destruction, Paris, 13 January 1993, in force 29 April 1997, 1974 UNTS 45 ("CWC"), art. 1.

[149] *Nicaragua*, para. 218.

[150] ICRC, Increasing respect for International Humanitarian Law in Non-International Armed Conflicts, February 2008, p. 9, www.icrc.org/eng/assets/files/other/icrc_002_0923.pdf.

[151] Ibid., p. 10; ICRC CIHL Study.

b. To whom does the (NIAC) law apply?

It is frequently stated that "all parties to non-international armed conflicts – whether State actors or armed groups – are bound by the relevant rules of IHL".[152] Common Article 3, for example, begins "[i]n the case of armed conflict not of an international character ... each Party to the conflict shall be bound to apply, as a minimum, the following provisions ...". The reference to each party to the conflict obviously includes the non-State party, and the use of the word "bound" suggests the imposition of a legal obligation on State and non-State parties alike. Additional Protocol II is less direct, applying to "all [non-international] armed conflicts" of a certain intensity;[153] the only reference to "parties" is to the High Contracting Parties to the Geneva Conventions or the Protocol. The determination by some States to avoid language that might confer any kind of legitimacy or recognition on insurgents led to the deletion from an earlier draft of all references to "the parties to the conflict".[154] Despite this, the AP II applies to each party; any other interpretation would contravene the principle of the equality of the parties to the conflict, and would be inconsistent with the Protocol's express statement that it "develops and supplements" Common Article 3, which clearly does apply to all parties.[155] Thus "[the Protocol's] rules grant the same rights and impose the same duties on both the established government and the insurgent party".[156] And finally, it is now well established that customary international humanitarian law also binds each party to a non-international armed conflict.[157]

So far as the State party is concerned, how the law – whether treaty or custom – applies and binds the State is clear and well understood in international law. The State is an international legal person and a subject of international law, with the capacity to bring and be subject to international claims;[158] it is, or may be if it chooses, a party to a treaty regarding international humanitarian law, and as a matter of international law it will be bound by any relevant rule of customary international law.[159] If it violates its international legal obligations, its international legal responsibility will be engaged and it will be obliged to make appropriate reparation to the injured party.[160]

But how, precisely, does international humanitarian law apply to and bind an armed group? Armed groups, not being States, are not (and cannot be) parties to the relevant treaties; and as they would appear to have questionable international legal

---

[152] Ibid., p. 10
[153] AP II, art. 1(1); see above Chapter 3 for a discussion of the threshold criteria for the Protocol's application.
[154] AP Commentary, para. 4415.   [155] AP II, art. 1(1); ICRC CIHL Study, vol. I, p. 497, commentary to r. 139.
[156] AP Commentary, para. 4442.   [157] See e.g. ICRC CIHL Study, vol. I, 495, r. 139.
[158] Crawford, *Brownlie's Principles of Public International Law*, p. 115.
[159] Subject to the rare exception of the persistent objector, which is unlikely in this field but might arise if, for example, the US continues with its objections to the customary status of some of the rules identified in the ICRC study on customary IHL.
[160] See ILC Articles on State Responsibility.

personality, it is not immediately obvious on what or whom the obligations legally
rest, and how they may be enforced. Several theories attempting to answer these
questions have been advanced, although none is entirely satisfactory.[161] They are
briefly summarised in the following paragraphs.

The first, which is most commonly referred to, is the "legislative jurisdiction"
theory: that a State has competence to legislate for all its nationals and all those
within its territory, who will be bound by and subject to that legislation. The
argument is that by analogy a State has a similar right to enter into treaties on
behalf of its nationals and those within its territory, and that those individuals will
similarly be bound by and subject to the provisions of the treaty.[162] The analogy has
also been extended to rules of customary international humanitarian law.[163] This
doctrine has several positive features, notably that the State and the armed group
will be bound by the same rules, and the fact that the armed group may not have
consented to the rules is immaterial, just as lack of consent to legislation is
immaterial to its binding force.[164] On the other hand, the doctrine may not encourage compliance with the law by armed groups, particularly those seeking to overthrow the established government; if an armed group has not consented to the
particular rules, it is unlikely to accept the power of the State to "legislate" on its
behalf and bind it anyway.[165] Further, it implicitly assumes that the conflict is
taking place on the State's territory or involves the State's nationals; it would not
apply neatly in the case of an non-international armed conflict taking place outside
the State's territory and involving other States' nationals. In that case application of
the law would depend on other States' treaty obligations, if any.

Another criticism is that the doctrine seems to confuse, or not adequately differentiate between, State legal systems in which treaties are self-executing and those
that require treaties to be implemented in domestic legislation before they will have
binding force on the individuals within the State.[166] Thus, according to this view,
the conceptual equation between legislation and treaty-making is flawed because it
does not explain how the armed groups themselves – the equivalent of individuals
subject to domestic legislation – are automatically bound by the provisions of a
treaty as soon as the State becomes party to it, even in a State where a treaty has no
domestic legal effect in the absence of implementing legislation.[167]

---

[161] Fleck, "The Law of Non-International Armed Conflict", pp. 585–6; Jann Kleffner, "The Applicability of
International Humanitarian Law to Organized Armed Groups" (2011) 93(992) IRRC 443; Cedric Ryngaert
and Anneleen Van de Meulebroucke, "Enhancing and Enforcing Compliance with International Humanitarian Law by Non-State Armed Groups: an Inquiry into some Mechanisms" (2011) 16(3) *Journal of
Conflict and Security Law* 443.

[162] Sandesh Sivakumaran, "Binding Armed Opposition Groups" (2006) 55 ICLQ 369 at 381–382.

[163] For example, Kleffner, "The Applicability of International Humanitarian Law to Organized Armed
Groups", 446.

[164] Ibid., p. 445.   [165] Ibid., p. 446.

[166] Ibid., pp. 446–8; Sivakumaran, "Binding Armed Opposition Groups", 383–4.

[167] For a counter-argument see Sivakumaran, "Binding Armed Opposition Groups", 384–5.

A second theoretical explanation as to why armed groups are bound by IHL is that the members of an armed group are bound as individuals, and since the group is a collection of individuals, the group itself is also bound. It is clear that IHL applies to individuals; it has long been accepted that individuals can be prosecuted for war crimes. The criticism of this theory is that it fails to distinguish between the individual and the collective: many provisions of IHL hinge on the existence of the group, from the very existence of an armed conflict to the duties of an armed group that are owed independently of its members. It does not therefore follow, it is said, that because individuals are bound by IHL, the armed group of which they are members must also be bound.[168]

A third theory of much narrower application is that if the armed group "exercises effective sovereignty" – governmental control – over a part of a State that is a party to a particular treaty, the armed group will be bound simply because it is acting as a government or quasi-government.[169] In this situation the armed group is either striving to become, or has become, the government of a State, and will thereby be bound by the treaty obligations of the State. It is closely related to the principle of State responsibility under which an insurgent group that succeeds in becoming the government of a State will be responsible in international law for all its prior acts and omissions.[170] If the insurgent group does not become the government, the State itself remains, in principle, not responsible for the insurgents' acts.[171] A significant flaw in this theory is that many armed groups will never reach the stage of exercising "effective sovereignty" over territory, and this theory fails to explain why those groups would or should also be bound by IHL.

A fourth, stronger theory is that armed groups are bound by customary IHL, by virtue of the international legal personality they possess.[172] Usually cited in support of this view is a UN commission of enquiry into the situation in Darfur in 2004; the commission's report included the assertion that "all insurgents that have reached a certain threshold of organization, stability and effective control of territory, possess international legal personality and are therefore bound by the relevant rules of customary international law on internal armed conflicts".[173] One objection to this theory is that it explains only customary IHL and does not explain how armed groups are bound by treaty law: a significant number of rules of IHL are not yet of customary status.

Another objection is the more fundamental issue of whether armed groups do indeed possess international legal personality. Many States will not accept this,

---

[168] Kleffner, "The Applicability of International Humanitarian Law to Organized Armed Groups", pp. 449–51.
[169] GC I Commentary, p. 51.   [170] ILC Articles on State Responsibility, art. 10.
[171] Ibid., commentary to art. 8.
[172] Kleffner, "The Applicability of International Humanitarian Law to Organized Armed Groups", pp. 454–6.
[173] Report of the International Commission of Inquiry on Darfur to the United Nations Secretary-General Pursuant to Security Council Resolution 1564 of 18 September 2004, 25 January 2005, para. 172, www.un.org/News/dh/sudan/com_inq_darfur.pdf.

preferring to regard all insurgents as criminals under domestic law and not entities with international legal status, and there are strongly divergent views among jurists as to whether armed groups have international legal personality.[174] Some say that following the reasoning in the *Reparation* case,[175] an entity will have the international legal personality that it needs to function; an armed group needs sufficient personality to "be able to hold rights and be subject to obligations afforded to them by the rules governing internal armed conflict".[176] Others point to the circularity of this reasoning: an armed group will have international legal personality because it needs to comply with international humanitarian law; but international humanitarian law is binding on an armed group only (according to this theory) because it has international legal personality.[177]

A last theory to mention is that IHL binds armed groups if they consent to it, or more precisely, if they have expressly consented to particular rules of IHL. One of the objections to the other theories is that they ignore the need (whether legal or practical) for an armed group to voluntarily agree to be bound by IHL, as such agreement is much more likely to translate into actual compliance. There are already many mechanisms by which armed groups can express such consent, from Common Article 3 which encourages the parties to a non-international armed conflict to enter into a special agreement to apply all or some of the other provisions of the Geneva Conventions in their conflict, to unilateral undertakings or commitments.[178] Many of these unilateral commitments are made to the ICRC or other organisations such as Geneva Call, which persuades armed groups to sign a "Deed of Commitment" of three kinds (to date): banning the use of anti-personnel mines (which forty-eight groups have signed), protecting children from the effects of armed conflict (thirteen) and prohibiting sexual violence (twelve).[179] However, from the theoretical viewpoint, relying on consent as a basis for the binding effect of IHL has some difficulties, the most obvious being that it would exclude the binding application of any rules to which the armed group had not consented.

None of these theories fully explains how or why armed groups are legally bound by IHL. International law is constantly evolving but is still State-centric in the way in which it is made and applied: treaties are made by States (and to a lesser extent, international organisations), and customary law is formed primarily by State practice and State *opinio juris*;[180] international law still struggles to recognise entities

---

[174] See e.g. Sivakumaran, "Binding Armed Opposition Groups", 373–4.

[175] *Reparation for Injuries Suffered in the Service of the Nations*, Advisory Opinion, ICJ Rep. 1949, p. 174.

[176] Sivakumaran, "Binding Armed Opposition Groups", 374.

[177] Kleffner, "The Applicability of International Humanitarian Law to Organized Armed Groups", p. 456.

[178] See further below, pp. 263–4.

[179] Geneva Call, *Deed of Commitment*, www.genevacall.org/how-we-work/deed-of-commitment/.

[180] The ICRC CIHL Study lists the practice of armed groups under the heading "Other": "[t]he practice of armed opposition groups, such as codes of conduct, commitments made to observe certain rules of international humanitarian law and other statements, does not constitute State practice as such. While such practice

other than States and international organisations as international legal persons. There is, therefore, no satisfactory conceptual explanation for the supposedly binding effect of IHL on armed groups. Nevertheless, armed groups do have a role distinct from their individual members, particularly in the implementation and enforcement of the law, as illustrated in the next section.

c. Implementation, enforcement and accountability

Many of the implementation, enforcement and accountability mechanisms in non-international armed conflict are the same as, or mirror, those in international armed conflict discussed above. The earlier discussion on the obligation to respect humanitarian norms, for example, applies equally to non-international armed conflict and is therefore not repeated here. Similarly the role played by the United Nations Security Council in applying sanctions on individuals and members of named groups has been covered in section 9 above. This section therefore focuses on the range of mechanisms, from dissemination of the law through to prosecutions in international criminal courts and tribunals, that are of relevance to non-international armed conflict.

i. Dissemination

The discussion earlier in this chapter on dissemination applies equally to State dissemination of the law applicable in non-international armed conflict. The express obligations contained in each of the four Geneva Conventions[181] refer to dissemination of "the text of the present Convention", which includes Common Article 3 applicable to non-international armed conflicts.[182] In other words, States are required to inform and educate their armed forces, and "if possible"[183] the civilian population, on the laws applicable to NIACs as well as international armed conflict – and to do so in times of peace as well as war. In addition, AP II contains the simple requirement that the Protocol "be disseminated as widely as possible".[184] This obligation applies to both the State and non-State parties to a NIAC, although in practice it will usually apply to an armed group only once the conflict breaks out since the group may not exist at all in peacetime.[185]

The ICRC and NGOs play a critical role in this area – talking to and educating armed groups (and States fighting them) on their IHL obligations. The ICRC will

---

may contain evidence of the acceptance of certain rules in non-international armed conflicts, its legal significance is unclear and it has therefore been listed under 'Other Practice' . . .": ICRC CIHL Study, vol. I. p. xlii.

[181] GC I, art. 47; GC II, art. 48; GC III, art. 127; GC IV, art. 144.

[182] Sivakumaran, "The Law of Non-International Armed Conflict", p. 431.

[183] GC I, art. 47; GC II, art. 48; GC III, art. 127; GC IV, art. 144.   [184] AP II, art. 19.

[185] Sivakumaran, "The Law of Non-International Armed Conflict", p. 432.

formally inform all parties to an armed conflict, as early as possible, of the legal characterisation of the situation and of the applicable law; it will also remind the parties of their obligation to train their members and will offer to help in that regard.[186] Other organisations such as Geneva Call are also active in the field, engaging with, educating and training the leadership and members of armed groups and thereby assisting them to fulfill their obligations.[187]

ii. Special agreements

One of the tools employed by the ICRC in this work is the special, or bilateral, agreement. Common Article 3 expressly encourages parties to a NIAC to agree that in addition to the basic provisions of that Article, their conflict will be subject to all, or some, of the other provisions of the Geneva Conventions.[188] Even without this provision the parties to a NIAC can agree between themselves that certain rules will apply. Examples of such agreements – whether specifically Common Article 3 agreements or covering additional issues such as respect for human rights – facilitated by the ICRC include those in the 1960s in Yemen and Nigeria, El Salvador in 1990, Bosnia and Herzegovina in 1992, and the Philippines in 1998.[189] Making these agreements does not guarantee compliance with their provisions, any more than the existence of a law guarantees obedience to it, but particularly where the agreement has been concluded with the assistance of the ICRC, it may provide a basis for continued monitoring and follow-up by the ICRC.[190] Special agreements are relatively rare; far more common are unilateral commitments made by armed groups, as described in the next section.[191]

iii. Unilateral undertakings or commitments

Armed groups quite commonly declare unilaterally that they will abide by international humanitarian law, or particular rules of IHL. They may do this for any number of reasons, including the purely political, for example seeking respectability in the eyes of the local population or the international community. The declaration may simply restate the minimum obligations of Common Article 3, or may assume greater obligations; the ICRC emphasises that whatever is expressly stated, the minimum rules will always be applicable.[192] The ICRC encourages unilateral

---

[186] ICRC, *Increasing Respect for International Humanitarian Law in Non-International Armed Conflicts*, p. 15.
[187] One of Geneva Call's many tools is a small brochure summarising the basic humanitarian norms in pictorial form, in many different languages: see e.g. Geneva Call, "15 Key Rules of Behavior for Fighters in Internal Armed Conflict", www.genevacall.org/wp-content/uploads/dlm_uploads/2014/05/GenevaCall_IHL_A6Booklet_English.pdf.
[188] Common Article 3 to the Four Geneva Conventions, penultimate paragraph.
[189] ICRC, *Increasing Respect for International Humanitarian Law in Non-International Armed Conflicts*, p. 15.
[190] This applies equally to other humanitarian organisations: Ibid., p. 18.   [191] Ibid., p. 17.
[192] Ibid., p. 19. See also Sandesh Sivakumaran, "Lessons for the Law of Armed Conflict from Commitments of Armed Groups: Identification of Legitimate Targets and Prisoners of War" (2011) 93 IRRC 463, 463–82.

declarations because they have a number of indirect benefits in addition to their express commitments: a declaration may provide the leadership of an armed group with a vehicle for internal education and discipline, and the process of making the declaration, especially where this occurs with the assistance of the ICRC or other humanitarian actors, can start a longer process of dialogue with and monitoring of the armed group.[193] And as with the special agreements mentioned earlier, there is also the hope that armed groups will feel more inclined to adhere to humanitarian rules where they have actively consented to them. Whatever may be the formal legal position, many armed groups may be tempted to reject or disregard the existing rules of IHL because they, as non-State actors, have had no role in their creation. Geneva Call focuses on this in its work persuading armed groups to sign its Deeds of Commitment.[194]

The legal effect of a unilateral declaration or commitment is not settled. To the extent that it merely restates the obligations already applicable to an armed group, the situation is no different to that discussed in section 10(b) above. But if greater obligations are assumed, it is not clear whether (and how) the armed group is legally bound and if so, how the obligations may be enforced. One suggestion is that unilateral commitments should be binding on armed groups in the same way as unilateral statements are binding on States in certain circumstances: when made publicly on behalf of the State by a person in a position of authority, on a subject within that person's competence, and with the intention of being bound.[195] In this connection it could be noted that a declaration made by a national liberation movement under Article 96(3) of Additional Protocol I, but not satisfying all the substantive and procedural requirements, might be construed as a unilateral commitment to adhere to the Geneva Conventions and that Protocol.[196]

iv. Accountability through International Criminal Law

The accountability of individuals under international criminal law is described in section 6 of this chapter, and as explained, applies to offences committed in non-international as well as international armed conflicts.[197] It might however be recalled that, however uncertain the legal position of armed groups may be in some

---

[193] Ibid., p. 19.

[194] Geneva Call, *Deed of Commitment*, www.genevacall.org/how-we-work/deed-of-commitment/.

[195] ILC, Guiding Principles Applicable to Unilateral Declarations of States Capable of Creating Legal Obligations, Report of the 58th Session, UN Doc. A/61/10 (2006) legal.un.org/ilc/texts/instruments/english/draft %20articles/9_9_2006.pdf; *Nuclear Tests (Australia v. France; New Zealand v. France)* Judgment, ICJ Rep. 1974, pp. 267–8, paras. 43 and 46 and pp. 472–3, paras. 46 and 49; Ryngaert and Van de Meulebroucke, "Enhancing and Enforcing Compliance with International Humanitarian Law by Non-State Armed Groups", p. 446; Andrew Clapham, "Focusing on Armed Non-State Actors", in Andrew Clapham and Paola Gaeta (eds.), *The Oxford Handbook of International Law in Armed Conflict*, (Oxford University Press, 2014), p. 783.

[196] See Chapter 3, pp. 55–8.   [197] See also Section 7 above.

contexts (such as precisely how they are bound by IHL), the existence or otherwise of a group can be relevant in international criminal prosecutions – in addition to the task of classifying the conflict.[198] For example, one of the elements of a crime against humanity as defined in Article 7 of the Rome Statute of the International Criminal Court[199] is that the act must be part of an attack that is "pursuant to or in furtherance of a[n] . . . organizational policy to commit such attack".[200] The Court in 2012[201] confirmed that this requires the existence of an organisation, and that it must satisfy much the same criteria as those set by the ICTY for an armed conflict to exist, i.e. that there must be (as well as intensity of fighting) an organised armed group.[202]

11. CONCLUSION

This chapter has considered the different ways in which international humanitarian law is implemented and enforced, and how individuals – and States – can be held accountable for violations of the law. The mechanisms are many and varied: they start with education, so that all participants are aware of their obligations; they can include subtle behind-the-scenes work by the ICRC, Geneva Call and similar actors, or political pressure by those actors or States; they can be legal or quasi-legal, as in the special agreements and unilateral declarations by non-State armed groups; they can involve economic coercion, as in targeted Security Council sanctions, or (in very limited circumstances) physical coercion, in the form of belligerent reprisals or UN-authorised military force; and when prevention has failed, they include prosecution and punishment of individual violations of the law as well as State-to-State claims on the basis of State responsibility.

Although it is not clear that the prospect of a potential future international criminal prosecution is an actual deterrent when an individual is about to violate the law, the trials that have taken place in the *ad hoc* international criminal tribunals have unquestionably restored some public faith that those guilty of atrocities may, eventually, face punishment. But those tribunals were obviously limited to particular conflicts (Yugoslavia and Rwanda) and will be wound up when their current trials and any appeals are complete. Thereafter there will only be the International Criminal Court, which is likely to remain the only truly international criminal court. Its record of prosecutions to date is encouraging, but the backlash from African States described in section 7 above is of serious concern. If the Court

---

[198] See Chapter 3 in relation to classification of the conflict. [199] Set out at n. 98 above.
[200] Rome Statute, art. 7(2)(a).
[201] *Prosecutor* v. *William Samoei Ruto, Henry Kiprono Kosgey and Joshua Arap Sang*, ICC-01/09-01/11, Decision on the Confirmation of Charges Pursuant to Article 61(7)(a) and (b) of the Rome Statute 23 January 2012, paras. 183–5, www.icc-cpi.int/iccdocs/doc/doc1314535.pdf.
[202] See Chapter 3, pp. 63–6.

loses international support, the fight against impunity will be set back a generation and future atrocities will be punishable only in the domestic courts of willing States, or in another *ad hoc* international tribunal if the Security Council has the necessary political will to create one. The role of education and prevention, and the good offices of organisations like the ICRC, will be even more vital.

SUGGESTED READING

Cassese, Antonio and Paola Gaeta, *Cassese's International Criminal Law*, 3rd edn (Oxford University Press, 2013)

Krieger, Heike (ed.), *Inducing Compliance with International Humanitarian Law: Lessons from the African Great Lakes Region* (Cambridge University Press, 2015)

Meron, Theodor, *The Making of International Criminal Justice: The View from the Bench: Selected Speeches* (Oxford University Press, 2011)

Schabas, William, *The International Criminal Court: A Commentary On The Rome Statute* (Oxford University Press, 2010)

DISCUSSION QUESTIONS

1. Has the growth of international criminal law been a positive development?
2. The Organisation for African Unity has condemned the ICC as "biased" and "anti-African"?[203] Do you agree? How would you defend against such an allegation?
3. Critically evaluate the various mechanisms for implementation and enforcement of IHL – how effective (or not) are they?
4. How are non-State armed groups bound by IHL?
5. How could compliance with IHL by State forces be improved?
6. How could compliance with IHL by non-State armed groups be improved?

---

[203] Faith Karimi, "African Union Accuses ICC of Bias, Seeks Delay of Cases Against Sitting Leaders", *CNN*, 12 October 2013, edition.cnn.com/2013/10/12/world/africa/ethiopia-au-icc-summit/.

10 Conclusions

The law of armed conflict seems torn between two fundamentally contradictory impulses – the need, on the one hand, to wage war effectively, and the desire, on the other hand, to protect people and property from the ravages of such warfare. The law of armed conflict attempts to reconcile these impulses, in a fundamentally pragmatic way.[1] IHL compels States and non-State parties alike to do their utmost to protect and preserve the life, limb and property of civilians and others *hors de combat*, while at the same time giving parties to a conflict leave to commit acts of violence within certain boundaries.

However, when those boundaries are transgressed, when perpetrators of war crimes are not brought to account for their transgressions, there is a natural impulse to dismiss IHL as lacking any "real" normative force. This is an understandable response, but it fails to grasp the complexities of IHL, and, indeed, international law more generally. As Falk has noted, there is an "ironic tendency for people to expect law in international affairs to do more for the order and welfare of the community than it does in domestic affairs ... when these extravagant expectations [of international law] are disappointed the contributions actually made by law to world order are extravagantly neglected."[2] Because we expect so much of IHL – that it not be violated ever – when it is broken, we might be inclined to think the entire system broken.

However, such an approach fails to recognise that the law has made life for those persons caught up in armed conflicts demonstrably better than if the law had never existed. Such an dismissal of IHL would diminish the great strides made by States

---

[1] Geoffrey Best puts it eloquently, arguing that IHL is fundamentally about "accepting war as a more or less regrettable recurrence in the mixed moral experience of mankind, without abandoning hope of sooner or later reducing its incidence to near-vanishing-point; in the meantime, restricting the extent of its horrors by observing the laws and rules of war, appealing partly to the softer side of human nature, partly to plain self-interest" (*Humanity in Warfare: The Modern History of the International Law of Armed Conflicts* (London: Methuen, 1983), p.15.

[2] Richard Falk (ed.), *The Vietnam War and International Law*, 4 vols. (Princeton University Press, 1968–76), vol. 4, p. 127.

and non-State groups alike, by the ICRC, by the UN, the ICJ, the ICC and the criminal tribunals in reminding all persons that the use of force is unlawful; that even in wartime, there are laws that must be followed, and when those rules are broken, consequences will follow. Those consequences may not always be criminal trials or incarceration, but there will be consequences, whether through sanctions, embargoes, public condemnation, loss of international reputation and standing, or through domestic redress, such as the removal of offending administrations from political office.

This is not to say that IHL is a perfect set of laws – far from it. The continuing reluctance of States to adopt more comprehensive laws on non-international armed conflicts, or to ban certain weapons, like nuclear weapons, clearly demonstrates gaps in the normative régime that should be addressed. Furthermore, constant developments and advancements in technology, like autonomous weapons systems, will no doubt bring new pressures to bear on IHL. However, IHL is a robust and vibrant field of law; the fundamental motivations that lead to the adoption of the first Geneva Convention in 1864 – to mitigate the brutality of war – were present again in 1949 and 1977. The fundamental principles espoused in the Preamble to the 1868 St Petersburg Declaration – humanity, distinction, military necessity, prohibitions on unnecessary suffering and superfluous injury – can be found in the manifold treaties on armed conflict that were adopted decades later.

It is always incumbent on any legal system to evaluate whether it continues to adequately address the situation it was adopted to regulate. As we have seen in these nine chapters, States and non-State actors continue to evaluate and examine the law of armed conflict, to gauge its effectiveness and adequacy, and to call for reaffirmation and development of the law when necessary. Consensus on such reaffirmation and development may seem at times fitful and sporadic; however, what remains a constant is the widespread acceptance of the value of the law. The foundations of IHL are strong, and have endured for over one hundred and fifty years, in the face of unprecedented social, political and technological change. It seems reasonable to believe that the fundamental principles will continue to endure, whether they are found in treaty law or customary law, for the next hundred and fifty years, and beyond.

BIBLIOGRAPHY

Abi-Saab, G, "Wars of National Liberation and the Development of Humanitarian Law" in R. Akkerman, P. van Krieken and C. Pannenborg (eds.), *Declarations on Principles: A Quest for Universal Peace* (Leiden: Sijthoff, 1977)

Ainley, Kirsten, "The International Criminal Court on Trial" (2011) 24 Camb Rev of Int'l Aff 309

Akande, Dapo, "Clearing the Fog of War? The ICRC's Interpretive Guidance on Direct Participation in Hostilities" (2010) 59 *ICLQ* 190

Akhavan, Payam, Goldman, Robert K., Meron, Theodor, Hays Parks, W. and Viseur-Sellers, Patricia, "The Contribution of the Ad Hoc Tribunals to International Humanitarian Law" (1998) 13 *AUILR* 1510

Al-Damkhi, Ali Mohamed, "Kuwait's Oil Well Fires, 1991: Environmental Crime and War" (2007) 64 *International Journal of Environmental Studies* 31

Aldrich, George, "Customary International Humanitarian Law – an Interpretation on Behalf of the International Committee of the Red Cross" (2005) 76 *BYBIL* 503

"The Taliban, Al Qaeda, and the Determination of Illegal Combatants" (2002) 96 *AJIL* 891

Ambrose, Stephen, *D-Day June 6, 1944: The Climactic Battle of World War II* (New York: Touchstone, 1994)

Amnesty International, *Behind a Wall of Silence: Prosecution of War Crimes in Croatia* (London: Amnesty International Publications, 2010)

Andrew, David, "Over a Century of Service: The .303 Projectile and its Wounding Capabilities – An Historical Profile" (2003) 12 *Australian Military Medicine* 144

Arai-Takahashi, Yutaka, "Preoccupied with Occupation: Critical Examinations of the Historical Development of the Law of Occupation" (2012) 94 IRRC 51

The Law of Occupation: Continuity and Change of International Humanitarian Law, and its Interaction with International Human Rights Law (Leiden: Martinus Nijhoff, 2009)

Australian Red Cross campaign, *Make Nuclear Weapons the Target*, 2013, targetnuclearweapons. org.au/#/petition

Bacon, Sir Reginald, *The Life of Lord Fisher of Kilverstone, Admiral of the Fleet*, 2 vols. (New York, Doubleday, Doran & Co., 1929)

Bartels, Rogier, "Timelines, Borderlines and Conflicts: The Historical Evolution of the Legal Divide between International and non-International Armed Conflicts" (2009) 91 *IRRC* 61

Bassiouni, M. Cherif, "The History of Universal Jurisdiction and its Place in International Law" in Steven Macedo (ed.), *Universal Jurisdiction: National Courts and the Prosecution of Serious Crimes under International Law* (Philadelphia: University of Pennsylvania Press, 2004)

Baudens, Lucien, *La Guerre de Crimée: Les Campements, Les Abris, Les Ambulances, Les Hopitaux etc etc* (Paris: Michel Lévy Frères, 1857)

"Une mission médicale à l'Armée d'Orient", *Revue des Deux Mondes*, XXVIIth year, February 1857

Baxter, R. R., "So-Called 'Unprivileged Belligerency': Spies, Guerrillas, and Saboteurs" (1951) 28 BYBIL 323

"The Municipal and International Law Basis of Jurisdiction over War Crimes" (1951) 28 BYBIL 382

Beale, Joseph, "The Recognition of Cuban Belligerency" (1896) 9 *Harvard Law Review* 406

Beevor, Antony, *Crete: The Battle and the Resistance* (London: John Murray Ltd, 1991)

Bellal, Annyssa, Giacca, Gilles and Casey-Maslen, Stuart, "International Law and Armed Non-state actors in Afghanistan" (2011) 93 *IRRC* 51

Benvenisti, Eyal, *The International Law of Occupation* (Princeton University Press, 2004)

Berman, Nathaniel, "Privileging Combat? Contemporary Conflict and the Legal Construction of War" (2004) 43 *Columbia Journal of Transnational Law* 1

"Sovereignty in Abeyance: Self-Determination and International Law" (1988) 7 *Wisconsin International Law Journal* 51

Best, Geoffrey, *Humanity in Warfare: The Modern History of the International Law of Armed Conflicts* (London: Methuen, 1983)

"The Restraint of War in Historical and Philosophic Perspective" in Astrid Delissen and Gerard Tanja (eds.), *Humanitarian Law of Armed Conflict – Challenges Ahead* (Dordrecht: Martinus Nijhoff, 1991)

Bethlehem, Daniel, "The Methodological Framework of the Study", in Elizabeth Wilmshurst and Susan Breau (eds.), *Perspectives on the ICRC Study on Customary International Humanitarian Law* (Cambridge University Press, 2007)

Biddle, Tami Davis, "Dresden 1945: Reality, History, and Memory" (2008) 72 *The Journal of Military History* 413

Blank, Laurie, and Noone, Gregory, *International Law and Armed Conflict: Fundamental Principles and Contemporary Challenges in the Law of War* (New York: Wolters Kluwer, 2013)

Blum, Gabriella and Heymann, Philip, "Law and Policy of Targeted Killing" (2010) 1 *Harv Nat'l Sec J* 145

Boisson de Chazournes, Laurence and Condorelli, Luigi, "Common Article 1 of the Geneva Conventions revisited: Protecting Collective Interests" (2000) 837 *IRRC* 67

Boisson de Chazournes, Laurence and Sands, Philippe (eds.), *International Law, the International Court of Justice and Nuclear Weapons* (Cambridge University Press, 1999)

Boothby, William, "'And for Such Time As': The Time Dimension to Direct Participation in Hostilities" (2010) 42 *NYU J Int'l L & Pol* 741

Conflict Law: The Influence of New Weapons Technology, Human Rights and Emerging Actors (The Hague: Springer, 2014)

The Law of Targeting (Oxford University Press, 2012)

Weapons and the Law of Armed Conflict (Oxford University Press, 2009)

Borelli, Sylvia, "Casting Light on the Legal Black Hole: International Law and Detentions Abroad in the 'War on Terror'" (2005) 87 *IRRC* 39

Bothe, Michael, "Article 3 and Protocol II: Case Studies of Nigeria and El Salvador" (1982) 31 *AULR* 899

"Targeting", in Andru E. Wall (ed.), *International Law Studies – Volume 78: Legal and Ethical Lessons of NATO's Kosovo Campaign* (Newport, RI: US Naval War College, 2002)

Bothe, Michael, Partsch, Karl and Solf, Waldemar (eds.), *New Rules for Victims of Armed Conflicts: Commentary on the Two 1977 Protocols Additional to the Geneva Conventions of 1949* (The Hague/Boston/London: Martinus Nijhoff, 1982)

New Rules for Victims of Armed Conflicts: Commentary on the Two 1977 Protocols Additional to the Geneva Conventions of 1949, 2nd edn (Leiden: Koninklijke Brill NV, 2013)

Bouvier, Antoine, "Assessing the Relationship between Jus in Bello and Jus ad Bellum: An Orthodox View" (2006) 100 *ASIL Proceedings* 109

Boyle, Alan and Chinkin, Christine, *The Making of International Law* (Oxford University Press, 2007)

Bugnion, François, "Birth of an Idea: The Founding of the International Committee of the Red Cross and of the International Red Cross and Red Crescent Movement: From Solferino to the Original Geneva Convention (1859–1864)" (2012) 94 *International Review of the Red Cross* 1299

"Droit de Genève et droit de La Haye" (2001) 83 *IRRC* 901

Red Cross, Red Crescent, Red Crystal (Geneva: ICRC, 2007)

The ICRC and the Protection of War Victims (Geneva: ICRC, 2003)

"The International Committee of the Red Cross and Nuclear Weapons" (2005) 859 *IRRC* 511

The International Committee of the Red Cross and the Protection of War Victims (Geneva: ICRC, 2003)

Cameron, Lindsay, "Private Military Companies – Their Status under International Humanitarian Law and its Impact on their Regulation" (2006) 88 *IRRC* 573

Cameron, Lindsay and Chetail, Vincent, *Privatizing War: Private Military and Security Companies under Public International Law* (Cambridge University Press, 2013)

Cannizzaro, Enzo, "Contextualising Proportionality: *Jus ad Bellum* and *Jus in Bello* in the Lebanese War" (2000) 864 *IRRC* 779

Carnahan, Burrus, "Lincoln, Lieber and the Laws of War: The Origins and Limits of the Principle of Military Necessity" (1998) 92 *AJIL* 213

Carnahan, Burrus and Robertson, Marjorie, "The Protocol on Blinding Laser Weapons: A New Direction for International Humanitarian Law" (1996) 90 *AJIL* 484

Carr, Jeffrey, *Inside Cyber Warfare* (Sebastopol, CA: O'Reilly, 2012)

Cassese, Antonio, *International Law*, 2nd edn, (Oxford University Press, 2005)

Self-Determination of Peoples: A Legal Reappraisal (Cambridge University Press, 1995)

Cassese, Antonio and Gaeta, Paola, *Cassese's International Criminal Law*, 3rd edn, (Oxford University Press, 2013)

Cavanaugh, K. A., "Rewriting Law: The Case of Israel and the Occupied Territory", in David Wippman and Matthew Evangelista (eds.), *New Wars, New Laws? Applying Laws of War in 21st Century Conflicts* (Dordrecht: Martinus Nijhoff, 2005)

Chickering, Roger, and Förster, Stig, "Are We There Yet? World War II and the Theory of Total War", in Roger Chickering, Stig Förster and Bernd Greiner (eds.), *A World at Total War: Global Conflict and the Politics of Destruction, 1937–1945* (Cambridge University Press, 2005)

Cicero, Marcus Tullius, Oratio *pro Tito Annio Milone*, trans. John Smyth Purton (Cambridge University Press, 1853)

Clapham, Andrew, "Focusing on Armed Non-State Actors", in Andrew Clapham and Paola Gaeta (eds), *The Oxford Handbook of International Law in Armed Conflict*, (Oxford University Press, 2014)

Human Rights Obligations of Non-State Actors (Oxford University Press, 2005)

Clarke, Richard and Knake, Robert, *Cyber War: The Next Threat to National Security and What To Do About It* (New York: Ecco, 2010)

Cluster Munition Coalition, *A Timeline of Cluster Bomb Use*, www.stopclustermunitions. org/en-gb/cluster-bombs/use-of-cluster-bombs/a-timeline-of-cluster-bomb-use.aspx.

Conner, Johnathan and Bebarta, Vikhyat, "White Phosphorus Dermal Burns" (2007) 357 *The New England Journal of Medicine* 1530

Corn, Geoffrey, "Hamdan, Lebanon, and the Regulation of Armed Conflict: The Need to Recognize a Hybrid Category of Armed Conflict" (2007) 40 *Vanderbilt Journal of Transnational Law* 295

"Snipers in the Minaret – What Is the Rule? The Law of War and the Protection of Cultural Property: A Complex Equation" (July 2005) *The Army Lawyer* 28

"Thinking the Unthinkable: Has the Time Come to Offer Combatant Immunity to Non-State Actors?" (2011) 22 *Stanford LPR* 253

Corn, Geoffrey, Hansen, Victor, Jackson, Richard, Jenks, Chris, Jensen, Eric Talbot and Schoettler, James Jr., *The Law of Armed Conflict: An Operational Approach* (New York: Wolters Kluwer, 2012)

Cottier, Michael, "Article 8(2)(b)(xi)", in Otto Triffterer (ed.), *Commentary on the Rome Statute of the International Criminal Court*, 2nd edn (Oxford: Hart, 2002)

Craven, W. L. and Cate J. L., (eds.), *The Army Air Forces in World War II*, 7 vols. (University of Chicago Press, 1948–58), vol. 5

Crawford, Emily, *The Treatment of Combatants and Insurgents Under the Law of Armed Conflict* (Oxford University Press, 2010)

"Unequal Before the Law: The Case for the Elimination of the Distinction Between International and Non-International Armed Conflict" (2007) 20 *Leiden Journal of International Law* 441

Crawford, James, *Brownlie's Principles of Public International Law*, 8th edn (Oxford University Press, 2012)

The International Law Commission's Articles on State Responsibility: Introduction, Text and Commentaries (Cambridge University Press, 2002)

Crowe, Jonathan and Weston-Scheuber, Kylie, *Principles of International Humanitarian Law* (Cheltenham: Elgar, 2013)

Cryer, Robert, *Prosecuting International Crimes: Selectivity and the International Criminal Law Regime* (Cambridge University Press, 2005)

Cullen, Anthony, "Key Developments Affecting the Scope of Internal Armed Conflict in International Humanitarian Law" (2005) 183 *Military Law Review* 65

The Concept of Non-International Armed Conflict in International Humanitarian Law (Cambridge University Press, 2010)

Dalton, Richard, "Libya", in Chatham House, "The Legal Classification of the Armed Conflicts in Syria, Yemen and Libya" (2014) *International Law PP* 2014/1, 38

de Martens, Fyodor, *La Paix et la Guerre* (Paris: Arthur Rousseau, 1901)

de Vattel, Emmer, *The Law Of Nations, Or, Principles Of The Law Of Nature, Applied To The Conduct And Affairs Of Nations And Sovereigns, With Three Early Essays On The Origin And Nature Of Natural Law And On Luxury, 1797*, trans. Thomas Nugent 2008 (Indianapolis, IN: Liberty Fund, 2008)

de Zayas, Alfred, *The Wehrmacht War Crimes Bureau, 1939–1945* (Lincoln, NB: University of Nebraska Press, 1989)

Deeks, Ashley, "Administrative Detention In Armed Conflict" (2009) 40 *Case W Res J Int'l L* 403

Demarest, Geoffrey, "Espionage in International Law" (1995–1996) 24 *Denver Journal of International Law and Policy* 321

Detter, Ingrid, *The Law of War*, 3rd edn (Oxford: Ashgate, 2013)

Dinstein, Yoram, "Legitimate Military Objects Under the Current Jus In Bello: The Principle of Distinction and Military Objectives", in Andru E. Wall (ed.), *International Law Studies – Volume 78: Legal and Ethical Lessons of NATO's Kosovo Campaign* (Newport, RI: US Naval War College, 2002)

The Conduct of Hostilities under the Law of International Armed Conflict, 2nd edn (Cambridge University Press, 2010)

"The Dilemmas Relating to Legislation under Article 43 of the Hague Regulations and Peace-Building", Background Paper prepared for the Informal High-Level Expert Meeting on Current Challenges to International Humanitarian Law, Cambridge, 25–27 June, 2004, www. hpcrresearch.org/sites/default/files/publications/dinstein.pdf

"The Distinction between Unlawful Combatants and War Criminals", in Yoram Dinstein and Mala Tabory (eds.), *International Law at a Time of Perplexity: Essays in Honour of Shabtai Rosenne* (Leiden: Martinus Nijhoff, 1989)

"The ICRC Customary International Humanitarian Law Study" (2006) 36 *Israel Yearbook on Human Rights* 1 *The International Law of Belligerent Occupation* (Cambridge University Press, 2009)

"The Israel Supreme Court and the Law of Belligerent Occupation: Deportations" (1993) 23 *IYHR* 1

Dörmann, Knut, *Elements of War Crimes under the Rome Statute of the International Criminal Court: Sources and Commentary* (Geneva: ICRC, 2003)

"The Legal Situation of 'Unlawful/Unprivileged Combatants'" (2003) 85 *IRRC* 45

Doswald-Beck, Louise, "Private Military Companies under IHL" in S. Chesterman and C. Lehnardt (eds.), *From Mercenaries to Market: The Rise and Regulation of Private Military Companies*, (Oxford University Press, 2007)

Downes, Alexander, *Targeting Civilians in War* (Ithaca, NY: Cornell University Press, 2008)

Dufour, Guillaume-Henri, Moynier, Gustave and Lehmann, Samuel, *Le Congrès de Genève: Rapport adressé au Conseil fédéral par MM. Dufour, Moynier et Lehmann, Plénipotentiaires de la Suisse* (Geneva: Imprimerie Fick, 1864)

Dunant, Jean-Henry, *A Memory of Solferino*, 1862 edn, trans. by the American Red Cross (Geneva: ICRC, 1939)

Duraković, Asaf, "On Depleted Uranium: Gulf War and Balkan Syndrome" (2001) 42 *Croatian Medical Journal* 130

Erickson, Richard John, "Protocol I: A Merging of the Hague and Geneva Law of Armed Conflict" (1979) 19 *Va J Int'l L* 557

Evans, Christine, *The Right to Reparation in International Law for Victims of Armed Conflict* (Cambridge University Press, 2012)

Expert Meeting on Procedural Safeguards For Security Detention In Non-International Armed Conflict, Chatham House and International Committee of the Red Cross, London, 22–23 September 2008 (2009) 91 IRRC 859

Extraordinary Chambers in the Courts of Cambodia, *Case Load*, www.eccc.gov.kh/en/caseload

Falk, Richard (ed.), *The Vietnam War and International Law*, 4 vols. (Princeton University Press, 1968–76)

Fairlie, Ian, "The Health Hazards of Depleted Uranium" (2008) 3 *Disarmament Forum* 3

Feickert, Andrew, and Kerr, Paul K., *Cluster Munitions: Background and Issues for Congress* (US Congressional Research Service, 29 April 2014), www.fas.org/sgp/crs/weapons/RS22907.pdf

Feith, Douglas, "Law in the Service of Terror – The Strange Case of the Additional Protocol" (1985) 1 *National Interest* 36

Fenrick, William, "The *Targeted Killings* Judgment and the Scope of Direct Participation in Hostilities" (2007) 5 *JICJ* 332

Fenwick, C. G., "War without a Declaration" (1937) 31(4) *AJIL* 694

Fidler, David P., "The Use of White Phosphorus Munitions by US Forces in Iraq" (2005) 9 *ASIL Insights*, www.asil.org/insights/volume/9/issue/37/use-white-phosphorus-munitions-us-military-forces-iraq

Fisher, Louis, *Nazi Saboteurs on Trial: Military Tribunal and American Law*, 2nd edn (Lawrence, KN: University Press of Kansas, 2005)

Fitzgerald, Gerald, "Chemical Warfare and Medical Response During World War I" (2008) 98 *Am J Public Health* 631

Fleck, Dieter, "The Law of Non-International Armed Conflict" in Dieter Fleck (ed.), *The Handbook of International Humanitarian Law*, 3rd edn, (Oxford University Press, 2013)

Fletcher, George, "Black Hole in Guantánamo Bay" (2004) 2 *JICJ* 121

Fletcher, George and Ohlin, Jens David, *Defending Humanity* (New York: Oxford University Press, 2008)

Focarelli, Carlo, "Common Article 1 of the 1949 Geneva Conventions: A Soap Bubble?" (2010) 21 *EJIL* 125

Forrest, Alan, "*La Patrie en Danger*: The French Revolution and the First *Levée en Masse*" in Daniel Moran and Arthur Waldron (eds.), *The People in Arms: Military Myth and National Mobilisation since the French Revolution* (Cambridge University Press, 2003)

Forsythe, David, *The Humanitarians: The International Committee of the Red Cross* (Cambridge University Press, 2005)

Fox, Gregory, "Transformative Occupation and the Unilateralist Impulse" (2012) 94 *IRRC* 237

Gaeta, Paola, "Does President Al Bashir Enjoy Immunity from Arrest?" (2009) 7(2) *JICJ* 315

Gardam, Judith, "Necessity and Proportionality in Jus ad Bellum and Jus in Bello", in Laurence Boisson de Chazournes and Philippe Sands (eds.), *International Law, the International Court of Justice and Nuclear Weapons* (Cambridge University Press, 1999)

Gardam, Judith, *Necessity, Proportionality and the Use of Force by States* (Cambridge University Press, 2004)

"Proportionality and Force in International Law" (1993) 87 *AJIL* 391

Garraway, Charles, "Discussion: Reasonable Military Commanders and Reasonable Civilians", in Andru E. Wall (ed.), *International Law Studies – Volume 78: Legal and Ethical Lessons of NATO's Kosovo Campaign* (Newport, RI: US Naval War College, 2002)

Gasser, Hans-Peter, "The International Committee of the Red Cross" (2013) Max Planck Encyclopaedia of International Law

Gaudreau, Julie, "The Reservations to the Protocols Additional to the Geneva Conventions for the Protection of War Victims" (2003) 849 *IRRC* 143

Geneva Academy of International Humanitarian Law and Human Rights, "Afghanistan: Applicable International Law", 14 June 2012, www.geneva-academy.ch/RULAC/applicable_international_law.php?id_state=1.

"Rule of Law in Armed Conflict (RULAC), 'Qualification of Armed Conflicts'", 13 June 2012, www.geneva-academy.ch/RULAC/qualification_of_armed_conflict.php

Geneva Call, *Armed Non-State Actors*, www.genevacall.org/how-we-work/armed-non-state-actors/

Deed of Commitment under Geneva Call for Adherence to a Total Ban on Anti-Personnel Mines and for Cooperation in Mine Action, 2000, www.genevacall.org/wp-content/uploads/dlm_uploads/2013/12/DoC-Banning-anti-personnel-mines.pdf

Gerson, Allan, "War, Conquered Territory, and Military Occupation in the Contemporary International Legal System" (1976–1977) 18 *Harv Int'l L J* 525

Gibbons, Owen Thomas, "Uses and Effects of Depleted Uranium Munitions: Towards a Moratorium on Use" (2004) 7 *YBIHL* 191

Gill, Terry and Van Sliedregt, Elies, "Guantánamo Bay: A Reflection on the Legal Status and Rights of 'Unlawful Enemy Combatants'" (2005) 1 *Utrecht Law Review* 28

Gillard, Emanuela-Chiara, "Reparation for Violations of International Humanitarian Law" (2003) 85 *IRRC* 536

Gillespie, Alexander, *A History of the Laws of War*, 3 vols. (Oxford: Hart Publishing, 2011)

Glasstone, Samuel and Dolan, Philip (eds.), *The Effects of Nuclear Weapons* (Washington, DC: United States Department of Defense and the Energy Research and Development Administration, 1977)

Gonzalez, Alberto, Counsel to the President and William J. Haynes II, General Counsel of the Department of Defense from US Department of Justice, Office of Legal Counsel, Memorandum, Subject: Application of Treaties and Law to al Qaeda and Taliban Detainees, 22 January 2002

Green, Leslie, *The Contemporary Law of Armed Conflict*, 3rd edn (Manchester University Press, 2008)

"The Status of Mercenaries in International Law" (1978) 8 *Israel Yearbook of Human Rights* 9

Greenberg, Karen, *The Least Worst Place: Guantanamo's First 100 Days* (Oxford University Press, 2009)

Greenberg, Karen and Dratel, Joshua, *The Torture Papers: The Road to Abu Ghraib* (Cambridge University Press, 2005)

Greenspan, Morris, *The Modern Law of Land Warfare* (Berkeley/Los Angeles, CA: UCLA Press, 1959)

Greenwood, Christopher, "Customary International Law and the First Geneva Protocol of 1977 in the Gulf Conflict", in Christopher Greenwood (ed.), *Essays on War in International Law* (London: Cameron May, 2006)

"Scope of Application of International Humanitarian Law", in Dieter Fleck (ed.), *The Handbook of International Humanitarian Law*, 2nd edn (Oxford University Press, 2008)

"The Advisory Opinion on Nuclear Weapons and the Contribution of the International Court to International Humanitarian Law" (1997) 316 *IRRC* 65

"The Law of Weaponry at the Start of the New Millennium", in Leslie Green and Michael
   Schmitt (eds.), *International Law Studies – Volume 71: The Law of Armed Conflict: Into the
   Next Millennium* (Newport, RI: US Naval War College, 1998)
"The Law of Weaponry at the Start of the New Millennium" (1998) 71 *International Law
   Studies* 185
"The Laws of War (International Humanitarian Law)" in Malcolm Evans (ed.), *International Law*
   (Oxford University Press, 2003)
"The Relationship between *Ius ad Bellum* and *Ius in Bello*" (1983) 9 *Review of International
   Studies* 221
"Twilight of the Law of Belligerent Reprisals" (1989) 20 *Netherlands YB Int'l L* 35
Greppi, Edoardo, "The Evolution of Individual Criminal Responsibility under International Law"
   (1999) 835 *IRRC* 531
Gross, Emanuel, "Human Rights, Terrorism And The Problem Of Administrative Detention In
   Israel: Does A Democracy Have The Right To Hold Terrorists As Bargaining Chips?" (2001) 18
   Ariz J Int'l & Comp L 721
Grotius, Hugo, *De Jure Belli ac Pacis Libri Tres*, trans. Francis W. Kelsey, in James Brown Scott
   (ed.) *The Classics of International Law* (Oxford University Press, 1925)
Grunawalt, Richard, King, John and McClain, Ronald (eds.), *Protection of the Environment During
   Armed Conflict* (Newport, RI: Naval War College, 1996)
Gunderson, Brian, "Leaflet Dropping Operations in World War II" (1998) 45 *Air Power History* 28
Haines, Steven, "Weapons, Means and Methods of Warfare", in Elizabeth Wilmshurst and Susan
   Breau (eds.), *Perspectives on the ICRC Study on Customary International Humanitarian Law*
   (Cambridge University Press, 2007)
Hall, Christopher, "The First Proposal for a Permanent International Criminal Court" (1998) 322
   IRRC 57
Hall, John Spencer, *Battle for Crete* (London: White Lion 1962)
Hall, William Edward, *A Treatise on International Law* (Oxford: Clarendon Press, 1880)
Hampson, Françoise, "Teaching the Law of Armed Conflict" (2008) 5 *Essex Human Rights Review* 1
Harley, Naomi H., *et al.*, *A Review of the Scientific Literature as it Pertains to Gulf War Illnesses*
   (Washington DC: National Defense Research Institute/RAND, 1999)
Harrison, Mark, "Resource Mobilisation for World War II: the USA, UK, USSR and Germany,
   1938–1945" (1988) 41 *Economic History Review* 171
Hartigan, Richard Shelly, *Lieber's Code and the Law of War* (New York: The Legal Classics Library
   1995)
Hassner, Ron, *War on Sacred Grounds* (Ithaca, NY: Cornell University Press, 2009)
Haug, Hans, *Humanity for All: The International Red Cross and Red Crescent Movement* (Geneva:
   Henri Dunant Institute, 1993)
Hays Parks, W., "Joint Service Combat Shotgun Program" (1997) *The Army Lawyer* 16
   "Part IX of the ICRC 'Direct Participation in Hostilities' Study: No Mandate, No Expertise, and
      Legally Incorrect" (2010) 42 *NYU J Int'l L and Pol* 769
   "The ICRC Customary Law Study: A Preliminary Assessment" (2005) 99 *American Society of
      International Law Proceedings* 208
Hayashi, Brian Masaru, *Democratizing the Enemy: the Japanese American Internment* (Princeton
   University Press, 2004)
Heffter, August Wilhelm, *Das Europäische Völkerrecht der Gegenwart* (Berlin: Schroeder, 1844)
Heintze, Hans-Joachim, "Protecting Power", in the *Max Planck Encyclopaedia of Public
   International Law* (2009)
Henckaerts, J. M., "Study on Customary International Humanitarian Law" (2005) 87 *IRRC* 198
Henckaerts, Jean-Marie and Doswald-Beck, Louise (eds.), *International Committee of the Red
   Cross: Customary International Humanitarian Law*, 2 vols. (Cambridge University Press,
   2005)
Henderson, Ian, *The Contemporary Law of Targeting: Military Objectives, Proportionality and
   Precautions in Attack under Additional Protocol I* (Leiden/Boston: Martinus Nijhoff, 2009)

Hersh, Seymour, *Chemical and Biological Warfare: America's Hidden Arsenal* (Indianapolis, IN: Bobbs Merrill, 1968)

Hilmas, Corey, Smart, Jeffrey and Hill, Benjamin, "History of Chemical Warfare", in Martha Lenhart (ed.), *Medical Aspects of Chemical Warfare* (Washington DC: Borden Institute/US Department of the Army, Office of the Surgeon General, 2008)

Holquist, Peter, *The Russian Empire as a "Civilized State": International Law as Principle and Practice in Imperial Russia, 1874–1878* (Washington DC: The National Council for Eurasian and East European Research, 2004)

Human Rights Watch, "Genocide, War Crimes and Crimes Against Humanity: Topical Digests of the Case Law of the International Criminal Tribunal for Rwanda and the International Criminal Tribunal for the Former Yugoslavia", February 2004, Listing of Cases included, www.hrw.org/reports/2004/ij/icty/2.htm

"Meeting the Challenge: Protecting Civilians through the Convention on Cluster Munitions", November 2010, www.hrw.org/sites/default/files/reports/armsclusters1110webwcover.pdf

"Needless Deaths in the Gulf War: Civilian Casualties During the Air Campaign and Violations of the Laws of War", June 1991, www.hrw.org/reports/pdfs/u/us/us.91o/us910full.pdf

"Rain of Fire: Israel's Unlawful Use of White Phosphorus in Gaza", March 2009, www.hrw.org/node/81760

Ticking Time Bombs: NATO's Use of Cluster Munitions in Yugoslavia (Human Rights Watch, June 1999), www.hrw.org/reports/1999/nato2/nato995–01.htm#P77_13303

"US: Give Guantanamo Detainees Fair Process", 4 December 2007, www.hrw.org/news/2007/12/03/us-give-guantanamo-detainees-fair-process

ICRC, "Action by the International Committee of the Red Cross in the Event of Violations of International Humanitarian Law or of Other Fundamental Rules Protecting Persons in Situations of Violence" (2005) 87 *IRRC* 393

"Adoption of the Red Crescent by the Islamic Republic of Iran" (1980) 219 *IRRC* 316

"External Activities: Nigeria" (1967) 79 *IRRC* 535

Health Care in Danger, www.icrc.org/eng/what-we-do/safeguarding-health-care/solution/2013-04-26-hcid-health-care-in-danger-project.htm

"Help to War Victims in Nigeria" (1968) in 92 IRRC 571, (1969) 94 IRRC 3, (1969) 95 IRRC 81 and (1969) 96 IRRC 119

"How is the Term 'Armed Conflict' Defined in International Humanitarian Law?" ICRC Opinion Paper, March 2008, www.icrc.org/eng/assets/files/other/opinion-paper-armed-conflict.pdf

"ICRC Central Tracing Agency: Half a Century of Restoring Family Link", 7 April 2010, www.icrc.org/eng/resources/documents/interview/centra-tracing-agency-interview-070410.htm

IHL Database, www.icrc.org/IHL

"Increasing Respect for International Humanitarian Law in Non-International Armed Conflicts", February 2008, p. 15, www.icrc.org/eng/assets/files/other/icrc_002_0923.pdf

"International Humanitarian Law and the Challenges of Contemporary Armed Conflicts", October 2011, www.icrc.org/eng/assets/files/red-cross-crescent-movement/31st-international-conference/31-int-conference-ihl-challenges-report-11-5-1-2-en.pdf

"International Humanitarian Law and Terrorism: Questions and Answers", 1 January 2011, www.icrc.org/eng/resources/documents/faq/terrorism-faq-050504.htm

National Implementation Database, http://www.icrc.org/ihl-nat

Nuclear Weapons, www.icrc.org/eng/war-and-law/weapons/nuclear-weapons/index.jsp

"People on War: Even Wars have Limits", 1998, www.icrc.org/eng/resources/documents/film/f00392.htm

Protection of Victims on Non-International Armed Conflicts, Document presented at the Conference of government experts on the reaffirmation and development of international humanitarian law applicable in armed conflicts, Vol. V, Geneva, 24 May-12 June 1971

The ICRC's Mandate and Mission, www.icrc.org/eng/who-we-are/mandate/overview-icrc-mandate-mission.htm

Treaties and State Parties to Such Treaties, www.icrc.org/IHL

"Unpublished Documents relative to the Founding of the Red Cross: Minutes of the Committee of Five" (1949) 2 *IRRC* 127

"What is ICRC's Position on Terrorism?", 15 November 2002, www.icrc.org/eng/resources/documents/faq/5fmf6k.htm

"What Limits does the Law of War Impose on Cyber Attacks?", 28 June 2013, www.icrc.org/eng/resources/documents/faq/130628-cyber-warfare-q-and-a-eng.htm

Final Report to the Prosecutor by the Committee Established to Review the NATO Bombing Campaign Against the Federal Republic of Yugoslavia, (ICTY, June 2000), www.icty.org/sid/10052

International Law Association, "Reparation for Victims of Armed Conflict", www.ila-hq.org/en/committees/index.cfm/cid/1018

Use of Force Committee, Final Report on the Meaning of Armed Conflict in International Law, www.ila-hq.org/en/committees/index.cfm/cid/1022

International Law Commission, "Commentary to the Vienna Convention on the Law of Treaties" (1966) 2 *Yearbook of the International Law Commission*

"Draft Code of Offences against the Peace and Security of Mankind with commentaries" (1954) 2 *Yearbook of the International Law Commission* 134

"Fourth Report on the Law of Treaties" (1965) 2 *Yearbook of the International Law Commission*, 12

"Report of the International Law Commission on the work of its forty-eighth session" (1996) 2 *Yearbook of the International Law Commission* 17

"Summary – Draft Code of Crimes Against the Peace and Security of Mankind (Part II) – including the draft Statute for an international criminal court", 9 July 2014, legal.un.org/ilc/summaries/7_4.htm

Institute of International Law, Resolutions, "Examen de la Déclaration de Bruxelles de 1874", 30 August 1875, www.idi–iil.org/idiF/resolutionsF/1875_haye_02_fr.pdf; Manuel des Lois de la Guerre sur Terre, 9 September 1880, www.idi–iil.org/idiF/resolutionsF/1880_oxf_02_fr.pdf, Preface

Inter-American Commission on Human Rights, Third Report on the Human Rights Situation in Colombia, OEA/Ser.L/V/II.102, doc. 9 rev. 1 ch. 4, 53 (26 February 1999)

International Criminal Court, *Elements of Crimes*, 2011, ICC-ASP/1/3(part II-B)

International Humanitarian Fact-Finding Commission, www.ihffc.org/index.asp?Language=EN&page=home

Ipsen, Knut, "Combatants and Non-Combatants" in Dieter Fleck (ed.), *The Handbook of Humanitarian Law in Armed Conflicts*, 3rd edn (Oxford University Press, 2013)

Jenks, Chris and Jensen, Eric Talbot, "Indefinite Detention Under the Laws of War" (2011) 22 *Stanford L and Pol'y Rev* 41

Jinks, Derek, "Protective Parity and the Laws of War" (2004) 79 *Notre Dame Law Review* 1493

Johnson, A. Ross, "Yugoslav Total National Defence" (1973) 15 *Survival* 54

Judgment of the International Military Tribunal, in *The Trial of German Major War Criminals: Proceedings of the International Military Tribunal sitting at Nuremberg, Germany* (London, 1950)

Kalshoven, Frits, "Arms, Armaments and International Law" (1985) 191 *RCADI* 183

Reflections on the Law of War: Collected Essays (Leiden: Martinus Nijhoff, 2007)

Kalshoven, Frits and Zegveld, Liesbeth, *Constraints on the Waging of War: An Introduction to International Humanitarian Law*, 4th edn (Cambridge University Press, 2011)

Keith, A. and Rigby, H. M., "Modern Military Bullets: A Study of Their Destructive Effects", *The Lancet*, 2 December 1899

Kellenberger, Jacob, "Speaking out or Remaining Silent in Humanitarian Work" (2004) 855 *IRRC* 593

Kleffner, Jann, "Improving Compliance with International Humanitarian Law Through the Establishment of an Individual Complaints Procedure" (2002) 15 *Leiden J Int'l L* 237

"Protection of the Wounded, Sick, and Shipwrecked", in Dieter Fleck (ed.), *The Handbook of Humanitarian Law in Armed Conflicts*, 3rd edn (Oxford University Press, 2013)

"Scope of Application of Humanitarian Law", in D. Fleck (ed.), *The Handbook of International Humanitarian Law*, 3rd edn (Oxford University Press, 2013)

"The Applicability of International Humanitarian Law to Organized Armed Groups" (2011) 93 (992) *IRRC* 443

Kolb, Robert and Hyde, Richard, *An Introduction to the International Law of Armed Conflicts* (Oxford: Hart, 2008)

Koppe, Erik, *The Use of Nuclear Weapons and the Protection of the Environment during International Armed Conflict* (Portland, OR: Hart, 2008)

Koutroulis, Vaios, "And Yet It Exists: In Defence of the 'Equality of Belligerents Principle" (2013) 26 *Leiden J Int'l L* 449

Kramer, Michael and Schmitt, Michael, "Lawyers on Horseback? Thoughts on Judge Advocates and Civil-Military Relations" (2008) 55 *UCLA L Rev* 1407

Kretzmer, David, "Targeted Killing of Suspected Terrorists: Extra-Judicial Executions or Legitimate Means of Defence?" (2005) 16 *EJIL* 171

Kussbach, Erich, "The International Humanitarian Fact-Finding Commission" (1994) 43 *ICLQ* 174

Landmine and Cluster Munition Monitor, *Contamination and Clearance*, 2013, www.the-monitor.org/index.php/publications/display?url=cmm/2013/CMM_Contamination_And_Clearance_2013.html

Lanning, Michael Lee, *Mercenaries: Soldiers of Fortune, from Ancient Greece to Today's Private Military Companies* (New York: Presidio Press, 2005)

Lanord, Christophe, "The Legal Status of National Red Cross and Red Crescent Societies" (2000) 840 *IRRC* 1053

Larsen, Kjetil Mujezinović, Cooper, Camilla Guldahl and Nystuen, Gro, "Is There a 'Principle of Humanity' in International Humanitarian Law?" in Kjetil Mujezinović Larsen, Camilla Guldahl Cooper and Gro Nystuen (eds.), *Searching for a "Principle of Humanity" in International Humanitarian Law* (Cambridge University Press, 2012)

Lauterpacht, Elihu (ed.), *International Law Reports*, vol. 42 (Cambridge: Grotius, 1971)

Lauterpacht, Hersch, "The Limits of the Operation of the Law of War" (1953) 30 *British Yearbook of International Law* 206

Lemkin, Raphael, *Axis Rule in Occupied Europe* (Concord, NH: Rumford Press, 1944)

Lesh, Michelle, "The Public Committee Against Torture in Israel v The Government Of Israel: The Israeli High Court of Justice Targeted Killing Decision" (2007) 8 *MJIL* 373

Levine, James, "The Doctrine of Command Responsibility and its Application to Superior Civilian Leadership: Does the International Criminal Court have the Correct Standard?" 193 *Mil L Rev* 52 (2007)

Lewis, Michael W., "The Law of Aerial Bombardment in the 1991 Gulf War" (2003) 97 *AJIL* 481

Liivoja, Rain and McCormack, Tim, "Law in the Virtual Battlespace: The Tallinn Manual and the *Jus in Bello*" (2013) 15 *YBIHL* 45

Likosky, Michael, "The Privatization of Violence", in Simon Chesterman and Angelina Fisher (eds.), *Private Security, Public Order: The Outsourcing of Public Service and Its Limits* (Oxford University Press, 2009)

Lippmann, Matthew, "Art and Ideology in the Third Reich: The Protection of Cultural Property and the Humanitarian Law of War" (1998–9) 17 *Dick. J. Int'l L.* 1

Lovell, David and Primoratz, Igor (eds.), *Protecting Civilians During Violent Conflict: Theoretical and Practical Issues for the 21st Century* (Farnham: Ashgate, 2012)

Lubell, Noam, *Extra-Territorial Use of Force against Non-State Actors* (Oxford University Press, 2010)

Macedo, Steven (ed.), *Universal Jurisdiction: National Courts and the Prosecution of Serious Crimes under International Law* (Philadelphia, PA: University of Pennsylvania Press, 2004)

Magliveras, Konstantinos and Naldi, Gina, "The International Criminal Court's Involvement with Africa: Evaluation of a Fractious Relationship" (2013) 82 *Nordic J Int'l L* 417

Mallison, W. Thomas and Mallison, Sally, "The Juridical Status of Irregular Combatants under the International Humanitarian Law of Armed Conflict" (1977) 9 *Case Western Reserve JIL* 39

Mallison, William, "A Juridical Analysis of the Israeli Settlements in the Occupied Territories" (1998–9) 10 *Palestine YB Int'l L* 1

Major, Marie-France, "Mercenaries and International Law" (1992) 22 *Ga J Int'l & Comp L* 103

Maresca, Louis, "A New Protocol on Explosive Remnants of War: The History and Negotiation of Protocol V to the 1980 Convention on Certain Conventional Weapons" (2004) 86 *IRRC* 815

Marsh, J. Jeremy and Glabe, Scott, "Time for the United States to Directly Participate" (2011) 1 *Va J Int'l L Online* 13

Maslen, Stuart, *Commentaries on Arms Control Treaties, Volume I: The Convention on the Prohibition of the Use, Stockpiling, Production, and Transfer of Anti-Personnel Mines and on their Destruction* (Oxford University Press, 2004)

Maslen, Stuart and Herby, Peter, "An International Ban on Anti-Personnel Mines: History and Negotiations of the 'Ottawa Treaty'" (1998) 38 *IRRC* 693

Maurer, Peter, "Challenges to International Humanitarian Law: Israel's Occupation Policy" (2012) 94 *IRRC* 1503

McCormack, Timothy, "A *Non Liquet* on Nuclear Weapons – The ICJ Avoids the Application of General Principles of International Humanitarian Law" (1997) 316 *IRRC* 76

"International Law and the Use of Chemical Weapons in the Gulf War" (1990–1) 21 *Cal W Int'l L J* 1

McCormack, Timothy and Durham, Helen, "Aerial Bombardment of Civilians: The Current International Legal Framework", in Yuki Tanaka and Marilyn Young (eds.), *Bombing Civilians: A Twentieth Century History* (New York/London: The New Press, 2009)

McCoubrey, *International Humanitarian Law: Modern Developments in the Limitation of Warfare*, 2nd edn (Dartmouth: Ashgate, 1998)

McDonald, Avril, "Depleted Uranium Weapons: The Next Target for Disarmament?" (2008) 3 *Disarmament Forum* 17

"The Challenges to International Humanitarian Law and the Principles of Distinction and Protection from the Increased Participation of Civilians in Hostilities" Paper Presented at the University of Teheran at a Round Table on the Interplay Between International Human Rights Law, April 2004

McNaught, L. W., *Nuclear Weapons and Their Effects* (London: Brassey's Defence Publishers, 1984)

Melzer, Nils, *Targeted Killing in International Law* (Oxford University Press, 2008)

Meron, Theodor, *Human Rights and Humanitarian Norms as Customary Law* (Oxford: Clarendon, 1989)

Meron, Theodor, "International Criminalisation of Internal Atrocities" (1995) 89 *AJIL* 554

Moir, Lindsey, "Towards the Unification of International Humanitarian Law?", in Richard Burchill, Nigel White and Justin Morris (eds.), *International Conflict and Security Law: Essays in Memory of Hilaire McCoubrey* (Cambridge University Press, 2005)

Mokhtar, Aly, "Will This Mummification Saga Come to an End? The International Humanitarian Fact-Finding Commission: Article 90 of Protocol 1" (2003–4) 22 *Penn St Int'l L Rev* 243

Moorehead, Caroline, *Dunant's Dream: War, Switzerland, and the History of the Red Cross* (London: Harper Collins, 1998)

Morton, Jeffrey, "The Legal Status of Laser Weapons That Blind" (1998) 35 *Journal of Peace Research* 697

Mudge, G. A., "Starvation as a Means of Warfare" (1969–70) 4 *Int'l Lawyer* 228

Neumann, Klaus, *In the Interest of National Security: Civilian Internment in Australia During World War II* (Canberra: National Archives of Australia, 2006)

Nwogugu, Pius, "The Nigerian Civil War: A Case Study in the Law of War" (1974) 14 *IJIL* 13

O'Connell, D. P., *The International Law of the Sea*, 2 vols. (Oxford: Clarendon Press, 1982–4)

O'Connell, Mary Ellen, "Combatants and the Combat Zone" (2009) 43 *U Rich L Rev* 845

"Historical Development and Legal Basis" in Dieter Fleck (ed.) *The Handbook of International Humanitarian Law*, 3rd edn (Oxford University Press, 2013)

O'Keefe, Roger, *The Protection of Cultural Property in Armed Conflict* (Cambridge University Press, 2006)

Oeter, Stefan, "Means and Methods of Combat", in Dieter Fleck (ed.), *The Handbook of International Humanitarian Law*, 3rd edn (Oxford University Press, 2013)

Ohlin, Jens David, "The Duty to Capture" (2013) 97 *Minnesota Law Review* 1268

Oppenheim L., *A Treatise on International Law*, 3rd edn, 2 vols. (London, New York: Longmans, Green and Co., 1920–1)

International Law: A Treatise, 1st edn, 2 vols. (London; New York: Longmans, Green and Co., 1905–6)

Organisation of African Unity, OAU Council of Ministers' Committee of Legal Experts, Doc CM/1/33/Ref. 1 (1972)

Resolution AHG/Res. 49 (IV), Congo, 11–14 September 1967, www.africa-union.org/Official_documents/Heads%20of%20State%20Summits/hog/eHoGAssembly1967.pdf

Paroff, Sasha, "Another Victim of the War in Iraq: The Looting of the National Museum in Baghdad and the Inadequacies of International Protection of Cultural Property" (2004) 53 *Emory Law Review* 2021

Paust, Jordan, "Dr Francis Lieber and the Lieber Code" (2001) 95 *ASIL Proceedings* 112

"Permissible Self-Defence Targeting and the Death of bin Laden" (2011) 39 *Denv J Int'l L & Pol'y* 569

Perna, Laura, *The Formation of the Treaty Law of Non-International Armed Conflicts* (Leiden: Martinus Nijhoff, 2006)

Perrin, Benjamin (ed.), *Modern Warfare: Armed Groups, Private Militaries, Humanitarian Organisations and the Law* (Vancouver: University of British Columbia Press, 2012)

Pfanner, Toni, "Various Mechanisms and Approaches for Implementing International Humanitarian Law and Protecting and Assisting War Victims" (2009) 91 *IRRC* 279

Phillips, Christopher, "Syria", in Chatham House, "The Legal Classification of the Armed Conflicts in Syria, Yemen and Libya", *International Law PP* 2014/1, March 2014

Pictet, Jean (ed.), *Commentary to Geneva Convention I for the Amelioration of the Condition of the Wounded and Sick in Armed Forces in the Field*, (Geneva: ICRC, 1952)

Development and Principles of International Humanitarian Law, (Dordrecht: Martinus Nijhoff, 1985)

Humanitarian Law and the Protection of War Victims (Leyden: A. W. Sijthoff, 1975)

The Development and Principles of International Humanitarian Law (The Hague: Martinus Nijhoff, 1985)

Pilloud, Claude, "Protection of the Victims of Armed Conflicts: Prisoners of War", in *International Dimensions of Humanitarian Law* (Geneva: Henry Dunant Institute, 1988)

Plant, Glen, *Environmental Protection and the Law of War: A "Fifth Geneva" Convention on the Protection of the Environment in Time of Armed Conflict* (London: Belhaven Press, 1992)

Playfair, Emma (ed.), *International Law and the Administration of Occupied Territories: Two Decades of Israeli Occupation of the West Bank and Gaza Strip* (Oxford: Clarendon, 1992)

Pomerance, *Self Determination in Law and Practice: The New Doctrine of the United Nations* (The Hague: Martinus Nijhoff, 1982)

Project of an International Declaration Concerning the Laws and Customs of War, 27 August 1874, reprinted in (1907) 1 (Supp.) *AJIL* 96

Prugh, George S., *Law at War: Vietnam 1964–1973, Vietnam Studies Series*, (Washington DC: Department of the Army, 1975)

Pulles, Gerrit Jan, "Crystallising an Emblem: On the Adoption of the Third Additional Protocol to the Geneva Conventions" (2005) 8 *YIHL* 296

Pustogarov, Vladimir, "Fyodor Fyodorovich Martens (1845–1909) – a Humanist of Modern Times" (1996) 312 *IRRC* 300

Quigley, John, "Iran and Iraq and the Obligations to Release and Repatriate Prisoners Of War After the Close of Hostilities" (1989) 5 *American University International Law Review* 73

Radsan, A. John, "The Unresolved Equation Of Espionage And International Law" (2007) 28 *Michigan Journal of International Law* 595

Ratner, Steven, "Law Promotion Beyond Law Talk: The Red Cross, Persuasion, and the Laws of War" (2011) 22 *EJIL* 459

Reeves, Jesse, "The Neutralisation of Belgium and the Doctrine of Kriegsraison" (1914–15) 13 *Michigan L Rev* 179

Ridlon, Daniel, "Contractors or Illegal Combatants? The Status of Armed Contractors in Iraq" (2008) 62 *AFL Rev* 199

Roberts, Adam, "The Equal Application of the Laws of War: A Principle Under Pressure" (2008) 90 *International Review of the Red Cross* 931

"Transformative Military Occupation: Applying the Laws of War and Human Rights" (2006) 100 *AJIL* 580

Roberts, Ian, "Saddam Hussein's Medical Examination should not have been Broadcast", Letter to the Editor, (2004) 328 *British Medical Journal* 51

Rogers, A. P. V., "A Commentary on the Protocol on Prohibitions or Restrictions on the Use of Mines, Booby Traps and Other Devices" (1987) 26 *RDMDG* 185

Law on the Battlefield, 3rd edn, (Huntington, New York: Juris, 2012)

Ronzitti, N., 'Resort to Force in Wars of National Liberation', in A. Cassese (ed.), *Current Problems of International Law: Essays on UN Law and on the Law of Armed Conflict* (Milan: A. Guiffrè, 1975)

Rosas, Allan, *The Legal Status of Prisoners of War: A Study in International Humanitarian Law Applicable in Armed Conflicts* (Helsinki: Suomalainen tiedeakatemia, 1976)

Rosenne, Shabtai, "The Red Cross, Red Crescent, Red Lion and Sun, and the Red Shield of David" (1975) 5 *Israel YB Hum Rts* 9

Ryngaert, Cedric and Van de Meulebroucke, Anneleen, "Enhancing and Enforcing Compliance with International Humanitarian Law by Non-State Armed Groups: an Inquiry into some Mechanisms" (2011) 16(3) *Journal of Conflict and Security Law* 443

Salzman, Zoe, "Private Military Contractors and the Taint of a Mercenary Reputation" (2008) 40 *NYUJILP* 853

Sandoz, Yves, Swinarski, Christophe and Zimmerman, Bruno (eds.), *Commentary on the Additional Protocols of 8 June 1977 to the Geneva Conventions of 12 August 1949* (Dordrecht: Martinus Nijhoff, 1987)

Sassòli, Marco, "Humanitarian Law and International Criminal Law" in A. Cassese (ed.), *The Oxford Companion to International Criminal Justice* (Oxford University Press, 2009)

"State Responsibility for Violations of International Humanitarian Law" (2002) 84 *IRRC* 419

"The Status of Persons Held in Guantánamo under International Humanitarian Law" (2004) 2 *JICJ* 96

"Transnational Armed Groups and International Humanitarian Law", Program on Humanitarian Policy and Conflict Research, Harvard University, *Occasional Paper Series*, Winter 2006, No. 6

Sassòli, Marco and Cameron, Lindsey, "The Protection of Civilian Objects – Current State of the Law and Issues de lege ferenda", in Natalino Ronzitti and Gabriella Venturini (eds.), *The Law of Air Warfare* (Utrecht: Eleven Publishing, 2006)

Sassòli, Marco, Bouvier, Antoine and Quintin, Anne, *How Does Law Protect in War? Cases, Documents and Teaching Materials on Contemporary Practice in International Humanitarian Law*, 3rd edn (Geneva: ICRC, 2011)

Saxon, Dan (ed.), *International Humanitarian Law and the Changing Technology of War* (Leiden: Martinus Nijhoff, 2013)

Scahill, Jeremy, *1 Dirty Wars: The World is a Battlefield* (London: Serpent's Tail, 2013)

Schaffer, Ronald, "The Bombing Campaigns in World War II: The European Theater", in Yuki Tanaka and Marilyn Young (eds.), *Bombing Civilians: A Twentieth Century History* (New York/London: The New Press, 2009)

Scheipers, Sibylle (ed.), *Prisoners in War* (Oxford University Press, 2010)

Schindler, Dietrich and Toman, Jiřì (eds.), *The Laws of Armed Conflicts: A Collection of Conventions, Resolutions, and Other Documents* 3rd edn (Leiden: Sijthoff, 1988)

Schindler, Dietrich, "International Humanitarian Law and Internationalized Internal Armed Conflicts" (1982) 22 *IRRC* 25

Schmitt, Michael, "Extraterritorial Lethal Targeting: Deconstructing the Logic of International Law" (2013) 52 *Colum J Transntl L* 79

"Foreword", in *William Boothby, The Law of Targeting* (Oxford University Press, 2012)

"Humanitarian Law and Direct Participation in Hostilities by Private Contractors or Civilian Employees" (2004–5) 5 *Chicago J Int'l L* 511

"The Interpretive Guidance on the Notion of Direct Participation in Hostilities: A Critical Analysis" (2010) 1 *Harv Nat Sec J* 5

Schöndorf, R. S., "Extra-State Armed Conflicts: Is there a Need for a New Legal Regime?" (2004) 37 *New York University Journal of International Law and Politics* 41

Schwager, Elke, "The Right to Compensation for Victims of an Armed Conflict" (2005) 4 *Chinese J Int'l L* 417

Schwebel, S. M., "Wars of Liberation – as Fought in UN Organs", in Norton Moore (ed.), *Law and Civil War in the Modern World* (Baltimore, MA: Johns Hopkins Press, 1974)

Scott, James Brown, *The Hague Conventions and Declarations of 1899 and 1907* (Washington, DC: Carnegie Endowment for International Peace, 1915)

Scott, James Brown, "The Work of the Second Peace Conference" (1908) 2 *AJIL* 1

Sherman, Gordon, "The Neutrality of Switzerland" (1918) 12 *AJIL* 462

Singer, P. W., *Corporate Warriors: The Rise of the Privatized Military Industry* (Ithaca, NY: Cornell University Press, 2003)

"Outsourcing War" (2005) 84 For Aff 119

Siordet, Frédéric, "The Geneva Conventions and Civil War" (1950) 3 *IRRC Supplement* 201

Sivakumaran, Sandesh, "Binding Armed Opposition Groups" (2006) 55 *ICLQ* 369

The Law of Non-International Armed Conflict (Oxford University Press, 2012)

Sofaer, Abraham, "Terrorism and the Law" (1985–6) 64 *Foreign Affairs* 901

Solf, Waldemar, "Development of the Protection of the Wounded, Sick and Shipwrecked under the Protocols Additional to the 1949 Geneva Conventions", in Christophe Swinarski (ed.), *Studies and Essays on International Humanitarian Law and Red Cross Principles in Honour of Jean Pictet* (Geneva: ICRC, 1984)

"The Status of Combatants in Non-International Armed Conflicts under Domestic Law and Transnational Practice" (1983–4) 33 *American University Law Review* 53

Solis, Gary, *The Law of Armed Conflict: International Humanitarian Law in War* (Cambridge University Press, 2010)

Sommaruga, Cornelio, "Unity and Plurality of the Emblems" (1992) 289 *IRRC* 333

Sosnowski, L., "The Position of Mercenaries Under International Law" (1979) 19 *Indian J Int'l L* 382

Statement of the Swiss Federal Department of Foreign Affairs, who act as repository for the Geneva Conventions, www.eda.admin.ch/eda/en/home/topics/intla/humlaw/gecons.html

Steindler, R. A., "The Case of the Mysterious Dum-Dum Bullet" (1983) 4 *American Journal of Forensic Medicine and Pathology* 205

Stockholm International Peace Research Institute, *SIPRI Yearbook 2013*, 2013, www.sipri.org/yearbook/2013/06

Swiss Federal Department of Foreign Affairs website www.eda.admin.ch/eda/en/home/reps/ocea/vaus/infoch/chhist.html

Thürer, Daniel, "International Humanitarian Law: Theory, Practice, Context" (2008) 338 *Recueil des Cours* 9

Tladi, Dire, "Cooperation, Immunities, and Article 98 of the Rome Statute: The ICC, Interpretation, and Conflicting Norms" (2012) 106 *AJIL* 307

Toebes, Birgit, "Doctors in Arms: Exploring the Legal and Ethical Position of Military Medical Personnel in Armed Conflicts", in Mariëlle Matthee, Brigit Toebes and Marcel Brus (eds.), *Armed Conflict and International Law: In search of the Human Face: Liber Amicorum in Memory of Avril McDonald* (The Hague: TMC Asser, 2013)

Tomuschat, Christian, *Human Rights: Between Idealism and Realism* (Oxford University Press, 2003)

Tudor, T. S., Walker, J. K., and Richards, N. S. (eds.), *Air Force Operations and the Law: A Guide for Air and Space Forces* (USAF Judge Advocate General's Department, 2002)

UK Ministry of Defence, *The Manual of the Law of Armed Conflict* (Oxford University Press, 2004)

United Kingdom, *The Law of War on Land being Part III of the Manual of Military Law* (London: HMSO, 1958)

US Department of Defense, "Final Report to Congress on the Conduct of the Persian Gulf War – Appendix O: The Role of the Law of War" (1992) 31 *ILM* 61

"Briefing on Geneva Convention, EPWs [Enemy Prisoners of War] and War Crimes, Office of the Assistant Secretary of Defence (Public Affairs)", 7 April 2003, www.defense.gov/Transcripts/Transcript.aspx?TranscriptID=2281

US Government, *Trials of War Criminals before the Nuernberg Military Tribunals under Control Council Law No. 10, Nuernberg, October 1946 – April 1949*, 15 vols. (Washington, DC: US Government Printing Office, 1949)

Van der Vat, Dan, *D-Day: The Greatest Invasion – A People's History* (Sydney: Allen and Unwin, 2003)

Vité, Sylvain, "Typology of Armed Conflicts in International Humanitarian Law: Legal Concepts and Actual Situations" (2009) 91 *IRRC* 69

Vogel, Ryan, "Drone Warfare and the Law of Armed Conflict" (2011) 39 *Denv J Int'l L & Pol'y* 101

von Clausewitz, Carl, *On War, 1832*, trans. J. J. Graham 1873 (London: Penguin Classics, 1982)

von Martens, G. F., *Summary of the Law of Nations*, trans. William Cobbett (Philadelphia: Thomas Bradford, 1795)

Vöneky, Silja, "Implementation and Enforcement of International Humanitarian Law", in Dieter Fleck (ed.), *The Handbook of International Humanitarian Law*, 3rd edn (Oxford University Press, 2013)

Walzer, Michael, *Just and Unjust Wars*, 3rd edn (New York: Basic Books, 2000)

Warner, Frederick, "The Environmental Consequences of the Gulf War" (1991) 33 *Environment* 6

Watkin, Kenneth, "Chemical Agents and Expanding Bullets: Limited Law Enforcement Exceptions or Unwarranted Handcuffs?" (2006) 36 *Isr YBHR 43*

"Opportunity Lost: Organised Armed Groups and the ICRC 'Direct Participation in Hostilities Interpretive Guidance'" (2010) 42 *NYU J Int'l L and Pol* 641

Westlake, John, *International Law*, vol. 1 (London: Sweet and Maxwell, 1904)

Wexler, Lesley, "'Limiting the Precautionary Principle' Weapons Regulation in the Face of Scientific Uncertainty" (2006) 39 *UC Davis LR* 459

Wheaton, Henry, *Elements of International Law*, 8th edn (Boston: Little, Brown and Company, 1866)

Wilmshurst, Elizabeth (ed.), *International Law and the Classification of Conflicts* (Oxford University Press, 2012)

Wilmshurst, Elizabeth and Breau, Susan (eds.), *Perspectives on the ICRC Study on Customary International Humanitarian Law* (Cambridge University Press, 2007)

Wilson, Heather A., *International Law and the Use of Force by National Liberation Movements* (Oxford: Clarendon Press, 1988)

Winthrop, William, *Military Law and Precedents*, 2nd edn (Washington, DC: Washington Government Printing Office, 1920)

Yoo, John, Deputy Assistant Attorney General, and Robert Delahunty, Special Counsel, US Department of Justice, Memo of January 9, 2002 to William Haynes, General Counsel, US Department of Defense (DoD) (excerpted in Karen Greenberg and Anthony Dratel (eds.), *The Torture Papers: The Road to Abu Ghraib* (Cambridge University Press, 2005)

Yung, Alvin, "Vietnam and Agent Orange Revisited" (2002) 9 *Environmental Science and Pollution Research* 158

Zegveld, L, "The Inter-American Commission on Human Rights and International Humanitarian Law: A Comment on the Tablada Case" (1998) 38 *IRRC* 505

INDEX